Ricardo's Law

Fred Harrison's

other works include

Wheels of Fortune (2006)

Boom Bust: House Prices, Banking & the Depression of 2010 (2005)

The Corruption of Economics (1994), with Mason Gaffney

Power in the Land (1983)

Ricardo's Law

House Prices and the Great Tax Clawback Scam

FRED HARRISON

SHEPHEARD-WALWYN (PUBLISHERS) LTD

First published in 2006 by
Shepheard-Walwyn (Publishers) Ltd
Suite 604, The Chandlery
50 Westminster Bridge Road
London SE1 7QY

British Library Cataloguing in Publication Data
A catalogue record of this book
is available from the British Library

ISBN-13: 978-0-85683-241-3
ISBN-10: 0-85683-241-3

Typeset by Alacrity,
Banwell Castle, Weston-super-Mare
Printed through Print Solutions, Wallington, Surrey

Contents

If we are frank about it, there is a group of people who have been shut out against society's mainstream and we have not yet found a way of bringing them in properly

TONY BLAIR (2006)

Evil men that can do no other than make just laws are safer than good men that must either make unjust laws or ruin themselves

JAMES HARRINGTON (1659)

Prologue

Civil War by Other Means

WESTERN civilisation has reached a point of crisis where we can no longer afford to accept the persistent failures of public policy. *Ricardo's Law* attempts to explain how the power of the state needs to be reconstituted.

The crisis is rooted in the evolution of a social organisation that deprived people of their primary birthright. In the 20th century, working people thought they had taken control of the state through the ballot box, and could compensate themselves for their losses. But the Welfare State fell short of what was possible because of the tools that were employed. The gains in material standards of living were far less than might have been achieved; and they were not distributed on the basis of just deserts. The tools employed – progressive taxes – could not deliver either justice or efficiency. As a result, the West is vulnerable because it cannot respond adequately to the economic challenge from the East.

Democratic politics failed to solve problems which were within its technical capacity to consign to history. Homelessness and unaffordable housing, for example, are absurdities, given the industrial economy's capacity to construct enough houses to meet demand. Yet we have patently failed to eradicate the problems that blight people's lives. The will existed, and it is not a problem of power: the state exercises sovereign authority, and its ability to use force is not contested, at least not in the realm of public policy. The persistence of failure can have one explanation only. It is structural: built into society's DNA – the laws and institutions that are the framework of our communities.

In the past, the West was able to recover from major catastrophes such as world wars. What is significant about the challenges of the 21st century that make the continuation of failure not the option that it once was? The West was able to recover from its previous breakdowns because of its command over global markets. It was able to buy or bully its way back to apparent prosperity. This time, neo-colonial strategies that worked in Africa and South America will not come to the rescue. So if Europe and North America are to survive as more than client consumer markets, a culture shift is imperative. Otherwise, large segments of these regions risk becoming appendages to the new centres of industrial power in India and China, with a few islands of prosperity to compensate, such as South-East England, the north-eastern states of America and a few metropolises in central Europe.

Time is not on the West's side. In its quest for prosperity, China is a predator that is brusquely pushing aside those who once dominated the world's economy. Just how impatient it is was illustrated by Shen Wenrong. He started life as a peasant farmer. In 2001, he purchased the mighty Ruhr-based ThyssenKrupp steel mill from Germany for its scrap price ($24m). Within a year, 250,000 tonnes of equipment were dismantled in double-quick time by 1,000 Chinese workers and the crates shipped to the Yangtze delta. The mill was reconstructed at a cost of 60% of a new plant. Now, cars designed in Germany may be manufactured with high-quality steel derived from German technology – but the car makers must buy that steel from furnaces on the other side of the world. Ten thousand German steelworkers lost their jobs.[1]

The fate of millions of families rests on how the West confronts such challenges. We must avoid the panic that would open the door to protectionism in the name of patriotism. The new globalisation affords opportunities for everyone. No one need lose, *provided the correct reforms are adopted*. To achieve their new status as a global economic (and therefore military) power, the communists had to dismantle their planned economy. That entailed a painful shift in the mind-set of both the people and their Politburo leaders in Beijing. A culture shift of similar proportions – and equally revolutionary in its outcomes – is now required by the peoples of Europe and North America.

The transformation need not be violent, but the mindset that shaped Western civilisation will be disturbed. Lest the reader be alarmed by this prognosis, I should stress that the one essential reform which I propose – to the tax system – is based on a principle to which we routinely adhere in our everyday lives. The institutional crises that have disgraced European civilisation for 500 years persist because of the deviation from this principle by our form of governance. The amendment to taxation which I elaborate in Part IV would deliver significant financial gains on a scale sufficient to enable society to compensate anyone who was deemed to lose under the new arrangements.

In Britain, for example, we can expect the reforms to deliver an increase in national income which, over the first 10 years, would amount to an additional £240bn. In the US, the short-term gains from the reform could increase average post-tax earnings per worker by about $4,000. Within 10 years, those earnings would be higher by an average of $7,000, rising to an additional $10,000 per year. These sums give us a sense of the losses we suffer under the current tax regime.

These are conservatively estimated gains, but they are appreciable and sustainable. Nonetheless, we can expect strong resistance to reform from interests that originated with the corruption of politics. That corruption needs to be confronted, for it continues to corrode communities that placed their faith in the state. That faith was misplaced. I shall show that our socially significant problems originated with the nation state. The political classes, whose hands are on the instruments of state power, are complicit. Politicians, of course, will not admit their role in the impoverishment of people's lives. The pressures that muzzle them are powerful. But by their silence and inactivity, governments in which we repose our welfare are unable to help us to face the profound challenges wrought by the next phase of globalisation.

The state needs to be reformed, literally from the ground up. The knowledge we need to execute this project has long been available, but I will show that governments are unwilling to share that information with their electorates. Thus, if we do not wish to become a Chinese takeaway society, we have no choice but to indict the state. This book provides the evidence to enable voters in democracies to sit in judgement in the court of public opinion.

The historical context is the Enlightenment and the values and institutions that subsequently emerged and are now fossilised in our system of taxation. Poverty and exploitation were embedded in the foundations of the absolute monarchies of Europe, aspects of which survived in their most pronounced forms in the Anglo-American model of property rights and public finance. There could be no justification for the continued reproduction of mass deprivation. With the concession of universal suffrage, the people held their destinies in their own hands. Didn't they?

No, they did not. Although they tried (in the first decade of the 20th century), they were not able to restore the birthright that was removed from them during the formative stages of the modern state. So we find ourselves in the grotesque situation in which people are now co-opted into sanctioning their own impoverishment.

We need a starting point for our analysis. This is provided by what historian J.G.A. Pocock describes as 'a moment of historical exhaustion and opportunity'.[2] He was referring to the collapse of the state in England in the 1630s, but his description captures the condition of the West today. There is both exhaustion (of governance) and opportunity (in economics and in the formation of culture).

Pocock drew attention to the work of political philosopher James Harrington (1611-1677). Previous social ruptures inspired philosophers to wrestle with the problems in terms of utopianism: Plato in the ancient world, Thomas More (with his *Utopia* [1516]) and Sir Francis Bacon (in *New Atlantis* [1624]). These writers visualised ideal communities created anew on fictional islands set apart from the society that was corrupted.

Harrington was not in the business of utopianism. *The Commonwealth of Oceana* (1656) employed little fiction. His was a hard-headed attempt to prescribe the terms for a constitutional settlement for England. Neither he nor those who had taken up arms against the king wanted to abandon the monarchy in favour of republicanism. Civil war and regicide came about because the state no longer had the resources to discharge its obligations. That episode, a breakdown of power, is pregnant with lessons for us today.

Why did the state lose control over its territory, and what was the basis for restoring order? Harrington offered a fundamental analysis of the nature of power. That is why *Oceana* and his other writings are important – not because his programme for a republic helped to shape the constitution of the USA.[3]

Harrington saw that power – as defined by the possession of arms – flowed to those who controlled land. He described a triadic relationship in which land tenure entailed duties to the community which legitimised (but put conditions on the exercise of) the use of force (see Figure 1). Anyone holding land had a duty to both protect the territory from external aggression and serve the community (for example, by defraying the costs of enforcing law and order). In a 'balanced' society, those who held land would acknowledge the public duties that went with its possession. The ability of society to enforce those responsibilities, however, depended on whether land was concentrated in the hands of the few, or diffused among the people.

Figure 1

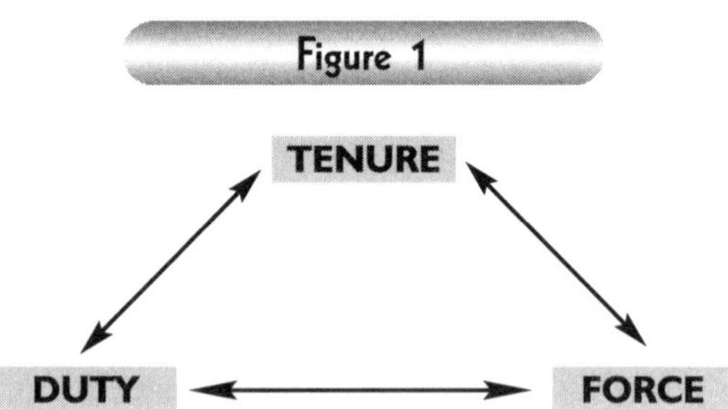

By the time of Charles I, the English state had lost control over its space. The state was divided against itself because the land had been alienated in a way that subverted the social interest. Land – more precisely, the income from land – was being privatised. This meant that the duties traditionally attached to the possession of land were not being fulfilled. Now, the gentry, a new landowning class in the counties, exercised power without responsibility. The reciprocal of this was a state that exercised responsibility with diminishing power. This was a recipe for disaster.

And so the 'commoners' of the House of Commons came into conflict with the royalists (the peers in the House of Lords) in civil war. This outcome became unavoidable once the state had begun to subvert the material basis of its authority. In plain English, this is what was happening: the land rents that had previously funded the state's functions were being drained away by the new landowners. The outcome was civil anarchy.

The UK is still living with the legacy of that anarchy. The settlement which led to the restoration of the Stuart dynasty failed to remove the causes that led to civil war. Today, that civil war is perpetuated by other means; but those means are every bit as violent as when Cromwell's army pitted Englishmen against Englishmen and sacked towns in Ireland.

Ricardo's Law is not intended as a work of historical detection. But because our analysis has to be fundamental, we have no choice but to reopen – for those who are interested in pursuing a mystery – the case of why the English resorted to regicide. I will explain that they were driven to it by the failure of the state to balance everyone's interests in a fair and efficient way, and that this is the problem that confronts us today. To disentangle the interlocking pieces, I assemble the evidence so that the reader may reflect on four indictments. These need to be tested against our everyday experiences. For if people are now obliged to take direct control of the future, they first need to know where to point the accusing finger.

We can summarise the choices in terms of the two theories of the state that continue to engage the Western mind. The first is associated with Thomas Hobbes (1588-1679). He argued that people had to surrender part of their liberties to an all-powerful sovereign, *The Leviathan* (1651). In this social contract, the individual negotiated protection for himself and his property. The other version of the social contract treats the individual as sovereign. This theory of the state (championed by philosophers like John Stuart Mill [1806-1873]), does not yield sovereignty to the state; but, rather, grants power to the state in return for protection of one's personal liberties.

The second version is associated with the concept of democracy. But the democratic project of the 20th century fell far short of its promise. Much work remains for those who claim to *think* about these issues, let alone for those who claim to represent people in places like Westminster and Washington's Capitol Hill. All too often, academic philosophers are less than helpful because, while they stress the sanctity of the individual (as in their discourses on human rights), they fail to offer a sufficient definition of the relationship between a person's private space, and the public space now staked out by the state.[4] The issues appear to be complex. We need to lay the foundations for a deeper understanding of how the present system operates before we can renegotiate the terms of the interface between the public space and the private space.

To produce evidence in sufficient authoritative detail, we need to interrogate a single case. I have chosen the United Kingdom, for three reasons. I have already alluded to the first one: the UK, in common with the USA and the rest of Europe, is locked into 'a moment of historical exhaustion and opportunity'. If we wish to avoid the embrace of a new Lord Protector – few people would want to yield democracy for another Oliver Cromwell – we need to relearn the terms of the balanced society.

Secondly, the people of England failed Harrington's challenge in 1660 when they accepted the soft option of inviting Charles II to occupy the throne. That debate, on the terms of the post-civil-war settlement of 350 years ago, was reopened in the context of President George W. Bush's 'war on terrorism'. In response to terrorism on the streets of London, new laws that would qualify the liberties of the individual were proposed by the Blair government in the name of security. The rule of law does have to be re-established in the UK; but on what basis?[5]

And, thirdly, the UK is held up as an exemplar to other members of the European Union. Over the course of his three administrations, Tony Blair and his Chancellor of the Exchequer, Gordon Brown, have portrayed Britain as the role model for the continental countries. They have repeatedly insisted that the UK was superior to Germany and France in economics. Furthermore, they have argued that those two countries ought to emulate aspects of the American economy, and especially its labour market.[6]

Despite the eulogies on its behalf, however, the UK is embarrassed by a growing gap between the rich and the poor, both at the inter-personal and the regional levels. A comparison of the 30 member countries of the Organisation for Economic Co-operation and Development (OECD) reveals that, between 1996 and 2001, only Turkey had a bigger spread of growth rates between the strongest and weakest regions.[7] The United Kingdom is a nation disunited; as such, it affords lessons for others. If the Anglo-American version of capitalism is so good that it should be emulated, why – comparatively speaking – is its performance unacceptable to millions of people at the level of the street?

If we wish to inform the public on the choices that confront us all, we cannot retreat to the safety of allegorical island communities. We have to ask the hard questions.

- After the regicide of Charles I, why was Parliament not able to represent the interests of all citizens? Who gained from the termination of the republic? Who had the most to gain from the Restoration?
- Why was it necessary to resort to the fictions of an 'unwritten' constitution? What had to be covered up? Who gained by not leaving a paper trail?

- Did the anarchy of the mid-17th century carry over as institutionalised deception against the people in general? If so, what form did this legalised violence take? Is it operating to this day? If so, what can be done about it?
- Is Western democracy sufficiently mature for these questions to be comprehensively explored? Have people reached the point at which they feel motivated to restore their birthrights?

Armed with the economic concepts provided in Part I, readers will be equipped to interrogate evidence from the other OECD countries. We apply these concepts in Part II, which is a forensic examination of the United Kingdom. I review the American model in Part III. The fundamental remedy, which I believe would strengthen all nations through the spirit of co-operation, enhanced prosperity, political security and personal liberty, is explored in Part IV.

The price of failure does not bear thinking about.

REFERENCES

1 James Kynge, *China Shakes the World: the Rise of a Hungry Nation*, London: Weidenfeld & Nicolson, 2006.

2 James Harrington, *The Commonwealth of Oceana and A System of Politics* (J.G.A. Pocock, ed), Cambridge: Cambridge University Press, 1992, p.xvii.

3 Barbara Goodwin and Keith Taylor, *The Politics of Utopia*, London: Hutchinson, 1982, p.43.

4 Karma Nabulsi, 'Don't sign up to this upside down Hobbesian contract', *The Guardian*, March 3, 2006), addresses the competing visions of the social contract in terms of the Blair/Bush doctrine of the state and its legislative responses to terrorism. Ms Nabulsi, a politics fellow at the University of Oxford, opposed the policies of the Bush and Blair administrations and argued for the need to 'cede the public space back to its owners', without explaining what that notion of 'public space' entails. The failures of political discourse stem primarily from this failure of philosophy.

5 Among those opposing Tony Blair's anti-terrorist laws was the Earl of Onslow. The peer reminded the Conservative Party that 'From our beginnings in the Restoration Parliament as defenders of church and king, we have seen ancient liberties as the key to the advancement of our fellow citizens ... From the Stuart kings to the modern, mass-political democracy, our great party has defended our constitution and benefited out country' in 'An open letter to the Conservative leader', *The Observer*, April 23, 2006. For Tony Blair's defence of his legislation – which he deemed necessary because the state's 'traditional processes ... are leaving the innocent unprotected and the guilty unpunished' – see the exchange of e-mails between the Prime Minister and Henry Porter in 'Britain's Liberties', *The Observer*, April 23, 2006, pp.20-2.

6 To oppose the Blairite vision of their future, German and French employees staged public protests in 2005 and 2006.

In France, university students provoked tear-gas responses from the security forces as they called for strikes to protect their version of social democracy. According to one reporter, 'it is clear that the current situation is the latest expression of the growing revolt against the authoritarian market society France has become and the elite that wishes to take the Thatcherite project further' (Naima Bouteldja, 'Fearful of exploitation', *The Guardian*, March 22, 2003). The mass protests in the streets by trades unionists and students forced President Jacques Chirac to sue for a negotiated peace; one that would shy away from the 'neo-liberal' model that the French associate with the UK.

7 Chris Giles, 'Forgotten Britain: how Labour has presided over a deepening divide', *Financial Times*, March 20, 2006.

Four Indictments

I DO NOT allege a conspiracy against the people. I wish it were that simple. Conspiracies are conscious, covertly perpetrated actions by identifiable individuals in particular times and places. They can be penetrated, exposed and destroyed.

I allege something far more problematic. A social process exists that now survives by co-opting people into exploiting themselves. This makes the challenges of the 21st century – lopsided demographics, the shortfall in money for the retirement years, vulnerable immigrant communities, the exodus of high-value jobs to China and India – all the more difficult to surmount.

The nation state is central to this process, so it is part of the problem rather than the solution. We can assert this on the basis of a 200-year record. The state has presided over many persistent problems, some of which, in the 20th century at least, it did try to eradicate from the social landscape; but failed.

The primary obstacles to reform are not associated with private enterprise. The persistent shortfalls in (say) housing are not due to the unwillingness of the construction industry to equate supply with demand. Nor (for most people) is unemployment a voluntary state of deprivation. And people do not wilfully deprive themselves of adequate incomes for their retirement years.

These and other challenges are built into the foundations of the Western form of social organisation. They can be corrected by modifying a few of the buttresses that support the system. The remedial policies have always been available, but they have been resisted because, ultimately, the state as an institution is corrupt. So before we can develop a template for reform, we must define and document that corruption; and identify the agents who perpetuate the rules and practises that deprive people of their natural rights.

We will adopt the definition of the state offered by German sociologist Max Weber (1864-1920), who specified it as the institution which claimed to exercise a monopoly of legitimate force within a territory.[1] To select and test the evidence, we also need a definition of corruption as it can be applied to the state. We will employ the one offered by Joel Hurstfield. As a professor of English history in the University of London he specialised in the diagnosis of corruption in early modern England.

> If we assume that the object of the state is the welfare of all its members, we may define corruption as the subversion of that object for other ends.[2]

To make the case that the state is not fit to help people to deal with the unique challenges of the third millennium, we have to show that

- a socially significant section of the community is routinely excluded from the benefits that accrue under the aegis of the state;
- personal aspirations are thwarted as a direct result of policies wilfully employed by the state; and
- 'other ends' – and especially the distribution of benefits because of privileged treatment by the state – result from discrimination against some to the advantage of others.

If we prove this case, we reopen political questions that people thought were resolved. If there is sufficient evidence for our charge, for example, the proposition that we are all equal before the law is a travesty of the facts.

One of our working assumptions is that everyone is equal. What do we mean by equality? The concept is traditionally related to opportunity, or to outcomes. A further use is that of equality of process, which refers to treating people in the same way. These are narrow definitions, and each has its problems. We shall adopt the definition proposed by the panel that was established at Tony Blair's behest to examine inequality in Britain. This stresses *capabilities,* which concentrates on what people are able to do or be in their lives. The Equalities Review panel wrote:

> [T]he first priority for action by all must be to ensure that every member of society has certain basic provisions and capabilities without which they cannot truly achieve any meaningful measure of equality. Without a basic level of income, shelter, education, cultural competence and social participation, to talk of people having equal life chances would be futile.[3]

Everyone should reach the 'capability threshold. This is a basic minimum set of capabilities which everyone has to possess in order to play a proper, autonomous part in society at all'.[4] This definition sets the benchmark without predetermining the rules by which a person's 'capabilities' are to be achieved.

As humans, we aspire to more than biological survival. Once our material needs are fulfilled, we seek contentment through cultural and recreational activity. Physical health and psychological well-being are intimately related. A fissure in the economic system, if it is sanctioned by law, may be the root cause of the social divide that leads to the breakdown in people's biological and mental welfare. Our investigation examines the evidence in terms of the wholeness of people.

We are not isolated individuals, but social creatures that *need* to live in wholesome communities. The advantage of the 'capabilities' approach is the comprehensive recognition of an individual's personality and the social context within which personality may evolve. As such, it necessarily encompasses an audit of the role of the state and its agencies, which are of paramount influence in determining whether an individual is enjoying the freedom to flourish.

Thus, we want to know who, or what, is responsible for the fact that the life expectancy of those in the higher classes is increasing faster than for people in the lowest classes. The latter are not congenitally incapable of living longer than they now do. The class difference cannot be attributed to personal proclivities. The Welfare State has had more than 60 years to erase class differences. Why has it failed? Is the state conniving against the lifestyles of millions of its citizens in a way that was never sanctioned by the democratic will of the people?

☞ Indictment I

The state is derelict in its duty to citizens

THE STATE derives its legitimacy from its ability to provide people with territorial security. This is its primary role, and it does seek to fulfil that military obligation. But the funding policy by which it does so – raising revenue to equip the army, navy and air force – abuses the welfare of the people who live on the territory. In providing for physical safety, the state undermines people's natural rights.

My analysis is not based on that of the Marxist or of the anarchist who wishes to see the withering away of the state. I accept the state (though not necessarily in its present form) as necessary to enforce laws through institutions that secure our liberties. I allege, however, that the state as we now know it is incapable of serving that purpose. The state abuses people's rights because its power is corrupt.

I do not side with those who claim that power, *per se*, is corrupting. Power is pure when it is consonant with justice. I allege that the state is continuously corrupting its power because of the tools that it employs – the tools of taxation – to establish that power in the first place. A *prima facie* case may be established in the following way.

In addition to defence, the state is also required to maintain law and order within the territory. This requires the provision of a police force and courts of law which have to be maintained out of public funds. From where is the money to come? The existence of these state-provided services adds value to society: in a lawless society, productivity is much lower because (for example) people would not be willing to risk their savings by investing in such a territory. Now, if it *is* the case that the state makes a direct contribution to increasing the nation's income, that added value is the legitimate source of its revenue.

Take the case of transportation. A police force does not just march on its belly any more than does an army; it also marches on roads. Even if those roads were funded out of private resources, their provision has to be facilitated through parliamentary institutions and courts of law. In providing these services, the state engages in activities which add value to the wealth of the nation. That value is sufficient to pay for the defence of the realm and the enforcement of law and order.

We shall explain how this added value crystallises in the land market, where it may be measured and collected to pay for the capital investment in services that people choose to share in common. This value is technically called the *economic rent* of land. One of Britain's most distinguished economists, Alfred Marshall, perceived that, for the sake of clarity in public policy, that value should be characterised as the 'annual public value of the land'.[5] But this is where the crisis begins. *The state fails to collect that public value*. It permits a privileged class of people to appropriate it. This privilege sets them apart from the rest of us. *The state, by its dereliction, disunites the kingdom. We are not equals before the law of the land.*

This dereliction of its financial duty is our primary reason for contesting the legitimacy of the state's use of force. How, if it abandons its claim to the public value which it helps to create in association with citizens, can it fund the military, the police and the law courts? It does so by coercively capturing people's earnings. This is an abuse of the right of the individual to earn a living and save out of that income to meet personal needs all the way through to retirement. The outcome is the redistribution of income from the poor to the privileged (Chapter 1). The Welfare State has perfected the art of abusive taxation. By this means, it undermines itself by its perverse policies. Instead of collecting the revenue which it creates, it hands that public value to others – and then victimises the losers by taxing their earnings. Some scholars claim the concept of the state is complex and elusive (others deny that it even exists).[6] But for lay people there is nothing elusive about the way money is forcibly removed from their pay packets!

We need a name for the way some people manipulate the perverse power of the state to arrogate these privileges unto themselves. Economists call it 'rent-seeking'. By manipulating laws and regulatory power, the liberties of some are circumscribed for the benefit of others. Our investigation will focus sharply on the historically most serious of all cases of rent-seeking. We are not concerned with personal corruption (such as the willingness of a law-maker or a civil servant to accept bribes). We are concerned with the rules that systematise the exploitation of people. The most grievous abuse occurs when the state sanctions the mal-distribution of the money that people pay for access to the amenities we share in common. This cannot be justified on grounds of either economic efficiency or justice.

☞ Indictment II

Parliament has failed to use its democratic mandate to remedy the injustices of the Tax State

IT WOULD be too easy to direct our accusations exclusively at an impersonal institution called 'the state'. But that monolithic institution is administered by people and agencies. So it is incumbent on us to name names, if our proposals for substantive reform of taxation are to be credible and receive public support. Therefore, we have to determine the role of the law-making institution in the abuse of the people.

To plumb the depths of institutionalised abuse, we need to recall the historical context in which corruption was ingrained into politics. Hurstfield notes that

> a relatively narrow social and political group of *élite*, at the centre of government and in the counties ... controlled patronage and advancement. And, as Parliament grew increasingly important, these men sought also to control elections, by persuasion, force and fraud in the 16th and 17th centuries, and by the familiar process of bribery of voters in the 18th. This too was corruption.[7]

These practices were designed to enshrine in law the fiscal folly that characterises the modern state. The corrupted feudal aristocracy embedded its selfish interests in the laws of the land and thereby polluted the political process that evolved into democracy. The corruption of the nation's finances was not ameliorated by the reforms that culminated in universal franchise. The outcome is a state with divided loyalties. It now claims to represent the welfare of all citizens, but it protects the rent-seeking interests of a privileged group.

The state is administered by politicians who are not self-serving individuals. The majority of them are sincerely intent on serving those who elect them to office. As a class, however, they betray the people. By their subservience to the prejudices inherited from the past, they are responsible for the abuse – inflicted day by painful day, like a never ending Chinese torture – of people who trust them with their care.

The formal event that expresses that betrayal is the annual endorsement of the nation's budget. We shall expose the complexion of the state by assessing the character of budgetary policies. We shall see that the state *cannot* serve the public's interest. Its taxes *reduce* the welfare of the nation while raising the value of the wealth of a privileged minority. This outcome is an affront to the principle of equal treatment under the law.

The aristocracy and gentry hijacked Parliament and promoted doctrines that justified the laws that served their private interests. But the hijackers had to go further if they were to consolidate their privileges. The land magnates, reinforced by their lawyers and placemen in Parliament, shaped the public's consciousness with notions that served as bulwarks to their financial interests. This was necessary if they were to be relieved of running battles every year over the contents of the public purse. People had to be made to view the world through *their* eyes, to serve *their* interests. The people's view of the state had to be coloured against *their* best interests.

Is this pushing our accusations too far? Joel Hurstfield, who studied state-sponsored propaganda through the official histories, warned:

> We should never forget that, until comparatively recent times, the historian was the servant of the state who testified to its greatness, and this is still true in many places in the world.[8]

The foundations of the state were grounded in the propagandistic manipulation of people's minds and emotions (and even their souls) through the use of religion as well as secular doctrines. As Hurstfield made clear, 'the control and creation of opinion was sought, and in some measure gained, by the government itself; that proclamations, statutes, homilies, officially sponsored pamphlets were aimed at forming and guiding opinion ... Of course the restraints were sometimes thwarted and broken, of course there was criticism in speech and print. But the power of repression in most cases could silence the voice of dissent'.[9] Today, the state does not rely exclusively on historians. It has added 'spin doctors' to the bureaucracy.

Our concern with history is not out of arcane curiosity. That history evolved in a way that delivered a particular set of decision-making institutions. Today, Western civilisation is at risk from a clear and present danger – largely of its own making. I allege that remedial action will remain beyond our democratic reach unless we question the legitimacy of some of the pillars that support the state. This means we have to apply our forensic tools to the most recent attempts to reshape that civilisation from within; the most determined case of which is the Third Way experiment in the United Kingdom.

☞ Indictment III

Tony Blair's New Labour administrations were constructed on a grand deception

IT WORKED. The people were beguiled by the sparkling personality that emerged out of the backbenches of Parliament to proclaim the rebirth of the nation. Tony Blair promised that, if granted power, New Labour would restore the virility of youth to the kingdom's institutions. The general election of 1997 was a landslide victory for Blair's project.

No time was lost in betraying The People's Mandate. In 1998, Blair's finance minister, Chancellor of the Exchequer Gordon Brown, modified the tax on capital gains. This consolidated the perversities of the Tax State. The change shifted the income of the nation further in the direction of the privileged class, the one that accumulated wealth without working for it.

The Treasury's Code for Fiscal Stability (published in November 1997) illustrates the linguistic illusions conjured up by policies in the realm of finance. The code was rigged against the people who most needed the protection of the state. The language, of course, was soothing. The public's finances would be managed in a principled way; the Treasury would be transparent in handling taxpayers' money – by disclosing and quantifying all decisions that affect the nation's economic and fiscal prospects; and it promised best-practice methods in the presentation of the public's accounts.

I claim that the public was hoodwinked. The words camouflaged the denial of vital information that people needed to judge whether their government was delivering value for their money. Furthermore, the financial affairs of the taxpayers were not administered on the basis of *principles*. The horse-trading that had delivered fortunes to the privileged ones in the past continued to dictate tax policy.

This was not what Tony Blair intended. The proclamations that tumbled out of the Treasury promised to reverse the injustices of the past. But it was business as usual, with the predators leeching the public value out of the economy to serve their private interests. Instead of confronting this historic problem, Blair placed the blame for society's problems on 'problem families' in a Downing Street speech towards the end of his reign.[10] And he defended his legacy by provocatively challenging his critics in these terms: 'If there is a better idea, let's hear it'.[11]

The reader is invited to suspend judgement on my indictment – and Blair's record on his changes to the UK's laws and institutions – until all the evidence we offer has been reviewed.

☞ Indictment IV

Experts who advise government muzzle our collective consciousness

HOW COULD the Blair government escape censure – Tony Blair led his party to victory on a record three successive occasions – when it encouraged people to hold it accountable for its actions? Dissenting voices of the kind that might have altered the course of history were not heard. But one class of people had a special responsibility to offer an impartial assessment of public policies. They were the experts who were paid handsomely by taxpayers to do so. They, too, need to be brought before the bar of public opinion.

Enormous sums of money were spent by Blair's government on consultants for advice on issues ranging from transport planning to the provision of housing. A veritable army of experts drawn from the universities, commercial consultancies and policy think-tanks was enlisted to assess current practices and identify solutions. They did not warn Blair that his government was on a course for failure.[12]

A tragic example concerned the decision to demolish 168,000 homes in the Midlands and the North to make way for dwellings at prices that people could afford. The Office of the Deputy Prime Minister (ODPM) paid £165m to consultants (up to the beginning of 2005) for advice which included testimony on how to go about this wrecking operation. The charity SAVE Britain's Heritage calculated that the consultancy fees could have restored 8,000 homes. The programme was doomed to failure from the start (Chapter 9). But the experts having pronounced, the local governments and state agencies that were organised into 'Pathfinder' projects, charged with driving the bulldozers, were not about to raise objections.

> Importantly, once the consultants' reports have been written, the Pathfinders seem loath to question them even if they bear little relevance to the reality of the situation on the ground.[13]

Thus is our collective consciousness damaged. Our allegation has profound implications. We claim that the intellectual landscape has been so distorted that rational people are co-opted into abusing their welfare (see Box 1). Technically, this process is called 'socialisation'. Lay people would employ a more colourful description: brainwashing. The reader, by accompanying us on our investigation, will form his or her judgement as to whether this allegation is tenable.

Box 1 Tyranny of the Experts

LANGUAGE and logic have been corrupted in a way that inhibits us from acting in our best interests. An example is provided by the Organisation for Economic Co-operation and Development.

After World War II, the richest nations decided to fund a think-tank to serve them. The OECD was located in Paris, and the best brains were hired. Every year, a report is issued on the state of economic health of each member country. The advice is accepted as well-intentioned, and based on a thorough compilation of all the available evidence.

In 1998, the OECD assessed the Blair government's planned reforms. These included additions to 'The new fiscal policy framework', which was supposed to guide decisions over the medium term. Blair and Brown welcomed the help they needed to deliver value-for-money governance.

What was the contribution from the OECD? It helped to shroud the mental horizons of both the government and the people. It did so by claiming that it was difficult to specify rules that would deliver the goals that could be set for tax policy. Why was it difficult? '[F]iscal policy,' it reported, included goals that embraced 'efficiency, equity and macroeconomic stability objectives.' But, unfortunately, 'Fiscal rules *cannot* embrace all these objectives...'*

This was a false pronouncement. For more than two centuries, the fiscal rules of good governance, which would simultaneously deliver economic efficiency and stable growth for the nation, and fairness between individuals, were known to economists. These are restated and developed in Part IV below

No one false statement, issued by individuals or agencies in authority, closes our minds. But the cumulative impact of persistent falsehoods and half-truths exercises a corrosive effect because the public tends to defer to the authority of the experts. The outcome is a tyranny of the state's servants who claim to know best.

***OECD Economic Surveys 1998: United Kingdom*, Paris, 1998, p.47. Emphasis added.

I AM CALLING for the public – through the institutions of civil society – to initiate a debate on these four indictments. I contend that our political representatives have disqualified themselves from leading that debate on the fundamental question of our liberties. If, as Blair has attested, there is an estrangement of 'the political and legal establishment' from 'the reality of people's lives',[14] the time has come for a fundamental review of the philosophy of the state itself; and for the people to take control of the debate that leads to reform.

Blair wished to take the lead with changes to the liberties of the individual as part of his programme for modernising Britain. But the changes that are needed cannot be delivered by government fiat. The breakdown in our communities has proceeded too far for a conventional law-led transformation. People themselves have to effect the changes in their homes, on the streets and in their neighbourhoods. On top of this comes the need to renegotiate the social contract that binds communities.

But how do we reconstitute our communities? On what principles do we formulate new rules and relationships? Attempts to rush such transformations led to the Terror of revolutionary France in the 18th century and the Terror of Soviet Russia in the 20th century. These events occurred because people did not understand what it would take to restore their fundamental liberties. So we begin by offering an exposition on how to think about economic issues in a way that will equip people with the tools that will enable them to address the unfinished business that began with the Enlightenment.

REFERENCES

1 Max Weber, *The Theory of Social Organisation*, London: Macmillan, 1964, pp.155-6.
2 Joel Hurstfield, 'Political corruption in modern England: the historian's problem', *History*, Vol. LII (174), 1967, p.19; Joel Hurstfield, *Freedom, Corruption and Government in Elizabethan England*, London: Jonathan Cape, 1973, p.141.
3 The Equalities Review, *Interim Report for Consultation*, March, 2006, p.77 (www.thequalitiesreview.org.uk).
4 *Ibid.*, p.8.
5 Alfred Marshall, *Principles of Economics*, London: Macmillan, 8th edn, 1930, p.434.
6 John Hoffman, *Beyond the State*, Cambridge: Polity Press, 1995.
7 Hurstfield, 'Political corruption…', p.30.
8 Joel Hurstfield, *The Historian as Moralist: Reflections on the Study of Tudor England*, London: Athlone Press, 1975, p.6.
9 *Ibid.*, pp.18-19.
10 Alan Travis, 'Blair spells out his masterplan for a safer, fairer society', *The Guardian*, January 11, 2006.
11 Tony Blair, 'No more coded critiques – let's have an open debate on where we go next', *The Guardian*, June 27, 2006.
12 The disintegration of the Blair government's 10-year Integrated Transport Plan is documented in Fred Harrison, *Wheels of Fortune*, London: Institute of Economic Affairs, 2006. For an assessment of the fiasco associated with the 'multi-modal studies', for which the transport experts were paid £32m, see pp.45-51.
13 Adam Wilkinson, *Pathfinder*, London: Save Britain's Heritage, 2006, p.71.
14 E-mail from Tony Blair to Henry Porter, 'Britain's Liberties', *The Observer*, April 23, 2006, p. 21.

Part I

THE TAX STATE

1

The Tax Clawback Scam

1.1 Fifteen Million Victims

IN BRITAIN, fifteen million people – a quarter of the population – are permanently locked into poverty by their elected politicians. To humiliate them further, the income that is taxed out of those 15m people is substantially transferred to the 15m people who are the richest in the nation. Sandwiched in the middle are 30m people who are deceived into thinking that 'progressive' taxes help them to acquire the health and education services they need. This is a perpetual process of torture-by-taxation.

The Welfare State, according to conventional wisdom, is a permanent feature of society, and it has to be funded out of taxes. I will show that the Welfare State, whatever the intentions of those who fathered it, is no such thing. Far from being part of the solution to poverty and the enlightened distribution of life-giving chances, *it is part of the problem*.

The middle classes are also trapped in a whirlygig of taxation-and-subsidies that lower their standard of living. Government intervention contributes directly to problems like:

- adults who cannot afford their own homes, so many of them have to live with their parents long after they should have flown the nest;
- pensions that are below what they should be after a lifetime's hard labour;
- mothers who are driven into the labour market not out of choice but to try and make ends meet for their children.

Since 1945, in the name of social justice, politicians have ratcheted up the amount they taxed and spent to nearly half of the nation's income. This was driven by a philosophy of 'progressive' equalisation of people's rights and living standards. It was a gigantic sham. Table 1:1 reveals some of the evidence.

First, focus on direct taxes such as those on wages and salaries, and the payroll tax which is deceptively called employees' National Insurance Contributions (NIC). People at the bottom of the income scale pay 9.5% of their gross wages as taxes. Those at the top end pay 23.7%. That seems fair – until we add in the indirect taxes. Most of these may be called *stealth* taxes. The poorest 20% are required to fork out 28.5% of gross income in taxes. The richest people only pay 11.3% into the public coffers.

Table 1:1

Taxes as a Percentage of Gross Income
All households, quintile groups (2002-3)

	Bottom	*2nd*	*3rd*	*4th*	*Top*
All direct taxes	9.5	12.2	17.0	20.4	23.7
All indirect taxes	28.5	20.1	17.7	15.0	11.3
All taxes	37.9	32.2	34.7	35.5	35.1

Source: Simon Briscoe, *Britain in Numbers*, London: Politico's, 2005, p.252.

If we add direct and indirect taxes together, we find that the poorest people hand over 37.9% of their gross income to the tax man compared with 35.1% from the richest people. What is 'progressive' about *that*?

But it gets worse. The traditional analysis of the distribution of after-tax income is calculated to mislead the losers. I will explain that *the richest people do not pay taxes at all*. They are the free riders on the backs of the people on the lowest incomes. *The poor subsidise the high life of the rich, an injustice that is driven by a tax system which governments administer in favour of wealthy people*.

How is the scam worked? Over the past 50 years, governments rigged taxes so that they escape the naked eye. We cannot see that they discriminate against those on the lowest incomes. The redistribution of income from the poor to the rich is camouflaged to avoid censure for this injustice.

The rich never cease to protest that they are heavily taxed. The truth comes as a shock to people weaned on the doctrines of the Welfare State. Taxes paid by top-rate taxpayers are cancelled out by covert government-funded rebates. What can be called a slush fund for the rich is a very public event, but the language we use to discuss politics and economics has been so perverted that no one challenges the legitimacy of that slush fund. How does it work?

When government invests taxpayers' money, it creates a huge economic value. That value can be measured, and it runs to billions of pounds of annually created wealth. That value, as income, can be – and is – taken to the bank.

But although it is funded out of the general pot of taxpayers' money, the proceeds are not distributed equally among all taxpayers. The lion's share goes to the minority who own the bulk of debt-free property. And that value escalates over time, so that the rich become relatively richer with the passage of time. The gap between the poor and the rich, when it is properly measured, is *continuously* widening.

This exercise is executed in the name of *fairness*, driven by *progressive* taxation, in a society that claims to champion every person's *human rights*. That language is pounded into our collective consciousness day in, day out, the drip feed of brainwashing that makes it possible for politicians to claim that black really is white. What does that language conceal?

When government invests taxpayers' money in capital-intensive infrastructure, such as railways, it creates a value which it fails to recapture. That value is allowed to cascade down on to the country, where it is netted by the land market. The territory of the United Kingdom is one giant sponge for soaking up that value as it flows out of taxpayer-funded services such as highways and hospitals.

That value is not left to lie unclaimed on the ground. People come along and pocket it. And why shouldn't they, if the government is derelict in its duty to taxpayers? But the collection is not a random event, like wins on the lottery. If it were, we might excuse it on the grounds that we all had an equal chance at winning. In fact, because of the way that the law of the land is written, that value can only be collected by one group: the owners of land.

Now, let's probe a little deeper into this system.

Low income people who do not own land are obliged by the state to yield part of their income to pay for the services that we share as a community. In exchange for their money, they receive benefits. Their children go to public schools or use public hospitals; and they enjoy the security of the military defence of the kingdom. That is a fair deal. Low-income earners pay their way. *But they don't get a share of the additional value – which their money helps to create – that cascades to the ground from the heavens.*

Let us consider the significance of that fact by examining the financial fate of someone who owns his home and who expects to pay substantial tax out of a handsome salary. Let's imagine someone who is married with two children. He earns £50,000 a year. This is not a super salary, but it is double the average wage.

- *The tax obligation.* Income tax liability on this salary in 2005 was £11,957. The employee's National Insurance liability came to £3,237, which meant that £15,194 was deducted from the salary.

That revenue, we are told, is used in part to cushion the conditions of people on much lower incomes. Fair? We need to probe beneath the official veneer that is wrapped around this doctrine.

What kind of a house does this person own? At a multiple of four or five times the salary, his home is likely to be worth at least £250,000. For illustrative purposes, I will adopt the standard price of houses in London used by Halifax, the mortgage-lending bank. This was £44,446 in 1984. Twenty years later it had increased to £242,296. Over those 20 years, Halifax found that the average annual increase in London house prices was 10%.

- *The capital gain.* During 2005, a 10% increase in the value of a house worth £242,000 was over £24,000. This windfall gain *more than covered what the home owner paid as tax on his salary – £15,195.*

Our home-owner lived a tax-free life! After tax deductions 'at source', he was better off to the tune of £8,800. He did not have to 'monetise' his capital gain immediately. But he *could* have borrowed against the enhanced asset value and spend the money as if it were earned income. And that money would be tax free.

He pays tax on some of the goods and services that he buys. But as we have seen, the burden of indirect taxation falls more heavily on low-income people than on people who receive handsome salaries. That is why indirect taxes are regressive. Those that fall on our home-owner are modest relative to the capital gain that he reaps, thanks to the government's slush fund.

The conclusion is astonishing. *Our comfortably-off home owner receives the use of the transport system, schools and hospitals for nothing.* He is the classic free rider. He rides on the back of the tax-paying tenant family that is not able to store up capital gains for a glorious spend-up in the future.

Our home owner does not *intend* to sponge off the poor. He would be horrified to learn that this perverse tax regime punishes people on low incomes while enriching those who own land. But the facts of life are inescapable. And they are all the more intolerable, in a democratic society, because politicians impose most of their taxes on the poor by stealth.

1.2 Stealthily Does It

POLITICIANS who legitimise this outrageous redistribution of the nation's income do it by subterfuge. Direct taxes take from the rich to help the poor. People at the bottom have about 10% of their gross incomes taken as taxes, compared with more than 20% for those on the top incomes. But this effect is more than cancelled out by the indirect taxes, which are shrouded in the small print that most of us fail to read. Those on the lowest incomes pay between 20% and nearly 30% of their incomes when they purchase the goods and services that they need, compared with an 11% tax-take for those on top incomes. The net effects:

- the poorest people subsidise the rich
- the rich have their taxes cancelled out by the windfall gains which they receive by courtesy of the government's wealth distributing tax-and-spend policies

The process of immiseration is not the fault of the free market, but everything to do with the philosophy of 'welfare' taxation. The housing market is the primary conduit for the worst abuses. To understand how this outrage discriminates against those who add value to the nation, we need to distinguish between land and the buildings that stand on it. The value of land operates on a different level compared to bricks and mortar.[1] We will track the way this mechanism works across a kingdom disunited by courtesy of Her Majesty's Government.

Taxes were increased during the years of Tony Blair's administration. But the benefits were not shared out to close the gap between the rich and poor. One result surfaced in the classroom. Researchers found that, in the reading skills of children, the gap in achievement widened between those receiving free school meals and the rest. A full explanation would describe how families on the lowest incomes had less choice – for example, in their mobility (fewer cars) and in the range of schools from which they could choose. But refine the description with whatever detail you like, in the end it boils down to the fact that their incomes are low and they are forced by taxation to transfer part of their wages to the rich.

The rich laugh all the way to their banks. As their homes escalate in value they withdraw equity and splash out on the finer things in life. They purchase holiday homes in France and Spain, and four-wheel-drive vehicles in which to deliver children to the schools of their preference. The high achieving schools give their children the best start in life; this is reflected in the higher income earning capacity that these children will achieve, perpetuating the divide into the next generation. That is why people are willing to pay more for the locations in the catchment areas of good schools. So the school's performance is partly measured by the value which is *externalised* (this is a technical term that we shall explain later in this study). If that value were captured and recycled back into the school, government would not need to tax people's wages and savings. But government does not do so. That is why low-income people are discriminated against: they pay their taxes, which they cannot recover as property prices rise in the vicinity of the school to which they send their children. This is part of the scam which works because government and its agencies bias the statistics to withhold the truth from taxpayers (see Box 1:1).

But there was a consolation prize for the poor. In July 2005, the then Secretary of State for Education (Ruth Kelly) announced that a bag of books would be delivered to parents for children when they reached the age of three. It remains to be seen whether children on free school meals will benefit. Their mothers tend to be working parents, tired at the end of the day, many of them without the energy to provide private tuition for their offspring. The two-income family has become a routine feature of family life, the result of the escalating cost of financing a mortgage.

The discrimination between home-owners and those who rent goes even deeper. Take the problem of the cost of money. Interest rates are sometimes driven up as part of government policy. For home owners, a rise in interest rates is offset by the windfall gains that continue to accrue to them. The total value of homes in 2004 was estimated by the Office for National Statistics to be £3.2 trillion, an increase of £352bn over 2003. That was an increase of 12% in 12 months, a rate of increase three times greater than the increase in people's wages. The Blair government's Pensions Commission, chaired by Adair Turner, conceded that people could draw on that value to fund lifestyles in their years of retirement. But that option is not open to people who spend their working lives paying rent to landlords. The injustices of this arrangement did not escape Adair Turner. He noted that the windfall gain for the present generation would be a windfall loss for the next generation that would have to buy houses at ever increasing prices.[2]

Thus, we see a pathological system at work. Through the land market, parents are turned into predators, devouring the livelihoods their children had hoped to enjoy when they grew to maturity. Instead of having a fair start in life, the offspring of today's generation have to vault the hurdle of the housing market. Some of them survive and land on their feet. They acquire property. They will have to pay a higher share of their wages to buy their homes, so that their parent's generation can retire in comfort. But at least they have an asset that will rise in value, courtesy of the taxpayer. However, the millions of young people who are excluded from the possession of property will have their lives permanently crippled.

Box 1:1 Government's 3-Card Trick

WE ALL add value to the wealth of the nation over and above what we take home in wages and salaries. That value ends up as land value, but it is not shared out between us. To conceal this injustice, government invokes the doctrine of progressive taxation. By selective use of statistics, taxes are deemed to be 'fair'. Take a closer look at the numbers.

On May 12, 2006, the Office of National Statistics (ONS) offered its analysis of taxes and subsidies. People in the lowest 20% income bracket received an average wage of £4,300. This was bumped up by state subsidies to an average of £13,300, a gain of £9,000. The average income of those in the top 20% bracket was £66,300, which after taxes was reduced to £47,400 – a loss of £18,900. So the rich fund a better lifestyle for the poor. Right?

Wrong.

The £18,900 paid by the average top earner is *more than offset by the rise in the value of his property*. That rise is funded by taxpayers, and disproportionately so by those on the lowest incomes who do not own property. The ONS, in computing the tax-and-benefits share-out, audits what is transferred to the poor (such as incapacity and child benefits), but ignores the windfall gains that are allocated to the rich out of the government's slush fund.

High-income earners, insists the ONS, 'pay more in tax than they receive in benefits'.[1] True or false? The answer depends on how you cook the books. *The Financial Times* reported the ONS figures in these terms: 'The figures show how the tax system is progressive, with the richest paying more of their income in direct tax than the poor'.[2] In fact, the Tax State has rigged the rules so that the rich claw back more than they pay into the public coffers. But nobody notices: that is the government's 3-card trick in action.

1 National Statistics, 'Taxes and benefits – the effect on household Income', May 12, 2006; www.statistics.gov.uk/taxesbenefits.

2 Scheherazade Daneshkhu, 'Tax and benefits make deep impact on income inequalities', *Financial Times*, May 13, 2006.

1:3 Bonanza for the Asset Rich

TAX POLICIES give the run-around to people on middle incomes.

Caroline Lakin of the Office for National Statistics examined the flow of income back and forth between government and the middle quintile group whose original income was, on average, £19,320 (Table 1:2).[3] What these households pay as direct and indirect taxes is all but cancelled out by what they receive in handouts of cash and kind. At the end of the tortuous process, they are better off by a fraction, with a final income of £19,750. Was it worth going through the bizarre system to end up with little more than £400 better off? The personal costs of filling in the tax returns, and the losses inflicted on them by the costs of collecting the taxes, more than cancel that benefit. Why not let them live a tax-free, subsidy-less life?

Table 1:2

Whirligig Taxes
Middle quintile household group income (2002-3)

Before-tax Income			£19,320
Taxes:	*Direct*	4,000	
	Indirect	4,180	
Benefits:	*Cash*	4,250	
	Kind	4,370	
After-tax Income			£19,750

How do governments get away with it? They claim that they are obliged to use broad-based taxes to minimise the distortions to the way people work, save and invest. The truthful way to translate this message is as follows: *governments seek to deceive people into thinking that they are not paying taxes, in the hope that they do not alter their behaviour in negative ways that result in the under-production of wealth and welfare.* This exposes the anti-democratic character of taxation, but also the cynical attitude of politicians. Governments, by avoiding the obligation to make taxes transparent, avoid being held accountable for their actions.

People are not deceived. They sense that taxes are unjust. But they also know that they must pay their way in life. All they want is fair play on a level field. But that equality of opportunity is not afforded them, and their democratically elected representatives are ultimately to blame. Parliament fixes the rules of the economic game.

Table 1:3

Windfall Gains from House Values

@ 5% per annum

	Renters	*Owners with houses worth*		
		£100,000	*£500,000*	*£1m*
In 1 Year	0	5,000	25,000	50,000
Over 10 Years	0	63,000	314,000	629,000

The cruel discrimination of the land-and-tax scam is highlighted by the data in Table 1:3. This compares the fate of people who rent their homes with those who own their properties. The cumulative effect is to enrich the wealthy disproportionately, and grind down those who are asset poor. I use a conservative 5% per annum growth rate for house prices. Over the course of 12 months, families that rent their homes are no better off. The owners of homes worth £500,000 are wealthier by £25,000 – this is about the average wage in the UK. People with more modestly priced homes – mainly to be found in the 'peripheral' regions of the North, Wales and Scotland – are better off by a modest £5,000. For many of them, that is not enough to claw back the taxes they pay during the year.

Now reflect on the fortunes of people who live on Millionaire's Row. They pocket a handsome £50,000 at the end of Year 1. At the end of 10 years, the owner of what was a million-pound dwelling now finds himself occupying a house that has risen in value by £629,000. Compare that with the £63,000 increase received by the owner of the house that was originally valued at £100,000.

This is not the result of either skill on the part of the home owner, or the random luck of a lottery. It is the result of tax-and-spend policies that discriminate against those who do not own land, or whose sites are not located in the best areas. The discrimination is sanctioned by Parliament.

The real-world impact of this process is enormous. Halifax estimated that the value of the UK's private residential housing stock, which was £3.3 trillion at the end of 2004, had increased by 15% in that year. That was more than 50% higher than three years earlier, and it was three times the value of the housing stock in 1994.[4] Families that rented their homes were excluded from these windfalls. In fact, far from sharing in those windfalls, the cost of renting their accommodation was higher than if they were buying their homes (see pages 87-8).

Families that rent their homes are locked into a vicious spiral of deprivation. Wages are now tied closely to the rate of inflation. The core retail price index (RPIX) rose by 28% over the 10 years to 2004. Living standards were tailored to this rate. But the value of residential property increased by more than 200%. This gave incomparable buying power to people who owned homes, setting them apart from taxpayers who were excluded from the tax-financed bonanza of the property market.

1.4 What's Going on Here?

THE EXPLANATION used by social scientists to account for the unequal distribution of income was inherited from Karl Marx. Class conflict is supposed to drive the process. But as we are now beginning to see, class theory offers an inadequate representation of the way in which people are victimised. The ogre of the Marxist narrative is the capitalist. Our competing explanation identifies the state as the villain. The housing market offers evidence that reveals a complex reality at work.

Draw a straight line on a map from the centre of London to (say) the North-Eastern corner of England, and we traverse six statistical regions. If we plot the value of houses on a graph, we perceive remarkable regional variations (Graph 1:1). The riches are concentrated in the South-Eastern corner of England. But over the decade to 2004, the value of the housing stock did not rise equally across Britain. House prices rose by 246% for Greater London compared with 197% for the North. Over the long run, the gap between people who own land in the South East and those who own it in the North increases inexorably. This discrimination is the result of the failure of the state to employ policies that equalise the benefits which it creates, with taxpayer money, for the benefit of all taxpayers.

In identifying the state as culpable, we acknowledge that society needs government to deliver services that people cannot provide for themselves. The state does contribute to the nation's wealth and welfare. Government spending on infrastructure increases the productivity of the economy. But because of the way that the market economy works, the consequence is the externalisation of part of that value out of the hands of the people who fund it. *The impact of this is the nub of the economics of wealth production and distribution which receives all but no attention from economists.*

Today, economists rely on a one-dimensional model of income distribution. The highest incomes are at the top of the scale and the lowest incomes are at the bottom. But this does not *explain* how income on the bottom rungs is transmitted to the top. For that, we need a spatial dimension to measure what is going on across the territory. If we place this dimension on a horizontal axis, the evidence reveals a horrifying tale of social exploitation that is driven by governments in the name of the people.

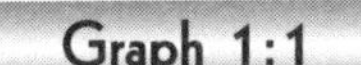

Value of UK Private Housing Stock
By region, £bns (2004)

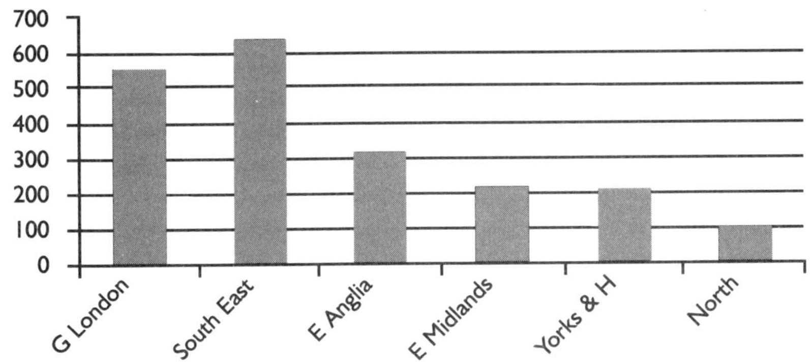

Source: Halifax, 'Value of UK Residential Housing Stock hits £3.3 trillion in 2004', Press Release, February 5, 2005.

Figure 1:1 offers a stylised portrait of the forces at work. When low-income earners in North-East England pay taxes, the net gains from the public investments which they help to fund surface as an increase in the value of assets owned by high-income people in London. The contra flow of welfare payments to the North East is poor compensation for the value that haemorrhages out of the region.

This seemingly magical transformation of the income of one section of the population, in one place, for the benefit of asset-rich people in another place, is not a necessary outcome of the market economy; and it was not legitimised by a democratic mandate. Low-income families that struggle to make ends meet do not voluntarily hand over their hard-earned cash for the benefit of the rich. The process is driven by forces that governments have chosen to foster.

There are two reasons why we should abandon the flat Marxist theory of class in favour of the dynamics of the spatial distribution of wealth. First, the deeper appreciation of how the economy works leads to commonsense answers to the questions of *what* and *why*. Challenging the power of the state is a daunting task, an exercise not to be undertaken frivolously. Previous attempts at changing the rules of the financial game (trying to redesign the structure of society by altering some of its key financial buttresses) failed because people did not fully comprehend the forces that were at work.

Second, the new understanding leads to policies that synchronise economic efficiency with the principles of justice. To achieve an outcome that

Figure 1:1

The Spatial Redistribution of Income and Wealth

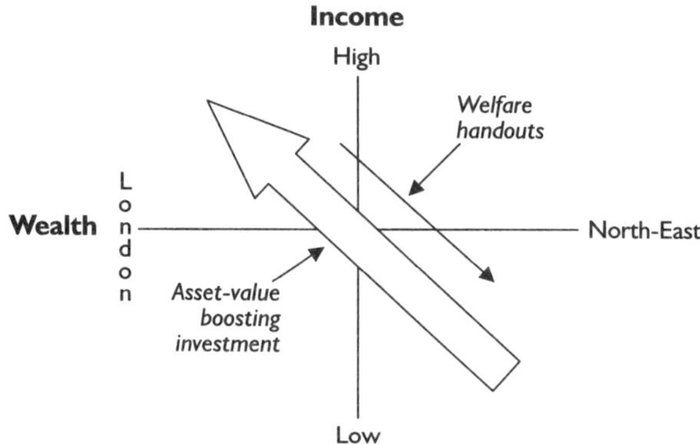

is fair and efficient from everyone's point of view, however, the doctrinal prejudices that shaped the tax system must be expunged. The prices that governments charge must conform to the principles of the code that has guided humans through evolutionary timescales. But before we introduce this code into our analysis, we need to equip ourselves with the theoretical tools that expose the mismanagement of people's money by the state.

To make sense of this spatial scale, and to understand how the political scam works, we need a piece of theoretical knowledge. The theory must explain, in scientific terms, why and how wealth is distributed across the surface of the nation. The theory was provided by David Ricardo. If we master the economic logic of Ricardo's Law, we can unlock the secrets that are withheld from taxpayers.

REFERENCES

1 For a description of the difference, see Fred Harrison, *Boom Bust: House Prices, Banking and the Depression of 2010*, London: Shepheard-Walwyn, 2005, Appendix.

2 Chris Giles, 'Pension hope as value of homes leaps', *Financial Times*, July 26, 2005.

3 Caroline Lakin, 'The effects of taxes and benefits on household income, 2002-03', *Economic Trends*, London: Office for National Statistics, June 2004.

4 Halifax, 'Value of UK Residential Housing Stock hits £3.3 trillion in 2004', Press Release, February 5, 2005.

2

Ricardo's Law

2.1 The Theory of Rent

DAVID RICARDO turned to the scientific study of economics rather late in life. Endowed with a fortune that he made from the stock exchange, he retired from business to contemplate the anatomy of the new wealth machine that was changing the world.

Ricardo was born into a Jewish family in London in 1772, four years before Adam Smith published *The Wealth of Nations*. He retired from the financial world in 1814. His first foray into economics was with essays on money. He published his seminal *Principles of Political Economy and Taxation* in 1817, followed by his election to Parliament in 1819. He died in 1823, but his name lives on as the economist who gave scientific precision to the concept of economic rent.

His theory of rent was integrated into classical economics, and was part of the working apparatus of the economist throughout the 19th century. But although it was not discredited by the scientific evidence, land and rent as distinct categories were eliminated by the post-classical school of economists in the 20th century. The enormity of this error is indicated by the fact that rent serves, in human society, a similar function to the dark matter that binds the universe together. The rent of land may have been vaporised from view, by the experts, but it continues to shape the destiny of communities as the glue that holds together the parts that constitute civilised society.

Economic rent is not what we pay when we sign a lease to become tenant of a landlord, when we rent a house or shop. Economic rent is the difference between the costs of production, and the revenue from a value-adding enterprise. Put another way, economic rent (which I shall shorten to the concept of *rent*) is a surplus. It is what is left after paying people's wages and the costs of using capital equipment, the raw material and all the other inputs of an enterprise. Thus, this is the amount which an enterprise (or an individual) can hand over for the use of land.

Rent emerges only where people have devised ways of raising their productive output above subsistence. As such, it is the material basis of civilisation: it is the income that releases people from manual labour, which makes possible the development of the aesthetic senses in its rich variety of forms – the religious sensibilities, artistic achievements and mental voyages ever deeper into the intellect.

Rent, in other words, is the excess income over the minimum that people need on which to live.[1] Such reasoning led the classical economists to distinguish between land, labour and capital. The latter is the concept for the man-made tools that are needed to grow food and manufacture goods in workshops and factories.

How did these three factors interact? In *The Wealth of Nations*, Adam Smith offered a robust description of the labour and capital markets, and he explained that the enterprise economy would be best served by integrating government into production through a tax on land – that is, the rent that owners charged those who wished to use their land. Rent was what Smith called the 'peculiarly suitable' source of revenue for commercial society, since payments out of it did not distort people's incentives to work, save and invest.

Figure 2:1

The Nation's Income

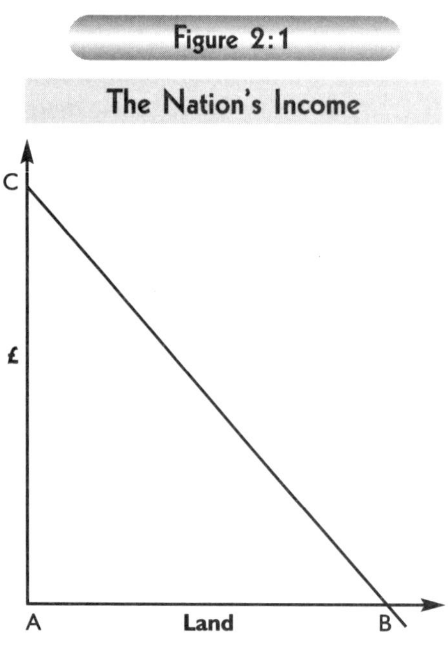

But this model was incomplete. Smith had noted that efficiency was achieved when labour specialised according to the variable skills of employees, but that was an insufficient description of the capitalist economy's organising principle. Something more was needed. Consider this issue in terms of our first abstract representation of the economy (Figure 2:1). This measures the nation's aggregate income. The value of units of output is measured by the vertical axis. The amount of land that is used by the economy is shown on the horizontal axis (AB). If we add up the value within the area ABC, we arrive at the total income of the economy.

The two questions that concern us are: (1) how were the factors of production combined to maximise the output of wealth and welfare? And (2) how was the nation's income distributed?[2] This was the point at which Ricardo stepped in with his theory of rent. He explained why there would be a downward sloping curve on the graph that measured the productive capacity of the economy. The sloping line implies that productivity varies as between both people engaged in production, and the land and capital inputs that they use to manufacture the goods that are sold in the markets. But the variations were not random events. In time, these would shake themselves down into a spatial pattern. Simply stated, specialisation would lead to high-value activity being located at the centre of production (near location A on Figure 2:1), graduating away to lower value activity at the periphery of the economy (denoted by B on our figure).

A number of questions arise from this representation of production. First, notice that the downward sloping line intersects the horizontal axis (at the point B). This implies that some people are working on land that does not yield an income sufficient to cover costs of production. That is an irrational state of affairs; people do not expend energy for nothing. We would expect them to stop working at the point where they were just able to generate sufficient income to cover the cost of living. Thus, something is missing from this model: an organising principle that ensures the use of resources up to the point where people can at least support themselves with sufficient wages, while they are working, to cover the costs of food, clothing, shelter and the other basics of life.

David Ricardo provided the formula that enables us to see how the parts fit together. His key was the rent of land. Land is defined to include all of nature's resources, including petroleum, water, coal, and so on, not just the surface that is used to grow food or on which to construct buildings.

Ricardo explained how human aspirations and propensities converged to adjust the combinations of land, labour and capital in an orderly manner, finally reaching a point called the *margin of production*. Beyond that point, land would not be used for economic purposes because people could not subsist on it. Within that margin, however, the commercial society operated constantly to rearrange the combination of land, labour and capital to optimise the output of goods and services that consumers wanted to purchase.

We must refine Graph 2:1 to identify a margin (this concept is fully explored in Chapter 3). This is shown on Figure 2:2. Production will take place on land up to the location denoted by X. This is where wages and interest are just sufficient to cover the inputs of labour and capital. But as we have shown it, the prices that consumers are willing to pay for the products produced on this land do not yield a surplus: the enterprise cannot pay rent for the use of the land.

To illustrate the theory, it would be helpful to work through a numerical example.

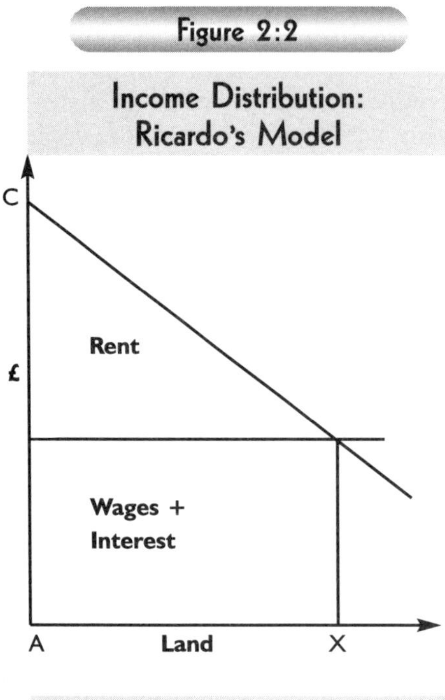

In our hypothetical economy, we shall assume that the minimum acceptable wage is £40 a week. Anyone who can earn more than this is, by definition, relatively more productive. That additional productivity is translated by the market economy into the rents that people are able and willing to pay for the use of land. Through competition, wages are equalised across the economy. Everything in excess of those wages is shaved off as the rent of land (the variations in remuneration due to skill are discussed in Chapter 3). The same applies to the interest that can be charged for the use of capital. People who lend money to entrepreneurs for investment in production would not expect to receive a higher rate than is available elsewhere: super-profits would soon be chiselled away by the competition from other people's savings. And so, as in Figure 2:2, we use a horizontal line to denote the distribution of income: the income below that line is reserved for labour and capital, and the surplus is paid as rent.

We have now identified one of the key elements of Ricardo's theory. Spatially speaking, the rent of land is shown as declining across the economy. The further we move from the centre (A), the lower the rental surplus. Why? What prevents the rent of land from being equal across the whole territory? Instead of Figure 2:2, why can't output be represented in the shape of a box (Figure 2:3)? This would require productivity to be equal across the land, wherever people located themselves.

An anthropological perspective will help to elucidate the answer. When people migrate to a new territory, they naturally gravitate to areas where the fruits of nature are most abundant, or because of other topographical advantages (such as access to rivers that can serve as transport links to the rest of the world). Why work heavy-going soil to produce your daily bread, when you can enjoy a full stomach with half as much labour on more fertile soil? The implication of this is that, the further people moved from the favoured spatial centre (as when population expanded), the fewer were the advantages of the land on which they relocated.

Besides soil fertility, there are other reasons why we would not expect the rent profile to be uniform across the economy. Take the case of transportation. The further away the farm is from the distribution centres where produce is sold, the higher the costs of carriage to market. Those costs have to be deducted from total revenue. In terms of Figure 2:2, transport costs are low near location A, and high for people located at X. So even if soil *was* uniformly fertile across the economy, the *rising* costs of transport (for enterprises located further away from the market) mean that there is a *declining* surplus that can be paid as rent. The profile of income suggested in Figure 2:3, then, does not fit the facts of life.

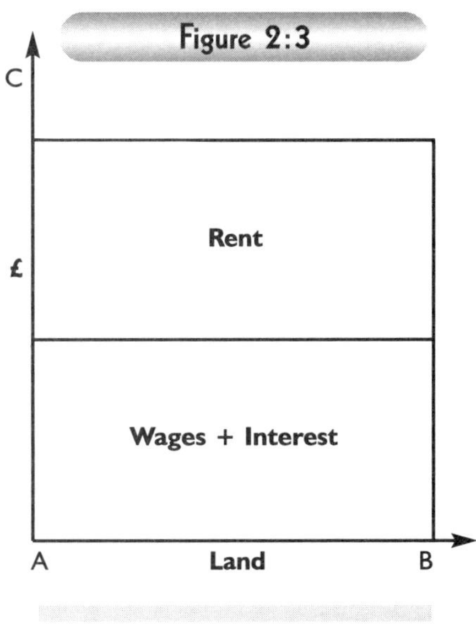

If people behave rationally, they would continue to recombine resources in different quantities until production reaches the point where, no matter how we try, we cannot increase the output. At this point we have maximised wealth and welfare, and we are not wasting resources. That point is determined by the margin. Here, people achieve maximum satisfaction, but without generating a surplus to pay for the use of land. But since land is a 'free gift of nature', in principle it does not matter that rent is not being paid at this location; people can still make a living, and may even be glad to be far away from 'the madding crowd'!

We shall defer further exploration of the concept of the margin to Chapter 3. First, it is important that the reader holds in mind the big picture provided by the Ricardian model.

2.2 The Price of Civilisation

RICARDO IDENTIFIED an organising principle that is akin to the laws of nature. Magnetism is the organising principle for lines of power on and inside our planet. Gravity is the organising principle for orbiting planets in space: thanks to the work of Newton and Einstein, we now understand how solid masses relate to each other, and the speed of their interaction. The tidal movements of oceans, for example, are explained by gravitational pull, as is the flow of water down a mountain to the sea. We need to understand these laws to make sense of everyday realities. Through our deeper comprehension of the forces of nature, we can work *with* nature to achieve ever deeper accomplishments in the human voyage through time and space.

Ricardo's Law explains the pull and push of land, labour and capital in the economy. With this law, we can begin to understand the various quantities of those factors that are used; and the reasons for the distribution of the income that flows from productive activity.

The framework within which this interaction occurs is provided by the principles of *co-operation* and *competition*. We are social creatures. We cohabit in settlements. Through our communities, we work together to achieve our human potential. This propensity to engage in social activity is balanced by the self-interest that surfaces, in the market economy, as the competitive spirit (or, on the playing field, as the attempt to achieve personal excellence in sport). The spirit of gregariousness and the quest for self-fulfilment make it possible for humans to elevate themselves and their communities above the level of subsistence.

By engaging in the enterprise economy we help each other to raise productivity to the point where we can all pay our way through life, and even generate the surplus that is needed to fund the finer achievements of complex societies. People can be released from working in fields and factories to concentrate on the arts, science and religion. Rent is the price we pay to participate as paid-up members of civilisation.

Wage rates are adjusted across the economy because we harness the principles of co-operation and competition. Mobility is the willingness of people to move to places of opportunity where they can improve their well-being. That is why people in low-productivity areas (near the margin) migrate towards the spatial centre. In doing so, they deliver a downward pull on the wages in towns when there is a risk that they will rise above the prices that consumers are willing to pay. At the same time, there is a push in the opposite direction. Investment in science and technology creates a demand for higher skills, which delivers an upward push to wages. Through co-operation and competition – as played out in the personal interactions that constitute the marketplace – wage (and interest) rates are equalised across the economic space that we inhabit.

But Ricardo's Law is not driven by natural phenomena alone. It operates at a much more complex level than the magnetic field or gravitation. It is a social law. As such, there is the danger that it will be manipulated by people who wish to gain an advantage at the expense of others. That manipulation, if it succeeds, may deprive people of a fair chance of earning a decent living. Before exploring that issue, however, we must pause to ask: how realistic is Ricardo's theory today, 200 years after he formulated it?

If Ricardo's Law remains relevant to the post-industrial Information Age, we would expect productivity to be highest at locations furthest away from the territorial periphery. We shall put the theory to a rigorous test. In

Chapter 1 we bisected England to cover six statistical regions. We visualised a straight line that began in the financial centre in London, where David Ricardo used to do his deals in the coffee houses, running up to the North East. The reason why we selected those six regions for detailed examination is explained in Chapter 4.

The value added to the UK economy by each region reveals a trend that conforms to the prediction of Ricardo's Law. The peak is in London and the South East, and the line descends to the lowest point in the North East. Now, if South-Easterners occupy the most productive locations in England, they can pay higher prices for land. North-Easterners, on the other hand, who are supposed to be least able to yield part of their production for the use of land, would pay the least for the use of land. The data in Graph 2:1 confirms Ricardo's theory. The highest surplus is produced in London, followed by the South East, East of England and so on down the line to the North East.

Now compare the profile of this graph with Figure 2:2 on page 36. We see that, in terms of the downward sloping curve, the empirical evidence confirms the theory in a robust way so far as the variable distribution of rent is concerned. We address the issues relating to the share received by labour and capital (that value shown below the horizontal line in Figure 2:2) in Chapter 3.

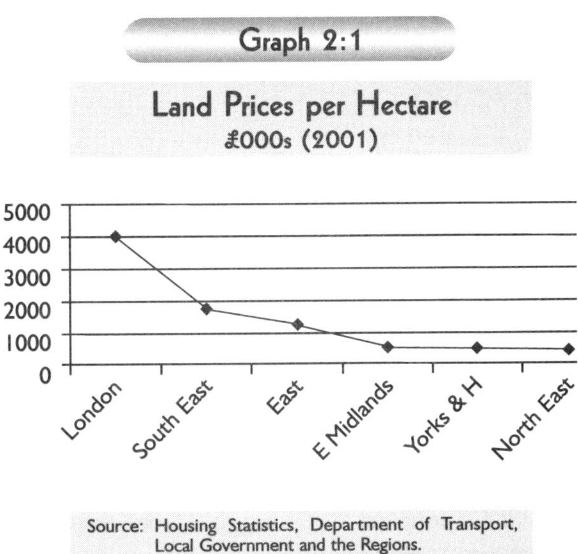

Source: Housing Statistics, Department of Transport, Local Government and the Regions.

2:3 The Domesday Book

RICARDO'S LAW is the interaction of natural forces with people in their communities. How can we be sure about this? What if the trend in land prices was unique to modern, complex societies? A detour into the history of early settlements in the British Isles may offer some answers.

By their settlement patterns, the prehistoric peoples who migrated from mainland Europe disclosed the varying attractions and productivity of the land. The thin dispersal of people was noticeable in the North. People concentrated in greatest numbers in the South where the farming land was superior. Given the level of their technologies of production, however, they were not able to produce much of a surplus.

However, by the Roman conquest in AD 43, 'Britain … was primarily agricultural and sufficiently productive (though probably only just) to support the gradual emergence of an unproductive upper tier in society'.[3] We should not underestimate the capacity of those early settlers to produce a surplus for religious and military purposes. Before the Romans, England was divided into tribal units that were continually at war with each other.

> Tribal warfare was dependent on an economic surplus because the surplus fed the leaders and warriors. If inter-tribal warfare was terminated and armed resistance quashed the surplus could then be re-directed into supporting towns; similarly the members of the tribal elites would seek to assert their influence and power within the structure and offices of local government.[4]

The first 400 years of the first millennium is the story of urbanisation. This was when the Romans extracted a surplus to support the legions which protected the western-most flank of the Empire. Every town dweller in the Roman era was supported by 13 or 14 people in the rural sector. But the town dwellers were not equally distributed throughout England. A map of Romano-British urban settlements reveals that towns were concentrated in the central and southern parts of the province.

> It can hardly be coincidence that this was also the part which was the most agriculturally fertile, or in economic terms, the least marginal. Here the land was generally good enough to allow the regular production of a surplus. In the north, west and extreme south-west this was not so true, though these areas were more productive than was once thought.[5]

The people of the North may have been relatively disadvantaged by the natural fertility of the land they occupied, but they enforced a measure of equity in the way they distributed and used land. This was so both during the tribal system of economics, and in the feudal organisation that followed it. William conquered England in 1066 after triumphing at the Battle of Hastings. Might was right, but public expenses – defence of the realm and the enforcement of law and internal order – were funded out of the rents of the kingdom.

William dispossessed the Anglo-Saxons of land to provide 170 baronies for the leading captains – Norman, French, Breton and Flemish – who teamed up in the mission to conquer England. Some of the baronies were small, but others were bestowed with rich rewards. One of them, Hugh, the *Vicomte* of Avranches, was allotted almost the whole of Cheshire. He was also allotted manors in richer locations in Lincolnshire, Suffolk and Oxfordshire.

William needed to know the rental capacity of his kingdom, if he was to administer it efficiently. He ordered the Domesday juries in 1086 to compile the famous record of the annual value of manors and estates of England. They came up with a figure of £73,000 a year (excluding the revenue from towns). Their findings were divided into regions by historian William Cobbett (Graph 2:2).[6]

The way William restructured land tenure and allocated the rents from the manors reveals the character of England during the three centuries when feudalism was at its peak as a social organisation. Of the £73,000 revenue, £30,350 a year was provided for the 170 barons who were expected to do military service on behalf of the king. These military fiefs formed the cornerstone of the new English social system. The land was held on the same conditions of tenure as the baronies in Normandy. The new tenure required homage to the king, the provision of fully equipped knights if summoned, to serve in the king's army, and aiding the king with money for certain specified events.

Rural Rents: the Domesday Findings
(1086)

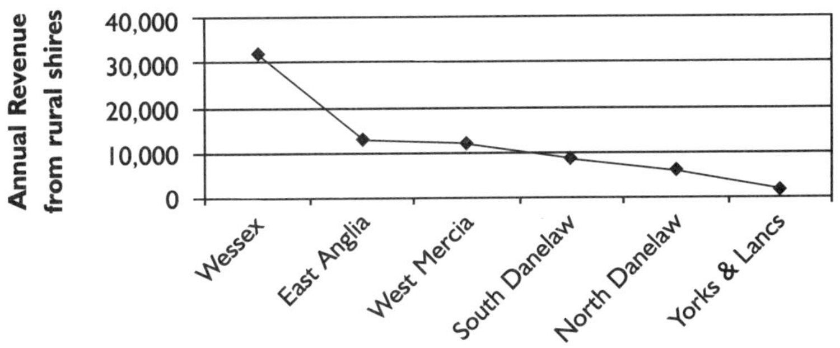

Source: William John Cobbett, 'The development of the Duchy of Normandy and the Norman conquest of England', *The Cambridge Medieval History: Contest of Empire and Papacy*, Vol. V, Cambridge: The University Press, 1926, p.507.

Cobbett suggests that there was a tendency for the king to claim that fiefs were indivisible and to insist on enforcing a rule of primogeniture.[7] Formerly, some of the cultivating classes had been free to select and change their laws. This freedom was swept aside by William.

> [T]he men in every manor, whatsoever their social status, became bound to their lords by an hereditary tie ... To a great extent the freer classes were merged into the less free, absorbed into manors,

> and compelled to do unfree services ... William in fact, whether consciously or not brought about a reconstruction of society on a new legal basis, and so in a sense turned England into a feudal state.[8]

The allotment of tenure rights was the linchpin of this new social order. Cobbett describes it as 'the most revolutionary of his measures; for it established in England the cardinal feudal doctrines that all land is held of the king, that all occupiers of land except the king must be tenants either of the king himself or of some lord who holds [land from] the king, that the ties between the lord and his tenants is hereditary, and that the extent of each man's holding and the nature of his tenure determine in the main his civil and political rights'.[9] William, however, did maintain intact the courts of the shire and hundreds, and even the Anglo-Saxon system of police. Taxation was not feudalised. The obligation on all freeholders to pay 'gelds' was maintained.

The outcome was a monarchy with absolute power which could ignore all provincial differences of law and custom. As a result, England was united in a way that was unknown under the Saxon kings. And that kingdom would be financed out of the rents of land.

The regions are not strictly comparable. Wessex, 10 shires south of the Thames, contributed about £32,000 to the total of £73,000 a year. East Anglia, which delivered £12,950, was made up of three shires. On the basis of the shires, the productivity of the southern rural communities was roughly the same. But as we move northwards, the productivity declines sharply. The eight West Mercian shires contributed £11,000, and the seven shires of the Southern Danelaw, lying between the Thames and the Welland, about £9,400. The shires of the Northern Danelaw between the Welland and the Humber reported annual revenue of £6,450. The territorially vast areas of Yorkshire and Lancashire between them were worth an annual £1,200. The downward trend in productivity is clear.

This remarkable evidence was subsequently confirmed after the civil war of the 17th century, when Parliament introduced the Land Tax. The rental yield of the land was assessed, which confirmed the findings of the Domesday Book. Northern counties like Cumberland and Westmoreland were lightly assessed to reflect the relatively lower yield of the land. The highest rates were applied throughout the southern and eastern counties (at the rate of 4s in the pound).[10]

It will seem strange to a modern audience to be told that, for all our cultural sophistication and scientific progress, our behaviour conforms to laws of nature. That is because the modern mind has had screened out of it knowledge of the primary drivers that motivate human behaviour. Whether this amnesia was accidental or on purpose is a matter for the reader to contemplate once all the evidence in this book has been assimilated. But the chronological sequence of events as they unfolded in the legal system, and

Box 2:1 The Rules of *Whose* Law?

ARISTOTLE, the ancient Greek philosopher, explained that humans were governed by natural laws. These were universal in that everyone was affected. Grafted on to natural laws were man-made laws that made provision for the particular needs of time and place.

In Britain, following the exodus of the Romans, anarchy made life difficult for the tribal communities until feudal law was applied from the 9th century. William conquered England in 1066 and enforced the Norman version of feudal law, which linked land rights and obligations to the manorial economy. The English common law was brought into being, administered in feudal courts. Then, after the 17th century flirtation with republicanism, the Parliament of landowners restored the monarchy but abolished feudal payments to the Crown. From then on, statute laws passed by Parliament superseded other forms of law.

With the supremacy of statute law, the concept of natural law was systematically eliminated as a guiding force in the law of the land. This was a curious turn of history.

- Philosophers like John Locke used the law of nature to justify the individual possession of land, which was deemed to have been given by God for everyone's equal use. The social contract, into which people freely entered to secure protection for their property under the rule of law, was the device they used to justify land privatisation. But private possession was not unqualified.
- This bequeathed an awkward problem to the land barons. Natural law could be a competing authority, and could be invoked to justify the restoration of people's common rights to land. Should we be surprised that the Parliament of landlords, having secured the whip hand over the monarchy on policy, cast natural law aside?

Today, we are locked into a long list of international treaties, declarations and constitutions that secure everyone's enforceable right to everything under the sun except the land they need on which to sustain their lives. People who do not own land are now tenants of the new, post-feudal class of owners.

the creation of privileges that paralleled the legal evolution, suggests that something more than coincidence was at work (see Box 2:1).

For an even deeper appreciation of the natural processes at work in our relationship with land, we need to go back to the ancient world.

2.4 The Riches of Babylon

BABYLON IS FAMOUS for its decadent period, but long before its eclipse it glowed as a refined city at the centre of one of the earliest civilisations. In the midst of an arid territory, the hanging gardens bloomed and people prospered. What was its secret? The people harmonised natural laws in the spheres of both economics and morality. In doing so, they delivered a surplus income that could be used for the common good.

This surplus was possible because the people invested in the key piece of infrastructure that their communities needed. Water had to be channelled through desert. Irrigation canals had to be constructed and maintained. In common with the other Near Eastern civilisations of antiquity, which pooled that surplus through the temple or palace, Babylon developed a network of canals that irrigated the fields. From these fields grew the dates and corn that could be traded in exchange for the riches of other civilisations; and which could be invested in the capital-intensive projects like the temples and palaces for the priests and princes who functioned as political leaders and the bureaucrats of their city state.

By pooling the surplus, Babylon grew prosperous. They did not have a theory of rent. Instead, they developed a cosmology that suited the state of their knowledge. Theology, rather than science, provided the guiding principles. Nonetheless, the outcome was as if they could articulate the laws of the land in terms of Ricardo's Law.

The evidence for this was excavated by archaeologists and tomb raiders and deposited in archives such as the British Museum in London. I examined some of that evidence with the assistance of Dr Cornelia Wünsch, a scholar dedicated to transcribing clay tablets on which were etched the commercial transactions of the Egibi family. The archive originally contained up to 3,000 tablets that spanned the lives of five generations of that family. The period dated from the reign of Nebuchadnezzar II to the beginning of Xerxes's rule (6th and early fifth centuries BC).

The clay tablets included contracts for the sale of land. These indicated the location, names of the neighbours, size of the plots and the quality and price of the land. From these records we can construct a graph of rents that follows the same gradient displayed in the Domesday Book written 1,500 years later.

In Babylon, there was a market for date orchards. Orchards within the city walls fetched higher prices than those outside but close to the city.

Orchards further afield were the least valuable. Transport costs had something to do with the difference, as did soil fertility. But the orchards within the town, which were most secure from thieves or marauding armies, also benefited from the urban infrastructure – the walls. Thus, on clay tablets excavated from the desert in the early 1870s, we can 'read off' the commercially sophisticated lives of the Babylonians from the way they conformed to Ricardo's Law.

A similar profile of land values along the canals also emerged from the clay tablets. Land closest to the water fetched the highest rents. Moving away from the canal side, the quality of the soil deteriorated. This was reflected in lower rents.

Payments to the temple or palace corresponded to the value of land. In other words, the ancient civilisations funded the cultural explosions in the arid regions of Mesopotamia out of what would be called a Land Tax in 17th century Britain.

This evidence from antiquity confirms my claim that Ricardo's Law articulates universally valid principles. It was by harnessing that law that these peoples were able to emerge from the hunter-gatherer lifestyle. They developed urban centres and with the surplus product they invested in the skills of arts and crafts which produced jewellery and artefacts that continue to amaze us with their exquisite splendour.

The lessons from Babylon in its formative period drive home a special feature associated with Ricardo's Law. To deliver the best results, the production of a surplus had to be linked to a moral code. This required that the benefits that could be funded by the surplus should be equalised throughout the community. Societies that abuse that code ask for trouble. Poverty came to blight the earliest civilisations. Landlessness became a feature for the first time. The rulers responded with the concept of the Clean Slate proclamation. When a new prince was enthroned, for example, he would issue the proclamation so that land was restored to the original owners, and debts that stemmed from taxation were cancelled (commercial debts had to be honoured). This was the formula for long-run stability in a society that would otherwise crumble into the desert sands of Mesopotamia. It is the lesson that the West needs to re-learn if it is to come to terms with the new economic dynamism of the East.

REFERENCES

1 Subsistence is a shifting concept. It defines the condition near the biological minimum for survival, in a tribal society that depends on hunting and gathering for its food and tools. Today, a sophisticated education and high standards of personal and public health are part of the 'subsistence' that people need if they are to function in the complex society.

2 We add 'welfare', because people regard non-material benefits – such as leisure time – to be an important part of their lives. Adam Smith well understood this, and was as concerned with the psychological health of employees as with the number of pins they could turn out on the factory conveyor belt.

3 Guy de la Bédoyère, *Roman Towns in Britain*, London: BT Batsford, 1992, p.15.

4 *Ibid.*, p.39.

5 *Ibid.*, p.79.

6 William John Cobbett, 'The development of the Duchy of Normandy and the Norman conquest of England', *The Cambridge Medieval History: Contest of Empire and Papacy*, (Vol. V), Cambridge: The University Press, 1926, p.507.

7 *Ibid.*, p.512.

8 *Ibid.*, pp.513-14.

9 *Ibid.*, p.514.

10 J.V. Beckett, 'English landownership in the later 17th and early 18th centuries', *Econ. Historical Review*, Second ser., XXX, 1977, pp.573-4; cited in Barry Coward, *The Stuart Age: England, 1603-1714*, London: Pearson, 3rd edn., 2003, p. 488.

3

Living on the Edge

3.1 The Margin as Place

THE HIGHEST concentration of wealth and the greatest opportunities for the mega-billion dollar deals are found at the centre of the economy. Here, surely, is where the fate of the nation is largely determined? That is the popular belief, but it is incorrect.

The fate of the nation – economically and sociologically – is sealed at a place called 'the margin'. In this place, people pit themselves against the toughest challenges. Here, they have to exercise ingenuity and determination to pare down their costs of production to remain economically viable. If they are not 'up to the job', the consequences do not just fall on their heads. The results are felt in communities throughout the territory. At the margin, the price of labour and of capital is determined in a way that shapes people's living standards throughout society. That is why it is in all our interests to make sure that life at the margin is good in all its senses.

We claimed in Chapter 2 that wages at the margin set the benchmarks for wages throughout the economy. If people in the North of England will work for £X a week, workers in comparable jobs in the South would need remarkably good reasons to be paid more than £X. Why? Because in an open society, northerners will migrate south to take up jobs that pay higher wages than they can get back home. The free-flow of people ensures that wages are equalised throughout the economy.

This interaction also applies to the capital markets. A moneylender in the South cannot expect a higher rate of interest than he can receive if the money was borrowed in the North. Why? Because owners of capital would move rapidly to take advantage of the higher interest rates available elsewhere. Through this reallocation of capital across space the rates of interest are equalised.

If that is the effect on wages and interest, why can't the rents of land be similarly equalised? Try moving a plot of land from a low-value industrial location in Newcastle to highly desirable residential locations in the South East. It can't be done!

It is the freedom to transfer one's labour or capital to places where the best returns can be earned that assigns a role of major importance to people at the margin. They make sure that we all operate at the edge, with the keenest prices on offer to consumers. In a strong sense, they discipline the market economy. They force people who live and work *within* the margin – people who enjoy special advantages, which might encourage them to become slothful – to remain on their toes. Without that discipline, enterprises drop their guard and fail to operate at optimum levels of efficiency.

The margin plays a similar role in the public sector, but this brings us to the question that is not predetermined by Ricardo's Law: who has the legitimate claim on the surplus which a community generates in the competitive economy? On moral grounds, it could be argued that this surplus *ought* to belong to everyone, since we all participate in its production. If socialised, rent becomes the fund out of which to defray the costs of the services that people share in common. I shall argue for this rent sharing outcome, but on the basis of strictly functional policies. In Part IV, I will present the case for a reform of the pricing system which does not disturb anyone's private property; but which requires people to pay for the benefits that they receive at the locations where they live and work. Philosophers have argued that we cannot derive ethical propositions out of the facts of life: we cannot derive an *ought* proposition from an *is* – a fact of life. I shall not attempt to do so. Rather, the principles that underpin the pricing mechanism which I prescribe is consistent with the norms of behaviour to which people now comply in their everyday lives; *but the outcomes are similar to those that would result from ethically-driven behaviour*.

If rent, then, is akin to a social fund, it is in all our interests to maximise it, so that we can enjoy the best possible public services. How do we generate the optimum flow of rental income through time? By adopting the correct rules for the economics of the margin, we find that competition+co-operation delivers the most efficient allocation of resources in private markets. But there is a complimentary effect through the impact on politics: the economics of the margin can also deliver efficiency in governance. For a start, the stream of income that politicians can tap would not be open-ended or arbitrarily defined, as it is now. Under the current tax regime, finance ministers decide how much they want to spend on whatever projects the government wants – and then the money is raised. That introduces the risk and uncertainty which play havoc with investment decisions and divides the governed from the government.

The fact that sovereign governments do not have to compete for revenue makes them slothful. But a new discipline is introduced when public spending is funded by rent. There is a finite stream of income. And to get the best possible value-for-money out of that income, policies must be tailored to meet people's needs in the most efficient way, which consequently increases what they are willing and able to pay as rent.

In raising the issue of how governments fund public services, we have foreshadowed the primary solution to the problems of modern society. We needed to register this point, briefly, to stress the comprehensive nature of the economics of the margin. But we must first concentrate on what happens in the labour and capital markets as a result of the distortions that flow from taxes on people's wages and savings.

Our foregoing account is based on the arrangement in which markets are not obstructed by monopoly power. Where obstacles exist, they prevent people from enjoying the full benefits of competition. There is a feedback effect that transforms life at the margin into a living hell.

The margin is a complex concept that needs to be broken down into three levels of reality. Each must be understood if we are to agree to reform the rules so that the economy is moved closer to the state of freedom, a state in which people can earn their living without the intrusion of others. The margin represents a place, a material condition and a state of mind.

As a *geographical space*, the margin is the location where working people can just cover the costs of living. As we plot it on a graph, it appears that the margin is a place where there is no surplus product. If this were the reality in modern society, two groups of people would be disappointed. First, landowners would not receive rents for their land. Second, there would be no income to invest in infrastructure or the higher forms of cultural pursuits. The margin would be a desperate place in which to live.

There need be no such place. Thanks to science and technology, people can earn more than the biological minimum wherever they live in the Western world. Awkwardly, that claim is challenged by the fact that there are neighbourhoods whose populations depend on the transfer of income from other places. Aren't they 'marginal' in the pure, theoretical sense of not being able to generate a bare living income for the residents? They are, but not because the people are incapable of doing so. As we began to explain in Chapter 1, taxes drive people below the margin, where they are prevented from earning enough to pay their way through life.

Before venturing into that terrible zone of deprivation, we need to understand how the margin interacts with economic activity in places that are located nearer to the centre. Given that we now live in the Age of Globalisation, we shall apply Ricardo's Law in its international context.

China provides the most testing challenge to Western nations. Our analysis begins at the margin *within* China. Graph 3:1 shows that hourly wage rates are lowest in the rural areas. Wages are four times greater in

Shanghai, the city at the heart of the coastal region which led communist China into capitalism. In 2005, the average hourly wage rate was $1.1 for urban China. That rate is held in check by the exodus of workers from the countryside pouring into the town.

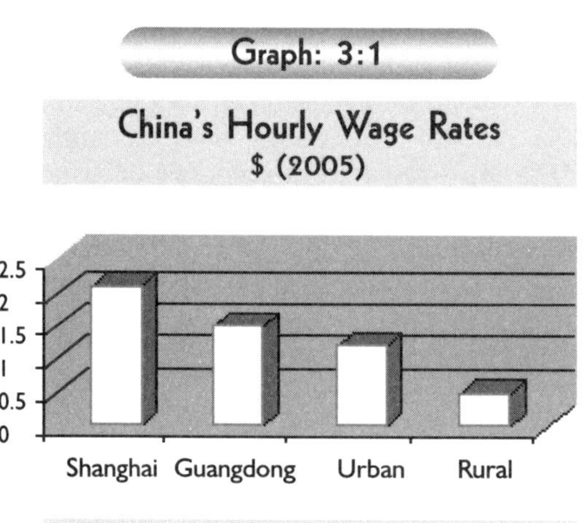

Why aren't wage rates equal throughout China? There are several reasons. One is that rural jobs are not equivalent to the skills that are needed in the urban-based factories. Those additional skills command a premium. Second, rural rates are depressed by the over-supply of workers who are legally prevented from moving off farms. Time is needed for wages to equalise through the country, but the change continues at a relentless pace. The Chinese Academy of Science predicts, in its *China Modernisation Report 2006*, that 500m peasants will be relocated to cities by 2050. Despite the giant strides towards modernisation in the 25 years to 2005, there are still 80m people living below the government's poverty line of less than 668 yuan (£48) a year.[1] This pressure at the economic margin constrains urban wages. Despite astonishing annual growth rates of 9%, the urban workforce cannot demand 'unrealistic' wages: people are disciplined by the knowledge that others would like their jobs.

This interaction in the labour market within China has a ripple effect on wages in Europe and North America. Graph 3:2 suggests that the average Chinese wage rate of 70¢ per hour delivers a downward pull on rates in the European Union (EU) and in the US. The evidence for this is disturbing the living standards of once generously rewarded workers. In Britain, for example, Rover car workers found themselves hostage to a Chinese manufacturer in 2005. Rover was closed down and the company's intellectual property rights became the property of a Chinese corporation. A similar story is being played out in the relationship between the US car market and Chinese automobile workers. Employers in the West are negotiating remuneration terms for their employees based on their ability to transfer production to Asia. The threat from the margin was not a hollow one. In the US, both General Motors and Ford announced plans to reduce their workforces by 30,000. In Germany, Daimler-Chrysler announced a plan to cut its corporate bureaucracy to save €1.5bn (£1bn), and VW revealed plans to cut up to 20,000 jobs over the three years to 2009.

The apparent beneficiary of the shift in global economic power was the consumer. Suddenly, shops were awash with high-tech products at cut-rate prices. But the increase in real disposable incomes did *not* necessarily mean higher living standards. Ricardo's Law reveals the outcome: the net gain from increased productivity across the economy is a rise in the prices that people are willing to pay for the scarcest of all resources – land.

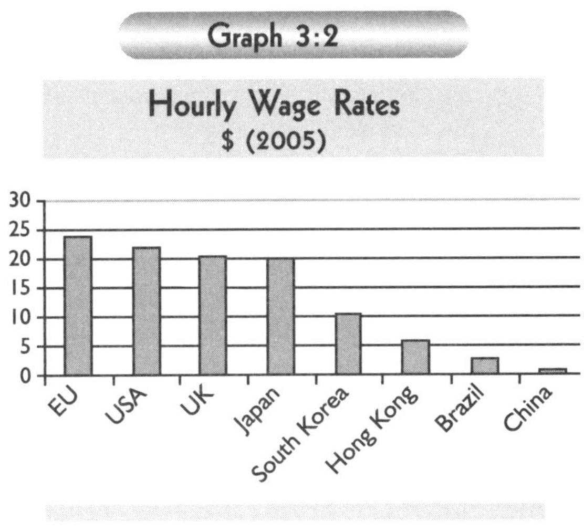

Mervyn King, the Governor of the Bank of England, described the chain reaction from the economic margin in China that affected property prices in the South-East of England. As consumers, King told an audience of business men in Kent

> We have benefited from falling prices of goods made in China and elsewhere in Asia. Between 1995 and 2005,the prices of imported manufactured goods fell by a sixth and, relative to the price of domestically produced output, by no less than a third. So over the past decade we have been able to increase consumption by more than the increase in production.[2]

The heightened tempo in global trade raised living standards at the Chinese margin and exercised a direct impact on one of the centres of the global economy – London and the surrounding Home Counties. King described one of the mechanisms for transmitting the benefits of increased productivity to real estate: interest rates were lowered. That increased the capital value (the selling price) of property. The increase in house prices in 2004 exceeded 20%.

King did not use the word *land*. That is because the post-classical school of economics of which he is an exponent abandoned land as a distinct factor of production a century ago. But media commentators understood the connection. Anatole Kaletsky, writing in the London *Times*, came close to calling a spade a spade. He noted that the addition of two billion new workers to the capitalist system had reduced the wages of manual workers around the world and thereby contributed to the increase in house prices. And that increase in asset values was stupendous.

> The average British family earned £2,000 in the first week of this month ... simply by sitting in their house ... given that £2,000 is more than four times average weekly earnings ... the story of instant enrichment for homeowners raised some perennial questions about the state of modern Britain.[3]

The world is criss-crossed with this dynamic interaction. Within the EU, for example, the automobile sector also has to respond to competition from the former Soviet bloc countries of Eastern Europe. Why is German investment migrating to Slovakia? Because the hourly wage rate in Germany is €29 and €5 in Slovakia.[4] The fluid shift of capital across national borders is the animating effect of the margin as a place.

If marginal areas pay their way, this outcome benefits everyone. The constant search for efficiency across the whole economy has the ultimate effect of maximising the surplus that is available for investment in infrastructure and culture. Why, then, do people generally fear competition from people who live at the edge? The answer to that question is to be found in the artificial limits imposed on people's freedoms. Fear is the product of the civil war that is constantly tearing apart people's lives. The margin is the best place to visit to observe that process in action.

3.2 The Margin as Political War Zone

PLAGUE WAS the scourge of the Middle Ages. With the Industrial Revolution, a new plague arrived. According to the Rev. Thomas Malthus, the sexual proclivities of the propertyless people reduced the population to the biological edge. Some people continue to believe that this is the explanation for poverty: that people are the architects of their own impoverishment.

This doctrine leads to a paradox. Why should rational people degrade their lives even as the nation develops techniques for producing wealth in previously unimagined quantities? According to Malthus, people kept breeding beyond the point where they could afford to support their children.

Ricardo engaged in a lively correspondence with Malthus. He, too, wanted to know what left people suspended at the margins of existence. He was not a theological moralist who censured the procreative activities of the propertyless. Ricardo approached the problem in scientific terms.

Classical economists understood that their new discipline was not just concerned with the production of income. It also had to prescribe ways of securing the correct distribution of income. But as Ricardo emphasised in the title of his book, *Principles of Political Economy and Taxation*, at issue was not just private enterprise; the government's role, through taxation, also had to be integrated into the analysis. This insight enables us to evaluate the forces that determined the quality of life at the margin.

Leftwing mythology demonised competition as the mechanism that drives wages down to subsistence levels. Our competing explanation places responsibility on the tax policies of government. To test this proposition, we shall consider what happens when government introduces a tax of (say) 10% on wages. According to our thesis, some people who are just able to pay their way find that labour costs – wages+tax liability – exceed the revenue generated by the goods or services they can offer for sale. That must lead to the loss of employment. Let us rehearse this point from what we have learnt so far.

We have argued that people *can* earn enough to live at the margin. They can create sufficient value to provide themselves with shelter, food, clothing and the other necessities of life. But this assumes that taxes are not levied on their labours. Now (with the aid of Figure 3:1), we shall consider what happens when government steps in with a tax on earnings.

Figure 3:1

The Imploding Economy

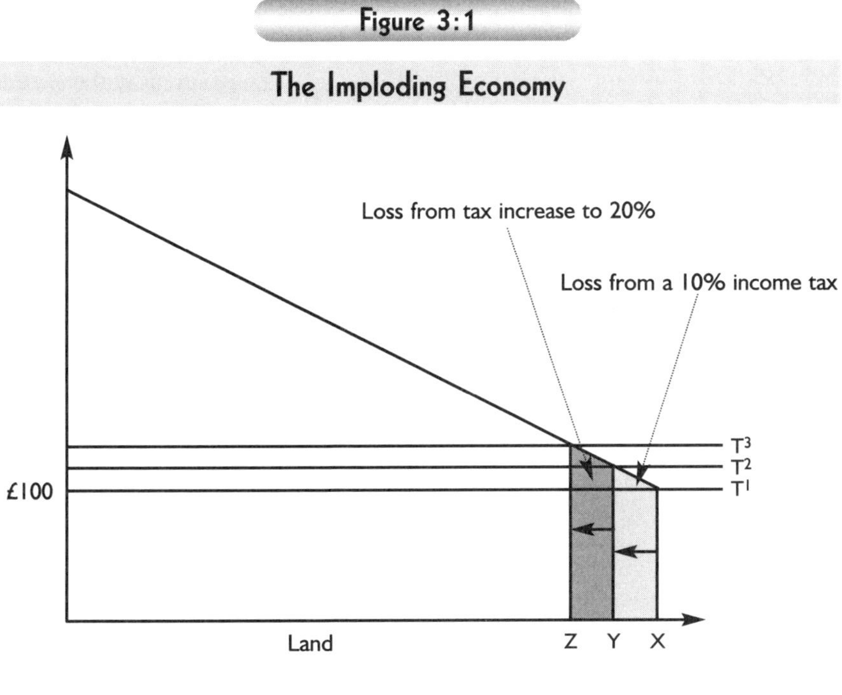

We start with a worker who earns £100 a week. This is denoted by the horizontal line T^1. He lives at point X in the economy: this is the spatial margin. He does not produce a taxable surplus, but his living standard is equal to those of other workers across the country who perform similar tasks. Now the government introduces a 10% tax on everyone's wages, which raises labour costs (shown by line T^2). It is impossible for our marginal worker to make a living. The cost of employing him, to his employer, has risen to £110. But that worker's productivity is £100. So he is out of a job. Government, by levying the tax, causes jobs to disappear.

Two centuries ago, that worker had to fend for himself. His options were limited. He could resort to crime, or work in the tax-dodging 'black' economy. Today, he is rescued by the Welfare State. As a society, we accept that help should be extended to people who are in need. But under the current economic philosophy, the response is to ratchet up the tax-take to fund unemployment benefits. What happens now? We show this in Figure 3:1. The line T^3 denotes an additional 10% increase in the income tax. This renders even more people unemployable. In the diagram, we show that the viable jobs market, and total income, shrinks inwards to point Z.

The margin exposes the ugly secret that finance ministers prefer to conceal. Taxes reduce the productivity of the economy. They deprive people of income that they would otherwise have produced if government had not been so inept with its revenue-raising policies. But more than wages are lost. From Figure 3:1 we see that this surplus – the total amount that would have been paid as rent – is also reduced. The loss is measured by the tinted area. And so on: *the implosion continues as government invents ever more ingenious stealth taxes designed to conceal the tragedies that it imposes on people*.

Here, we should introduce a word of caution. The reader should not take away the impression that the squeeze on people's economic welfare is limited to a place far from the great urban centres. The richest of cities need low-value workers to carry out economically marginal tasks. So the impact of taxation is also damaging to sections of the workforce in locations like London where, in some wards in boroughs like Tower Hamlets, we can find concentrations of some of the poorest people in the country.

This state of deprivation is not the outcome of a natural process. It is the result of an historical process, a grand larceny in which people's independent livelihoods were destroyed when they were deprived of their land rights. One consequence is that the margin is prevented from playing its constructive part in the equalisation of economic activity. People are locked into a captive labour force. They are prevented from bargaining to secure their interests, reduced to the state of dependency which employers are able to exploit. The margin, in other words, has been politicised and transformed into a war zone. How did democratic governments find themselves in this mess? We have to go back to the legal and institutional changes that obliged government to tax wages instead of using the rent of land to pay for public services. A summary of that history is offered in Parts III and IV.

3.3 The Margin as State of Mind

THE PREDATORY effect of taxation may be viewed as a process that devours people's minds. For when people are cheated of a fair deal in life, the damage is to their mental as well as their physical health. That damage can be profound. Epidemiologists trace the impact along 'psycho-social stress pathways', the term they use to link tensions in the mind to death-dealing ailments such as cancer.

The death gap is growing. In Britain in the 1990s, death rates among the most deprived individuals did not decline. These people lived in rented accommodation, had no access to a car and were unemployed. In marked contrast, the rates of death declined substantially among people who owned their homes, had access to a car and were employed.[5] To plumb the depths of this process we need a sophisticated analytical framework.

New Labour, instead of developing a complex appreciation of life at 'the margin' – which includes the negative impact of government policies – remained committed to the crude doctrines of a simple geographical North/South divide.[6] The redistribution of incomes across that divide remained the tool for combating injustice. But 'progressive' taxes were the major cause of damage to people's economic prospects, and therefore their psychological and physical welfare. Far from ameliorating the disparities, New Labour strengthened the dead hand that rests on communities across the nation. The architect of some of those policies was Gordon Brown, Tony Blair's Chancellor of the Exchequer.

Brown was sincere in wanting to help low-income people and their children. His novel device was tax credits. These were supposed to 'tackle child poverty and help make work pay'. The outcome was traumatic for millions of people. Many of them were driven deeper into debt. Of six million recipients, 1.9m were paid too much in the first year of the scheme. The bureaucracy launched a massive operation to claw back £1.9bn. Thousands of people who did not understand the complexities of the calculations had already spent the money. With life on the margin yielding them no spare cash to save, they found they could not repay the taxman – 'they have been plunged into poverty by the very policy that was designed to prevent it,' according to the economics editor of *The Financial Times*.[7]

For the millions who live in the tax-induced zone of despair, one of the escape routes is narco-land. A drugged existence is tempting to some because it provides them with relief from the humiliations of life in the sub-marginal twilight zone. Such human tragedies demand clarity of thought about the dynamics of the margin. Unfortunately, the knowledge people need, on which to base judgements about reforms, is bedevilled by crude concepts that cloud rather than clarify the causes of deprivation at the margin. This is the view of academics who contest the received wisdom about the marginal regions of Italy.[8]

3.4 Zone Beyond the Margin

IF NO ONE need live under the conditions of simple subsistence, why are millions of people driven *beyond* the margin?

To confirm the existence of that terrible place, note the evidence of history. People quit their homelands not out of choice, but because they were dispossessed of their ancestral lands. In colonial times, Europe disposed of those unwanted people through emigration to other peoples' territories.

The world beyond the margin is 'out there', another place, and yet bolted on to our communities by the political policies that we condone, an artificial social construct, No-man's Land. The chain of causation that creates this place is a complex one. We trace some of the routes into the sub-marginal zone with the help of Figure 3:2. We can illuminate the destructive process further by reviewing the strategies used by organised labour that are meant to oppose the malevolent forces that obstruct the legitimate aspirations of working people

Through their collective action – such as by striking against their employers – some trades unions are able to force firms to raise wages. One reason why a union would exercise that power is to raise wages to cover the tax-take (from Y to Z on Figure 3:2), leaving them with the same take-home pay (Y). But the collateral damage to others is immense. Non-unionised people lose their jobs. The numbers who are rendered unemployed is implied by the shift in the margin from X to W on Figure 3:2.

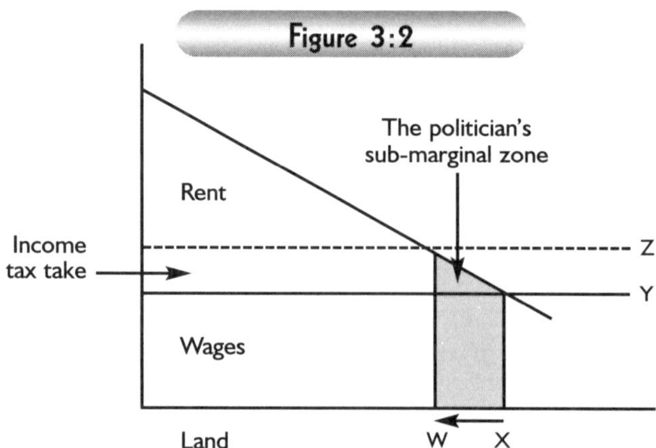

Consumers do not gain from the politicisation of the workplace, for higher gross wages are passed on as higher prices. Through this interaction in the markets, the population as a whole is left with less in its pockets. The aggregate loss is shown on Figure 3:2 as the tinted area.

Culture is degraded. For by driving the economic margin inwards, the aggregate output – the gross national product – is reduced. This means that there is a smaller surplus that can be deployed as rent. And when the nation's rental income is shrunk, the arts and sciences are impoverished.

The relationship between employers and their employees is converted into the nature of a civil war. Britain exploded into near insurrection in the 1970s (when the miners' union challenged the Labour government). The disunited kingdom was reduced to working a three-day week. Then, in the 1980s, the unions lined up against the Press barons. These conflicts were generated by the tensions at the interface between Rent, Wages and Interest. But Rent was not allowed by commentators to intrude into discussions over the ideological contest. The mythology of capitalism was that of a battle between Labour and Capital. The rent-seekers were excluded from the equation, free to plunder the nation's wealth and welfare without fear of being censured.

Margaret Thatcher faced down the unions. Blair's New Labour government continued to pay lip service to the 'values' of its predecessors, and presided over a decline in the share of national income contributed by manufacturers. This dropped from just over 21% in 1997 to under 15% in 2003. During those Labour years, a million jobs were lost from the value-adding industries of a nation that once exercised the industrial power to conquer the world.

The losses to the nation can be quantified, and we shall offer some estimates in Part IV. Needless to say, it is not in the interests of finance ministries to promote public awareness of the scale of these losses. And when they acknowledge such losses, their calculations are suspiciously low. Britain's Treasury, for example, grossly understates what is called the 'excess burden' of taxation. But if we take its measure, Britain was denied wealth and welfare valued at about £138bn in 2005/06. *Over the nine years since New Labour came to power, the loss of wealth to the nation was more than £1 trillion. It was as if every working man and woman in Britain stopped work for one year during Blair's Premiership.* For that year, no one earned a living. To survive, they would have to live off savings. No one can afford to lose one year's income out of nine, but that is what the Disunited Kingdom does to itself because of the way that it pays for public services.

The lesson is this. Ricardo's Law delivers the best results when people locate their behaviour in a code of practice that secures their freedoms. This means that rent should be made available to the community through a market-based pricing mechanism that is efficient, one that does not deprive people of their earnings, and which requires everyone to pay their way in life. This is no more than what reasonable people want for themselves. It is towards this end that we need to develop governance as a science.

REFERENCES

1 Jonathan Watts, 'China's powerhouse vision for 2050', *The Guardian*, February 10, 2006.
2 Mervyn King, Speech, Kent Messenger Group/Kent Business, January 16, 2006.
3 Anatole Kaletsky, 'Why are house prices rising even as the economy falters? Good Question', *The Times*, January 19, 2006.
4 Gail Edmondson, 'Detroit east: Eastern Europe is becoming the world's newest car capital', *Business Week*, July 25, 2005, p.50.
5 A. Reid and S. Harding, 'Trends in regional deprivation and mortality using the Longitudinal Study', *Health Statistics Quarterly*, (5) 2000.
6 *Sharing the Nation's Prosperity. Variation in Economic and Social Conditions Across the UK*, London: Cabinet Office, 1999.
7 Chris Giles, 'Why Brown must overhaul the tax credits system', *Financial Times*, July 29, 2005.
8 Robert Lumley and Jonathan Morris (eds), *The New History of the Italian South*, Exeter: University of Exeter Press, 1997.

Governance as a Science

4.1 The Nature of Society

WHEN THE GODS turned against Rome, something had to be done to placate the people. Free bread and the circus appeared to do the trick, for a while.

The crisis in Roman civilisation originated with the change in the status of the peasant farmers, and the acquisitive character of the land-owning aristocracy. The latter appropriated the most fertile land which they turned into great plantations worked by their slaves. The free peasants were driven onto marginal land and, eventually, into serfdom.[1] In increasing numbers they gravitated to the city where they lived off Rome's version of the Welfare State. To contain the discontent, they were deluded into thinking that all was well, that they could continue to glory in the victories of the empire. But because people did not have to pay for bread, or for their entertainment, an increasing proportion of their disposable income was captured as higher prices for residential property. The landlords of Rome were not going to let ordinary folk enjoy their amusement Scot free![2]

The rents of housing in Rome rose in line with the decay in employment prospects. As slaves were forced to fight to the death in the arena to amuse the citizenry, so the price of land rose for the folk on the grandstands. And as the rents rose, the discontent intensified in the back streets until, one day, the rotten core of that culture was ready for the plucking. The marauders from the wastelands of the north could not have overrun that great city's fortifications if the barbarians from within had not drained the life-blood from a once proud civilisation. Then, as now, the leadership lacked a theory to *explain* how the parts work in relation to the whole.

One of the essential elements of the social jigsaw puzzle – land, and its economic rent – has been degraded to such a lowly status that it is considered to be of little interest to social scientists. The process of expunging land from our mental horizons did not come about by accident: it was a necessary ploy by those who wished to remain 'free riders'.[3] So we are left to ask why politicians, who do wish to improve people's life-chances, make decisions that exploit those who elect them to power.

The land issue is treated with caution in everyday political discussion because the elites do not want the victims to ask the searching questions that challenge the integrity of the laws. The bread-and-circuses technique is used to distract people from penetrating below the surface of society, to gaze upon a system that incubates the behaviour of the barbarian.

When he came to power in 1997, Tony Blair declared an intention to erode the inequalities that discriminate between people in the most fatal of ways.[4] Spreading opportunity and social mobility was a core commitment for his party. But in 2004, New Labour's re-election supremo, Alan Milburn, admitted that opportunity and mobility had declined over the previous 20 years.[5] The experiment in egalitarianism had achieved some benefits for children of some working class families, but by the end of the century the Welfare State had exhausted itself as a means of social improvement.

In 2005, a Department of Health report conceded that the gaps between the rich and the poor, measured by infant mortality and life expectancy, continued to widen despite the £75bn annual expenditure on the National Health Service.[6] Epidemiologists such as Prof. Sir Michael Marmot, who chaired the scientific group that endorsed the report, confirmed findings by other scholars that life expectancy in the rich nations correlated with levels of equality. When the gap between the periphery and the flourishing centre is wide, life expectancy is lower for the poor. But where the gap in incomes is relatively narrow, as in Greece, with half the GDP per head, people enjoy longer lives than citizens in the US, the richest country in the world but also the most unequal.[7]

The hard facts stare us in the face, but we need to know the meaning of the statistics. What causes the disparity in people's life-chances? Prof. Marmot, the government's chief adviser on the epidemiology of the nation's health, declined to speculate on causes. He offered, instead, what looked like a safe platitude: 'Health inequalities arise because of the nature of society'.[8] *The nature of society?*

After seven years of New Labour patronage, the take-home income of the poorest 5.8m Britons had fallen. Weekly real income after tax, welfare and housing costs decreased from £91 in 2001-2 to £88 in 2003-4. This erosion of the take-home pay was monitored by *Households Below Average Income*, a report produced by the Department of Work and Pensions.[9] What was it in the nature of society that drove this outcome?

We argued, in Chapter I, that the conjunction of property rights and taxation redistributes income from the poor to the rich. This is reflected in the spatial distribution of people's health prospects (discussed in Chapter 8), a difference that is not natural. It is not the consequence, say, of a genetic flaw in the population's DNA which, by coincidence, happens to be spread unequally across England. But at the same time, the provision of 'free' health services available at the point of need did not eliminate unequal outcomes between people on a regional basis.

Remedial action is needed, but what kind of action? Recall the words of Michael Marmot, the professor who was knighted for the services he rendered: *health inequalities arise because of the nature of society*. If babies are condemned to shorter lives because they are born on the periphery of the United Kingdom, we have here a *social*, not a *personal*, problem, and one that is of a magnitude that overwhelms people's lives.

Thus it was that, in 2005, the Blair government agonised over the shorter, brutish lives of people who lived at the bottom of the income scales. To leave us in no doubt that the poor were personally responsible for their predicament, the government endorsed the view that 'individuals are primarily responsible for their own and their families' health'.[10] Solutions were tailored to that assessment. The government despatched personal 'health trainers' to the most deprived parts of England. At a cost of £200,000 apiece, these trainers were supposed to guide people towards healthy ways of living 'to tackle the deep-rooted causes of poor health'.

Twelve areas were selected for the health trainers, an initiative announced in the government's White Paper *Choosing Health*. This report was overseen by the Department of Health's scientific reference group, 'made up of independent experts on health inequalities' and chaired by Sir Michael. According to the Department of Health's Press Release, 'health trainers will identify barriers to individuals making healthier choices and help find solutions to get over them'.

What were those barriers? The Blair government did not ask fundamental questions. Instead, it piled more money and bureaucratic initiatives on top of existing attempts to compensate for 'the nature of society'. The problem (and its resolution), evidently, was not a political one; but a personal challenge for the individual. The spirit of Thomas Malthus continues to roam the kingdom. Few politicians would *publicly* associate themselves with the critique of the poor by the 19th century cleric, of course, but their actions speak more profoundly than their words. When the chips are down, the verdict is clear: the poor are to blame for their plight.

Some scholars are aware that poverty is not a personal failing, but rather the institutionalised outcome of the rules of society; and that these rules – or rather, the *comprehension of their significance* – had to be camouflaged. As one of them acknowledged, 'when inequality is institutional' we have a "veil of ignorance' [which] is ignorance about the distribution of power. There is inequality because the more powerful individuals in society choose the rules and institutions which constitute the social contract'.[11]

People are distracted by cherished beliefs that offer a plausible, if incorrect, explanation for large-scale problems such as poverty. People are encouraged to believe that responsibility for persistent economic crises may be attributed to 'market failures'. Hence, say the politicians, the state must intervene to champion those who lose out in competitive markets.

The market economy, if it were really free, does not promote inequality or poverty; it is the mediating mechanism that enables people to enjoy the fruits of freedom and prosperity (see Chapter 14). But that mechanism cannot operate freely and efficiently while carrying on its back the free rider.

4.2 Free Riders

THERE IS one essential difference between free riders and highway robbers: the former do not have to draw pistols to take what belongs to others. The laws that constitute 'the nature of society' deliver purse-snatching rewards to them without having to resort to threats.

Consider what happens when science raises the productivity of the economy. This happened with the invention of digital technology and the world wide web. As a consequence of the virtuous features of the market economy, reductions in the cost of production are isolated as *net gains* and measured in the market for land.

This effect is diagrammatically illustrated in Figure 4:1. Assume that new technologies lead to improvements in the transport network. The costs of distributing goods to consumers are reduced. There is a general increase in productivity. The first effect is felt in the labour market: new jobs are created. People find work on the additional land that comes into use: the margin moves from B^1 to B^2. But wage *rates* do not rise. Competition tends to equalise wages across the territory, on a job-for-like-job basis. But what happens to the additional surplus income? It is pooled into the land market (the tinted area in Figure 4:1). If this was recycled back into funding the nation's infrastructure –

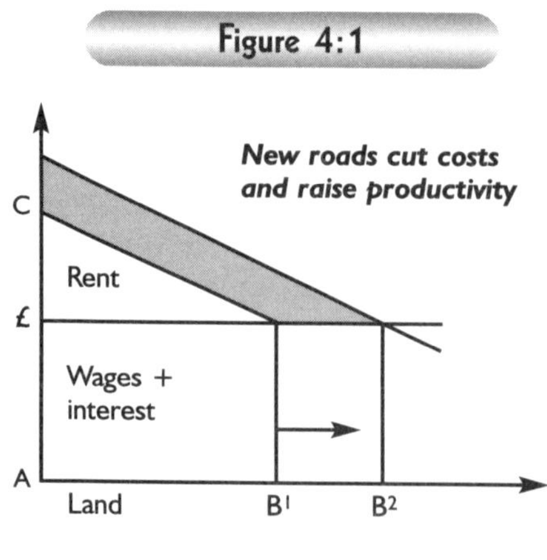

such as the transport systems that helped to create that value – everyone would share in the net gains. But it isn't: the law dictates that the surplus income is delivered as a windfall to the owners of land. Thus, the transport sector is transformed into a sophisticated mechanism for redistributing income away from low-income taxpayers who funded infrastructure to asset-rich people. This is how the trick is performed in relation to railways:

Government Tax on Wages and Consumption → Subsidies to Railways → Strategically Located Sites rise in value → Windfall Gains pocketed by Landowners → Shortfall in Funds to renew infrastructure → Government raises rates of Taxes on Wages and Consumption ...[12]

By increments, the vicious spiral implodes the enterprise economy. Because of the payroll taxes, some people are priced out of work. So government increases taxes to compensate the losers, which creates even more losers. Either some people's living standards, or science and technology, have to be squeezed harder just to keep the economy going on a barely increasing growth path.

We can trace the ripples as they spread destruction deeper into our communities. The windfall gains to landowners from a new road or railway elevates house prices beyond the reach of some people. This prevents low-income 'key workers' from moving into communities where they are needed to administer hospitals and schools or to man the fire brigades or enforce law and order. So a transport system that is supposed to enhance mobility achieves the opposite effect. It becomes an instrument for discrimination against those on the lowest incomes. Immobility is frozen into the structure of the community.

Few people notice. Instead, the pursuit of the 'unearned increment' from land becomes a 'national obsession', as the president of the Campaign to Protect Rural England put it. What fuels that obsession? Housing, he wrote, 'offers a better chance of turning a tax-free profit than any other form of (taxed) personal investment'.[13] Ours is supposed to be a culture of enterprise. For many, however, it is driven by a parasitism that undermines freedom. We institutionalise as *normal* the processes that create and segregate the rich from the rest who are materially, culturally and psychologically impoverished.

Because this chain of events is now regarded as normal, it is invisible. We are not conscious of its pernicious influence, which is why it is morally and materially corrosive. We celebrate the most sophisticated form of pillage because we do not recognise it as such. The free riders are free to rip off the majority without retribution. And most of them do not even realise what they are doing.

4.3 The First Law of Social Dynamics

FREEDOM is the core requirement of the market economy. This was understood by Adam Smith, whose *Wealth of Nations* was written as an attack on the free riders of his time. These were the mercantilists. If people were to derive the maximum benefits from co-operation and competition in the industrial economy, they needed to be free of the state's arbitrary constraints. In the 18th century, the state operated a trade-restricting policy in favour of rent-seeking merchants. That reduced the liberty to exchange goods in the global markets, with the pernicious effect of reducing people's living standards.

Smith figured that if people were co-operating by pooling their labour and savings to mass produce goods, the quality of their lives would rise. But co-operation and competition would not yield the optimum benefits if government failed to play a constructive role. It should not wield its sovereign power to accord privileges to particular enterprises. But if the mercantilist merchants were to lose the privileges which they purchased from the Crown, how was revenue to be raised to pay for the services provided by the state? Adam Smith identified the solution. The Land Tax was the dynamic solution for the enterprise economy.

The tinted area in Figure 4:2 illustrates Smith's recommendation. Assume that government decided to abolish the taxes that injured people's employment prospects and base its revenue on (say) a 50% charge on the nation's land rents. How would that affect people who lived at the margin (location B)? *It would have no negative effect at all!* Why? Because they occupy no-rent land. This means they would live tax-free lives.

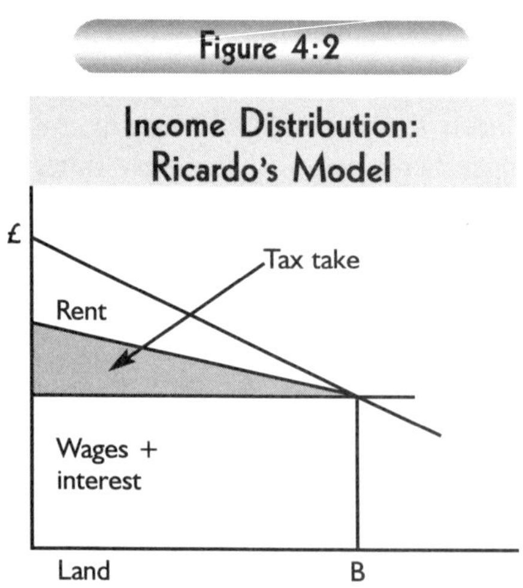

People who enjoy the benefits of living within the margin, however, and were therefore generating a surplus, would contribute in proportion to their capacity to pay. Thus, Adam Smith identified a revenue tool that was 'progressive' – people who generate high incomes paid more than those on low incomes.

This method of raising revenue supports the commercial economy. People with savings invest without having to dodge the taxman. People who want to work overtime would not be criminalized by the tax authority – they would pocket what they earned. It is this conjunction of efficient prices – in the spheres of both private and public goods – that is at the heart of the science of governance.

But scholars now claim that such a science is not possible. Francis Fukuyama, the author of *State Building: Governance and World Order in the 21st century*, asserts that 'there is no optimal form of organisation, both in the private sector and for public sector agencies. That there are no globally valid rules for organisation design means that the field of public administration is necessarily more of an art than a science'.[14] Those words provide comfort for the corrupt politician and protection for the corrupt system. Art legitimises personal judgement; and in politics, the freedom to judge what is in other people's best interests may be exercised with integrity or with contempt.

Fukuyama's assessment is based on an incomplete model of governance. In particular, he fails to take account of the consequences of a correctly constructed pricing mechanism. He is right to argue that people should 'design' their institutions to accommodate local needs. But the *principles* on which their institutions are built should conform to rules that are universally valid.

The institutions which buttress society need to be carefully framed. Caution should be shown before tampering with time-honoured arrangements. Since we will propose a radical departure from some of the key arrangements for property rights and public finance, we need to explain how these are an improvement on the present policies. We shall do so on the basis of an account which we believe to be a realistic description of the social structure within which the earliest civilisations evolved. Indeed, we contend that civilisation is impossible without adherence to this structure.

There are two elements to the social structure. The first has been discussed theoretically in terms of the economy. Nature's resources need to be used efficiently. Energy needs to be concentrated in those places where it can deliver best results. Ricardo's Law provides a modern expression of that principle, revealing symmetry within the social structure in terms of the distribution of people and their natural and manufactured resources. Freedom of the individual is the precondition for achieving this balance through time. Personal liberty entails the right to associate with others in joint enterprises by means that are in the service of the consuming community. In a commercial society, this principle is realised through competition and co-operation.

The outcome is the highest returns for the lowest inputs of time and energy and the materials placed at our disposal by nature. But to achieve this aggregate effect, one-third of the value that is added to the wealth of the nation must be distributed in a way that benefits everyone, either directly or indirectly. This added value, or rent, we recall, was perfectly described as the 'public value of land' by Alfred Marshall, one of the architects of the 'marginalist revolution' in economics at the beginning of the 20th century.[15]

The spatially unequal production of rent (or public value) need not lock people into an unequal distribution of rent. The application of our rational faculties, and the sense of fair play, would ensure that Ricardo's Law delivered outcomes that complimented the norms of justice. If efficiency leads to the disproportionate concentration of resources at the centre, justice requires the re-circulation of that surplus on the basis of the principle of equality. The equalisation of rent among all citizens secures a balance to the present community structure and its resilience into the future. But we have to stress that equalisation of rent is required not just out of a sense of fairness; it is imperative if we want to ensure that all the latent resources that become available through time are constantly redistributed to secure economic efficiency.

This creative relationship between efficiency and ethics delivers what I call the First Law of Social Dynamics. Some people born in the social periphery may be attracted to the centre, but their extraordinary productivity – recognised in higher personal remuneration – is also shared with those in the periphery who, to flourish, have to enjoy access to the cultural riches that are funded out of public value.

We can now visualise a structure in which justice is the complimentary framework for biological imperatives. It is when people are willing to share the public value on an equal basis that culture emerges and then flourishes. In the commercial society, it is the genius of the market to concentrate the surplus in ways that makes its efficient collection possible so that it may be equalised in ways that accommodate the differences in each community. The pricing mechanism for achieving this is market based, and will be elaborated in Chapter 15.

Having presented our social template in terms of the ideal structure, the sceptic may think that this is unattainable. One way to gauge the realism of this model is to examine the consequences of impediments to it. If we can measure poverty on a socially significant scale, we may infer that this is the logical result of our being denied the benefits of the arrangements that are practicable in a moral society.

We shall consider, for example, how the restriction on personal freedom limits our ability to produce wealth. If the public value is less than what we can actually achieve, given the level of knowledge and technology, we would also expect culture to be impoverished. And if that is the case, the constraint on culture implies a process of dehumanisation, for we define civilisation as the realisation of one's full creative potential. By permitting a minority to monopolise the public value, we would expect pathological reactions at several levels. The personality of the monopolist, for example, is afflicted by unseemly characteristics such as greed and an atrophied sense of morality and community spirit. Those deprived of their share of the surplus are similarly damaged in both psychological and biological ways.

By removing the impediments to the ideal structure, we shift society in the direction of that hitherto ill-defined goal, the 'sustainable' community. This is the social organisation that expresses the symmetry of the spatial environment with our sense of justice. When we combine the two, we generate a synergy which surfaces in the creative intensity of the individual and the associational benefits of people who, through co-operation, experience life to the full. Thus the two principles which constitute the basis for a science of governance are *competition with co-operation* (see Box 4:1).

4.4 The Roman Road to Wallsend

IF THE RATIONAL pricing mechanism is not applied alongside Ricardo's Law, we would expect the mal-distribution of public value to surface in a variety of ways, such as spatially determined health and happiness. Without the personal responsibility to pay for the benefits that people receive at the locations which they occupy, we would expect the statistics that track people's wealth and psychological welfare to follow a similar trajectory to the distribution of rent. Rent, as we have seen in the graphs, displays a downward sloping profile. But if the benefits of rent are equalised across the country through public spending policies, we would expect the statistics to plot a horizontal impact across the graph, to indicate that people's life chances were on an equal footing across the country.

We shall test this proposition by assembling the evidence from the UK. We shall journey across the land to observe what is happening on the ground. But to prepare us for this journey, we need to abandon the idea that Britain is divided into two halves by an invisible wall. According to the myth, the wall runs from east to west, approximately located between The Wash that faces the North Sea and the River Severn that flows into the Atlantic. Social scientists make it tangible like the wall of China (built to keep out the Mongol hordes), or Hadrian's Wall at the top of England (built to keep out the barbarians from the highlands of Scotland).

Doreen Massey and two other professors of geography affirm this version of the spatial divide.[16] The imagery is that of the escarpment. England is divided by a sharp precipice that divides London and the South East from the rest of the kingdom. Rather than a continuum which begins in London and slopes to the periphery, theirs is a flat terrain at two distinct levels separated by the cliff face.

Box 4:1 The Science of Governance

POLITICS as 'the art of the possible' is a doctrine tailored to protect the vested interests of rent-seekers: the people who manipulate the state to appropriate privileges that impair the rights and freedoms of others.

In a rational society, governance is treated as a science. The degree to which it meets the standards of integrity associated with science, and the accountability associated with democracy, ultimately depends on the ability of the community to unite two principles.

- *Competition* in the free market. This is the tool for optimum use of resources and the rents that people will pay for amenities that are available in particular locations.
- *Co-operation* among free people. Justice unites people around the common good when the ethical system assures people of 'fair play'.

Policy analysts like Francis Fukuyama, whose *The End of History and the Last Man* is a eulogy to Western democracy, deny that governance can conform to the rigours of science. In analysing 'failing states' in the developing world, Fukuyama claims that 'there can be no science of public administration despite recent efforts by economists to establish one'.* He relies for this contention on weaknesses in the 'public choice' theory of economics.

Advocates of the public choice doctrine are blind to the principle of cooperation as we define it. Public officials are assumed to be self-serving agents who disregard 'the common good'. But if the principle of paying for benefits received were also applied to the delivery of public services, the outcome would be harmony between a person's private interests and shared communal interests. This proposition is explored in Chapter 15.

* Francis Fukuyama, *State Building: Governance and World Order in the 21st Century*, London: Profile Books, 2005, p.xx.

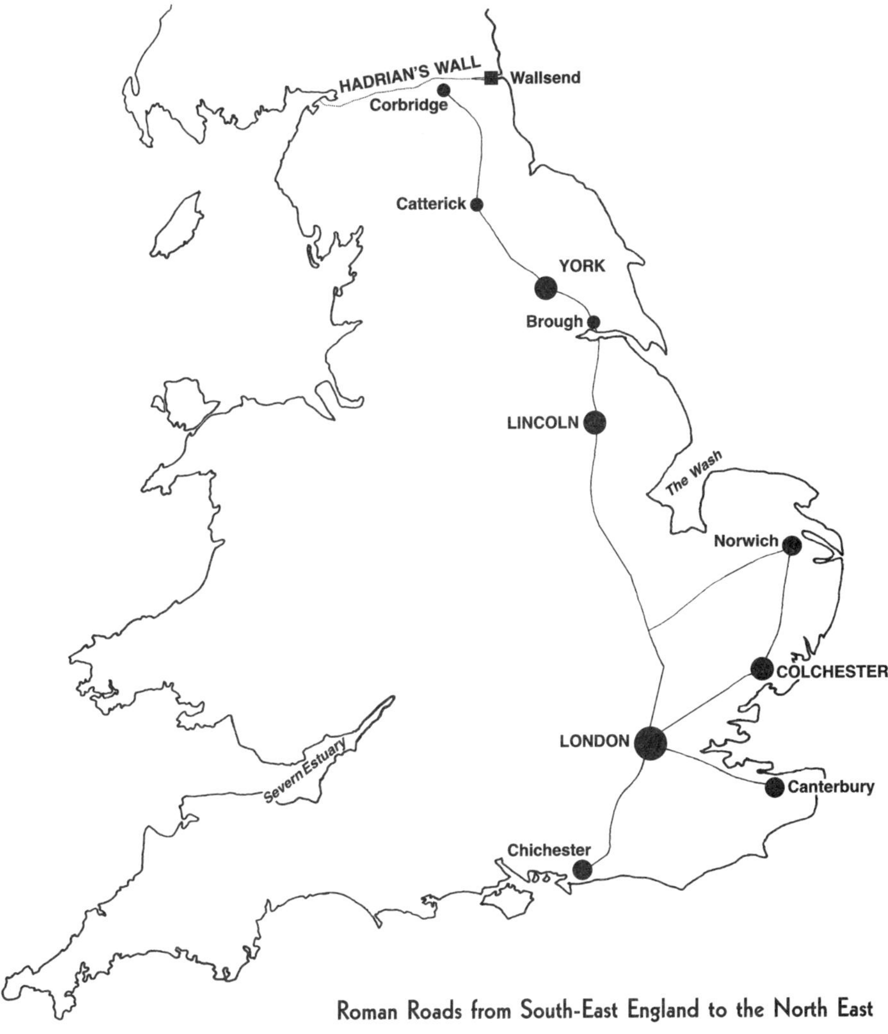

Roman Roads from South-East England to the North East

Their account of the divide relies on the reference back to the political power of feudal monarchs and their courts. London became important because of the fashionable season when the aristocracy gravitated from their castles, palaces and manorial estates to London to indulge in seasonal preoccupations. There was horse racing at Ascot, the boating Regatta at Henley and the debutante balls in fashionable West End homes. These social events were the decorative icing on the political horse-trading within walking distance of Parliament. Excluded from this privileged concentration of power and play was the rest of the country. This 'spatial grammar' was carried over from the feudal to the democratic eras without change.

This treatment of the North-South divide relies on the constant renewal of political habits and memories. Our competing thesis relies on the differential economic potential of a territory which, when combined with a perverse tax system, automatically favours the centre and continuously reproduces itself without relying on class habits and memories. There is no 'magic roundabout' on which the professors of geography rely for their thesis.[17]

To interrogate our competing thesis, we must cut a cross-section through England: a straight line from the centre of London to the farthest corner of the kingdom. We will follow one of the Roman roads that bisect the nation (see map on page 69). With the exception of a few dog-leg detours, these were constructed as straight as an arrow flies. Our destination is Wallsend, which is at the eastern end of Hadrian's Wall.

We chose this route across the country for two reasons. First, tying ourselves to the Roman road constrains us from zigzagging to select evidence that happens to accommodate the theory. Second, this highway traverses the maximum possible number of regions, as defined by government statistical agencies.

England is divided into 9 statistical regions. We shall subject six of them to a forensic examination. Our trail leads us through a wide spectrum of social, economic and health measures that reflect the distribution of income. Table 4:1 lists the regions and the abbreviations we shall use for the five economies that are compared with London in Part II.

Table 4:1

English Regions and their Population Densities (2001)

	Population (million)	*Hectares (million)*	*Density (population per hectare)*	*Gross Value Added (£bn: 2002)*
North East (NE)	2.5	0.86	2.93	29.5
North West	6.7	1.41	4.77	93.1
Yorkshire & Humberside (Y & H)	5.0	1.54	3.22	65.7
East Midlands (E Mid)	4.2	1.56	2.67	59.1
West Midlands	5.3	1.30	4.05	72.9
East of England (East)	5.4	1.91	2.82	91.0
London	7.2	0.16	45.62	146.9
South East (SE)	8.0	1.91	4.2	147.8
South West	4.9	2.38	2.07	69.2

Source: ONS Census 2001.

On a GDP *per capita* basis, at the beginning of the 21st century the value produced in the North East was over 40% below that of London. This difference is not a temporary phenomenon. The evidence has been tracked back to the early 1920s, and it indicates that the present pattern of regional differentials has persisted at least since then.[18]

The further we traverse from London, the lower the productivity. We find ourselves on a toboggan slide down a *social process*. One of the questions we will consider is why, according to Robert Huggins, a Sheffield university economist, the gap between the rich and poor regions will widen, with the northern regions falling further behind.[19]

When we plot our six regions on a graph, we find a pattern that persistently reflects Ricardo's Law. The broadest indicator of economic performance is GDP *per capita*. Within England, this ranges from £16,000 and over for London, between £13,500 to £15,999 for the South East and East England, declining to £11,000 to £13,499 for the East Midlands and Yorkshire & Humberside, to below £11,000 for the North East.[20]

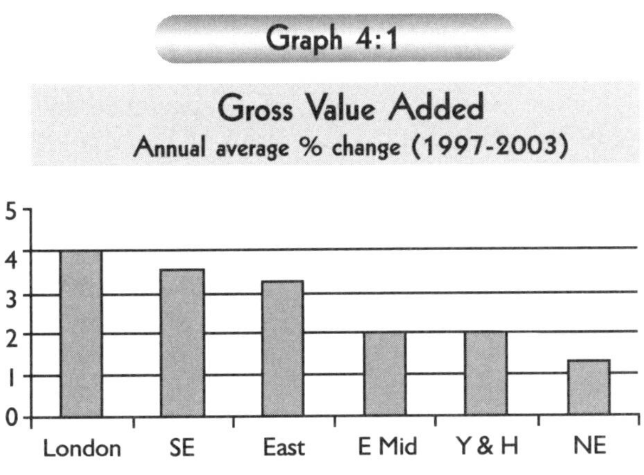

Source: Office of National Statistics; *Financial Times* calculations, reported in Chris Giles, 'Forgotten Britain: how Labour has presided over a deepening divide', *Financial Times*, March 20, 2006.

We are not just concerned with the static picture. The modern economy is a dynamic one, constantly changing, and the direction of change favours a widening gap between London and its hinterland regions. Why, we want to know, can't they grow at equal rates? Margaret Thatcher's reputation for favouring market economics has branded her as responsible for entrenching the wealth gap across the UK regions. But why did that gap grow even wider during Tony Blair's years in power? Graph 4:1 shows that in the six years after New Labour came to power, London's economy grew at an average annual rate of 4% (as measured by gross value added) compared with 1.3% for the North East. The gap widened despite record levels of public funding in the economies of the outer regions. Gordon Brown had committed himself (in 2003) to improving the prosperity of the regional economies as 'the government's main priority'. If this was a litmus test of his economic policies, he failed.

To uncover the explanation for this distribution of wealth and welfare, ours must be a multi-layered journey of both the mind and the soul. We shall embark on some brief excursions into the past, to glimpse some of the events that made the kingdom what it is today.

You will have two guides. One is David Ricardo. The other is the present author. I will point out some of the landmarks of importance. But if our journey is to be successful, we need you, the reader, to be more than a back-seat passenger. Now that you are equipped with the basic tools of Ricardo's Law, you can reinterpret the landscape. In doing so, you will enrich your life and, if you are so motivated, contribute towards a better future for yourself and others.

We will find ourselves questioning the Welfare State. This was intended to compensate for the inability of intelligent, able-bodied people to raise all the income they need to pay their way through life. From cradle to grave, about 40% of the population is now apparently so incapacitated that they depend on the transfer of income from the two-fifths of households that enjoy substantial incomes. Are there really so many economically incapable people in Britain? I believe that they do not need the cradle-to-grave paternalism of the state.

From the evidence assembled in Part II, we shall be driven to the conclusion that the state is the cause of most of the major problems in people's lives. In Part III, I shall explain that this problem is not peculiar to Britain: the US is similarly afflicted by the policies of the disabling state. And in Part IV, I will explain how, if the UK wishes to achieved a state of maturity as a nation, it needs to adopt reforms that would abolish people's state of dependency.

REFERENCES

1 Max Weber, 'Social Causes of the Decay of Ancient Civilisation', in *Max Weber: The Interpretation of Social Reality* (J.E.T. Eldridge, ed), London: Michael Joseph, 1970, pp.254-75.

2 The universality of this process was illustrated nearly two thousand years later by Winston Churchill. In a speech delivered at Edinburgh on July 17, 1909, he referred to the parish of Southwark, on the south bank of the Thames, where 'about £350 a year, roughly speaking, was given away in doles of bread by charitable people in connection with one of the churches, and as a consequence of this competition for small houses, but more particularly single-roomed tenements, is, we are told, so great that rents are considerably higher than in the neighbouring district. All goes back to the land, and the landowner, who in many cases, in most cases, is a worthy person utterly unconscious of the character of the methods by which he is enriched, is enabled with resistless strength to absorb to himself a share of almost every public and every private benefit, however important or however

pitiful those benefits may be'. Quoted in Winston S. Churchill, *The People's Rights*, London: Jonathan Cape, 1970, pp.122-3.

3 For an examination of how the school of post-classical economics emerged at the beginning of the 20th century to disparage the unique role of land and rent in the economy, see Mason Gaffney and Fred Harrison, *The Corruption of Economics*, London: Shepheard-Walwyn, 1994.

4 Department of Health, White Paper, *Saving Lives: Our Healthier Nation*, London: Stationery Office, 1999.

5 Michael White and Patrick Wintour, 'The man with a plan for Labour election victory', *The Guardian*, November 1, 2004.

6 *Tackling Health Inequalities: Status Report on the Programme for Action*, London: Department of Health, 2005.

7 Richard G. Wilkinson, *The Impact of Inequality: How to Make Sick Societies Healthier*: London, Routledge, 2005.

8 *Tackling Health Inequalities*, *op. cit.*, p.3.

9 Fraser Nelson and Allister Heath, 'The poor get poorer under Gordon Brown', *The Business*, April 3, 2005.

10 *Tackling Health Inequalities*, *op. cit.*, p.11, para. 1.8.

11 Patricia Apps, *A Theory of Inequality and Taxation*, Cambridge: Cambridge University Press, 1981, p.8.

12 Fred Harrison, *Wheels of Fortune: Self-funding Infrastructure and the Free Market Case for a Land Tax*, London: Institute of Economic Affairs, 2006.

13 Max Hastings, 'A national obsession', *The Guardian*, August 17, 2005.

14 Francis Fukuyama, *State Building: Governance and World Order in the 21st Century*, London: Profile Books, 2005, p.58.

15 Alfred Marshall was the distinguished professor of economics at the University of Cambridge. In the 8th edition of his *Principles of Economics* (London: Macmillan, 1920), he insisted that the annual value of land should be called its '*public value*' (p.433: emphasis in original). He stressed that 'we may speak of this annual public value of the land as "true rent"' (p.434).

16 Ash Amin, Doreen Massey and Nigel Thrift, *De-centering the Nation: A Radical Approach to Regional Inequality*, London: Catalyst, 2003.

17 *Ibid.*, p.18.

18 HM Treasury, *Productivity in the UK: Progress Towards a Productive Economy* , London, March 2001, p.8.

19 Ed Crooks and Roger Blitz (ed), 'North-South divide "grew wider in 2001"', *Financial Times*, August 21, 2003.

20 HM Treasury, *Productivity in the UK: 3 – The Regional Dimension*, November 2001, p.2. Graph 4:I is derived from p.7, Chart 1.4.

Part II

ANATOMY OF A DISUNITED KINGDOM

Pulling Power

LONDON

5.1 Dick Whittington's Streets of Gold

LONDON'S STREETS are paved with gold. That's what they told Dick Whittington, and that is why he was attracted to the capital. Children are reminded of his exploits every Christmas, as fact is merged with fiction in a pantomime that dramatises the life of the young gentleman who went in search of fortune.

The children who fill theatres particularly love the role played by Whittington's larger than life cat. How much is myth is difficult to say, but we do know that the son of a minor Gloucestershire landowner became Mayor of the City of London on three occasions, and a banker to the Crown (lending money to monarchs on no fewer than 58 occasions between 1388 and 1422). The cat may be no more than an entertaining fable.[1] But there is no doubt that, as a merchant, Dick Whittington did earn a fortune. And the streets of London were, indeed, a source of gold. Untangling the economics of the street is vital to an understanding of how London is enriched at the expense of the rest of the kingdom. At the heart of this process is the extraction of rents produced elsewhere and sunk into the infrastructure of the London economy.

The process has been going on for centuries, a redistribution of income from the outer regions in favour of the City which had an irresistible pulling power. People gravitated to London for the greater opportunities that were available. Looking back, we can see how there emerged an alliance between monarch, high finance and real estate. A symbiotic interest was created between these three, establishing a covert pact around the extraction of the rent of land from the people who created it.

The outlines of this model of exploitation may be perceived in the biographies of people like Dick Whittington in the 15th century. The personal relationship between the monarch and certain of his subjects was the basis of an emerging understanding about the nation's rents which tied them together in a new bond of power. In the 16th century, that relationship was symbolised by another Mayor of the City of London, Sir Rowland Hill (1492?-1561).

Like Whittington before him, Hill left his family's country estate (Hawkstone Park, Hodnet, in Shropshire) to seek his fortune as a merchant in London. Like Whittington, he was one of the king's creditors. He was chosen Lord Mayor in 1549 (the first Protestant to attain that distinction), all the time raking in the rents from 1,181 tenants.[2] Like Whittington he invested his rents in the construction and repair of several highways in the capital. Like Whittington, he generously bequeathed some of his tenants' rents to several of London's hospitals (£200 went to St Bartholomew's Hospital).[3]

London was grateful to people like Whittington and Hill. Their generosity raised the productivity of the capital's economy. But by drawing rents away from the regions, they gutted the economies (and culture) of the countryside. This destined England to a lopsided growth that retarded the welfare of the people in the regions. By this means, the streets of London were transformed into highways down which flowed liquid gold. One day, that investment in the infrastructure would transform London into one of the richest financial centres in the world. For when capital is invested in roads, the productivity of the economy is increased. That creates a multiplier effect, the largest benefits going to the owners of land under buildings in the City of London.

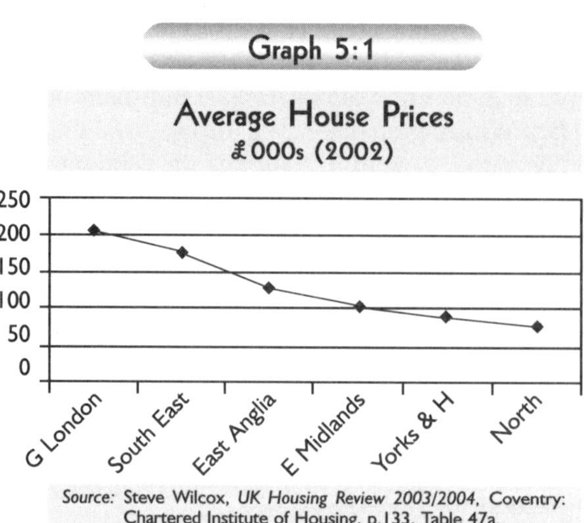

Source: Steve Wilcox, *UK Housing Review 2003/2004*, Coventry: Chartered Institute of Housing, p.133, Table 47a.

Residential and commercial sites serviced by the highways command higher rents because they improve the attractions of living in those localities. There would be nothing wrong with this if the people who benefited paid for their roads. But, as with the case of the Shropshire rents, much of the money that was sunk into London's infrastructure came out of the pockets of people who did not gain from the investment, and who did not voluntarily yield their surplus income for the benefit of Londoners.

Today, a snapshot of this financial process is offered by the cost of purchasing a home. House prices are greater in London than anywhere else in Britain (see Graph 5:1). The Greater London average for 2002 was £206,839 compared with the North's £79,457.

According to Ricardo's Law, the London economy was bound to be more productive as a location, yielding a higher rent than the other regions. But because of the discriminatory character of taxation, the gap between London and the North is wider than it need be. One result is the displacement of people out of the regions. London grows at a faster rate than elsewhere, and the distribution of additional households is patterned by Ricardo's Law (Graph 5:2). The gap would be narrower if people were not artificially expelled from the towns of their birth under pressure from the damage inflicted by taxation.

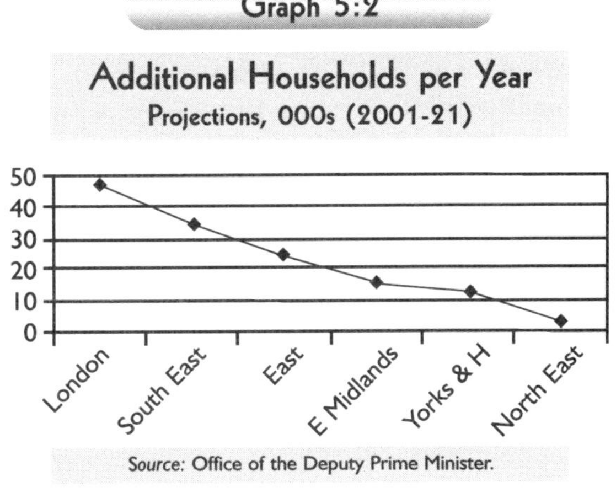

Source: Office of the Deputy Prime Minister.

London gets away with pillaging the provinces because over the centuries a variety of doctrines were used to justify the delivery of the rents to the capital. Today the fashionable explanation, which seeks to reassure us that the process is natural and should be encouraged, is known as *agglomeration*.

5.2 The Doctrine of 'Agglomeration'

THE THEORY of agglomeration explains the success of cities like London in terms of the benefits that arise from the clustering of enterprises engaged in similar lines of activity. The interaction between them delivers lower costs and/or higher productivity; so it is natural that such firms or individuals should gravitate towards each other. The banking districts, the garment districts, the concentration of lawyers in close proximity, all these are cases of agglomeration.[4]

But could the gravitational pull of London also be due to the rigging of the rules? Comparatively speaking, is London really as successful as the statistics suggest? We shall consider this issue in terms of London's power to attract a great deal more investment of taxpayers' money than the rest of the country. From Graph 5:3, we see that public expenditure on a *per capita* basis is more than twice the amount invested in the other regions in both the transport and housing sectors. Might this help to explain why the London economy is so much more productive?

London justifies its favourable treatment on the grounds that, pound for pound, it is more efficient than the rest of the UK in the way that it uses resources. In 1999, GDP *per capita* in London was 30% above the UK average and more than 60% higher than in the North East.[5] But while we would expect the London economy to generate a higher rental surplus, are the rules of public finance biased to give it an additional advantage? Identifying the bias in government decisions, and exposing the role of public money in the enrichment of London, requires a comparison of some statistics.

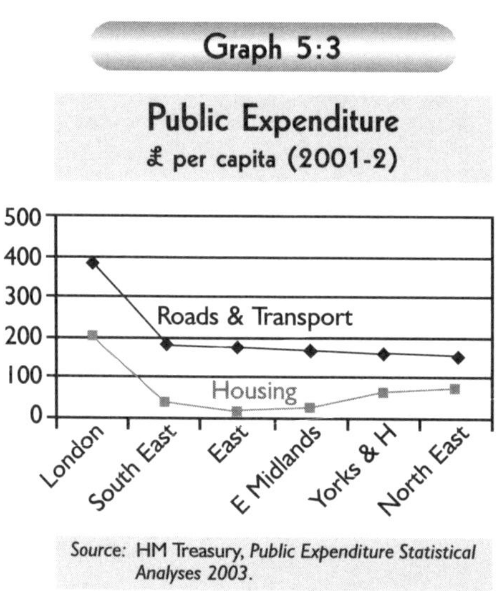

Source: HM Treasury, *Public Expenditure Statistical Analyses 2003*.

First, consider the productivity of the regional economies. The numbers presented above compared productivity on a *per capita* basis. If we look at the numbers per employee, we find that GDP in London exceeds the UK average by 17%, and it is approximately 30% higher than the North East, which is at the bottom of the productivity league table. We shall compare the fate of London and the North East. Bear in mind that 30% gap.

The next statistic we need is a measure of the losses that are directly attributable to taxation. According to the Treasury, when people's incomes and savings are taxed there is a loss of 30p for every £1 raised by 'bad' taxes. That 30% loss is the wealth and welfare that *would* have been produced if government had not raised its revenue by means of taxes that inflict disincentives. Using the Treasury's measure, that loss to Britain in 2005 was of the order of £138bn.[6] The loss is actually far greater, as we shall explain in Chapter 15. But, for present purposes, we shall take the Treasury's estimate at its face value: a 30% liability attached to investments paid for out of Exchequer funds.

According to the Department for Transport's website, government makes decisions on where and when to invest taxpayers' money on roads on the basis of 'good value for money'. This value-for-money policy has a built-in prejudice against the North East, while favouring London. How?

Pound for pound invested in tooling up employees, a Londoner generates 30% more value than the northerner. How does this affect investment decisions? When the Department for Transport assessed the costs and benefits of a new road or railway, it factored in the 30% loss inflicted by the way the Treasury raised the revenue that was to be spent on the project. In London, the loss was offset by the 30% higher productivity. In the North East, the 30% tax-induced losses are a hurdle that the region first has to overcome *before* it could begin to justify improvements to its infrastructure. Thus, London projects are *always* going to be more rewarding than those in the North East. This means – thanks to the tax system – that there was an automatic bias in favour of directing investment towards London.

Table 5:1 illustrates how the investments that may be funded by the Department for Transport are classified. As a result of its cost benefit analyses, if the return on investment is less than 1, the project will not to be funded. There is no sense in paying for an amenity which yields a lower return than its capital cost. But notice that a project which will yield £1.50 is also considered a poor prospect – at least, in the North East it would be. That is because, when you add in the 30p tax-induced loss to the £1 investment, there is no net gain. That project would certainly not be funded in the North East. But it *would* stand a chance in London, where the £1 investment is supported by the 30% productivity bonus. That productivity bonus offsets the losses that arise from the way government raises its revenue.

Table 5:1

UK Department for Transport's Value for Money Criteria

Value for Money Category	*Benefit to Cost Ratio*	*Prospects for Projects*
Poor	Less than 1	None
Low	Between 1 and 1.5	Very few
Medium	Between 1.5 and 2	Some, but by no means all
High	Over 2	Most, if not all

Source: Guidance on Value for Money, London: Department for Transport, December 15, 2004, paras 15, 31.

Projects that yield benefit to cost of up to £2 for £1 invested have only a medium prospect of being given the go-ahead. Again, the bias would be greater against investment in the North compared with a similar project proposed for London. With London receiving a favourable head start as a result of the tax-and-investment bias, it is not surprising that the capital appears to be more productive than the North East: the historic accumulation of capital in London's infrastructure ensures that it will always be ahead of the game.

London's response to the complaint of a bias in the system would be that, in the growth years, it makes a net contribution to the public coffers of between £2bn and £9bn.[7] This is disingenuous. The calculation ignores the capital gains that flow from public spending. Public money invested in London yields huge rewards to the private sector – in the appreciation in capital assets – that far exceed the financial subsidies that are transferred to the regions. How does this cause and effect work?

- A higher proportion of public spending in the regions is committed to welfare benefits to people who are rendered unemployable by payroll taxes. Those state subsidies are necessary to keep people alive. Unlike investment in (say) a new metro system, they do not produce windfall gains in the land market.
- In London, however, a higher proportion of public money is devoted to improving the quality of transport and schools. This raises the productive capacity of the population working in the capital. The spin-off takes the form of capital gains to land owners. And that means Londoners are more able to claw back the taxes they paid to the exchequer, leaving them with higher disposable incomes to be spent in the retail sectors – which, through the multiplier effect, gives a further boost to the London economy.

The productivity gap is increasing rather than narrowing. It accelerated further during the height of the dot.com boom at the end of the 20th century. This is not primarily due to the natural trends within the economy, but the conjunction of costs and benefits prescribed by government through taxation.

5.3 Capital Gains

THE BIAS that is built into taxation is grossly offensive to the official doctrine of equal treatment of everyone, but London's wealth is now heavily dependent on it.

The constant campaign to invest in transport, to maintain the City as a pre-eminent financial centre in the world, is an example. The greater the concentration of financial institutions, the greater is the demand for capital investment in the capital. This process establishes a treadmill effect with the self-fulfilling prophesy – in fact, a threat – that investment in London's infrastructure *always* falls short of need; therefore, government should pay more attention to the needs of the capital and channel more taxpayers' money into this region – or the City will lose its competitive edge.

The collateral damage of this process: less investment in the regions, which reduces their ability to compete with London for (say) inward investment from foreign sources. One illustration is of the favourable tax treatment directed at Docklands, which was deemed to be necessary to expand the commercial space available for insurance and banking corporations. £3.4bn was invested in the extension of the Jubilee Line, for example, to service Canary Wharf, while other centres of high population concentration (such as Liverpool) were denied a few hundred million pounds for the metros they needed.

We need to locate the contemporary evidence in its historical context, beginning in the 18th century with the construction of canals. Private investors provided the capital to create the transport network that could move goods on a mass scale. But those investors discovered that it was difficult to balance their books, because part of the value which they helped to create leaked out of their grasp. That value ended up in the pockets of land owners. The same thing happened with the railways in the 19th century, the highways in the 20th century, and the story is repeating itself around the airports of the 21st century Space Age. Land owners contributed nothing towards the increased value that accrued to their assets. The losses were incurred by uninformed investors; and then, in the 20th century, they were shifted onto taxpayers.

This financial scam continues to this day, and its victims include low-income communities in London. Not everyone who walked the streets of London ended up with gold in his pockets. It is worth probing further into the poignant story of Docklands.

In the 1980s, as the docks lost their economic value, a vast tract of land on the east side of the City lost its role as a transit hub. Wedged between the docks were traditional communities such as those on the Isle of Dogs. The Thatcher government decided that the area should be redeveloped. Its primary tool was a policy that stood justice on its head. Instead of imposing a public charge on vacant land – to force it into new uses – the government created an Enterprise Zone. One of the privileges was exemption from property taxation.

The result was predictable. Tax relief was capitalised into higher land values, and families which for generations had made the Docklands their home were pressured out of the area by the rising costs of living. Those who did not own land were the losers. The windfall gain did enrich some people. One of them was umbrella manufacturer Arnold Fulton. He purchased a plot of land in a derelict corner of Docklands for £650,000. Money rained down on him! Developers pursued him for the right to buy his plot, but he fended off their offers of £30m.[8]

Financiers wanted to move into Docklands – providing the transport links were upgraded – and the rents they were willing to pay were almost as much as the cost of commercial space in the City. The upward trend in the value of land paralleled the outward displacement of low income families. Viewed in terms of natural justice, there was no need to humiliate those workers by taxing their wages to pay for the Jubilee Line. The Jubilee Line raised the price of land by upwards of £10bn.[9] But instead of tapping it to pay for the investment, that value was allowed to leak into the pockets of landowners. And their ingenuity with 'tax shelters' ensured that they paid the minimum possible back to the public purse.

Families living in social housing did not collect a share of the capital gains dividend that followed the investment of taxpayers' money. They had to settle for the privilege of paying taxes to support the asset-rich. One result: after taking housing costs into account, 300,000 children, or 41%, were estimated to be living below the poverty line in London in 2003.[10]

But the London property market did not just discriminate against its own communities. Given the need to encourage entrepreneurial innovation, the tax-and-tenure arrangements favoured London against the regions. The mechanism for transmitting the bias is through the financial sector, which insists on using property as collateral for loans. This makes it relatively more difficult for entrepreneurs in the North East to secure loans to start the businesses with which to compete with London. People in London are more likely to start a new business than elsewhere, and particularly compared to the North East. Business creation rates in 2000 ranged from 21 new VAT registrations per 10,000 resident population in the North East, up to 65 per 10,000 in London.[11]

Thus, a self-serving mechanism operates. Taxation hammers people's economic prospects at the margin, in regions like the North East, while privileging the core economy in London. The boost to London's infrastructure out of the public purse spills over into higher land values, which then translates into easier financing arrangements for entrepreneurs who consequently secure an advantage over their competitors in the regions.

Periodically, however, the good times come to an end. And, again, it is London that is responsible for punishing the other regions on the principle that 'the bigger they are, the harder they fall'. It is speculation in property – both residential and commercial – that leads the way into the booms and busts that plunge the economy into recession. London's real estate is always the most overheated. When the government – and, now, the Bank of England – steps in and raises interest rates to try and 'cool' house prices, there is an unequal impact across the country. In the North East, where property prices are more stable, the market is not subject to the same ferocity of land speculation. And yet, its entrepreneurs are forced to carry the same increase in the cost of borrowing money as their London competitors – who, of course, have reaped most of the windfall gains in land values over the preceding cycle.

Disunited Kingdom (1): Citizenship

IF CITIZENSHIP is measured in terms of the benefits received from the state, some people are more equal than others. Nowhere is this more poignantly illustrated than in London, where those who own land near to major investments in infrastructure – transport hubs, and good schools and hospitals – reap the biggest windfalls.

The impact of successive waves of public investments is illustrated by Figure 5:1. Ploughing more taxpayers' money into raising the quality of schools and hospitals leads to more jobs (this is measured by the shift in economic activity from B to C in the figure). And as productivity rises, so the demand for land results in further rises in rents. How 'real' is this abstract account in terms of the London economy? We first examine the claim that investment in infrastructure raises the value of land. Consider this question in relation to the decision to locate the 2012 Olympic Games in East London.

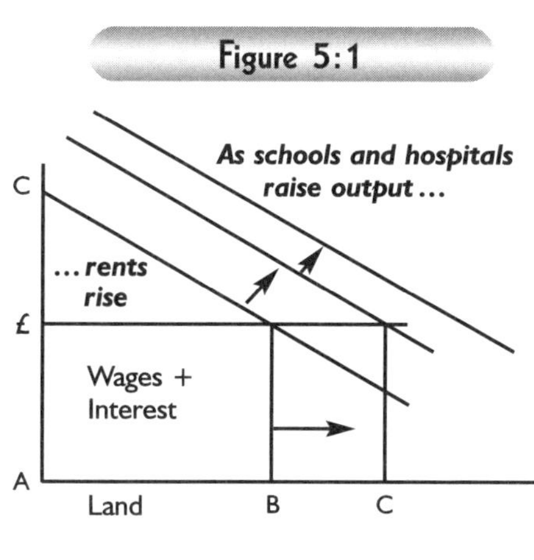

For East-Enders, locating the Olympics near the newly constructed Stratford rail terminal was a two-edged prospect. New employment prospects would be created, but the decision sent a volcanic shock through the property market. About £3.6bn would be spent on building the sporting facilities. The *Evening Standard* reported (July 7, 2005): *GOLD RUSH: Property prices in Games areas set to soar by 50%*. To make way for the Olympic Village, some properties would have to be demolished. One firm that expected to be displaced was a construction company located in Marshgate Lane, Stratford. Its owner, Michael Finlay, reported that an estate agency 'has estimated that the value of land where the Olympic Park will be sited will increase almost tenfold. The largest source of revenue for the world's most expensive two weeks of sport will not come from advertising or broadcasting rights, but from land disposal following the games'.[12]

The upward pressure on property prices was affirmed by London and Continental Railways (LCR), which owned the 180-acre site where the Olympic village would be built. After the games, LCR would reclaim the properties, sell 30% of the apartments at a discount 'to provide affordable homes', and then market the rest of the properties at up to £1m each.[13]

The empirical evidence supports the general proposition that, with further investment in the London economy, the net gains are captured by the rent-seekers. But what about the employees who live by their wages? We claimed in Part I that wages are equalised across the country; and we repeat this claim in Figure 5:1 by drawing a horizontal line which denotes similar wages across the national economy. How does this claim stand up to the facts of the London labour market?

The claim that wages are equalised as people respond to a rise in a localised demand for labour holds good as an analytical insight. But the theory has to be adjusted to take into account the distortions caused by the tax-and-tenure laws. These disturb the general tendencies. And if we want to find out what life is like under these laws, we could do no better than to turn to people who work for their living at the sharp end in London. Here, employees near the bottom of the income scales could not live on the wages of their colleagues in the North East. We see this when we break down wages relative to those in Tyne & Wear, in the North East. There is a difference, and Graph 5:4 reveals a downward trend that fits the Ricardian rent profile.

Graph 5:4

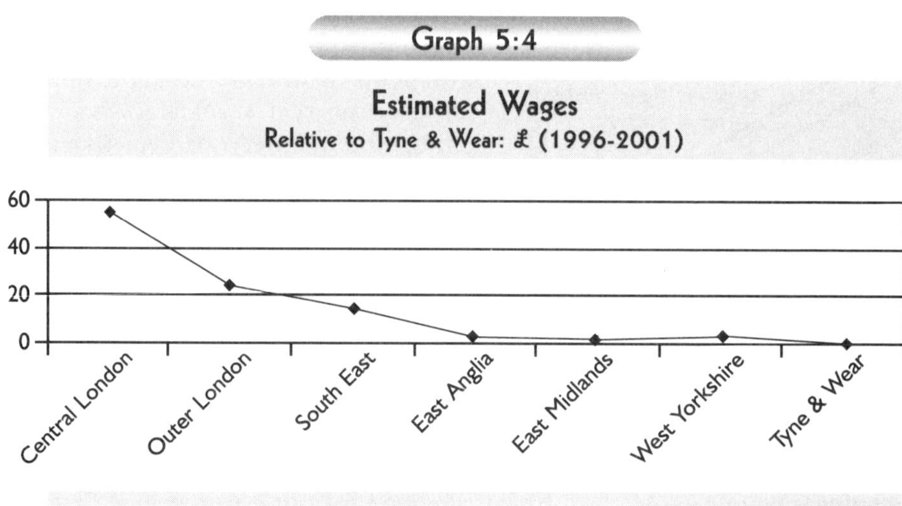

According to data from the *New Earnings Survey 2002*, analysed by the Office for National Statistics, private sector pay is 54% higher in London than in Tyne and Wear, 24% higher for workers in Outer London and 13% higher for workers in the rest of the South East. Why (if our theory is correct) are wages not equalised? Is it because northerners are reluctant to migrate to the South? That is not the explanation, because there *is* a demographic outflow from North to South.

But if wages are not equalised by competition, how do we account for the differences? They are attributable to additions to wage packets to compensate for the cost of living in the South East, including regional weighting and recruitment and retention supplements. But why do employers in London and the South East pay that extra money? They face problems when they try to hire 'key workers', including fire fighters, teachers and nurses. And the explanation for that difficulty is to be found, ultimately, in the cost of land. This is the primary determinant in the supply and price of houses. To confirm that fact, we have the testimony of one of London's residential property barons. Andreas Panayiotou owns 2,500 flats, a portfolio which he assembled by converting old buildings in the East End. But in 2006 he pulled out of the residentail sector, explaining in a rare interview (Matthew Goodman, 'Buy to let tycoon checks out hotels', *Sunday Times,* August 27, 2006): 'I have had a fantastic run. I just feel we are reaching the height of the market. My business model involves having a borrowing ratio of 50%-55% of value. But *the cost of land has increased* and I can't achieve the margins I want and still be at that ratio' (emphasis added).

Employees could not afford London house prices at northern wage rates. So the national wage has to be adjusted to take into account the costs of living in London. These costs have been calculated to determine what constitutes a minimum living wage in the capital. Any wage below around £6.15 an hour (in 2005) results in an income on or below the poverty line even when state benefits are taken into account. The national minimum wage (£5.05) is insufficient on which to sustain life. The difference between the national minimum rate and the London 'living wage' is largely accounted for, according to the London Mayor and his researchers, by the higher cost of housing in the capital.[14]

The facts reveal that this is not just a central London problem. From Graph 5:4 we see that the relative wage differential across our six regions follows a downward sloping curve. This tells us that the differential pressure on wages across the regions conforms to Ricardo's Law.

The interaction between the labour and property markets is a complex one. Recall, first, that land owners are able to claw back their taxes, because their payments to government are offset by the capital gains that flow from public investment in infrastructure. In the calculations on the London living wage, for example, a family with two wage earners on the minimum wage pay £54.50 a week in taxes. These are retrieved by the home owner, whereas the family that rents its home receives no such clawback.

But the inequities go deeper. Owner-occupiers on the lowest wages have to pay interest on their mortgages. Even so, their weekly mortgage repayments are less than the rents that families pay to landlords. Rents in London, for three-bedroom dwellings at the lower end of the housing market, are shown in Table 5:1.

Table 5:1

Bottom Quartile Rents in London for 3-bedroom Dwellings
(£ per week)

Owner Occupier	135*
Renting from Council	147
Renting from Housing Association	159
Renting from Private Landlord	149

*The cost of owner occupation based on repayment mortgage over 25 years at an interest rate of 5.14%

Source: GLA Economics/ The Living Wage Unit, *A Fairer London: The Living Wage in London*, London: Greater London Authority, 2006, p.32, Table A.4

The evidence leads to two conclusions. First, when we adjust wages to take into account the differential rents across the country, we find that incomes net of housing costs do tend towards equality throughout the economy. Second, there is a systematic bias against people who do not own land; they end up paying *more* for the roofs over their heads than people who own (or who are buying) the land under the bricks and mortar.

There was nothing that London could do to moderate these negative effects, given the tax policies administered by central government. That was why the Welfare State failed in its mission to provide the residential, educational and recreational amenities that were sorely needed in the East End, where most low-income families are concentrated.

A new approach is needed because the postwar socialist settlement has failed. That failure is being registered by East-Enders who were at the murderous end of Hitler's bombs. They had hoped that the Labour government's creation of the Welfare State would bring them into society. The outcome was less than perfect. The failure of the Welfare State was recounted to researchers who chronicled the decline in expectations.

> Throughout its history the East End of London had been at the bottom of the pile, on the margin of British society and excluded from mainstream opportunities ... Local people therefore saw the Labour victory at the 1945 general election as something that they had achieved and earned for themselves (and their ilk) rather than received from on high as yet more 'charity' ... State-managed social security would be a *right*, rather than a gift from superiors carrying the stigma of dependence ... High hopes soon led to disappointment.[15]

Hopes dissolved spectacularly in the housing sector. Working class Eastenders assumed that the Welfare State would at least ensure decent homes for themselves, and then their children. But the state was to disappoint them.

Blaming the successive waves of immigrants was a convenient way to avoid probing too deeply into public policy. The East End has traditionally been one of the first ports of call for waves of migrants seeking a new life in Britain. As they secured their economic future, they relocated to higher value areas, leaving behind them people who remained at the bottom of the pile. They were the ones under constant pressure, in their need for decent homes, but no one could offer them a rational explanation for their plight. Despite the Welfare State's redistribution of income on an epic scale, the people in Tower Hamlets, the borough within stone-throwing distance of the City of London, continued to be excluded from the huge wealth generated in the capital.

The London housing crisis is indicated by the projected increase in the number of households – 46,400 every year, according to estimates by the Office of the Deputy Prime Minister.[16] Mayor Ken Livingstone set a construction target of 30,000 homes, but who would pay for the schools and the transport facilities? Didn't the East-Enders have a right to an equal share in the land values which they helped to create with their tax-funded investments? Why not tap the values to fund the infrastructure that every community needs? If this revenue was captured, it would be possible to cut the income taxes that marginalised workers pay on the fringe of one of the richest cities on earth. Wasn't this strategy worth exploring by the Greater London Authority?

A new approach to funding infrastructure could have been given a central place in the Olympian bid to elevate the quality of life in the capital. That was one of the aspirations of Mayor Livingstone.[17] But, curiously, the Mayor's own think-tank, GLA Economics, was ambivalent. It assessed the policy options, peered into the future and concluded that a land value tax

> to incentivise development and lead to additional sites being released for housing – generating a receipt to landowners – may well not work in London. This is mainly because sites in London are being held back primarily owing to lack of infrastructure and to planning policy – for example on protection of Green Belt and employment land – and where this is profitable for the developer and landowner.[18]

Here was confused thinking just when London needed clarity. Might the shortage of infrastructure be explained by the fact that it was not funded out of the land values which the railways and schools create? GLA Economics was ill-informed. Otherwise it would not have published this statement: 'Taxing the landowner is not likely to increase the transfer of sites from other uses, especially where relative gains are fairly marginal and where costs and risks are substantial'. Dynamic adjustments in the land market are precisely what would be achieved if the land value-based pricing mechanism were correctly framed. There is a wealth of evidence from world-class cities around the world to prove it.

That London needed investment in its transport network is attested by the losses through congestion, which were estimated at £1.7bn a year. This was equivalent to a loss of £1,220 a year per person working in central London.[19] Funding is the key to the shortfall in the provision of services. Crossrail, for example, which would join East with West London, was proposed in the 1940s. In 2005, a further attempt was made to secure Parliamentary approval for it, but still no one knew where the money would come from.

GLA Economics took a lead in promoting the doctrine of agglomeration, a concept used by economists who did not wish to disturb conventional fiscal wisdom. A more dynamic concept is that of the *synergistic* city, the features of which were documented by Mason Gaffney.[20] He clarifies what the algebraic wizards who author textbooks are coy about explaining in layman's language.[21] There is no mystery about the economics of urban expansion and concentration. As another scholar put it in relation to the benefits of transport investment,

> the city as a whole generates an economic surplus from its productivity advantage. The surplus arises as workers who live closer to the city centre pay lower commuting costs. However, this surplus is all captured by rent/house prices so that, in equilibrium, the entire surplus accrues to owners of the immobile factor – land.[22]

Circumstances arise in which some workers may share in the productivity gains. But in the fullness of time, the general principle holds true: the ratchetting up of land values. This economic reality ought to contribute to the shaping of public policies. In general, it is ignored, to the advantage of London's land owners.

The large city can affect its residents in two ways. It can crush the people with the weakest earning power even as it enriches the privileged segments of the population. London has more than its share of victims. Or, alternatively, a correctly governed city can ensure a distribution of the benefits so that all residents share in the riches that flow from the clustering of the best skills in productive enterprises. But in Britain, citizenship is not based on the latter principle. That is why communities in the Disunited Kingdom are spatially fragmented. For the residents of the debilitated communities of the East End, the talk of agglomeration has the whiff of a classic story – 'the growth of Ancient Rome as an example in which rent-seeking citizens locate in the capital to take advantage of the benefits of imperialism in return for not rebelling against the Emperor'.[23]

INTERROGATION

MAYOR LIVINGSTONE supported the idea of tapping land values to fund transport projects like Crossrail. But the mayor had to compete with the influence of one of his economic advisors, whose views were aired for the benefit of the Treasury. Heading Livingstone's GLA Economics think-tank was Bridget Rosewell, who acknowledged that the doctrine of agglomeration originated with Alfred Marshall.[24]

The clustering of specialist workers generates a synergy which delivers a surplus that crystallises as land values. This, consequently, leads to a land market that transfers sites between competing uses to deliver the best allocation of resources. Marshall advocated the land value-based tax to pay for shared services.[25] Bridget Rosewell did not share Marshall's enthusiasm for land taxation.

☞ A land-value-based tax is levied in Sydney, one of the classiest and most productive cities where the Olympic Games were staged in 2000.[26] Is there something peculiar about London that disqualifies it from adopting the best practice policies of others to fund infrastructure by charging a public price for amenities delivered for the benefit of those who occupy particular locations?

☞ Bridget Rosewell believed that conventional taxes were sufficient 'so we don't need to go down the road to generate taxes from some different route'. She was 'very uncomfortable about suggesting that we can only engage in [new] investments if we can find new methods for value capture'.[27] Is the comfort zone of an economist a consideration when evaluating the best interests of Londoners?

☞ Taxing the cash flows of enterprises was preferable, argued Rosewell, 'because it is much easier to find them. We start from here, rather than a different perspective'. In view of this preference for taxes that damage the economy, should the mayor's think-tank publish its estimate of the ensuing losses that accrue from disincentive taxes on the wages, savings and investments of people who live and work in London?

REFERENCES

1 John Attwood, *Dick Whittington: Fact and Fable*, London: Regency Press, 1988, pp.89-90.

2 Leslie Stephen and Sidney Lee (eds.), *Dictionary of National Biography*, Vol. xxvi, London: Smith, Elder (1891), p.410.

3 Sir Rowland Hill 'Was truly designated "a grave and worthy father of the Citye", for by his munificence he added to its approaches, and by his charities enriched its hospitals'. Edwin Sidney, *The Life of Lord Hill*, London: John Murray, 1845, p.2.

4 GLA Economics, *Why Distance Doesn't Die: Agglomeration and its Benefits*, London: Greater London Authority, June 2006.

5 Patricia Rice and Anthony J. Venables, 'Equilibrium regional disparities: theory and British evidence', 2003, p.2 (www.econ.lse.ac.uk/staff/ajv).

6 Harrison, *Wheels of Fortune*, Ch. 1.

7 GLA Economics, *Growing Together: London and the UK Economy*, London: Greater London Authority, 2005, Ch. 5.

8 Nilufer Attik, 'A £650,000 gamble that turned into £30m', *Evening Standard*, October 7, 2002.

9 Don Riley, *Taken for a Ride*, London: Centre for Land Policy Studies, 2001.

10 Roger Blitz, 'Cabinet team to devise strategy for London', *Financial Times*, March 5, 2003.

11 HM Treasury, *Productivity in the UK: 3 – The Regional Dimension*, November 2001, p.25, para. 2.35.

12 Michael Finlay, 'Olympic Land Grab', *Daily Telegraph*, February 14, 2006.

13 Ian Pocock, 'London Olympic flats will be sold on for up to £1m', *The Sunday Times*, June 11, 2006.

14 GLA Economics/The Living Wage Unit, *A Fairer London: The Living Wage in London*, London: Greater London Authority, 2006.

15 Geoff Dench, Kate Gavron and Michael Young, *The New East End: Kinship, Race and Conflict*, London: Profile Books, 2006, pp.189, 193, 197.

16 Roger Blitz, 'Challenge builds on homes front', *Financial Times*, September 8, 2004.

17 The Mayor's transport authority, Transport *for* London, authorised its vice-chairman, Dave Wetzel, to discuss land value taxation with Sir Michael Lyons, who was enquiring into local government finance on behalf of the government. Transport for London Board Meeting, December 7, 2005, Minute No. 71/10/05 – Crossrail.

18 GLA Economics, *Our London, Our Future: Planning for London's Growth II*, Main Report, November 2005, p.86.

19 Oxford Economic Forecasting, *Time is Money*, London, GLA, 2005, p.32.

20 Mason Gaffney, 'The Synergistic City', *Real Estate Issues*, Winter 1978, pp.36-61; available on www.masongaffney.org.

21 Masahisa Fujita and Jacques-François Thisse, *Economics of Agglomeration*, Cambridge: Cambridge University Press, 2002; Masahisa Fujita, Paul Krugman and Anthony J. Venables, *The Spatial Economy*, Cambridge, Mass: The MIT Press, 2001.

22 Anthony J. Venables, 'Evaluating urban transport improvements: cost-benefit analysis in the presence of agglomeration', A revised paper written for the UK Department for Transport, June 2003, pp.3-4 (www.econ.lse.ac.uk/staff/ajv/).

23 Daniel J. Graham, 'Wider economic benefits of transport improvements: link between agglomeration and productivity', Stage 1 report, Imperial College, London, July 2005, p.22.

24 Alfred Marshall, *Principles of Economics*, London: Macmillan, 1898, Vol. 1, p.278.

25 Alfred Marshall, 'Rates and taxes on land values', Letter, *The Times*, November 16, 1909; reprinted in George J. Miller, *On fairness and efficiency*, Bristol: Policy Press, 2000, p.386.

26 The principles and practise of the New South Wales land tax may be reviewed

on the Valuer-General's website: www.lands.nsw.gov.au. See also R.V. Andelson, *Land Value Taxation Around the World*, 3rd edn, Oxford: Blackwell, 2000, Ch 25.

27 Bridget Rosewell's comments were made at a seminar convened by GLA Economics, Exploring the relationship between transport and London's economy, City Hall, February 15, 2006.

Castles in the Air

SOUTH EAST

6.1 Location, Location, Location

IF SOUTH-EAST England were an independent country, it would be the 20th largest economy in the world. With a population of eight million, it generates over 15% of total UK gross value added. Because of proximity to London, it has the highest quality of life in the UK. Here, the belief that an 'Englishman's home is his castle' is most deeply entrenched and staunchly aligned to the preservation of the 'green and pleasant land'.

The region's politicians are sensitive to the landscape's role in securing the inflow of capital and entrepreneurial talent. The clusters of high-tech business parks in the Home Counties deliver large rewards for employees, but they also attract a problem: others covet the Green Belt. The South East seeks to minimise the flow of migrants from regions like the North East with the aid of a policy of silent segregation. And yet, it is that inflow which secures the vitality of the region. So it employs a mechanism that balances the conflicting demands on the space that is the key to its prosperity.

The struggle over the economic value of the location began with the turnpikes in the 18th century. The highways opened up the London market to farmers from far afield. This caused panic among land owners who had traditionally grown the food for sale in London's Covent Garden and the Smithfield meat market. Wouldn't they now suffer from the competition coming down the road? They need not have worried: they possessed something more valuable than nature's soil fertility: location. With patience, the riches would pour down on them. All they needed was the technology to increase people's mobility. With the arrival of the steam age in the 19th century, the fields around the capital blossomed with new uses.

Railways raised productivity exponentially. One effect was that coalminers of the North East enriched the landlords of the South East. As the haulage systems reduced the cost of coal at seaports on the Tyne, the increased flow of coal down the coast reduced the prices to consumers in the capital. This increased the disposable incomes of households and made it possible for landlords to raise the rents of residential properties in the South East. The hazards of working at the coalface in the North East were compensated for by the high life that landowners could now enjoy in the villas they built beyond the overcrowded city.

Within a few decades Britain was a cobweb of steel tracks. Professional people could now escape from the smog of the inner city and live in suburbs where the air was not polluted. The villages around London acquired a new kind of resident: the commuter. He could live in the countryside and earn his salary in the City. Those who owned land extracted a share of the jump in the productivity of the capital by charging high prices for residential property. As trains grew faster and more comfortable, so the commuter belt extended from the outer suburbs to the ancient towns like Canterbury and Chichester, and then on to the coastal settlements that fronted the English Channel. The synergy was a two-way flow, for the availability of a workforce from the Home Counties increased the value of land within London itself. Guildford and Tunbridge Wells and the other towns that ringed the capital had the best of all worlds. The commuters enjoyed London salaries, working in the finance and media industries by day, while retreating to the pastoral delights of rural England by night.

The dwellers in the hamlets that nestled around the chalk downs prospered because they were able to share in the riches that percolated out of the capital, which was awash with cash. London's most remunerative employment sectors relied on attracting finance from the rest of the country. Much of what people saved for their retirement was sent to London to be invested. So were the billions paid in insurance premiums and deposited in banks for safekeeping. Money out of wage packets in the North East was transmitted to the City, where bankers and brokers took their cut as handling fees. Those financiers resided in the 'stockbroker belt' of Surrey and Kent. They relied on the thrift and the entrepreneurship of the people in the rest of the country for their prosperity.[1] So what erased this mutuality in favour of the apparent dependency of the North on the South? The answer is not to be found in any shortcomings on the part of northerners, but in the way governments spend the money it taxes out of the people of the North.

In addition to private money, the people of the South East also relied on the expenditure of public money. Just how dependent they were we shall shortly see. What mattered was not how much was spent *in* a locality, but what it was spent *on*. As we saw in Chapter 5, in the Blair years a record increase in public spending on health and education helped to lower unemployment rates in the northern regions, but a disproportionate amount was subsidies to people without jobs. In the South East, public expenditure was biased in favour of investment in infrastructure.

The formation of new businesses among people aged between 16 and 50 is highest in the South East. The rate for the North East is a third of what is achieved in the capital (see Graph 6:1). Economists claim that this is the consequence of people gravitating to the area with the most profitable opportunities. But in the age of rapid transportation, there is no good reason for this disparity in start-ups. The unequal distribution of opportunities is primarily due to the bias in taxation and public spending, not the defects in transport systems or the superior talents of people who start their working lives in the South East.

Graph 6:1

UK Entrepreneurial Activity
% starting own business (2000-4)

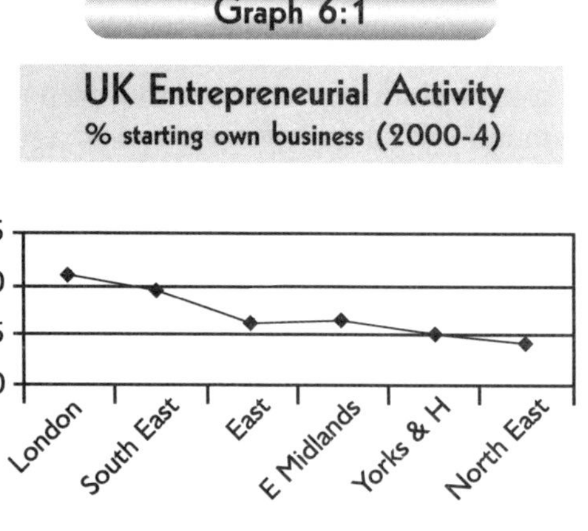

Source: Kingston University Business School.

To compensate for the differences in opportunities, one suggestion is that stock exchanges should be re-established in the regions. In fact, they did spring up in towns like Birmingham and Leeds in the 19th century, but that did not prevent the concentration of financial activity in London. Given the mobility of capital, there is no reason why any locality should be denied access to it at competitive rates, no matter where the financial institutions were located. Someone who wants a mortgage, for example, can just as easily secure it from a North-Eastern lender, if he lived in the South East, as from a lender in London.

The reason capital is not so readily invested in the North is that the privileged aggregation of rents at the centre creates benefits such as the public subsidies to transport, and the opportunity to claw back one's tax payments as capital gains. This set of incentives encourages the financial institutions to concentrate close to each other in these areas. The cumulative effect is bias in favour of the centre.

6.2 A Capital Conundrum

THE CLUSTERING of high-productivity enterprises in the South East need not deprive the regions of new businesses. Industries flourished throughout the kingdom during the early phase of the Industrial Revolution. The subsequent lopsided evolution of the economy was due to a flaw in the business model that was employed to fund the investment of capital in infrastructure. We need to take a closer look at the economics of the canals of the 18th century, which triggered the process.

Land owners knew that windfall gains were to be made not out of pioneering entrepreneurship, but by the simple expedient of transferring part of the income of those who produced the new wealth to themselves. Location was the key, and leading the way was the appropriately named Duke of Bridgewater. Canals were built on or contiguous to the land of aristocrats, to carry coal to the markets. This enabled landowners to capture the gains from the increased productivity as higher rents.

The model was an elegant one, but the productivity generated by railways was not so easy to capture. For the steel tracks had to traverse the properties of many owners, which meant that the windfall gains were diffused. The risks were therefore increased. Political deals would have to be cut in Parliament. A sophisticated financial and legal framework was needed to protect the family fortunes of landowners. Their tactics were as follows. First, they created a railway company and owned the shares. They paid for the capital works, reconfiguring the landscape and laying the tracks, and then publicising the venture as a commercial success. This boosted the price of their shares. As share prices rose to dizzying peaks, prudent landowners 'cashed out'. They sold to second generation investors, who naturally expected to make handsome profits from this wondrous business of transporting people and goods rapidly throughout the kingdom. In fact, they were left with big debts. Those debts arose from the original investments in the capital that was sunk into the land. So while shareholders struggled with the legacy of debt, the owners of land adjoining the railways who had recovered their original capital investment, with profits, could look forward to pulling in the higher rents that were made possible by the railways.

Parliament ought to have addressed the financial conundrum – how to link infrastructure investment with the value that it created – in the first half of the 19th century. But Parliament was dominated by landowners. Their failure to act in the best interests of the nation set the scene for the financial boom-and-bust crises that periodically brought the economy to its knees.

It was a legalised racket. Small-time savers used the stock exchanges that sprang up in their towns to buy shares in new railway ventures that were hyped as lucrative opportunities. They were not aware that many of the companies were financial traps. People who invested their savings were denied their share of the value which they helped to add to the wealth of the nation.

There was a systemic flaw in the financial architecture. The revenue generated by the freight trucks and the passenger coaches was sufficient to cover the operating costs (the wages of employees, the horses, the barges and the coal that fuelled the steam engines). But many investors lost their money as companies failed to pay a return that covered the debts on the capital invested in their enterprises. If the railways were a valuable addition to the new industrial economy, investors puzzled, why could they not make ends meet?

The truth is, they could. They generated an additional value equal to the cost of the capital that was invested in the infrastructure. This occurred by the process of increasing the productivity of the economy. But the net gains that flowed from that productivity were beyond the legal reach of the railways. That value was captured by owners of land. They charged higher rents for land around the canal wharfs and railway stations. So money that could have been used to defray the infrastructure costs leaked away through the land market. The losers were the urban merchants and people like widows who invested their pensions in the hopes of higher returns. The financial truth was concealed from them by the nation's duplicitous accounting system (see Box 6:1).

Property rights could have been adapted to serve both private and public interests. In London, entrepreneurs used land values to fund the construction of some of the capital's commuter railways. They bought land at agricultural prices in the Home Counties and then ran the tracks into the green fields. This raised the attractions of farmland for residential use. The profits from selling the land were used to fund the railway's infrastructure. This model could have been refined to serve everyone's interests; it wasn't.

In the end – we now know with hindsight – the railways were bound to collapse into the arms of the state. While they operated, they buoyed up the land values of the South East's commuter country, but because of the business model that was developed by the aristocracy in the 18th century, taxpayers were forced to subsidise the commuter lines in the 20th century. That is also why nationalisation failed. The financial arrangements were inherited from the past, unreconstructed. The essential difference was that taxpayers were substituted for shareholders as the fall-guys.

Whitehall's books could not be balanced. Westminster managed to conceal the losses through the national accounts for a few decades, but Margaret Thatcher's housekeeping economics exposed the problem. Why (she wondered) should taxpayers be 'bankrupted' (as it were) to keep railways running and coal pits operating that were 'losing money'?

Box 6:1 Was the Bishop's Castle Railway Really Bankrupt?

THE BISHOP'S CASTLE Railway Co. opened for business on October 24, 1865. Within months it was declared bankrupt. Its assets were seized and auctioned for £3,522. The company leased back the locomotive and carriages and operated for 70 years under the supervision of a Receiver. Its last locomotive took its final gasp in 1935.

The engines steamed back and forth between Bishop's Castle and the main line that connected Shrewsbury and Hereford. For the townsfolk of Bishop's Castle, the railway was a commercial boon. So was the railway really bankrupt for 70 years? It paid its employees their wages on Saturday afternoons, the coal was purchased at commercial rates, and the rent for the right to steam into Craven Arms Station was paid on time.

The debt arose over the financing of the infrastructure. The railway could not fund the original capital costs. But when we take into account the increase in land values for which it was responsible, we see that the railway was self-financing. It did not cost more to operate than it produced for Shropshire's economy.

Alarm spread on the occasions when, through legal action by landowners, its services were suspended. The cost of provisions and of the coal imported from Wrexham rose alarmingly. That indicates the efficiency of railway transportation. Savings were to be made, and these were captured as higher rents for dwellings in the town. Timber land also fetched higher rents, because the lumber could be shipped out on the railway's trucks. Cattle and the other products of farms that surrounded the market town also enjoyed lower transport costs. The reduced costs of freight were translated into higher rents paid by tenant farmers.

The *Bishop's Castle Advertiser* acknowledged (August 22, 1901): 'Bishop's Castle can never be styled a flourishing town but the little trade and development it has made during recent years is certainly owing to its railway service, which, although not of the best and most convenient, is fully appreciated by everyone.'

They were not a drain on the economy, of course; the total value which they contributed was such that they must be classed as self-funding. But a large slice of the value they created was missing from the audited accounts. It was leaking out through the gigantic sluice that was the land market.

The Thatcher philosophy prescribed the re-privatisation of the railways. That happened in May 1996 with the creation of Railtrack, which leased to private train operators the right to use the infrastructure which it owned. The shares attracted huge numbers of private investors. But because taxpayers had to be committed to funding investment in the infrastructure, the exercise was destined to fail. With the collapse of Railtrack in 2002, more than 250,000 private shareholders lost millions of pounds.

The Blair government replaced Railtrack with a not-for-profit company, Network Rail. The attitude of the civil servants towards the small investors who lost out was revealed when an e-mail from a senior Treasury advisor was disclosed. This dismissed the investors as 'grannies'. The official weighed up the pros and cons of compensating Railtrack's financiers, but not its shareholders, and he wrote:

> If lenders are seen to have been bailed out by Government in dealing with Railtrack's administration, this will make it harder to refuse to help out the shareholders: fat cat City bankers get 100p in the pound and grannies (who probably invested at privatisation) lose their blouses.[2]

This was a repeat performance of the 19th century financial fiascos. The costs were transferred to taxpayers while the owners of land around the commuter railways in the South East continued to pocket the windfall gains. But the major difference, this time, was that the windfall gains went into the pockets of middle-class home-owners rather than the aristocracy. This gave the new rich a tantalising taste of the noble lifestyle; one that literally gave their children a head start in life.

6.3 A Head Start in Life

THE VALUE of residential properties rose, so the commuters could supplement their salaries by borrowing against their land as collateral.

The value of that collateral was continuously being raised because of the inflow of migrants from abroad as well as the displaced peoples of other UK regions. The government was anxious to cope with the housing problems, because a large number of people could not afford to purchase their homes. However, that did not prevent owners from keeping nearly 700,000 residential properties vacant in England alone (2005).

Nearly 200,000 of these were in London and the South East, this at a time when there were insufficient houses for sale or rent at prices people could afford.

Every community needs nurses, policemen and firefighters to run vital services. And yet, these workers were being driven out of the housing market. All but five of the forty least affordable areas for 'key workers' are in London and the South East. But how could houses be provided for these workers without building on the green fields that contributed to the high values of existing properties? Local governments in Kent, Surrey, West Sussex and Oxfordshire combined forces to resist the government's targets for new construction. The government wanted hundreds of thousands of new dwellings built in the region. But even if existing home owners were willing to tolerate the expanded building programme, who would pay for the infrastructure that was needed to service the schools and hospitals of the new settlers?

South-Easterners had a great deal at stake. From a quality of life point of view, theirs was the most desirable region in the country. Generally, unemployment rates are lowest here. London has its pockets of high unemployment because of the concentration of migrant workers. The South East did not share in that problem: it merely took its slice of the City's good fortunes as handsome bonuses for the bankers and stockbrokers, and generous salaries for front and back office employees. Once outside the capital the trend in unemployment prospects begins its upward climb to the peak in the North East (see Graph 6:2).

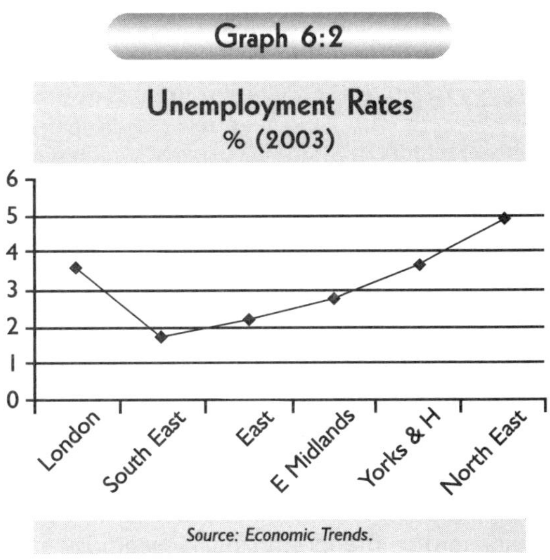

For the best head-start in life, rear children in the South East. The regional distribution of children who live in poverty is shown in Graph 6:3. About 45% of children in Inner London exist in households with the lowest disposable income. Outer London's figure drops by more than half. The lowest numbers are in the South East. Then the climb begins. Apart from Inner London, the highest percentage of children in the bottom 20% of households live in the North East.

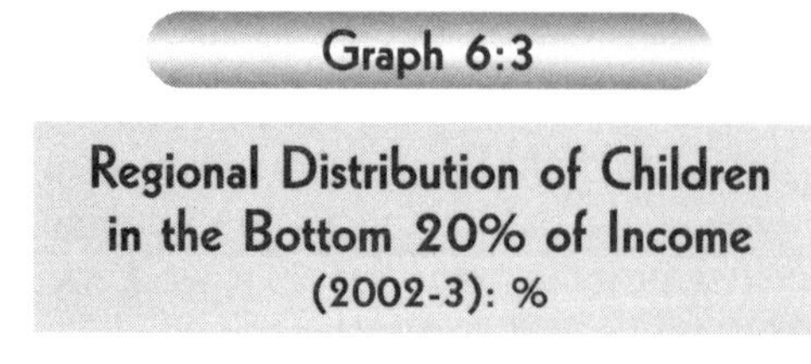

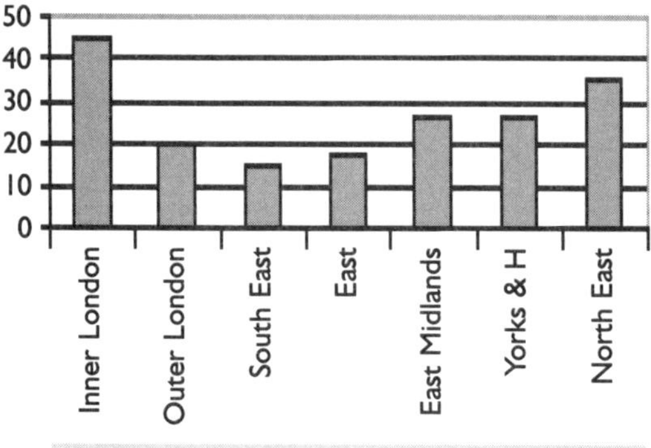

Source: *Households Below Average Income*, London: Department of Work and Pensions, 2004, p.48, Table 4.2.

This head-start in life in the South East is organically linked to a quality of life built on the back of the windfall gains in the housing market which are heavily dependent on the generosity of taxpayers. These windfalls delivered unprecedented wealth to the middle classes. And they are ready to circle the wagons to fend off any proposal that would intrude on that value. Just how delicate is the situation was the subject of a confession by one of the columnists writing in *The Daily Telegraph*.

Tom Utley's children are privately educated. On his taxed income, however, he could not afford the £20,000 a year that he pays to the private school attended by his two sons.

> I had a great deal of help – and that help came from my house. I have increased my mortgage five times over the past 10 years to help with the school fees … the only solid and meaningful stake that we hold in our country's economy is in the bricks and mortar of our homes. When Tony Blair and Gordon Brown seek to bump up taxes on property, therefore, they are playing an extremely dangerous game with middle Britain.[3]

The columnist did not hesitate to berate the Prime Minister and his Chancellor for threatening to increase the property tax on people's homes. This Englishman was beleaguered in 'his' castle, and he was going to defend it to the end. But there were flaws in the logic that Tom Utley used to justify the privileged education which he was able to purchase for his sons.

The first mistake was the belief that he owed his good fortune to bricks and mortar. It was the land beneath those bricks that gave him his windfall gains, and which enabled his family to live beyond his means. This is not pedantic nit-picking. If his bricks and mortar were located in one of the Welsh valleys, the value of his property probably would not pay for one year's fees at Dulwich College, to which he was sending his sons.

Box 6:2 Commuting to a Head-start in Life

FREELANCE WRITER Claire Alderson, her husband and two daughters moved to Cornwall in 1994. Property prices were low following the boom/bust at the end of the Thatcher years. She and her husband were able to relocate in the South West while continuing to work in London because of good transport links. They bought a run-down farmhouse for £180,000 which 'after some renovation work was sold five years later for £550,000'.

Their two daughters were growing up, and they wanted to move near to Truro School. This had 'great sporting facilities, an excellent academic record and, most importantly, encourages a healthy mix of fun and hard work. We also felt that travelling between Truro and London has improved so much, with bargain flights from Newquay and the trains system, that we could continue to juggle between the two cities.'

Their waterfront home in a small fishing village cost £350,000. They spent a similar sum on renovations 'that took full advantage of the views of the sea. Now, four years on, we have a home worth around £1m and a lifestyle that we would not swap for anything. We could not have chosen a better school if we had trawled the country.'

Reported Ms Alderson: 'All this and property prices are going up at an incredible rate in the Truro area.'*

Commuter trains are subsidised by taxpayers who fund the infrastructure costs of the tracks.

* Claire Alderson, 'Move to Cornwall has been a financial and lifestyle success', *The Daily Telegraph*, May 20, 2006.

The second mistake was his claim that he, like so many other parents, had a great deal of help in paying for the school fees 'from my house'. In fact, the money came from the taxpayers of Britain, who had invested in the infrastructure that raised the value of his land. Why does this matter? Many of those taxpayers do not own homes, so they do not enjoy the windfall gains reaped by owners like Tom Utley.

Utley's case is recounted not because his is an exceptional situation, but because it reveals the confusion surrounding public finance. He admitted that he could not provide his readers with an account of the best way to fund local government. He reviewed the Poll Tax (Thatcher's), the local Income Tax (proposed by Liberal Democrats, which he thought had some merit) and a local Sales Tax ('but I have no idea whether or not it would work'). Of one thing Utley was certain, however. The revaluation of people's houses should be scrapped so that owners – those whose properties had increased most in value – would not have to pay more into the public coffers.

Media pundits like Tom Utley influence the public's views. They articulate the interests of the middle classes who own their homes. They help to shape the ways in which the laws of the land are framed. That places a special burden on them to separate their private interests from their public pronouncements on the policies that determine the future of the nation.

By attacking politicians who target his property value, Utley undermines the welfare of those who have the weakest voices in the public debate. I am not suggesting that he intends to harm the poorest sections of the community in regions like the North East. But by reinforcing the prejudices of property owners who wish to preserve their capital gains, they make it difficult for informed voices to be heard.

What makes this obligation poignant is that the source of the prosperity tapped by people like Utley is also the cause of the deprivation of future generations of children. There is self-deception about house prices. People feel wealthier – but are reluctant to face the fact that a rise in the price of their homes does not mean that the wealth of the nation has increased. What *has* increased is the debt burden on the buyer. And as *Financial Times* columnist Martin Wolf noted: 'Higher prices merely redistribute income among residents, principally from the young to the old'.[4] But the young are not equally disadvantaged. Those whose parents have shrewdly tapped into the property market enjoy a head start in life (see Box 6:2).

6.4 The Disunited Kingdom (2): Community

THE NATION is divided into two kinds of communities. There are those where high land prices signal prosperity. The others are the communities where the quality of life is lower. Is this an unavoidable division of society?

Quality of life indices are more sensitive indicators of welfare than income, and some of them are literally about life. The opportunity for mothers to give birth to their children at home is an example. The trend displayed in Graph 6:4 shadows the pattern of wealth distribution. Personal choice is determined by what some commentators call the 'postcode lottery', but that concept is misleading. Gambling is not involved. The outcome is predetermined by the underlying forces that structure much of people's lives.

Mothers in the South East, in counties like Kent and East Sussex, are almost four times as likely to give birth at home as mothers in the North. We can follow the data along the east coast counties. The one anomaly in the pattern is London, where the births rate is half that of Kent. Does this reflect a personal preference that deviates from the pattern of wealth distribution? Apparently not. There is a shortage of midwives available to visit pregnant women in their homes. Is this because midwives are unwilling to live and work in London? According to Mary Newburn, Head of Policy Research at the National Childbirth Trust, the shortage of midwives is due to the unaffordability of houses.[5]

Graph 6:4

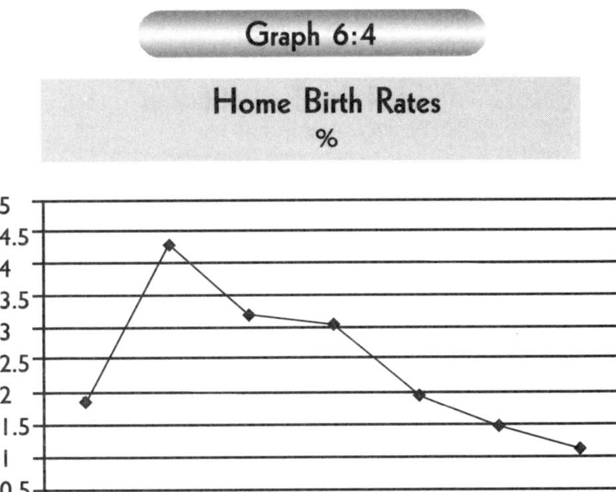

Source: Office for National Statistics data compiled by Birthchoice UK (www.birthchoiceuk.com).

The Blair government understood the importance of giving children a decent start in life, and the surest start was one that began at home within communities that met people's needs. But despite the plethora of government initiatives reaching almost into the cradle, it appears that, for many children, the prospects are getting bleaker. Since 1997, the percentage of 16 and 17-year-olds who were out of school but classified as economically inactive rose from 12% to almost 28% (in 2005). And the labour market was not getting easier. In 2005, 42% of the unemployed were under 25, a rise from 31% in 1992. Children are being born into a world that is getting tougher, and government is not making it easier for them. The difficulties, however, are not randomly distributed; but biased against the young in the outer regions.

With the erosion of demand for manual skills and the shift to the knowledge-based economy, further education would become crucial for people's employment prospects. But the divisions in the primary schools continue all the way through to the allocation of funds for postgraduate research. London in 2001 received total research funding of £806.4m – eight times

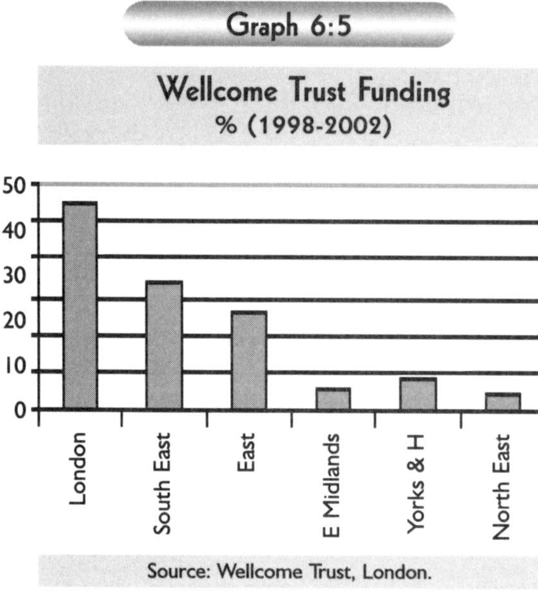

more than the North East's £109.5m. The allocation of funds is ostensibly based on support for projects of excellence. This is the criterion employed by the Wellcome Trust, a private charity. Graph 6:5 tracks the regional distribution of its grants between 1998 and 2002. The bias in favour of London and the South East is clear, not through prejudice against the other regions but in response to the distribution of educational opportunities on which future knowledge depends.

INTERROGATION

THERE WAS no excuse for governments of the 20th century to misread the economics of transportation. They had the benefit of the historical record, and the analysis by Alfred Marshall. Capital invested in rolling stock did not make big profits, but that did not trouble landowning investors. For as Marshall noted, when

> a group of land-owners ... combine to make a railway, the net traffic receipts ... are not expected to pay any considerable interest on the capital invested in making it; but which will greatly raise the value of their land.[6]

Parliament failed to utilise that lesson to formulate sound public policies. It did not do so in the 19th or 20th centuries, and – we now know, with foresight – it is not doing so in the 21st century. We see this with the need for new strategies to fund the nation's schools and hospitals, as well as the highways and railways. Instead of developing fresh solutions that might work, Parliament remains committed to the landlords' model of the 19th century.

The Private Finance Initiative (PFI) is ostensibly intended to direct private capital into public infrastructure to save money for taxpayers. In fact the PFI is a sophisticated accounting device to remove taxpayer-funded investments off the Treasury's books, without relieving the financial strain on taxpayers. Take the case of Network Rail's £23bn debt. According to Sir John Bourn, the Auditor General, in an interview with *The Sunday Telegraph* (July 23, 2006), this debt should be on the government's books.

As we have noted, the one essential difference with the 19th century model is that, instead of bequeathing the debts from capital investments to small-time investors, they are imposed on taxpayers. The one similarity with the 19th century model is that the value added to land continues to be privately extracted.

How the PFI works was documented by the public accounts committee of the House of Commons in a report on the Norfolk and Norwich Hospital, which was completed in 2001 on a 63-acre site. The private consortium which built the hospital decided to re-finance the project to take early profits. The outcome was that members of the consortium received a windfall of £115m. They gave £34m to the hospital trust and pocketed the rest. According to the Commons committee, this increased their rate of return from 16% to 60%. Furthermore, the hospital trust might now have to pay up to £257m more if it terminated the contract early. In May 2006, the hospital trust warned that it may have to axe 450 jobs because of debts that were caused, in part, by the PFI deal.[7]

 Why were hospitals locked into PFIs that committed them to fund capital investment out of operating revenue? This financial formula did not work under private enterprise in the 19th century, or during nationalisation in the 20th century, so why did the Treasury think it would work in a hybrid form in the 21st century? Could the Treasury have dedicated to hospitals some of the public value which they add in their catchment areas?

 Gordon Brown insisted on payments-by-results and patients' choice in support of the Treasury's value for taxpayers' money policy. But while he claimed credit for balancing the Treasury's books, was it fair that communities in the North suffered health care deficits while those in the South were over-funded?[8]

 What is the value of the principle of equal treatment under the law? People in the South East can withdraw equity from their homes to pay for private education and health treatment (their equity enhanced by taxpayers' money), while renters are obliged to rely on under-funded public services.

REFERENCES

1 Britain's pension crisis early in the 21st century is ominous not just for the people who face a shortfall in incomes during retirement, but also for the future of the City of London. Sir John Bond, chairman of HSBC, the world's third largest bank by market capitalisation, warned: 'We're all rightly concerned about individuals and the quality of their retirement and retirement age. But a corollary of the pensions debate is that it is actually one of the major underpinnings of London as a financial centre'. Peter Thal Larsen, 'HSBC chairman warns City to remain vigilant', *Financial Times*, December 24, 2004.

2 Alistair Osborne, 'Labour called Railtrack shareholders 'grannies'', *The Daily Telegraph*, June 25, 2005.

3 Tom Utley, 'An Englishman's home should be safe from Blair and Brown', *The Daily Telegraph*, April 22, 2005.

4 Martin Wolf, 'Dangers of the housing market delusion', *Financial Times*, April 17, 2006. Tom Utley, writing in the *Daily Mail* ('What earthly business is it of the Nanny State if I let my children eat strawberry-flavoured liquorice shoelaces?', June 30, 2006), presumably intended his question to be taken seriously. One answer may be as follows: if the state is funding his children's private education (through the capital gains it delivers to him via the land market), that *might* give the Nanny State some right to a say on their health. What Mr Utley calls '*my* house' needs to be qualified by the answer to this question: how much of the value of that property is attributable to the generosity of Britain's taxpayers?

5 Interview, 26 November, 2004.

6 Marshall, *op. cit.*, p.444.

7 Terry Macalister and John Carvel, 'Huge windfall for hospital's PFI investors as staff face job cuts', *The Guardian*, May 3, 2006. The Blair government used the PFI model to create 27 academies that were supposed to be part-funded by private sponsors. The sponsor was granted control over the curriculum, staffing and admissions in return for £2m a time donation towards the construction of the school. In May 2006, of the 27 academies that had been opened, 23 were still waiting to receive all the money that was pledged to them. Along with complaints that peerages had been offered in return for the pledged money, Blair's government had to explain how it could offer so much control over an educational establishment for sums that averaged under £1m for each academy.

8 The Healthcare Commission, which is responsible for policing standards in the NHS and private hospitals, discovered that the government short-changed patients in the poorest regions by denying their hospitals and GPs a fair share of resources. They were starved of cash because government ministers feared the consequences of re-allocating resources from prosperous regions that were overfunded. The health service in Easington, County Durham, for example, was getting £26.5m less in 2004 than it should under the fairness formula – a shortfall of 20%. In contrast, the NHS in Kensington and Chelsea was getting £30m more than its fair share – an overpayment of 16.5%. John Carvel, 'NHS funds for poor areas go to richest', *The Guardian*, July 8, 2004.

To CAP it All

EAST OF ENGLAND

7.1 People of the Commons

NARRATE THE TALE in Shakespeare's English, and you could imagine that you were walking across an English commons in the 17th century. The peasants were up in arms against the land-grab by the son of a peer of the realm who had enclosed the commons with a fence.

The traditions of the village of Hanworth in Norfolk reach back to Saxon times. The villagers believed that the common was theirs for ever more. Their brick and flint cottages snugly circle the duck pond. Merrie Olde Englande lived on in the land rights of yore, but the Honourable Robert Harbord-Hammond, younger son of the 11th Baron of Suffield, had different ideas.

This descendant of William the Conqueror decided to seize control of the 24 hectare (34 acre) common. As a reformed drug addict, and a champion of the poor for whom he wished to provide affordable homes, this noble gentleman decided that he possessed superior rights to those exercised by commoners.

Many of the houses in Hanworth still possess ancient grazing rights in their title deeds.The green was awarded to the villagers by the National Commons Commissioner in 1974. Four Trustees rent the land to a local grazier. The rent pays to maintain the common and pay a dividend – £1 a year for each resident in recent times.

Harbord-Hammond staked his claim on records showing the third Lord Suffield was granted the land in 1777 in return for giving £10 worth of bread to the poor. It was in this spirit of paternalism that the son of feudal traditions abandoned his high life in the City of London and returned to his roots to claim his heritage. A spot of land speculation on a putting green in the coastal town of Cromer came to nothing, but the new lord of the estate that stretched across North Norfolk was not finished with building his property portfolio. One of his ambitions was to sell the common in another village for development.

The villagers of Hanworth determined that they would go down fighting. They would challenge the feudal claim in court. The Liberal Democrat MP for North Norfolk, Norman Lamb, backed the peasants in this latest revolt of the commons of England. Of the claim by the baron's son, the MP is reported as stating: 'It's completely out of order. It strikes me as remarkably feudal. It is unacceptable to fence in common land this way'.[1]

England's peasants had yielded to the fencing of their commons for five centuries. The battle for Hanworth common was a reminder of an ancient injustice, but one that no longer featured at the centre of the theatre of politics. There was no need for such attention. The land barons had won the battle of the enclosures. But there was a minor victory for the residents of Hanworth when the Hon. Harbord-Hamond capitulated. He agreed to take down the barbed wire fence in August 2005 rather than face 100 rebellious latter-day peasants who had moved to take him to court to contest the ownership and access to the common.[2]

7.2 The Lord was No Protector

HE WAS called Lord of the Fens, a farmer whose powerful Puritan ethic drove him with such skill and ferocity that he achieved eminence on the battle field during the Civil War of the 17th century. The soft soils of the Fenland nourished a personality so hard that Oliver Cromwell became Lord Protector of England. For a brief interlude in the history of a monarchical state, England was transformed into a Republic. A revised version of the Parliamentary constitution of 1654-5 was followed by the offer of the crown to Cromwell which he declined. In 1658 the Protector died and his elder son, Richard, briefly succeeded him. In fact, within two years the experiment in republicanism came to an end when Charles II was restored to the throne. The political failure to carry through the reforms in the preceding 20 years was to shape the destiny of the nation in ways that need to be understood for the impact this will make on the lives of people in the 21st century.

Why, when he exercised absolute sovereign power and was uncontested on the battlefield, did Cromwell fail to put in place a political process that would have secured continuity of the Republic and the devolution of power to the people? The answer is to be found in the sub-text to the turbulent

20 years. This reveals the character of the struggle for power and wealth at the heart of the British constitution.

The backdrop to the events following the regicide of Charles I was the struggle to control land, the revenue from land, and the public purse. Having disposed of Charles I, the composition of Parliament was vital: control of it would deliver control over the land and the right to determine the revenue-raising policies – previously all land had been held of the king. The Lord Protector could have turned to his Bible for guidance. This sacred text made it clear that land was a resource to be shared by everyone. Leviticus leaves no doubt that profane politics, if it was to be made consistent with the theology of the land, would have to devise ways of ensuring an equitable distribution of God's natural resources. Cromwell had no excuse. If he had overlooked the theology of the land, James Harrington, who dedicated *Oceana* to him, spelt it out in detail.

The feudal aristocracy which had sided with Charles I – and lost the battle in the fields – had their revenge in Parliament. For when Parliament was convened on April 25, 1660, the elected members restored the House of Lords and accepted the terms of the Declaration issued by Charles II. This included the settlement of disputes about land sales. Property rights would not be shared out with the commoners; they would be protected by the new settlement.

The logic of the Restoration is revealed by the language that camouflaged the political reality. The common people of England were told that they were privileged to be represented by 'the greatest and learnedest and wealthiest and wisest persons that can be chosen out of the nation'. The landowners in Parliament were not chosen; they were self-selected. Charles II himself noted, 20 years later, that 'without the safety and dignity of the monarchy, neither religion nor property can be preserved'. But when reviewed objectively, neither religion nor property was preserved by the guardians of theology or natural law.

It is perhaps unfair to place the full burden of blame on Cromwell. He was not strong enough to defend the strictures of God or the common law which had originally ascribed access rights to all people as a matter of birthright. Cromwell was up against the petty princes on their feudal estates throughout the land. As a pamphlet of 1660 cited by historian Christopher Hill put it:

> This island … is … governed by the influence of a sort of people that live plentifully and at ease upon their rents, extracted from the toil of their tenants and servants, each … of whom within the bounds of his own estate acts the prince.[3]

The monarch as the steward of the interests of all his subjects was fatally weakened when, in 1660, feudal tenures were abolished and nearly all of the land held by the crown was sold. As Hill noted, this

> transformed the nature of the monarchy's power. It was no longer, in the medieval tradition, based on land, on personal relations between King and his rich subjects, or on the crown's ability to inflict economic harm. The court in the sense of the royal household was ceasing to be the centre of real power.[4]

Formerly, the rights of tenure linked the crown to the community in a direct way through the public purse. The public's services were funded out of the rents that people generated. Once that link was ruptured, the rents would be grabbed by the strongest. Once the feudal traditions were abolished, the landowners who consolidated their power over Parliament could tax people's wages to pay for the services that gave value to their land, thereby ensuring themselves a double win. They lost no opportunity in exploiting the new constitution by deepening their accumulation of the rents of the nation. In this, they were being consistent with the activities that prevailed during the years of the Republic. Under Oliver Cromwell, for example, the Army lost its revolutionary fervour as 'many officers speculated in 'debentures' (IOUs in which the troops had too often been paid), buying them up cheap and using them to invest in land'. The Army, in fact, became a socially destabilising force whose 'further land confiscations, rose to terrify the men of property'.[5]

Socialists like to idealise the revolutionary tendencies of the New Model Army and to recall wistfully the debates among the levellers, notably those that took place in a church in Putney in 1647. But if there was virtue in abolishing the monarchy in the cause of justice, such a project could succeed only if the tax-and-tenure rules were configured to harmonise with the interests of the people. Instead, the Puritanism that drove those who claimed to represent the people of England bequeathed an impure legacy, which tainted Parliament with a doctrine of private property and public finance that continues to prejudice the interests of the people of Britain to this day.

7.3 Farming the Taxpayers

THE INSTITUTIONALISED anarchy that passes for politics today has as its basis the struggle to preserve the interests of the people who own land; with, as a subordinate and contradictory project, the attempt to ameliorate the condition of those who are outcasts in the land of their birth. Driving through Cambridgeshire, one was forced to ruminate over the pathetic contests of the political parties to outbid each other in the policies they offered on property rights.

The Liberal Democrats have abandoned their 1905 tradition more or less completely. Now, they informed the electorate, if elected, they would abolish the tax on residential property altogether. In its place, they would introduce a new layer of income taxation.

The Conservative Party was more subtle. It promised to under-assess the value of residential property for revenue purposes. This would again shift more of the burden of taxation on to wage earners. Furthermore, the Conservatives promised to subsidise pensioners in a way that would privilege the assets that they would transfer to their children – again, at the expense of the landless.

As for New Labour, during its nine years in government it could have implemented reforms in favour of the generations whose forefathers were cast out of the commons. Instead, it avoided upsetting the voters by postponing a tax that would be levied when planning permission was granted for a change in the use of land. But in its manifesto, it promised the impossible – a million more homes would be built and ownership would be extended to many more people.

It was left to the minority parties to say something sensible on land and tax policy. Notably, the Greens prominently offered to abolish the taxes that harm people who worked for a living and it promised to raise revenue from the rent of land.

Such was the Parliamentary legacy of the Republic of the 17th century. And nowhere can one better observe the grotesque injustices to the working people of Britain than in the Fenland pastures to which a battle-weary Cromwell yearned to retire.

The agricultural revolution in the early 17th century required a modification to the rights of tenure. A commercial approach to property rights was appropriate if the economy was to benefit from the new ways of increasing the yield from the soil. Reform was not universally welcomed. Drainage of the Fens, for example, to take advantage of the new processes of cultivation and increase aggregate output, was met with resistance by Cromwell himself.

Today there is a unanimous belief that the feudal model was anachronistic and that it had to be abolished. So deeply embedded is this view that when power was devolved to Scotland by the Blair government, the new Assembly in Edinburgh promptly abolished the feudal tenures that had survived north of the border.[6]

The rational strategy was not to abolish feudal tenure but to modernise it. To foster investment and private enterprise, what matters is not freehold tenure but security of possession under the law. Leases are a model of property rights that work efficiently for the profit-seeking entrepreneur. The issue at stake, of course, is the fate of the rent that people are willing to pay for the use of land. For the aristocracy and gentry, feudalism had to be neutered if rents were to be channelled away from the public purse and into private pockets. The outcome is measured in the way in which landowners are less interested in farming as a way of growing food and more concerned with farming the taxpayer.

The landowners of East Anglia, as elsewhere, harvest huge revenues under the Common Agricultural Policy (CAP). The European Union allocates nearly half of its budget to subsidising landowners. The subsidies do not raise the wages of those who labour on the land. Nor do they boost the profits of the risk-takers who invest in combine harvesters and livestock. Under the CAP, income transferred from labouring taxpayers elevates the value of land. But the money-milking process sanctioned by Parliament would be difficult to sustain without centuries of doctrinal deception that has closed people's minds to the economic realities.

In Britain, the transfer of wages into the pockets of farmland owners was systematised after World War II with the aid of the manipulation of statistics. This dawned on a farmer in Scotland. Dr Duncan Pickard had previously lectured on animal physiology and nutrition at the University of Leeds before turning to farming. Starting with a smallholding in Yorkshire, he moved to a 1,100 acre arable and livestock holding in Fife. Then, in the general election of 2001, he attended a meeting of the National Farmers' Union which was addressed by Sir Menzies Campbell, who was seeking re-election as the Liberal Member of Parliament for Northeast Fife. Campbell stated that the average farmer's income in Scotland in 2001 was £73 per week. Farmer Pickard was shocked. He understood the economics of agriculture from the inside. And he wondered how such a statistic could be used by a parliamentarian to colour the minds of the electorate.

Pickard subsequently informed his MP that the statistic was based on a lie: farmers enjoyed far more generous standards of living than was portrayed by the Whitehall bureaucracy that championed their interests. So angry was he that he exposed the manipulation of statistics in *Lie of the Land: A Study in the Culture of Deception*.

> If Members of Parliament accept figures like these without question, it is not surprising that most other people – including some farmers – also believe what they are told. Even the Prince of Wales, at a press conference at St. James' Palace, said that average incomes were £5,200 per farm, and this meant that 'a way of life is at risk of collapsing'.[7]

Following the publication of his book, Dr Pickard campaigned against the manipulation of the collective consciousness of taxpayers. In his view, agriculture was being damaged by the tax burden and the mountains of paperwork required by the EU bureaucracy in Brussels. Abolish most of this and, in Pickard's view, the best interests of farmers would be served if they were simply required to pay the annual rental value of the land they used into the public's purse.

He failed to persuade the politicians to desist from manipulating the statistics. Nor did he receive a reply from his constituency MP, Sir Menzies Campbell. So in the election of May 2005 farmer Pickard decided to stand for Parliament himself. His natural affinity was with the Liberal

Party but it had strayed from its philosophical roots. So up went the posters in the byways of the constituency of Northeast Fife inviting the voters to back the candidate for the UK Independence Party. The angry would-be parliamentarian campaigned for votes while lambing his flocks in the hills. He was not elected; Sir Menzies was returned to the Commons, where, in due course, he would be elected leader of the Liberal Democrats, the rump of the party which once campaigned to restore people's birthrights in land.

7.4 The Disunited Kingdom (3): Democracy

ONCE UPON a time, people had to own land to qualify as a voter to elect a Member of Parliament. The property qualification was eventually abolished, but this was not sufficient to make all citizens equal before the laws of the land. Some are more equal than others, as Jim Speechley well knew from his close study of the economics of the land market.

Speechley did not come from a landowning aristocratic family, but he found himself in a political situation where he might still acquire a fortune. All he had to do was redraw a line on the map that lay before him on the table. He pulled the map closer and scrutinised it. Then he picked up a red pen and drew a new line. This, he told the planner who sat opposite him, would be the appropriate route for a highway. He then carefully marked the map with a cross: X marked the field which he had bought in 1971. Those two red marks on the map could deliver him a capital gain – providing he could bypass the rules of democracy.

Jim Speechley was out of luck: the two red marks on the map earned him a prison sentence of 18 months. The moral of his story is revealing for what it tells us about the privileges associated with land as an asset.

There was nothing exceptional about the field. It was located near the edge of the Lincolnshire village of Crowland. The 4.21 acres had cost Speechley £10,000 in 1971. It served the farmer well over the years. During this time its owner, a Conservative, rose through the ranks of the county council to become leader.

Then, suddenly, something remarkable happened to the field. A bypass was needed. The planners drew a line *through* Speechley's field. Had that proposal been confirmed by the planning authority, the owner would have been compensated. The field's agricultural value had risen over the years, thanks largely to Europe's taxpayers. In its current use as agricultural or paddock land, it would be worth up to £17,500.

What occurred next became the subject of dispute at Sheffield Crown Court. In March 2000, Speechley visited a council engineer and drew the alternative line on the map. This, he suggested, was the ideal route for the A1073. The line skirted the field. The road would become the physical boundary of the village.

At the stroke of a pen, the field was transformed. No longer was it merely a patch of soil. According to surveyor David Brown, the land would be worth £190,000 if it was put to industrial use. But what if the four acres were sliced into smaller plots for housing? Then, according to his evidence to the Crown Court, it would be worth £375,000.

Speechley, who had been honoured with the CBE (Commander of the British Empire) in 1993, was accused of changing the route of the £25m bypass so that it would enhance the value of his land. He denied a charge of misconduct in public office, but he was accused by the council's Chief Executive, David Bowles, of being a 'most deceitful and dishonest' person. Another council employee said in evidence that the former leader of the council could be 'crass, intimidating, nasty – a tin-pot dictator'.[8]

The case of the Crowland field illuminates the complex character of land as the repository of value. In no other market can an asset increase in price overnight by 375% without its owner doing anything to improve its physical condition or social appeal. The public value of land was elucidated by what happened at Lincolnshire County Council.

All societies regulate the use to which their land may be put, to one degree or another, and there is a duty on elected representatives to discharge their obligations with integrity. In the Lincolnshire case, auditors KPMG were brought in to examine the council's record. Its findings did not make palatable reading. They were the subject of a debate in the House of Commons. Gillian Merron, the Member for Lincoln, quoted KPMG as referring to Speechley as displaying 'examples of behaviour, which can only be categorised as both improper pressure, and misuse of power'. Speechley had intervened in the staffing of, and decisions in, the highways and planning department, which were censured as unacceptable. The 'bullying and systematic abuse of power', asserted Gillian Merron, was conduct that did not meet the standards of integrity that were expected of public servants.[9] The auditors' report had identified a breakdown in governance at the interface between public life and private markets.

Democracy is a set of rules that requires people to behave in a transparent and non-prejudicial way. Speechley thought he could bypass that process. All he wanted was a windfall gain of the kind that is pocketed every day by the owners of land. His mistake was to try and sidestep the democratic formalities that legitimised the mal-distribution of capital gains. For the sake of decorum, a ritual has been devised so that the unjust milking of taxpayers can be seen to be conducted in a fair way. People thought that, when the property qualification attached to the right to vote was abolished, democracy would unite the nation. In fact, it has been appropriated as a device to legitimise the continued disuniting of the population between taxpayers and the owners whose land captures the windfall gains.

INTERROGATION

THE FENS date back to the last Ice Age, a system of flat land under water which the Romans began to drain nearly 2,000 years ago. The result was rich soil and bountiful harvests, but no farmer could imagine in his wildest dreams that one day his farming techniques would yield dividends that had little to do with the fertility of the soil. Because of the power of the landowner, governments could be persuaded to rig the food markets to boost their rental incomes.

 Europe's CAP did not distribute the windfall gains equally among the regions. About 80% of the subsidies were concentrated in the rich regions in Germany, the UK, France and the Netherlands. The poorer regions in southern and eastern Europe received the leftovers. The richer regions also tend to be where the larger farms are located, which increases the inequality between them and the regions on the margins of Europe.[10]

 Cambridgeshire cereal farmer Oliver Walston had an answer to those who object to the lion's share of agricultural subsidies going to the big farmers. He explained: '80% of the land is owned by 20% of the farmers and the subsidy is paid on a per acre basis'. So, logically, there was nothing wrong with the lion's share going to the few farmers who received it as 'a reward for looking after the landscape and the environment'. Walston's subsidy cheque in 2004 totalled £170,523.[11]

 The EU tries to compensate urban dwellers with subsidies but these do not match the money paid to the owners of farmland. According to Oxford professor Iain McLean, who led a study on the regional distribution of taxpayers' money, the value of EU subsidies received by farmers in East Anglia far outweighed EU funds that were supposed to alleviate problems in high unemployment areas.[12] The EU, which is concerned about poverty in the developing world, pays a subsidy of $2.62 a day per cow, which exceeds the daily income of half the world's population.

REFERENCES

1 Patrick Barkham, 'Village revolt as common people take on City gent over land rights', *The Guardian*, April 28, 2005.
2 Sam Jones, 'Victory over Norfolk landowner who fenced in village green', *The Guardian*, August 16, 2005.
3 Christopher Hill, *The Century of Revolution 1603-1714*, London: Routledge, 2nd edn, 1980, pp.221-2.
4 *Ibid.*, p.223.
5 *Ibid.*, pp.135, 136.
6 Peter Gibb, 'Civil Society, Governance and Land Reform', *Geo*philos, Autumn 2000 (01).
7 Duncan Pickard, *Lie of the Land*, London: Land Research Trust/Shepheard-Walwyn, 2004, pp.7-8.
8 Sharon Edwards, 'A1073 a "parochial pet project" for south of the county leader', *Lincolnshire Echo*, February 13, 2004, p.19.
9 *Hansard*, 'Standards of Conduct (County Councillors)', June 12, 2002, Col. 314WH.
10 Fiona Harvey, 'CAP "increases divide between rich and poor"', *Financial Times*, August 19, 2005.
11 Oliver Walston, 'The peasant within', *The Guardian*, March 24, 2005.
12 Peter Hetherington, 'Mayor's regional robbery claim is denied', *The Guardian*, September 12, 2003.

8

The Economics of Life and Death

EAST MIDLANDS

8.1 Mortality and the System

DRIVING THROUGH the middle of England, one's thoughts turn to life and death. If my thesis is correct, the privatisation of rents should affect people's health in a spatial pattern that reflects, say, the price of houses. The relatively richer South East should enjoy a healthier lifestyle, with the indices on health fading away as we move further up the road to the North East.

The causal connection between wealth and health was established in the 19th century, when medical officers analysed the statistics that they assembled from impoverished parts of urban Britain and Ireland. This evidence was expertly located in its economic context by Dr George Miller in *On Fairness and Efficiency*.[1] This professor of epidemiology interrogated the origins of Britain's class system. He compared the distribution of occupations (on which the classification of social status is based) with people's health. *The lower down the class structure you are, the higher the prospects of suffering from ill-health and a shorter life.*

Miller dug deeper than those who went before him. He wanted to know whether the distribution of health was related to the degree to which rent was shared in the population. It was. But we can now add a new layer of evidence to his findings. To deepen his analysis, we will consider whether there is a spatial pattern to the health-based facts. The statistics suggest that we should begin our diagnosis by standing somewhere in the middle of the East Midlands. If Miller is correct, then, given the tax and tenure arrangements that shape life in England, we ought to be able to trace a deterioration in the quality of people's lives the further we move towards the North East.

We shall test this theory by taking two measures – male mortality and cancer rates – to see if there is a spatial relationship between health and income. Ricardo's rent slope is downwards: the reciprocal should be an *upward* slope as we traverse the highway from London to the North East.

Mortality rates are compared by using an *excess deaths* index. The yardstick is the mortality that would be expected if a region within the UK had the same age-specific mortality rates as for the UK as a whole. A relatively good quality of life would result in excess deaths per 100,000 people below the UK average (in this case, the number would have a minus sign in front of it). A relatively disadvantaged region would have excess deaths above the UK's. Scotland does not fare well. It has about 350 excess deaths from all causes in a year. England, on the other hand, has about 430 *fewer* deaths than would be expected. Within England, however, the differences are remarkable, and they reflect the pattern that is predicted by our theory.

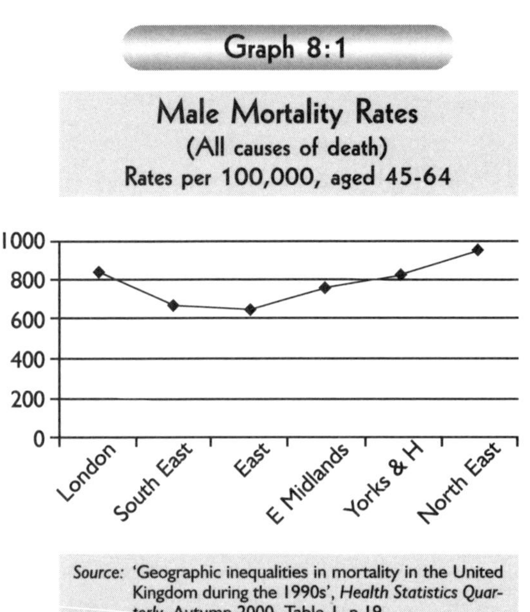

Source: 'Geographic inequalities in mortality in the United Kingdom during the 1990s', *Health Statistics Quarterly*, Autumn 2000, Table 1, p.19.

Parents naturally want the best for their children, but the place of birth automatically tilts the scales against a male child's prospects. That is the tragic reality embedded in the statistics that are summarised in Graph 8:1. The prospects for females born outside the prosperous end of England are similarly prejudiced.

The exception appears to be London, which reports higher mortality rates than those in the Home Counties. This contradicts what we would have expected, given the higher productivity and income levels in the capital. The explanation is to be found in the concentration of poverty among people located in deprived inner city boroughs. These affect the total figures. Tower Hamlets has the highest mortality rate, with excess deaths per year of 160. This compares with life-chances in the prosperous boroughs. Barnet, in the north-west corner of the metropolis, reports the lowest number of excess deaths per year as *minus* 240.

The moral appears to be clear: if you live in London, make sure you adopt the lifestyles of boroughs like Barnet and Chelsea, and avoid Tower Hamlets. And if you choose to migrate out of London, be aware that the closer you settle to Wallsend the greater the risk of premature mortality.

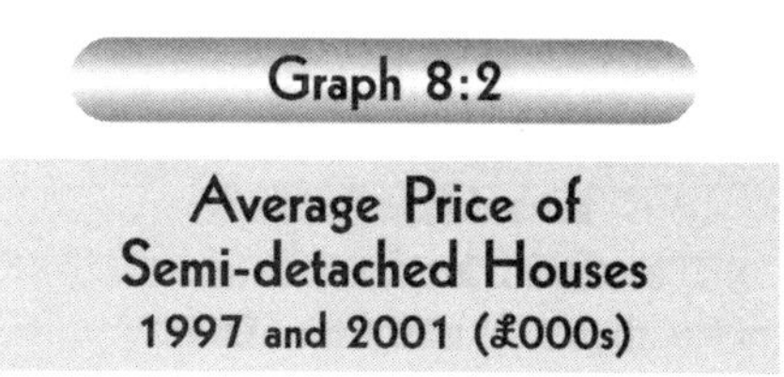

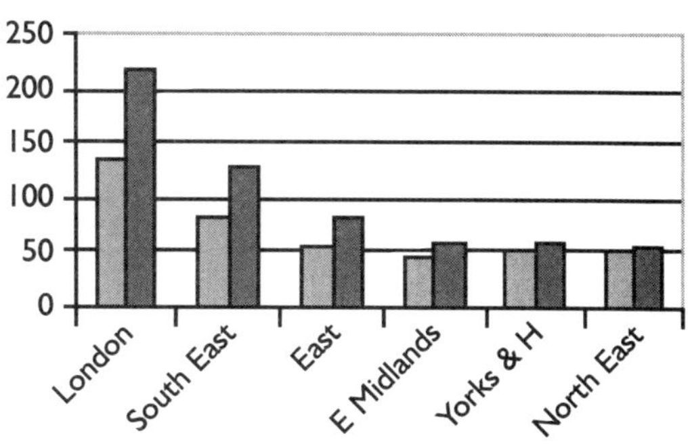

Source: Data from *Residential Property Price Reports*, London: Land Registry

The health statistics should be juxtaposed with the wealth of the nation during the Blair years. The first column in Graph 8:2 shows the average price of a semi-detached house during the first few months of Blair's New Labour government. New Labour was elected to inject fairness into society. The index of house price increases reveals how unequally the capital gains have been distributed. The second column shows the average price for the semi-detached property in early 2001 as British industry slumped into recession. Home owners in London and the South East enjoyed a dramatic leap in the value of their properties compared with properties down the road. Thanks to the ensuing property boom, the gap was narrowed between 2004 and 2006, but this was not sustained. And the wider differential would be increased with the onset of the next property crash.

The beneficial impact of wealth on people's life chances fizzle out by the time we reach the Midlands. Here, regional earnings have dropped to just above the level that prevails further north, having declined by a third from the rates prevailing in London. Now, the further north we go, the greater the risk of premature death.

8.2 The Clues in Cancer

CANCER IS an effective measure of one's life-chances because it reflects a complex range of factors. These include the food we eat, our habits (such as smoking), levels of education and recreation, and the quality of the ecological environment within which we live. In England in 2000 there were a total of 149,000 cases of cancer registered for males and 170,000 for females.[2] The victims, however, were not spread evenly throughout

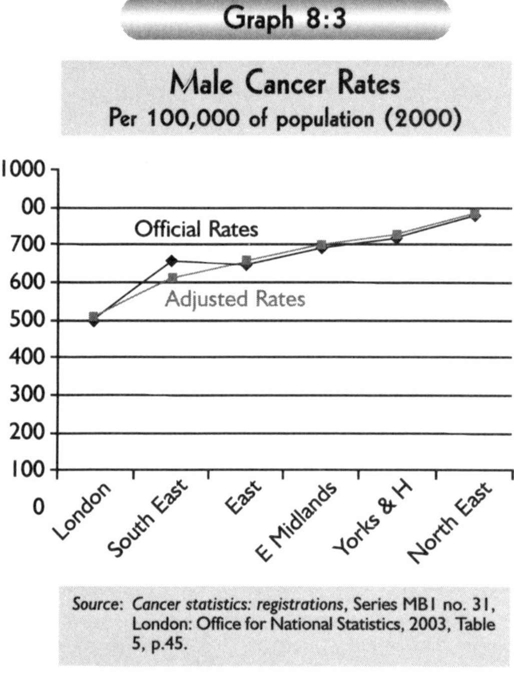

England. When we break the numbers down by region, we discover that the rate per 100,000 people is lowest in London and highest in the North East (Graph 8:3).

As we move northwards, we climb a deadly profile. As the economic surplus diminishes, there is a reciprocal increase in the negative impact on people's health. The rate of deterioration is not haphazard. There is a consistent pattern of prejudice against the spatially distributed people of England. The further they live from London, the greater the risk from cancer.

According to the statistics, however, there is one exception to the rule. We would have expected the rate of cancer to be lower in the South East than in the East of England. The official data contradicts this prediction. People living in the South East, who accrue more wealth, register a greater risk of cancer than people in the East of England. The statistics, however, are (not intentionally) misleading. The statistical blip can be explained in a way that brings cancer rates in line with our theory.

We expect the risk of cancer to be at its lowest in London. At 402 per 100,000 males, the rate is far below the North East's 676. But the number understates the risk of contracting cancer in London. In fact, the figures also slightly understate the lifetime risks in all the regions, while overstating those associated with living in the South East. But when we take migration and retirement patterns into account, the discrepancy corrects itself. For when people retire, some of them choose to relocate in warmer climes: they sell up and make a beeline for the south coast. This is the time of life when we are most at risk of contracting cancer, which is described as 'predominantly a disease of the elderly'.[3] London and our other four regions off-load some of their cancer cases on to the South East. The towns on the south coast that report high mortality rates, which would be accounted for by the migration habit, include Brighton and Hove, Bournemouth, Torbay, Hastings and Christchurch.[4]

So the 567 cases per 100,000 exaggerate the South East's *home-grown* risk factor. This number ought to be reduced by about 10%. By distributing 56 cases back to the other regions, the incidence in the South East's rate is decreased to 511. This is *below* the East of England's rate of 540. Our adjustment to the official figures delivers a graphic profile (the grey line in Graph 8:3) that is consistent with our theory.

Our contention is that the unequal distribution of life chances is ultimately grounded in the configuration of the rules of taxation and tenure. This explanation for problems like strokes and heart diseases does not feature in the academic research into the geographical variations in disease rates. It needs to be. We must distinguish between the failings that may be attributed to the individual (which require personalised solutions) and 'independent area-level effects' (which require political solutions). According to one heart specialist

> the widening gap between the rich and poor appears to be mirrored by a growing divergence of their residential environments, so that affluent people are increasingly living and interacting with other affluent people while the poor increasingly live and interact with other poor people.[5]

Without the correct diagnosis and political action, Britain will continue to be ghettoised into enclaves that are an affront to a society that supposedly treats everyone as equal. When examining the characteristics of a locality, we do need to consider 'the local availability of affordable fruits and vegetables, green areas, and physical activity facilities; area levels of criminal activity; and other indicators of environmental adversity'.[6] Ricardo's Law provides us with an elegant measure that summarises all these factors; they are factored into the *net* value that may be derived from living in those localities. The index of that net value is compiled by the people themselves. It is the price they are *willing* and *able* to pay for the use of land, after they have deducted the costs of the fruit and vegetables, recreation and so on.

That we should be less concerned about personal shortcomings, and more about systemic features, is clear from the medical evidence. For example, men born in the rest of Britain who move to the South reduce their risks of contracting coronary heart disease. This process also works in the opposite direction: men who move from the South to the rest of Britain increase their risk of contracting coronary heart disease.[7] This evidence confirms that we are not dealing with a genetic problem (which would be portable: migrants would take their risks with them). Diagnosis should be focused on causal agents that are independently located across the country. Furthermore, such evidence shows the risk is *graduated*. It is not randomly distributed, but significantly related to distance from London and the South East. So the *primary* problem must be located in a cultural context within which people are driven to adopt fatal habits such as the smoking and eating that leads to obesity. These are responses to an underlying tendency. With stroke mortality, for example, 'the low risk associated with living in Greater London was acquired by individuals who lived there and was not a consequence of early life factors or selective migration'.[8]

We are dealing with a life-and-death issue, but not one that is set in concrete. For there is

> the potential to avoid about one quarter of coronary heart disease and one third of stroke events occurring in the rest of Britain if conditions enjoyed by men in the south of England could be replicated elsewhere.[9]

It is the treatment of the differential surplus income (or public value) that ultimately leads to the gradation of people's health prospects.

I am not representing living conditions in the South as ideal. The risks of heart diseases in London and the South East are high by international standards. But the prospect of achieving a significant improvement in the health of the nation is more likely to arise if we equalise people's access to the nation's surplus income. We can deduce this by referring to mental illness rates. The distribution of income reveals a remarkable prejudice against those at the bottom of the income league table. Those within the highest 20% income band have a risk of developing a mental illness which is half the rate for women, compared with those in the poorest 5th of incomes; while the rate for men is one-third compared with the risks faced by males at the bottom of the income pile. For suicide, the rate among manual occupations is more than twice that of other occupations. But the income statistics, by themselves, tell part of the story only; we need to plot the health and income data on the map to discover the deeper ramifications on inequality.

8.3 Poverty of Place

WHY DID the Welfare State fail to unite the kingdom by equalising people's life chances? 'Free treatment at the point of need' for anyone in need of medical attention was the slogan by those who sought social solidarity through progressive income taxes.

The National Health Service (NHS) was launched to protect the post-war generation from the injustices of the past. Being born into a family with a low income would not continue to be a liability. We can measure the effect of 60 years of progressive taxation and state paternalism in the teeth of children born in the 21st century.

Five-year-old children born in South-East England have an average of under 0.5 teeth that have decayed. Move northwards to the East Midlands and that average rises to three decayed teeth. And then, at the end of the line, in the North, the average number rises to four. Testimony out of the mouths of children is likely to disclose the truth. A social process is at work which is biased against children in the regions that do not receive their equal share of the nation's surplus revenue.

The Blair government was shocked. It launched a Dental Health Taskforce in child oral health. The Department of Health acknowledged that adults in the North were twice as likely to have no teeth as those in the South.[10] But the experts assembled to advise the ministry focused attention on fluoride and on the need to instruct parents on the wisdom of using toothbrushes. Responsibility was shifted away from systemic failures and onto the individual.

The midwife of the Welfare State was a socialist party that was committed to central planning of the economy. It would remove the injustices inherited from the 19th century, most acutely represented by the gap between the rich and the poor. The Labour Party came to power determined to enact laws that would give government greater control over the people from cradle to grave. For 60 years Labour governments – supported in its welfare agenda by the Conservative Party – propagated the belief that it could reverse the trends of history.

The tools for this remarkable feat would be the taxes that would transfer income from the rich to those who were excluded from the riches of the nation. The experiment was a failure.

The Welfare State did enhance the general health of the population. Given the growth of national income over 60 years it would have been truly remarkable if there had not been some measurable effect. But the Welfare State's agenda was to *equalise* people's life-chances. So we have to judge its performance in terms of whether it overrode the hurdles that were placed in front of a large section of the population. On that count, the Welfare State has failed.

But were politicians solely to blame? What about the experts who presumed to advise the representatives of the people?

Reforms intended to elevate the welfare of the population were originally promoted by the Liberal Party at the beginning of the century. Liberals wanted to provide a safety net for the aged and infirm – and those who were temporarily without jobs – but it linked the costs of these measures to the rents of land and natural resources.

The Liberal government did place some of its employment and retirement policies on the statute book in its 1909 budget, which began to humanise the capitalist economy, but the financial foundations were missing. The landlords blocked the tax reform programme so the welfare agenda remained unbalanced. After another ill-fated attempt to restore the philosophy of rent as a basis for public revenue in 1931, the Marxist programme of the Labour Party began to assert itself in British politics. The opportunity came with the Second World War, when the Labour Party took control of Parliament and launched its socialist project.

The rationale for Labour's Welfare State was provided by a Liberal, William Beveridge. As soldiers laid down their lives on foreign fields, a report by Beveridge in 1942 exposed what he called the five 'giant evils' – disease, ignorance, squalor, idleness and want. He formalised his aspirations for the survivors of the war in *Full Employment in a Free Society* (1944). But missing from his influential diagnosis was the philosophy that explained the origins of these evils.

It is not surprising that politicians are reluctant to pronounce the Welfare State a social experiment that has run its course. But why did academics fail to see the failure coming? They are supposed to be the objective students of social welfare, objective in not just chronicling the facts but also explaining the outcomes. And yet, no one offered a coherent explanation for the inability of sovereign governments to crush the giant evils that continued to course through the kingdom.

In fact, one of the astonishing facts about the academic community is that it is shocked by the evidence of failure. It may be invidious to pick on particular individuals, given the general failure of scholars to serve the nation, but an event at the Royal Geographical Society conference in London in September 2005 is poignant for several reasons.

First, four distinguished scholars pronounced the Welfare State a failure when they disclosed the findings of their analysis of census data. *Life in Britain* did not reveal anything new. Geographical location as well as income affected the chances of obtaining a well-paid job. The gap between the rich and poor was as wide as it had been 60 years previously. 'Wide and persisting inequality is reflected in big differences between 'rich' and 'poor' areas in terms of housing, education and health care as well as economic wealth,' said Professor Daniel Dorling of the University of Leeds.[11]

Britain, they confirmed, was vulnerable to something called the 'inverse care law'.

- Areas with the highest levels of poor health had the fewest doctors, dentists and health professionals.
- Areas with the highest proportions of unqualified young people had the fewest teachers.

The scholars were dismayed that the inverse care law was still operating. But the biggest surprise is that they should have been shocked at all by their findings. According to Professor Dorling:[12]

- 'It is acutely *disappointing* to discover that so many opportunities and resources still depend on where people live.'
- '*Perversely*, people living in the poorest neighbourhoods with the greatest needs are often the least likely to have access to the services and support that would help them improve their lives and life chances.'

We italicise the words *disappointing* and *perversely* to highlight the fact that scholars had failed to realise that these outcomes were the logical consequences of the tax-and-tenure rules. This may be disappointing, but we cannot condemn as perverse the consequences of rules that programme our communities. Scholars who devote their lives to tracking the trends in the Welfare State ought to know that government cannot reverse the social trends that were inherited from the 19th century because the primary rules themselves have not been changed.

According to Prof. Dorling's co-worker, Dr Ben Wheeler, their analysis of the census data 'maps these differences and aims to stimulate discussion about ways in which policy-makers *can begin to bridge the divide*' (emphasis added). What entitled these academics to think that, using their conventional theories of deprivation, policy-makers can possibly hope to bridge the divide when they had tried so hard – and failed – over the previous 60 years?

In the case of the findings based on the census data, the sponsoring foundation, the Joseph Rowntree Foundation, admitted in its information sheet that 'the study demonstrates associations rather than proving causes'.[13] There is the problem. The poor do not need more statistics to prove the association between statistics. What they need is *explanations* for the causes that disqualify them from a decent life at the very moment of their conception.

Churning out statistics year after year does nothing to inform politicians, improve policy or alleviate poverty. So who do we hold responsible for the merry-go-round of statistics that have become the background noise that stops intelligent people from *thinking*? Britain has a well-funded poverty industry which appears incapable of achieving its mission. Prominent in this community of agencies that agonise about the unfair distribution of wealth and opportunities is the Joseph Rowntree Foundation. Every year, the Rowntree name is celebrated through the lush publications that lavishly display the scale of poverty 60 years after the inauguration of the Welfare State. Every year, the Foundation spends over £7m in sponsoring academics to collate the statistics and present them in technicolour graphics so that no one is left in doubt that Britain has a problem of poverty.[14] Those millions in grants fuel the busy academic bees who feed off the official statistics, all the time blinding us with 'evidence-led' analyses which are then presented to the public at plush conference centres in London to leave no one in any doubt that the Joseph Rowntree Foundation cares about the disadvantaged sections of society. We shall take a close look at the role of the Rowntree Foundation as we enter its home territory, in the Yorkshire and Humberside region.

8.4 The Disunited Kingdom (4): Health

TONY BLAIR was determined to subvert the 'inverse health law': the greater the people's needs, the fewer the facilities. Northern constituencies, one of which he represents, experience more than their fair share of discrimination. Whole communities suffer poor health and long-term illness alongside inadequate medical amenities. An example is the Owton residential estate in Hartlepool. Nearly half of its households had at least one person with a long-term illness. But it was 'a health and social care desert ... At its extreme, there is little evidence that we have a Welfare State there', in the words of Lord Adebowale, the Chief Executive of a social care charity that was working in Owton.[15]

Residents of Owton had access to two part-time doctors working out of a shop and another part-time practice. This availability of doctors was inverse to the needs of the community. But why should we be surprised? Ricardo's Law would tend to drive newly qualified doctors to the South, and the tax rules are rigged against high unemployment areas in favour of prosperous regions. How this operates can be seen if we compare the financial prospects of two doctors, one working in a hospital (say, in Hartlepool), the other as a general practitioner (GP) in (let us say) Hatfield, Hertfordshire.

The Hartlepool hospital doctor would spend his working life receiving his salary and a pension when he retired. This remuneration was earned by his labour service, caring for his community's health.

The Hatfield GP was destined for dramatically different prospects. As a self-employed contractor to the National Health Service, his salary is paid by taxpayers. He earns his keep in attending to the needs of his patients. But under the terms of his employment, he also receives the rent that has to be paid for the building that houses his surgery. If he bought that building at the beginning of his practice, taxpayers would effectively be paying his mortgage through the rental subsidy which continued until he retired. At the end of 30 years (say) a building which he had purchased for £100,000 would now be worth (say) £500,000. That gives him a windfall gain of £400,000. He did not pay for the building: the taxpayer did. But under government rules and the law, taxpayers have no property right in that capital gain. Even if the retiring doctor had to pay tax on the windfall, it would be a trivial return to taxpayers for their investment. Unlike the hospital doctor in Hartlepool, the GP embarks on a retirement with a handsome cash pile to spend on the good life, with the capital gain supplementing his pension.

Why should newly qualified doctors work in hospitals in the North when they can seek their fortune – courtesy of the taxpayer – in the South? Doctors located in London and the South East can claw back their lifetime's tax payments through their capital gains. In essence, they have received tax-free remuneration for their services.

The health service needs financial surgery, but Blair's government adopted a funding model that returned Britain to the 19th century. The PFI is a travesty that will further damage the health of people at the bottom of the income scales. It is not surprising that some of the nation's most ancient hospitals – like St Bartholomew's in London, the recipient of a donation from Sir Rowland Hill back in the 17th century – faced financial crises. They had to fund capital costs out of the revenue they were allocated to perform operations and care for their patients. That model did not work in the 19th century and no amount of juggling the books would make it work in the 21st century.

INTERROGATION

TONY BLAIR was puzzled by the fact that 2.8m people claim benefits on the grounds that they are incapacitated and cannot work. There was something seriously wrong with a welfare system that leads to 350,000 new claimants each year. 'Does anyone seriously believe that every year you have 350,000 more people completely incapacitated from any form of work?' he asked.[16]

Richard Layard, an advisor to the Blair government on mental health, reported that 15% of the population suffered from depression and anxiety disorders. The value of lost productivity was about £17bn, or 1.5% of UK gross domestic product. 'There are now more than 1m mentally ill people receiving incapacity benefits – more than the total number of unemployed people receiving unemployment benefits,' he wrote in the *British Medical Journal*.[17]

But the psychosomatic evidence does not provide a real sense of the profound flaw in the structure of society. Perhaps the best indicator of the crisis was offered by George Miller. He calculated that about 50,000 people die prematurely every year in England and Wales because of the impact of taxes. He analysed the chain of causation and published his findings at the time (2003) when he was not only a professor of epidemiology but also a member of the Senior Clinical Scientific Staff at the prestigious Medical Research Council.[18] Dr Miller's conclusions were submitted to the Department of Health and the Treasury. A deafening silence reverberated around Whitehall. None of Miller's peers, some of whom were consultants to the Department of Health, considered his analysis worthy of critical evaluation.

Miller called on government to investigate why the Welfare State and the NHS failed to close the gap in health and life expectancy. Tough questions needed to be answered about the way taxation favoured those who appropriated the rents.

 Despite a huge increase in spending on the NHS, there was still a cash shortfall. In one case, a new £6m ward was mothballed because the hospital could not afford to employ the staff.[19] Since the Prime Minister was concerned about the funding of the nation's health and wealth, wasn't the critique by a distinguished medical scientist worthy of examination?

 The House of Commons' public accounts committee reported that the chances of beating cancer depended on where the patient lived. This was the postcode lottery identified by the National Institute for Clinical Excellence.[20] Why was the NHS not delivering a fair deal to all citizens, especially those who live in the wrong areas or who could not afford private health care? Would a reformed tax system generate the right kinds of revenue to finally solve the problem of place?

 Hospitals with a good reputation help to boost nearby house prices. These hospitals are partly funded by taxpayers living nearby in rented accommodation. They are not able to claw back some of their taxes as capital gains in the way owners of freeholds living in the vicinity can. Was this discriminatory outcome intended by the champions of the working class who created the NHS and who vigorously promoted 'progressive' taxes?

REFERENCES

1 George J. Miller, *On Fairness and Efficiency: The Privatisation of the Public Income Over the Past Millennium*, Bristol: Policy Press, 2000.

2 *Cancer Statistics: Registrations*, Series MB1 No. 31, London: Office for National Statistics, 2003, p.13.

3 *Ibid.*

4 'Geographic inequalities in mortality in the United Kingdom during the 1990s', *Health Statistics Quarterly*, Autumn 2000, p.27

5 Peter McCarron, 'North, South: Changing Directions in Cardiovascular Epidemiology', *Stroke*, November 2003, p.2610.

6 *Ibid.*

7 S. Goya Wannamethee, A. Gerald Shaper, Peter H. Whincup and Mary Walker, 'Migration within Great Britain and cardiovascular disease: early life and adult

environmental factors', *International J. of Epidemiology* (31), 2002, p.1056-8.

8 *Ibid.*, p.1059.

9 R.W. Morris, P.H. Whincup, J.R. Emberson, F.C. Lampe, M. Walker and A.G. Shaper, 'North-South Gradients in Britain for Stroke and CHD', *Stroke*, November 2003, p.2607.

10 Anushka Asthana, 'Decay bites ever deeper into poor children's teeth', *The Observer*, September 4, 2005.

11 Sarah Womack, 'Rich-poor divide "as wide as 60 years ago"', *The Daily Telegraph*, September 2, 2005.

12 'UK's rich and poor "still live in different worlds despite the Welfare State"', Press Release, Joseph Rowntree Foundation, September 1, 2005.

13 Joseph Rowntree Foundation, 'The relationship between poverty, affluence and area', September 2005, p.2 (www.jrf.org.uk).

14 Grant commitments and support costs in 2005 were £8.8m, thanks to a rise in the market value of the Joseph Rowntree foundation's investment portfolio. The capital of £207m included £18m invested in property.

15 Peter Hetherington, 'Reality check', *The Guardian*, February 1, 2006.

16 Patrick Wintour, 'Blair defends reform of incapacity benefit', *The Guardian*, November 7, 2005.

17 Quoted in Sarah Boseley, 'Depression is UK's biggest social problem, government told', *The Guardian*, April 28, 2006.

18 George Miller, *Dying for Justice*, London: Centre for Land Policy Studies, 2003.

19 Nigel Hawkes, '£6m ward closed before it opens', *The Times*, April 6, 2006.

20 Sarah Boseley, 'Beating Cancer still depends on where you live, say MPs', *The Guardian*, January 26, 2006. According to a poll of Chief Executives of hospital trusts, the financial crisis meant that patients were receiving a reduced standard of care in 75% of NHS hospitals and clinics in England (John Carvel, 'Patients suffer in crisis for 75% of hospitals', *The Guardian*, January 19, 2006).

Brave New World

YORKSHIRE AND HUMBERSIDE

9.1 A Demolition Job

HE WAS the closest that a politician dare get to being a pugilist. John Prescott was known to throw a punch on the hustings. His pugnacious credentials as the champion of the underdog could not be doubted.

Prescott knew what it was like to live at the bottom of the pile. He began his working life as a steward on boats operating out of Hull, the seaport at the mouth of the Humber on the Yorkshire coast. From there he fought his way up to a fine £2.3m grace-and-favour home in Admiralty Arch, an imposing façade at one end of The Mall opposite Buckingham Palace. But despite his elevated status, as Deputy Prime Minister he would not forget his roots: he would do his best to renew Britain's communities. Workers were entitled to live in decent neighbourhoods.

As MP for Hull East since 1970, he knew that shelter was a problem for many people. Prescott's constituency is in the Yorkshire and Humberside region which upsets the downward trend on homelessness (see Graph 9:1). In 2002, high-price London reported 31,000 households as homeless, compared with the 6,460 in the North East. Yorkshire and Humberside broke the predictable trend with 13,980 homeless households. Does it offer a lesson on housing? Given that shelter is a primary need for every family, how is it possible for so many to be homeless in such a rich nation? In 2003, about 200,000 households were accepted as homeless by their local authorities, a quarter higher than in 2000. This rise was of households without dependent children. Behind the statistics is a process that leads to the fragmentation of families.[1]

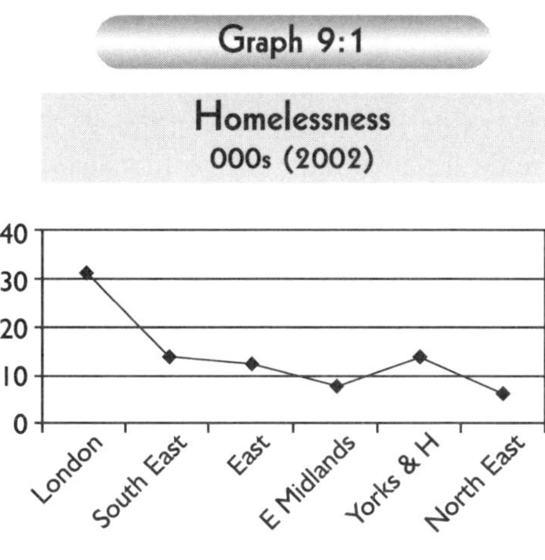

Source: Homelessness Statistics, ODPM; Wilcox (2003), Table 94a, p.185

Getting on to the 'housing ladder' has become all but impossible. The desperation begins for people reaching maturity between the ages of 25 and 29. That is when they should be starting their families and settling down in their careers. In London, they have to borrow a multiple of 8.5 times their income to afford a house (see Graph 9:2). Even in the North East, the multiple was higher than four times the average income for this age group.

House prices reflect the quality not only of people's lives, but also the character of communities. In the North East, people are most likely to live near their families (81%) compared with Londoners, who are least likely to be close to their families (49%). This is because, in the North, the young are trapped in their localities by poverty. In London they are displaced from their localities by high house prices. But being rooted in the place of their birth did not protect the northerners from the malevolent forces that were at work. Take the case of self-destructive behaviour. In the four years to 2004, alcohol-related deaths increased by 46.5% in Yorkshire and Humberside, which topped the death league followed by the North East (28.4%). This information, derived by the Office of National Statistics, showed that the deaths in London dropped by 4.2%.[2]

Graph 9:2

First Time Buyers
(Aged 25-29)
Income multiples

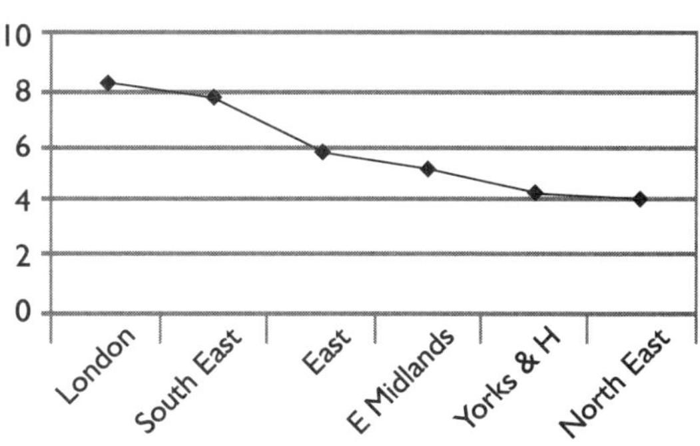

Source: National Housing Federation [*Daily Express*, 'Under-thirties hit by property squeeze', August 26, 2002].

John Prescott's dream was to override such problems by constructing 'sustainable communities' in the South East. He had a more dramatic recipe for the North: he programmed the demolition of 168,000 houses by 2016, ostensibly to build homes that people could afford.

Was the Deputy Prime Minister trying to hide something with his demolition job? Was this really the way to deliver a lasting solution to a problem that had blighted the nation since the beginning of the Industrial Revolution? Was it better to wipe out the evidence of failure rather than to rehabilitate existing communities?

Prescott gave his project a grand name: the Housing Market Renewal Initiative, a 15-year plan known as Pathfinder projects. Scattered around the great conurbations of the Midlands and the North were whole streets of houses that were boarded up, apparently because nobody wanted to buy or rent them. The larger-than-life John Prescott would bulldoze them to the ground and recreate neighbourhoods from scratch, with some houses refurbished where this was deemed to be desireable.

This was supposed to be in the interests of low-income families. But an examination of the operation reveals the scandal of the rent-seekers who would pocket the biggest gains from this exercise in social investment. The evidence was collated by SAVE Britain's Heritage, a charity that champions the built environment. Its report exposed the operations of the property market in a way that revealed how state institutions worked hand-in-glove with land speculators to extract the biggest capital gains out of investments funded by taxpayers. SAVE came close to alleging a conspiracy between public housing agencies and land-speculating building companies. But it stuck to a factual description of how the system works in the property market.

One curiosity was the heavy incidence of boarded-up houses owned by local governments or registered social landlords (RSLs). According to independent assessments, many of these properties could be restored as comfortable dwellings for much less than the cost of demolition and the construction of new houses. But by blighting an area and contributing to a decline in property values, richer pickings awaited those who engaged in new-build ventures.

Because of the incentive of government grants, as well as the speculative gains from demolition, SAVE conjectured that the Pathfinder programme may have driven some RSLs 'to seek to deliberately create circumstances where they can maximise development and speculation opportunities and conditions for entering into ventures with private developers'. It added:

> The evidence of this is all around Pathfinder areas, where all the decanting, 'tinning up', lack of investment, and running down of essential public services is highly visible for all to see. Liverpool has literally thousands of otherwise perfectly good properties boarded up, whilst between the council and the RSLs there is a housing waiting list of some 18,000 people.[3]

Councils and RSLs, by their failure to maintain services to an area, 'effected explicit and implicit policies for decline, for example by decanting and boarding up properties, not maintaining their properties, by suggestions and conjecture quietly threatening residents with demolition'.[4] This blighted the area and reduced the value of some of those properties whose owners would be entitled to receive compensation.

> The very agencies meant to serve these people, using a policy itself designed to help these people, are now seeking to prosper themselves, leaving the dislocated homeowner severely prejudiced and disadvantaged. Once the homes have been acquired cheaply and the population cleared, the buildings can be demolished ... The resultant site will be extremely valuable indeed, and can then be transferred to volume house builders in return for a significant uplift in value (Marriage Value).[5]

Public funds were available to finance such an operation. But while the public and the private housing agencies would profit, the costs would be borne 'by the dispossessed residents who, as a direct result, are now forced into lesser circumstances themselves than before'.[6]

SAVE believed that the 'marriage value' belonged to those from whom the land was compulsorily purchased, rather than the house builders and RSLs. But that is not how the Tax State operates. The bonanza gains are taken from low income taxpayers and transferred through the land market to those who have not earned them.

Many of the Victorian homes that would be levelled were suitable for rehabilitation.

> Houses are being condemned on the basis of cursory inspections. Lines are drawn on maps based on evidence that is in many cases out of date. Local wishes are ignored. Areas are blighted and communities are destroyed.[7]

Was this laying the foundations for Prescott's sustainable communities? In the early postwar years, structurally sound houses were demolished as 'slums' and whole communities scattered to soulless tower blocks which, in turn, have been demolished.[8] Could the £1.2bn cost of Pathfinder by 2008 be better spent in rehabilitating existing communities? Some of Prescott's Labour Party members thought so, and they were representing the views of their constituents. One of them was Ken Walker, a former Labour leader of Middlesbrough council who was suspended when he objected to the plan to demolish 1,500 homes in his ward. He was reported as saying: 'The only reason I have been suspended is that I am supporting the residents who don't want to see the end of their homes'.[9]

Prescott was embarrassed when his demolition was ridiculed by a TV company which paid £24,000 to refurbish a derelict Toxteth (Liverpool) terraced house. It would cost £100,000 to knock it down and build a new dwelling in its place.[10] Ringo Starr, the former Beatle who was raised in Liverpool, was not amused by news that 20,000 homes in his birthplace were scheduled to be demolished. He asked: 'Are they going to knock out the centre of Liverpool? That's what they did before. They moved everybody to high-rise apartments outside the city and forgot to rebuild'.[11]

Prescott's department, the Office of the Deputy Prime Minister (ODPM), contested the predictions on how many houses would be demolished. But one thing was certain: the investment of taxpayer's money would raise the value of adjoining land, once again triggering the process by which taxes on the incomes and consumption of the poor would be converted into higher asset values of the better off. But in the process, they would render even more people homeless in the Yorkshire and Humberside region. There was a tragic irony to this outcome. The region was the home of the one philanthropist who had identified land values as the possible source of the problems of the poor.

9.2 The Chocolate King

TWO ACADEMICS were singled out by SAVE as 'the fathers of Pathfinder'. Ian Cole is a professor at Sheffield Hallam University and Brendan Nevin is a visiting professor at Salford University. Both are influential as special advisors to the House of Commons Select Committee on Transport, Local Government and the Regions and the ODPM Urban Affairs Sub-Committee. Through their advice to politicians, and their academic studies, they helped to develop the policies that justified renewal by demolition.[12]

That Britain faced an enormous problem in the housing sector was beyond doubt. At the beginning of the 21st century, the number of empty homes ranged between 764,000 and 844,000.[13] But empty houses would not be the only victims of the preferred strategy for dealing with this problem. According to Brendan Nevin, quoted in the Pathfinder Report on North Staffordshire, 'the outcome of the market renewal process could be a lower population. But this is a price worth paying for a better quality environment and enhanced prospects for the area's population. For the people who are living there it will be fantastic. We should not be hanging on to population for its own sake'.[14] People could be dispensed with for the sake of the grand plan.

How did two professors, Cole and Nevin, come to exercise such influence over the government's urban renewal programme? They authored a study entitled *The Road to Renewal*. This was funded and published by a charity with a profound interest in Britain's property market. The Joseph Rowntree Foundation honours the memory of its benefactor by spending

£7m every year on research into social problems. It maintains an attractive website with the photograph of bearded Joseph Rowntree prominently displayed on the Home page. Was *The Road to Renewal* worthy of the Yorkshire manufacturer who cared about the welfare of his workers? The answer depends on what one deems to be the mission of the foundation today.

Curiously, the Joseph Rowntree Foundation shows little enthusiasm for the one policy which its benefactor highlighted in the memorandum which he bequeathed as guidance on how his money might be spent to help the poor. This is an interesting puzzle for students of the history of the social sciences. Is this lack of enthusiasm an example of a wilful preference for strategies that are proven failures?

In his memo dated December 29, 1904, Rowntree stressed 'the need to search out the underlying causes of weakness or evil' in society. He noted: 'Every Social writer knows the supreme importance of questions connected with the holding and taxation of land'. Rowntree did not want his legacy to be devoted to 'the more superficial manifestations of weakness or evil. While little thought or effort is directed to search out their underlying causes'. Having drawn attention to 'the Land question', he expressed the following wish:

> Such aspects of it as the nationalisation of land, or the taxation of land values, or the appropriation of the unearned increment – all need a treatment far more thorough than they have received.
>
> If one or other of the Directors and Trustees were able to collaborate with competent investigators and workers upon these questions, it would be quite suitable for *large sums to be appropriated in this direction* [emphasis added].

The trustees of the Rowntree Foundation do respect their benefactor's wishes. To guide the investment of the Foundation's £207m fortune, they bar investments in the shares of companies engaged in the manufacture of armaments, alcohol, and tobacco or gambling. But what about Rowntree's wish that large sums might be devoted to the study of the land question? Oddly, this topic is neglected.

Rowntree, who made his fortune out of manufacturing chocolate, did provide his trustees with an escape clause. While the land question was one of the topics 'which under present social conditions appear to me to be of paramount importance', nonetheless if such issues 'ceased to be vital and pressing in the interests of the community' they need not be pursued further. So has the land question ceased to be socially relevant? It appears so, for there was no analysis of it in the plenary papers presented at the conference in York to celebrate the centenary of the Joseph Rowntree Foundation. Land as a social problem was relegated beyond the intellectual landscapes of the social scientists who were contracted to explore the problem of poverty.

Since 1947, Labour governments have repeatedly attempted to promulgate socialist solutions to the land question. Repeatedly their laws were deleted from the statute book by Conservative governments, and their institutions (like the Land Commission) were terminated. These outcomes were not because land policy had fulfilled its purpose. Rather, the policies failed because they were driven by socialist doctrines. So if a prior land problem existed before the socialist experiment, it continued in the aftermath of that experiment.

That Britain continues to need a reform of the tax system in favour of a shift to the rents of land is attested by independent commentators. Two of them write for the *Financial Times*.[15] And yet tax reform as it affects the ownership and use of land is absent from the Rowntree research agenda. Instead, it chooses to sponsor publications such as *The Road to Renewal* which the authors, Cole and Nevin, used to good effect. They cited it at length in a memorandum to a Parliamentary Sub-Committee as 'the first independent study' of the Pathfinder programme, which was 'lodged in a discussion of the policy context for "low demand" and neighbourhood abandonment'. Missing was a review of the impact of fiscal policy on the property market.

Does the Rowntree Foundation have a special responsibility for devoting at least a modest share of its research grants to the policy implications of Ricardo's Law? Had it met that obligation to its benefactor, might it have helped Parliament to eradicate poverty long ago?

That taxation is relevant to the ownership and use of property cannot be contested. Houses, for example, would not be held vacant for long periods if their owners were obliged to pay for the public services that were delivered to their properties.

To determine the contemporary relevance of the land market on the fabric of urban Britain, we can visit York, the home town of the Rowntree Foundation which is also infamous for the insider dealings of the Railway King.

9.3 Railroading the Kingdom

THE RAILWAY revolution was an historical opportunity for Parliament to act as the steward of the common good. The nation's financial architecture needed to be fine-tuned. Laws concerning the access to land had to be revised to ensure efficient investment of all resources in the new systems of communication. And the infrastructure had to be funded, which also necessitated a fundamental review of the public's finances. If Parliament had risen to these challenges, it would not merely have served the interests of investors and travellers; it would also have entrenched a new approach to economic liberty.

James Morrison, a self-made millionaire, was determined to promote this reform agenda. Apprenticed to a London haberdasher, he ended up as the owner of three country homes and was a generous patron of the arts. He was also a Member of Parliament who saw the need to neutralise the monopoly power associated with the busiest routes between cities like Liverpool and Manchester. He was reluctant to invest in railways because he did not want to join those Members who owned shares in such companies. He wanted to be free to propose reforms in the public interest.

Morrison made three attempts at regulating the railways between 1836 and his retirement in 1847. The proposal with the potentially most dramatic historical significance was inspired by evidence from France. In suggesting the appointment of a select committee, he proposed that a financial partnership between state and private enterprise would generate income for the public coffers while levelling the field for those who wished to run railways. The state ought to assume responsibility for the more valuable lines which could be leased to private operators. This would generate a flow of rents – the prices that users would be willing to offer to monopolise the fixed supply of time-and-space travel slots on the rails.[16]

What might have transpired if Parliament had treated Morrison's leasehold proposal with sympathy? He identified a mechanism that would enable entrepreneurs to compete for the most valuable slots on the railway lines. If those slots had been auctioned to the highest bidders, the rents could have been collected and reinvested in the infrastructure. This financial model was practical politics. In January 1843, the Foreign Secretary, Lord Aberdeen, formulated such a model of public/private finance for Britain's most far-flung trading outpost – Hong Kong. Here were the elements of a model that was consistent with free enterprise, private property *and a diminished need to raise public funds by taxing people's wages and savings*.[17]

George Hudson (1800-71) was a vociferous opponent. He did not want to recast the financial fortunes of the railway industry on the basis of a sophisticated partnership between the state and private enterprise. The man who became one of the railway barons knew that land speculation was the secret to a fortune! Hudson, who represented Sunderland in the House of Commons from 1845 to 1859, and fellow MPs like Lord Granville of Somerset, interceded in favour of the *status quo*. They muzzled James Morrison. B*y design*, Parliament endorsed the systematic redistribution of wealth from unwary investors to those who could capture the productivity gains as windfalls. The incentives for avoiding Morrison's package of reforms was illustrated by Hudson's land deal in Whitby, a small town on the Yorkshire coast.

Hudson had learnt the economics of investing in infrastructure so that, by the time of the railway mania of 1844, he had more than 1,000 miles of line under his control. However, the big money was not made out of charging passengers to ride on the trains. It was made by capturing the value which the railways created but – thanks to competition – could not capture in the fares box.

In 1843, Hudson and his close colleagues at the York and North Midland Railway created the Whitby Building Company. Then he began to lay the tracks to the coast, completing the exercise on June 4, 1847, and the first train drawn by a locomotive pulled into the seaside town. Within a year, the Whitby Building Company acquired the fields on West Cliff as a speculation.[18] Shrewdly, Hudson calculated that the trains would carry holiday makers to Whitby where they would need hotel accommodation. So before people knew of their vacation intentions, Hudson & Co cornered the best sites. In effect, they captured the land values that were created by the railway.

Some would say that Hudson earned the windfall gains. But the consequence was that the railways would always be short of the capital needed to invest in new tracks. In the meantime, Hudson was able to indulge himself with his profits. His fortune enabled him 'to acquire land and the social cachet that went with it, and to play a leading role in London Society ... social contacts would aid a successful political career, which in turn might help him to a title, and full integration into the upper classes'.[19]

The consequences were fatal to the enterprise economy. As the infrastructure aged and needed renewing, so the financial stresses became intolerable until, in the 20th century, a once-proud industry was ready to fall into the arms of the state. This sidelining of private enterprise cannot be blamed on socialists. If the Tory Party had retained its hold on Parliament after the Second World War, as arch opponent of the doctrines of Karl Marx, I believe that investors in the railway industry would either have sought refuge in national ownership, or they would have appealed for state subsidies to keep the wheels turning on the tracks.

As for Hudson, he was crowned the Railway King by the media who loved to satirise a rogue. But his kingdom started to come apart after the end of the third bout of railway mania. His financial misdeeds (which included insider trading) were exposed and he went into voluntary exile.

9.4 Disunited Kingdom (5): Shelter

ACCORDING TO the experts, the capitalist economy is seriously incompetent. We are invited to believe that a process geared to the formation of capital has not learnt how to perform this operation efficiently. We can see how the problem of capital formation has arisen in the housing sector.

We can identify rules that prevent people from acquiring homes at the prices they can afford in the places where they want to live and work. Those rules are intrinsic to the market model. But they are evidence of political – not market – failure (see Box 9:1).

Box 9:1 Whose Failure Is it Anyway?

JOHN PRESCOTT'S housing demolition plan was based on the claim that the market had failed in areas where 'demand' did not exist for housing – which was supposed to explain swathes of vacant low-value properties. But how do we explain the housing problem in his constituency?

Hull had about 5,000 empty council homes (10% of the local stock). This was the highest rate in Britain. Although one of the richest municipalities in the country in recent years, thanks to the sale of its telephone company, Hull had an acute housing crisis which its elected representatives were unable to handle. In 2003, following a report by the Audit Commission, Prescott's home council suffered the indignity of losing control of its operations to the Deputy Prime Minister's own department. Housing policy was one of the failures identified by the Audit Commission.

Subsequently, Hull councillors clashed with their MP when they accused the government of having 'a 1960s mentality'. This was their response when Prescott's department, the ODPM, told Hull's housing renewal team that it was not demolishing enough homes in the city.[1]

Housing had also become a perplexing problem for Hull's residents. They were bewildered by the machinations involving their council and a property company. This involved a land deal that was supposed to yield profits that would be used to upgrade the social housing stock. But the council would not disclose the value of the land it had sold to the developer. And when the project failed to deliver the expected profits, the council blamed the housing market. One resident whose house was demolished said: 'This was a deal that was purely about real estate, not regeneration. Now it's backfired on them'.[2]

1 Charles Clover, 'Prescott's homes plan backfires in his own back yard', *Daily Telegraph*, April 4, 2005.
2 Paul Humphries, 'Private grief', *Guardian Society*, May 23, 2001.

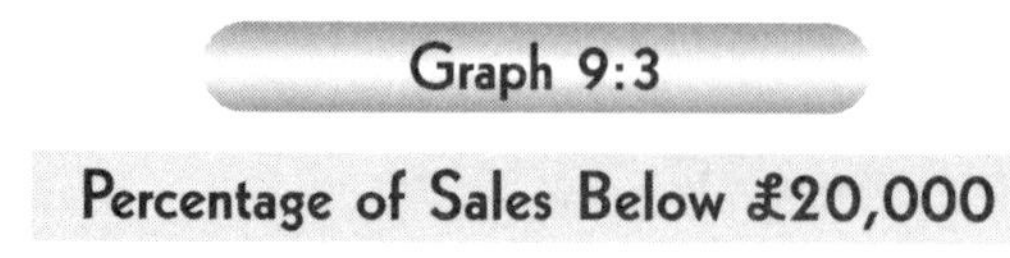

Percentage of Sales Below £20,000

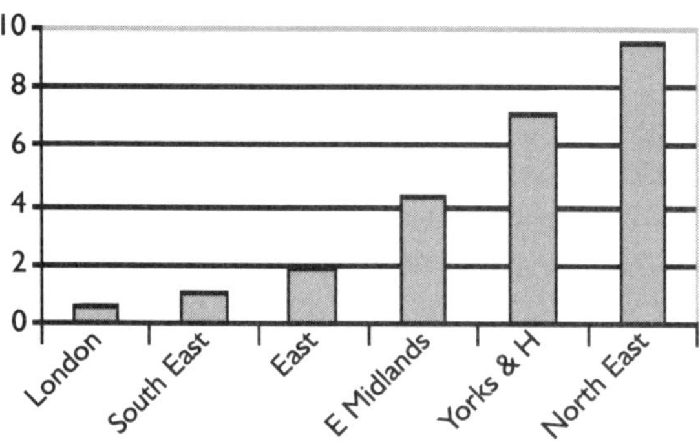

Source: Katharine Mumford and Anne Power, *Boom or Abandonment*, Coventry: Chartered Institute of Housing, 2002, p.18.

The doctrine of market failure is implausible, because the failures are not random. They follow a clear pattern. This suggests the unfolding of a logic that is prescribed by rules that are beyond the control of individual entrepreneurs. In the housing sector, the experts claim that failing local property markets – mainly concentrated in the Midlands and the North – are evidenced by low-value properties for which there is no demand. In fact, the distribution of low-value residential properties across England can be predicted according to Ricardo's Law. From Graph 9:3 we see that the fewest houses worth less than £20,000, according to Land Registry data, are to be found in London (0.5% of total sales); rising steadily to a peak in the North East (9.5% of sales).

Pockets of derelict neighbourhoods are to be found in urban centres throughout the country. This is the rational result of the pursuit of maximum capital gains from land. But it is not the market that is failing: it is performing its role with efficiency. If there is inequity in this model, the fault is with government. But in that case, what prevents us from *understanding* that we are dealing with a failure of governance rather than with the market? The answer is to be found in the way that the rule-makers – or those who benefit from the rules – camouflage the defects by disparaging those who question the way the system operates. This is illustrated by the reaction to the criticism of John Prescott's house-demolition project.

SAVE Britain's Heritage is a respectable charity which is performing valuable work in championing the nation's built environment. It works with both public and private sector agencies to rehabilitate buildings and secure the townscapes that make urban living an enjoyable experience. Its critique of the Pathfinder programme (referred to above, pp.16, 134) was serious in intent and based on methodical interrogation of the facts. One would have thought that its report was worthy of a considered reaction. The official response reveals much about the way the power structure cuts down critics who come close to exposing systemic failures at the heart of governance.

Prescott's department, the ODPM, attacked SAVE in a manner more consistent with fighting in the streets than with engaging in serious discourse. The technique was to discredit by playing fast and loose with the facts. Some examples illustrate this technique.

SAVE reported that £168m was spent on consultants. The ODPM, in its press release on January 26, 2006, used language like 'utter nonsense' and 'ridiculous' to defend its policy. On the fees paid to consultants, it said that 'this is not a figure we recognise'. Journalists invited to report on the dispute could be forgiven for thinking that this was a denial that such a sum had been spent on consultancy fees by the ODPM. And yet, one of the ODPM's own ministers, the Right Hon. Lord Rooker, who was then Minister for Regeneration and Regional Development, stated in evidence to the ODPM Parliamentary Committee, in answer to a question on how much had been spent on consultants, replied: 'At the moment it is £165m.'

What of SAVE's claim that, on existing trends and policies 168,000 houses would be demolished by 2016. This was 'ill-informed scare-mongering, not the facts', according to the ODPM. The prediction was 'complete nonsense'. And yet, SAVE drew its report from *Moving Forward the Northern Way*, a document endorsed by the ODPM which gave the figure of 167,000 houses to be demolished, and called for more houses to suffer that fate.

And what of the response of the academics who helped to rationalise the renewal-by-demolition programme? Messrs Cole and Nevin reacted brusquely, branding the SAVE allegations as 'nasty' and its report as reading like 'an extract from Monty Python's *Life of Brian*'.[20]

An observation attributed to physicist Albert Einstein is pertinent to this discussion: 'a problem cannot be solved with the same thinking that created it'. It does appear that the academic community, and the civil servants who implement public policy, have difficulty in stepping outside the ruts of conventional wisdom to analyse persistent problems that are insoluble because of defective policies.

The provision of shelter presents no logistical challenge for the capitalist economy. And yet, there continues to be a problem of equating demand with supply. This brings to mind another observation attributed to Einstein: insanity is 'doing the same thing over and over again and expecting different results'. In the past 100 years, the frustrations caused by the perpetual housing crisis have surfaced as brutal attacks on the urban environment. After World War I, homes would be provided 'Fit for Heroes'. Swathes of dwellings were demolished to make way for a construction programme that would solve the problem of shelter. It didn't. Then, after World War II, with more war heroes to house, the slum-clearances wrecked large parts of Britain's cities on the basis that, finally, in the Welfare State, we could build a Brave New World. We didn't. Prescott's programme of bulldozing neighbourhoods to provide affordable homes will be no more successful.

MPs, it has to be admitted, are protected from the worst excesses of the housing market by the generous Parliamentary allowances which they receive. In Prescott's case, he claimed more than £70,000 in taxpayers' money to pay interest on and for furnishings of his eight-bedroom home in his Hull constituency. This was for a house on which he took out a mortgage of £62,000 in 1992. As taxpayers covered the cost of funding the mortgage, Prescott pocketed the enormous capital gains that resulted from the land boom during the years in which he was Deputy Prime Minister.[21]

INTERROGATION

SOCIAL SCIENTISTS tend to neglect the pathological relationship between tenure and taxation. Do conventional taxes encourage the demolition of structurally sound dwellings and favour speculative building (rehabilitating an old house attracts VAT at 17.5%, while knocking down and rebuilding a house is zero-rated)?

In spotlighting Suzanne Fitzpatrick, we do not intend to identify her work as inferior to that of her peers. Our interest stems from the fact that she analysed the connection between poverty and place as the Joseph Rowntree Professor of Housing Policy at the University of York. Did this patronage encourage her to take a look at the clues offered by Joseph Rowntree himself?

In *Poverty of Place*, Fitzpatrick sought to explain why deprivation was concentrated in particular locations. We apparently need 'a new, or at least a refined, "story"'.[22] This story would feature the North-South poverty divide: census statistics confirmed 'deepening concentrations of both wealth and poverty'. Spatial segregation is heavily influenced by people's 'highly self-conscious' choices. Individuals chose neighbours with lifestyles similar to their own, creating a 'social distance' between themselves and others. This self-selection – 'area effects' – included people in deprived communities who preferred to live cheek-by-jowl with similarly disadvantaged people.

 Does this diagnosis focus too much responsibility on the psychology of the individual? Fitzpatrick contends that 'we should not await a more egalitarian society before attempting to ameliorate the problems of those who suffer poverty-related hardship'. But might second-best policies – such as state-sponsored residential

communities that locate low income families closer to the rich – tighten the grip of whatever it is that creates the social divide in the first place?

 Housing can 'provide a point of intervention to weaken segregation'. Is this wishful thinking? If government could diminish place-based deprivation with its existing policies, it would have done so in the last 60 years when it 'progressively' redistributed income, replanned the urban landscape and promulgated anti-poverty laws by the truck load. And yet, poverty remains concentrated on the margins of society.

 Social scientists who are daunted by intransigent problems resort to preaching the need for a trade-off: we can have more of one good thing if we agree to have less of another good thing. For Fitzpatrick, the trade-off is between social justice and the freedom to choose where we live. Why are the experts reluctant to accept that we can have both of these at the same time? Might tax reform tied to location benefits deliver both outcomes simultaneously?

REFERENCES

1 Housing charities accused the government of under estimating the extent of homelessness in England. One of them, Crisis, claimed that 500,000 people were without a proper home when children were taken into account. Shelter said the figure was more like 230,000. Peter Hetherington, '500,000 homeless, claims charity', *The Guardian*, December 14, 2004.

2 'Alcohol-related deaths rise 18%', *Financial Times*, August 16, 2005.

3 Adam Wilkinson, *Pathfinder*, London: SAVE Britain's Heritage, 2006, p.63.

4 *Ibid.*, p.65.

5 *Ibid.*, p.66.

6 *Ibid.*, p.64.

7 SAVE Britain's Heritage, Press Release, January 26, 2006.

8 Two million houses were demolished in England alone, and 4m people were displaced. Peter Hetherington,'Razed expectations', *Society Guardian*, March 10, 2004.

9 Charles Clover, 'Labour threat to housing dissident', *Daily Telegraph*, October 21, 2005.

10 Charles Clover, 'Has Prescott got his sums right on housing crisis?', *Daily Telegraph*, May 16, 2005.

11 Charles Clover, 'Ringo attacks demolition of city homes', *Daily Telegraph*, May 24, 2005.

12 Prof. Cole acknowledged the influence of Brendan Nevin and his colleagues at the University of Birmingham's Centre for Urban and Regional Studies, whose work 'was very influential in determining the selection of the nine Housing Market Renewal Pathfinders'. See Ian Cole, Paul Hickman and Kesia Reeve, *Interpreting Housing Market Change:*

The Case of Leeds, Sheffield Hallam University, 2004, p.4; available from www.shu.ac.uk/cresr.

13 House of Commons Select Committee on Transport, Local Government and the Regions, Sixth Report, March, 2002, Paras 2-3.

14 ODPM Website, 'Market Renewal Programme: Learning Lessons,' Manchester 2003.

15 Samuel Brittan, 'A tax idea that cannot be buried', *Financial Times*, April 15, 2005; Martin Wolf, 'Grounds for a New Way to Look at Land Use', May 14, 2004, and 'Why Livingstone is a Tax Genius', August 6, 2004.

16 Robert S. Sephton, '"Small Profits on a Large Trade": James Morrison MP [Part 1]', *J. of the Railway and Canal Historical Society*, Vol. 34, Pt. 6 (186), November 2003, p.367.

17 Fred Harrison (ed.) *The Losses of Nations*, London: Othila Press,1998, p.ix.

18 A.J. Arnold and S. McCartney, *George Hudson: The Rise and Fall of the Railway King*, London: Hambledon and London, 2004, p.55.

19 *Ibid.,* p.134.

20 'Study digs into renewal rows', *The Times, Public Agenda*, February 7, 2006.

21 Stephen Swinford and Tom Baird, '"Black hole" in the ministers' home expenses', *Sunday Times*, March 26, 2006.

22 Suzanne Fitzpatrick, 'Poverty of Place', §Keynote address, Joseph Rowntree Foundation Centenary Conference, University of York, December 14, 2004, p.4.

10

The Constituents of Tony Blair's Mind

NORTH EAST

10.1 Formation of the English

THE ROMAN ROAD that wends north from Brough on the Humber river is shown on the Ordinance Survey map as passing close to Sedgefield, the small town that gives Tony Blair's constituency its name. We visited the constituency during the general election of May 2005. The Prime Minister was not being given an easy time by his community newspaper, the *Newton News*, which declared in an editorial: 'Strictly speaking he is a failure as an MP!'[1]

The class divide was getting wider and the Prime Minister's constituents were puzzled. This was not what they had expected from their MP. The North was making headlines for the wrong reasons. *The Financial Times* reported 'North-South incomes gap is widening' (April 30, 2005), while research by Halifax showed that households in Sedgefield would pay the highest residential property tax in Britain. This contrasted with the lowest tax, which was paid by Blair's Downing Street neighbours in Westminster.[2] These anomalies are the logical outcomes of the rules of tax policy. If the Venerable Bede could return to his monastery today, he would be appalled at the state of his native corner of England.

Bede (672-735) wrote *The Ecclesiastical History of the English People* in Jarrow. This is the town which is celebrated in the annals of working-class history as the starting point for unemployed miners who marched on London in 1936. Theirs was a crusade against the unemployment which had blighted the region. And yet, from this fertile soil had emerged the first piece of literature to identify the English spirit.

How, in what is today considered by southerners as a backwater of England, did a monk manage to compile the narrative that gave the tribes their first collective consciousness? Why was Bede relieved of the need to work in the fields? Who paid for him to sit in a library and write a historical account that continues to inform scholars to this day? For the answers, we have to turn our attention to the peasants who tilled the land. They were the first and most honourable of patrons of the intellectual and aesthetic activities of the English.

It could not have been otherwise. The people who work are the ones who produce the surplus that is needed to finance the time it takes to learn from books, and to think, and then to wield the pen, the paintbrush and the chisel to create the abstract images that express the mind and the emotions.

It was the genius and humanity of the northern peasants that made it possible for high culture to emerge in Northumbria, for poetry and music to find its highest expression in Hartlepool and Whitby on the east coast and for history and science to emerge in Jarrow.[3]

After the Romans, and following the decay of militant heathenism, England was at a cultural crossroads. Monasteries were the centres of learning, and the greatest achievements were by the people of the North. Historian Sir Frank Stenton was emphatic when he drew attention to 'the rarity of outstanding scholars in the southern churches of this period … the learning which gives unique distinction to the English church of this age was centred in a small group of Northumbrian monasteries'.[4] The grants of land to the monasteries, and the willingness of peasants to yield up food-rents to keep the monks working, made it possible to shed the light that brought the Dark Age to an end.

The pooling of food-rents was not the result of coercion. The peasants wanted the sacred to illuminate their lives, and they were willing to pay with the rents that would free Bede and his fellow monks to work in their cells instead of the fields. The earliest Anglo-Saxon reference to the household payment of resources to support the church appears in the law code of King Ine of the West Saxons (688-726). This was issued about 690. Bede provided evidence that a similar system applied in Northumbria. No matter how remote the villages and hamlets in mountains or dense forests, the inhabitants contributed their share to support the advance of culture.[5] The monks reciprocated by diffusing knowledge. As Bede noted in his *Letter to Egbert*, 'the bishop who lives a holy life should not neglect the duty of teaching'. The spiritual leaders earned their daily bread by pushing outwards the boundaries of knowledge secular as well as sacred.

Thanks in part to the work of Bede, the collective consciousness made it possible for King Alfred to unite England around 886. Alfred occupied

London at a time when 'the free peasant formed the basis of society ... he was required to join with others of his class in supporting his king by contributions to a *Feorm*, or food-rent'.[6] The peasants evolved a tenure called folkland, 'which meant land from which the king drew food-rents and customary services. The definition of folkland as land subject to the rents and services by which the whole people had once maintained its king [had] the merit of simplicity'.[7]

When the Normans crossed the channel and conquered England in 1066, they found that the tradition of pooling surplus resources had evolved through three stages. The earliest tribal communities delivered food-rent to their leaders. This was followed by the manorial organisation, which saw the change from food-rents to labour services. Peasants worked for a certain number of days on the lands of the lord in return for the benefits they received from him. By 1066 and William's victory at the Battle of Hastings, labour services were converted into money rents. Old England had evolved an organised financial system at what Stenton describes as 'a date exceptionally remote'.[8]

Alfred's political and military skills rescued Old England from the Danes, whose invasions had destroyed the ability of people to pursue arts, including poetry. Although the peasants were willing to continue to fund civilisation, the institutions on which the flow of rents relied were dislocated by the Danes. They extracted the rents as tribute from the peoples whom they suppressed. Alfred restored high culture by enabling the free peasants to restart the flow of material resources to the centres of learning. But that came to a halt with the conquest of the Normans.

William dispossessed the English nobles, replacing them with his lieutenants. This was a classic land grab. William ordained himself not only king but owner of all the land of England. Those who held land were now his tenants. The political culture of England was militarised. The surplus product did not go to scholars and musicians. It was reserved for knights of the battlefield. Thus began the centralisation of power and the gradual transformation of the public's finances. The outcome was predictable: the distraction of native talents from the pursuit of civilised activities. The Normans, noted Stenton, 'were a harsh and violent race. They were the closest of all Western peoples to the barbarian strain in the continental order. They had produced little in art or learning, and nothing in literature, that could be set beside the work of Englishmen'.[9]

Northerners can be proud of their contribution to English history in the first millennium, and they were central to the advance of science and technology in the second millennium. But today, as we embark on the third millennium, the prospects appear bleak. Their region has been annexed to the rich South and their people disparaged as dependents on welfare handouts. They are represented as a people whose culture must be imported from elsewhere and funded out of the profits of gambling (the national lottery). This is a demeaning outcome for the noble people who gave us the self-consciousness of the English.

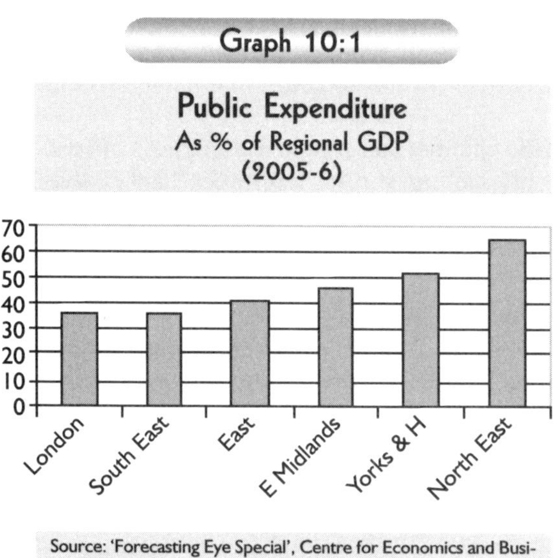

Graph 10:1

Public Expenditure
As % of Regional GDP
(2005-6)

Source: 'Forecasting Eye Special', Centre for Economics and Business Research, London, May 29, 2006.

The facts cannot be contested, but they demand explanation. For the North Eastern economy is almost twice as dependent on the public sector as London. The London-based Centre for Economics and Business Research has calculated public spending as a share of regional GDP and adjusted the figures so that they could be compared with public spending in other countries. The results are shown in Graph 10:1. The proportion spent in the North East (64.9%) is greater than Sweden's 56.1%. The share of Yorkshire and the Humber region (51.5%) is greater than Slovenia's 46.4%. Since the proportion is greater than the numbers for former communist countries like Hungary, Poland and the Czech Republic, the people of the North East are told that they are 'dependent on the state as some Soviet bloc countries were at the time communism collapsed',[10] and made to feel like beggars living on 'handouts' compared with Londoners (whose share of public spending was 35.6%).[11] These epithets overlook the fact that the quality of the expenditure varies. As we saw in Chapters 6 and 7, London and the South East receive a disproportionate share of the value-enhancing investment in infrastructure, while the northern regions rely disproportionately on body-and-soul spending which does not enhance the economy's productivity.

But it was not always like this. High culture can flourish in lands of relatively low productivity, providing the public policies are correctly framed. The North was a rich country in Bede's day, not because the soil was abundantly fertile but because the people knew how to deploy their surplus products for the common good. This contrasts with the condition of large swathes of the North today, where communities exist below Ricardo's economic margin. Incomes are so low that many people cannot afford to sustain themselves, let alone fund science and the arts. Because of the tax-induced poverty trap, they are priced out of the opportunity to work. So they remain at home, the recipients of rations from the state's larder.

Tony Blair has such a community in his constituency. In Chapel Row, in the mining village of Ferryhill, people are obliged to make ends meet on the edge of society. According to the Land Registry, this was the street with the lowest property prices over the five years leading up to Blair's historic accomplishment – securing a third term in government for his New Labour Party.[12] Driving north along the A167 out of Newton Aycliffe, Ferryhill is on your right. Its shameful secret is screened from the affluent residents of Sedgefield by the A1(M). The slagheaps are no more, camouflaged by mysterious green eruptions on the landscape, the excretions of industrialisation no longer an offence to rural sensibilities.

The identity of the English nation originated here, but today the native culture is haemorrhaging away with emigration – people voting with their feet, admitting that they lack confidence in their home country.

10.2 The Aristocratic Double-take

SAILING SHIPS lashed the world together in the First Age of Globalisation, and railways provided the lattice-work of steel tracks for the Second Age of Globalisation. The steam engine that made the railways possible was invented in England's North East by geniuses like George Stephenson (1781-1848). Their technologies reduced the costs of extracting and transporting the coal from the rich seams that stretched from the hillsides out into the North Sea, coal that powered the conveyor belts of the industries that gave Britain its leading edge in the world economy in the 19th century.

The explosion in innovative ingenuity and entrepreneurial *nouse* in this region was symbolised by the founding of the Stockton and Darlington Railway Company. The coal seams beneath 100,000 acres which had previously been inaccessible were now opened up. George Stephenson developed his first locomotive in 1814. It could haul 30 tons of coal at 4 mph. Through experimentation he developed a locomotive that could traverse the route between Stockton and Darlington at 16 mph (in 1825). The rest is history.

The railways raised productivity in quantum leaps. The costs of transportation crashed from 7*d* per one ton of goods per mile by canal, to 1*p* on the railway. As a result, the price of coal fell by more than 6*s* a chaldron (a unit of capacity equal to 36 bushels). The mail could be carried at an astonishing 20mph, at one-third of the former cost.

The biggest winners were the dukes and earls who owned the coal. The enhanced productivity was also reflected in the increased value of urban land. So when the railway needed to construct a branch line to Middlesbrough, the Bishop of Durham was paid £333 an acre for farmland that was worth £5 an acre. New towns were built to accommodate the factory workers, but the surplus value coalesced into higher rents for the use of land.[13]

Londoners relied heavily on the coal that was transported to the coastal ports. Boats carried their cargoes to the Southerners who needed the heat to cook food and keep them warm in winter. But the railways became one of the instruments for exploiting the families that lived by their labour. Men and their children spent their working lives at the coalface, sacrificing a civilised existence to hew energy out of the bosom of nature. Their reward was housing which they could not afford. Thus originated the back-to-back jerry-built houses in which people died from diseases, the bacteria incubated in airless hovels.

As the landowners grew richer, competition from migrant workers drove down wages. Government added to the burden with taxes. The men who dug the coal never had a chance. They mobilised themselves into combinations of workers, but the landlords' parliament fought back with the power of the state.

Tony Blair committed himself to reverse this history. The North East has more than its share of the 1.1m people who are a lost generation of 16 to 24-year-olds who are not in education, employment or training. These are the people whom Blair's government believe were individually responsible for their plight. About 85,000 of them leave school and join that welfare-dependent group every year. But, ironically, the emphasis that Blair placed on education to rescue this generation discriminated against the majority of his constituents and preserved the divisions in English society.

10.3 Tony Blair's Magic Mantra

POLITICIANS SECURE power by persuading people that they can solve problems. This is achieved by manipulating public discourse on a day to day basis. The psychodynamics of democratic politics may be illustrated by the slogan adopted by Tony Blair when he sought a mandate to govern Britain in 1997.

New Labour's mantra was 'Education, Education, Education'. Equipping people with knowledge would deliver personal fulfilment and equip Britain to deal with the 21st century's challenges. This was an honourable aspiration, and to assist him in constructing his Third Way agenda Blair enjoyed the support of eminent sociologists. The government increased spending on education. Unfortunately, he failed to reverse the trends.

That Britain continued to slide in the education league tables is not the issue that I wish to stress. The important point is that the Blair government at the end of its second administration was no nearer to understanding the *causes* of the nation's problems.

After eight years of the Blair project, the evidence on mobility was not consistent with the script written by the Masters of Spin who orchestrated the public's perception of government performance. Researchers at the London School of Economics compared the mobility of children in eight European and North American countries. Here was a test for the claim that the Anglo-American model of economics was more robust than the 'social market' economies of continental Europe. The research revealed a lower rate of social mobility between the generations in the UK and USA than in the high-tax countries. Data that tracked the mobility of people since 1970 showed that Denmark, Sweden, Finland, West Germany and Norway delivered greater scope for self-improvement than in the two countries that eulogised individualism. Wealth was more clearly linked to educational attainment in the Anglo-American countries, with children from poor backgrounds destined to attend poorly performing schools and less likely to continue their studies. Inter-generational mobility fell markedly over time in Britain, with a similarly poor performance in the US. This was particularly offensive to the US, where the notion of 'the land of opportunity ... clearly seems misplaced'.[14]

How do we account for these differences? Champions of the doctrines that underpin the Anglo-American model castigate the continental European models, which favour a denser role for the public sector in people's lives. The European model was characterised as sclerotic; but this is not an assessment endorsed by the evidence of people's freedom to work their way up the social and economic ladders.

Here was a conundrum for those who walked the corridors of power in Westminster and Whitehall. Leading sociologists such as John Goldthorpe, a professor at Nuffield College, Oxford, were represented in Downing Street as holding the view that 'using policy measures to promote higher rates of social mobility may be a considerable challenge. Goldthorpe's view is that changing social mobility through policy intervention is likely to be very difficult'.[15] Their views on social mobility were distilled for the Prime Minister at a Downing Street seminar. Stephen Aldridge, as the chief economist for the Cabinet's Performance and Innovation Unit, presented a briefing paper after consulting some of the most eminent academic sociologists in Britain. Among those attending the seminar was one of New Labour's gurus, sociologist Anthony Giddens, the Director of the London School of Economics.

The collective wisdom of the sociologists came with a health warning: 'The determinants of and barriers to relative social mobility are not well understood'.[16] Three centuries of empirical evidence, a period during which the class system emerged to divide the nation, was insufficient for the sociologists to pronounce with confidence on the causes of social scleroticism. The sociologists could only offer a checklist of symptoms which they labelled as *determinants*. Among the list were:

- Educational attainment
- Childhood poverty
- Negative attitudes including aversion to risk
- Defensive professional strategies that obstruct competition (such as those employed by the legal and medical professions)

But why had some people suffered from these obstacles to personal advancement? Was it a personal failing? Why were they prevented from receiving the rewards they merited? Sociologists agonise endlessly over the meaning of the meritocratic society, highlighting what they perceive as some of the problems that might arise if people were properly rewarded. One unattractive feature of meritocracy, they claim, is the risk of downward mobility with no one to blame but their own lack of ability and commitment, which could create unhappiness and resentment. What the sociologists could not visualise was a rewarding system that was free of inequalities. 'The winners or upwardly mobile could scoop all the rewards leaving little for the rest. Egalitarians, who would prefer there to be no losers, are therefore generally critical of the concept meritocracy.'[17]

Given this doctrinal struggle over the nature of freedom, there was little left for Blair but to hang on to the platitude about the importance of education. For the public school and Oxford-tutored Blair, education was the key to upward mobility. It enabled young people from the lower classes to achieve higher status and living standards compared to those of their parents. This proposition was crafted by academic sociologists who helped to design the New Labour project. But the sociologists were blind to the key variable that would affect the destinies of millions of young people: the way in which the state conspired with the law of the land to divide society in the classroom itself.

10.4 Disunited Kingdom (6): The Class Divided

WHEN I REFER to class divide, I mean it literally. The class society is incubated by fiscal policies and nurtured in the classroom. Through the classroom, we inflict a double humiliation on the most vulnerable sections of our communities. The economics of education are rigged to fragment society. The process begins with the funding of schools.

In Britain, most children attend state schools. In theory, educational opportunities are available on an equal basis. In practice, the access rights of some are more equal than for others. The process needs to be clearly understood if we are to persuade politicians to stop riding roughshod over children's lives.

Schools help to raise the productivity of the workforce. Part of that increased value surfaces as public value. We need to break this chain of events down into its parts. The elements that concern us relate to the way in which the net benefits are unequally allocated. The analysis begins with the impact of schools on land values.

Nationwide, the mortgage lending bank, studied the impact of schools on the housing market. For England as a whole, parents paid a premium of 1.3% (£2,122 on the average £167,407 property in 2004), to live close to a primary school that out-performed the average by 5%. If the schools whose pass rates for 7-11-year-olds was 10% higher, the price of a property was bid up by 2.6% (£4,270).[18]

But the national average conceals the enormous influence of good schools in London. Here, wealthy parents are able to bid up the price of houses to an astonishing degree. The influence was measured by two London University economists in relation to primary schools. The number-crunching exercise for the Greater London region revealed that, at 2004 prices, 'parents can expect a move from an average dwelling outside a weak school, to one outside a top over-subscribed school, to cost around £61,000 ... a similar move to an under-subscribed top school would cost, on average, about £49,000 – some £12,000 less!'[19] The distribution of benefits conforms to Ricardian principles. The highest land values are closest to the top schools: 'Each 100m distance to a school erodes the performance premium by about 8.4% relative to its initial level, so by 600m the premium is halved'.[20] In contrast, under-performing schools depress land prices: the closer the school the lower the land value attributable to 'school-run' traffic congestion, playground noise and the environmental problems associated with them.

Thus, income stratification delivers a bias against the poorest pupils who would like to enter top-performing schools. Now, reflect on the social humiliation inflicted by this financial arrangement. The schools are funded by all taxpayers, including those whose homes are rented, and by those whose incomes are at the bottom end of the scales. But the surplus value generated by good schools is distributed to those who own their homes and who can therefore capture the enhanced productivity as a rise in the value of their locations.

The inequity between schools of varying performance is compounded within the classroom. Because they are state schools, the best establishments do include children from low income families. But that does not make all children equal. Lower ability children from asset-rich families are able to overtake higher ability children from asset-poor families by the age of six. The evidence was documented by Tony Blair's Equalities Review panel, which cited the way in which class status shaped divisions within the classroom.[21] It concluded that 'the single largest contributor in most cases is without doubt the socio-economic group into which we are born'.

Box 10:1 Class in the Classroom

IN THE BUDGET he presented to the House of Commons on March 23, 2006, Gordon Brown announced that he had adopted a new target: he would spend £8,000 per pupil (up from £5,000) in state schools. The aim was to match the amount spent on children in private education. Where was the money coming from, and who would benefit?

Consider these questions in terms of a 'failing' school whose children were not achieving the desired exam pass marks. Assume that the extra taxpayers' money, in patching up leaking roofs, reducing the teacher/pupil ratio and installing extra IT equipment in the classroom, was so successful in raising standards that the school became a magnet for parents.

- For renting families, their extra tax investment in the school is money well spent. Their children receive an improved education.
- For property-owning families, however, there is an extra bonus. Because the school is now an attraction, the value of nearby residential property rises. So these families receive back, as a capital gain, *their* portion of the extra taxes invested in the school. Their children enjoy a free education. Only the poor pay.

The inequity goes deeper, however. As house prices rise in the school's catchment area, the rents that landlords charge for accommodation are driven up. So the renting families that contributed to the improved performance of the school are double-taxed. Far from enjoying a windfall gain, they pay higher rents out of post-tax incomes. This *reduces* their disposable incomes, and therefore living standards, even as existing home-owners enjoy an increase in disposable incomes, and asset values, and therefore a rising living standard. The tax policies that cause this rising gap consequently give an advantage to lower-ability children from high income homes.

The state promotes the class divide through the classroom. Gordon Brown, in using the amount of funding in private schools as his financial yardstick, distracts parents from the financial reality: the Treasury's policies damage the education opportunities of children.

Thus, through the tax-and-tenure nexus, the class system is nourished in the primary school. The inequities are the result of state policies which propagate distributional injustices (see Box 10.1). Children whose parents rent their homes are abused by government through a tax regime that not only discriminates against them at birth, but locks them into an iniquitous fiscal system for the rest of their lives. If government were honest, it would not only publish the grades of educational attainment in schools; it would also publish a league table of property prices linked to each school. The financial impact is significant, for 'the main effect of performance is 3% on prices for each 10 percentage point improvement in the proportion of children reaching the target test grade'.[22]

According to the philosophy of the Welfare State, 'progressive' taxes redistribute income from those who have, to those in need. Superficially, the statistics seem to confirm this, as may be observed by comparing London and the North East. They appear to have something in common. In *per capita* terms, government statistics show that they receive almost as much as each other in the distribution of taxpayers' money (see Graph 10:2). But the North East support is out of sympathy for its tax-induced liabilities, whereas London's pay-out is to reinforce the capital's good fortunes.

For an example of the North East's liabilities, we exit Blair's constituency and return to the A1, the main highway to Newcastle. It is congested. The North-East Chamber of Commerce argues that under-investment in this highway retards economic growth. It estimates that additional funding to relieve the congestion could attract £1bn of investment, which would increase employment by 10,000 jobs.[23] If the civic representatives of the North East want a fair deal, they need to find ways to end the tax-funded subsidies controlled from London and demand the right to a direct claim on their share of the nation's rents. Otherwise, they will continue to suffer the consequences that flow from the mal-distribution of public value. Current taxation guts communities like the villages in Blair's constituency. And the young are quarantined in a backwater.

Graph 10:2

Public Expenditure

£000 per capita (2001-2)

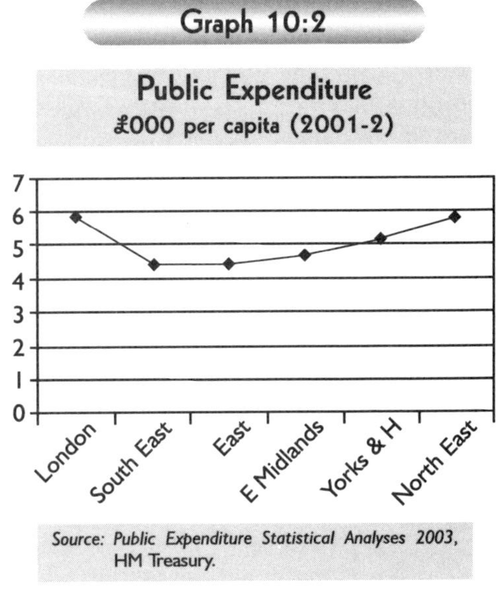

Source: Public Expenditure Statistical Analyses 2003, HM Treasury.

If the North East wants better transport, it could fund this out of the value that would be created by the improvements to highways like the A1. By sinking funds into road improvements, some of the added value surfaces as a rise in the value of land. If the North East captured that value and recycled it back into public services, it would achieve two outcomes. First, the region would take an independent grip over its destiny instead of being dependent on subsidies from Westminster. Second, its regional leaders could negotiate with government for a reduction in the taxes that damage their economy.

INTERROGATION

GOVERNMENTS HAVE experimented with the suspension of taxes. This happened in the 1980s with the Enterprise Zones, in which property was privileged with the suspension of the property tax. The leaders of the North East should seek power to experiment with the abatement of taxes on labour.

The Blair government was committed to the devolution of power so that decision-making was as close as possible to the people who were affected. Political devolution is of little value it if is not associated with direct control of tax policy. Local and regional governments need to reduce the costs of employment. There is enormous potential just waiting to be harnessed – not least, the relatively cheaper cost of using land. And this fits with the ideal way of transforming the public's finances.

The peoples of the periphery are not helpless; but they need to re-sculpture the power structure by adding a pricing mechanism that is fair to everyone. They can re-build their communities by evolving new ways of living and novel social institutions that would re-awaken the energies that are latent in their populations.

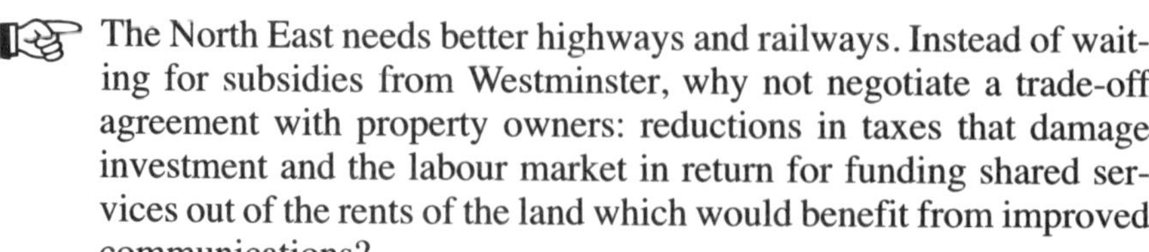

☞ The North East needs better highways and railways. Instead of waiting for subsidies from Westminster, why not negotiate a trade-off agreement with property owners: reductions in taxes that damage investment and the labour market in return for funding shared services out of the rents of the land which would benefit from improved communications?

☞ In 2005, National Health Service trusts began sacking nurses and managers because they could not balance their books. In one two-week period, 4,000 health workers were made redundant, including 700 in County Durham whose hospital served Tony Blair's Sedgefield constituency. According to Frank Dobson, a former Health Secretary: 'The government is spending hundreds of millions of pounds on management consultants and franchising operations to the private sector. Paperwork used to cost 4% of the NHS budget, but now costs 15-16%'.[24] Why not raise funds locally out of a charge on properties whose values depend on decent hospital services?

 Instead of selling land at strategic locations (such as at the junctions with motorways), local governments can lease out their land and attract inward investment by offering entrepreneurs a workforce not burdened by the payroll tax. Is there a good reason why London should be protected from tax competition from the North East?

REFERENCES

1 'Will it be easy for Tony Blair?', *Newton News*, April 8, 2005, p.2.

2 Patrick Collinson and Rupert Jones, 'Soaring council taxes rake in £18.9bn', *The Guardian*, April 25,2003.

3 F.M. Stenton, *Anglo-Saxon England*, Oxford: Clarendon Press, 3rd edn., 1971, Ch. VI.

4 *Ibid.*, p.183.

5 Bede, *The Ecclesiastical History of the English People*, Edited with introduction by Judith McClure and Roger Collins, Oxford: University Press, 1969, p.347.

6 Stenton, *op. cit.*, p.278.

7 *Ibid.*, p.311.

8 *Ibid.*, p.643.

9 *Ibid.*, p.687.

10 David Smith, 'Brown hand-outs create a "Soviet" North', *Sunday Times*, April 24, 2005.

11 David Smith and Claire Newell, 'Britain's northern "soviets" swell on Brown handouts', *Sunday Times*, May 28, 2006.

12 Property analysts reviewed 2,480 transactions for www.houseprice.com, an internet property website. The average price for houses in Ferryhill as a whole was £44,359.

13 N. Moorsom, *The Stockton and Darlington Railway: The Foundation of Middlesbrough*, Middlesbrough: J.G. Peckston, 1975.

14 Jo Blanden, Paul Gregg and Stephen Machin, 'Inter-generational Mobility in Europe and North America', London: Centre for Economic Performance, LSE, April 2005, p.7.

15 Stephen Aldridge, 'Social Mobility', Discussion Paper, London: Cabinet Office, April, 2001, p.31, para. 74 (www.cabinet-office.gov.uk).

16 *Ibid.*, p.3.

17 *Ibid.*, p.30, para. 71.

18 Scheherazade Daneshkhu, 'Premium for houses near best primary schools', *Financial Times*, September 16, 2004.

19 Stephen Gibbons and Stephen Machin, 'Paying for primary schools: admission constraints, school popularity or congestion?', *The Economic Journal*, March, 2006, pp.C88-C89.

20 *Ibid.*, p.C90.

21 Equalities Review, *op. cit.*, p.28.

22 Gibbons and Machin, *op. cit.*, p.C85.

23 Chris Tighe, 'Business chiefs warn over highways policy', *Financial Times*, November 17, 2005.

24 John Carvel and Will Woodward, 'Thousands of jobs go in NHS cash crisis', *The Guardian*, March 24, 2006.

BARBARIANS WITHIN

11

Beyond Hadrian's Wall

11.1 Cometh the Barbarians

OUR JOURNEY through England came to an end on top of an ancient wall. From it, you can scan the landscape of the Borders to catch a glimpse of what the Romans feared, the barbarians who dwelt in the highlands. But to understand the symbolism of Hadrian's Wall, you need to peer deep into a reality that is beyond the gaze of tourists who visit the monument every year. Armed with the conceptual tools provided in Part I, from these ramparts you can see a place that corrodes the mind and tempts the soul. Evil lurks to corrupt the flesh in dark corners. *No-Man's Land.*

This zone of despair is the sub-marginal terrain in which civilisation is demolished. We all fear it, because the place is transportable. It is located in pockets anywhere, everywhere – even in the midst of the richest cities like New York or the most cultured, like Paris. It is not a natural place. It is a political creation. Unless we can visualise it, and understand the policies that give rise to it – a continuous process of creating a living hell for the victims trapped inside it – there is no hope of change. This is the place where people live beyond the margin, the margin of economics.

Hadrian's Wall was more than a defensive fortification. It was a symbol that reminded people that theirs was a civilisation physically separated from the sub-human life of the tribes that they could not pacify. People who did not submit to the laws of Rome were regarded as inferior. That meant those people were barbarians, in the eyes of the citizens of the Empire.

Today, hundreds of thousands of people beyond Hadrian's Wall subsist below the margin. Through no fault of their own, they do not earn their living by labour of brain and brawn. Is this still the land of the barbarian? Will they breach the wall and overwhelm our cities? The stuff of nightmares envelopes you as the haunting thought creeps into the mind: *are they already inside the walls of our cities?* The notion may appear fantastic, but before dismissing it, reflect on the shocking evidence.

- The United Nations reports that Scotland is the most violent country in the developed world. More than 2,000 people are subject to a violent attack each week, more than 10 times official police figures.
- The World Heath Organisation documents the statistics which reveal that Scotland has the second highest murder rate in Western Europe. Scots are more than three times more likely to be murdered than people in England.
- Glasgow is the murder capital of Europe, with about 70 killings each year. Many of the slayings are the result of turf wars between gangs struggling to control the drugs trade.[1]

And yet, this is the land of the Enlightenment. Historians publish books which show that the Scots invented the modern world. In the 18th century, Edinburgh was at the heart of a philosophical discourse that extended our mental horizons. Glasgow was one of the merchant capitals of the world, spreading commerce to the farthest corners to enrich the nation and contribute to the emergence of the mightiest of empires.

How, then, could this country beyond Hadrian's Wall be the land of barbarians? To make sense of the evidence, we need to work with our hypothesis (Chapter 10.1) that rent is the material basis of civilisation. Every subsistence society, organised on tribal lines, had first to learn how to generate a surplus before it could evolve into a civilisation. The accumulation of surplus was a precondition for change. But *how* that surplus was shared determined the character of the complex society that replaced the hunting-and-gathering community.

For the British Isles, rent came not just from domestic resources, however. It was also plundered from abroad. The Act of Union, which united Scotland with England in 1707, gave the merchants of Glasgow access to the lucrative trading routes that England was spanning around the globe. This produced a handsome rental surplus. If such a surplus was available to elevate the culture of its people, how could that population have possibly degenerated into such a disgraceful state as is now recorded in the UN statistics? Is it possible to incubate the barbarian *within* the gates of the city? That idea was advanced by Henry George who, while working as a journalist in San Francisco, began his analysis of Western civilisation with the aid of Ricardo's Law. He folded the economics of the efficient production of wealth into the principles of natural justice. This opened a vision of the kind of society that we could all enjoy; but it also exposed the awful truth about the malevolent forces that were debasing human beings in the United States. Writing in *Progress and Poverty* (1789), which became the first global best-selling economics text, he traced the conditions that would nurture the barbarian within society.

> One of the characteristics of barbarism is the low regard for the rights of person and property.[2]

The breakdown of civilisation was reflected in the debasement of law and religion, but the process began with the mal-distribution of income.

> Now, the tendency in this direction is an increasing one. It is shown in greatest force where the inequalities in the distribution of wealth are greatest, and it shows itself as they increase. If it be not a return to barbarism, what is it?

The Romans who looked beyond the territorial boundaries of their society for the clues were deceiving themselves. The people who *lived* the decline of culture were incubated within the home borders.

> Whence shall come the new barbarians? Go through the squalid quarters of great cities, and you may see, even now, their gathering hordes!

Beguiled by the idea of social progress, as the Scottish philosophers encouraged us to be, we, too, have deluded ourselves with the idea of forward momentum. Look closely: see the debilitation of culture, in the arts and personal tastes, in the way people are exhausted by the need to pay their way through life, and in the breakdown of the biological building blocks of society, the family.

> Everywhere is it evident that the tendency to inequality, which is the necessary result of material progress where land is monopolized, cannot go much further without carrying our civilization into that downward path which is so easy to enter and so hard to abandon.

If communities are constructed on principles grounded in injustice, the outcome is predictable.

> ... though knowledge yet increases and invention marches on, and new states are being settled, and cities still expand, yet civilization has begun to wane when, in proportion to population, we must build more and more prisons, more and more almshouses, more and more insane asylums. It is not from top to bottom that societies die; it is from bottom to top.

Barbarism is not something that can be quarantined with walls and barbed wire. It is the condition that we nourish when we deprive people of justice, consigning them to a state of dependency on others for their biological, spiritual and aesthetic existence. This is the state of many people beyond Hadrian's Wall. And yet, these people gave us philosophers like Adam Smith and David Hume, poets and writers like Burns and Boswell, architects like Robert Adam who built neoclassical settlements such as the fine structures that grace the New Town of Edinburgh. Many of them, through the diaspora, left their mark on North America, South Africa and Australasia.[3] How can these achievements be equated with the notion of barbarism beyond Hadrian's Wall?

The statistics tell a story, but these cannot be understood without the historical context.

Of the 10 UK local authorities with the lowest male life expectancy at birth, seven are in Scotland. The shortest lives are lived out in Glasgow – under 70 years, compared with an expectancy of more than 80 years for people born in the London borough of Kensington and Chelsea (see Table 11:1). Our journey northwards through England led us to the realisation that the cultural forces at work are not random. The evidence can be plotted on the downward sloping line on graph paper.

Retrace the journey on which we embarked from central London. In the capital of the Disunited Kingdom, babies born at the beginning of the third millennium can expect, on average, to live more than 80 years. Drive into the lush flatlands of eastern England, and the lifespan begins to drop: by one year, in South Norfolk. Circumvent The Wash and we pass through Rutland where Margaret Thatcher was born and raised (a respectable average of 79.6 years). Heading north, we drop into the regions where people can expect to live six or seven years fewer than the residents of Chelsea. By the time we reached Newcastle upon Tyne, the average life span is under 75 years (in nearby Gateshead the figure drops to 71.7 years). Then, crossing Hadrian's Wall, we find ourselves in Border country. Turn northwest through North Lanarkshire, and you can observe children in the school playground who can expect to live an average life of 72 years. But the worst is to come. Coast into the City of Glasgow, and the birthright is little more than 69 years.

Table 11:1

Life Expectancy at Birth
(Years) by local authority (2002-4)

Kensington & Chelsea	*South Norfolk*	*Rutland*	*Darlington*	*Newcastle-upon-Tyne*	*North Lanarkshire*	*Glasgow City*
80.8	79.7	79.6	74.7	74.4	72.4	69.3

Source: National Statistics, 'Life expectancy at birth by health and local authorities in the UK, 1991-1993 to 2002-2004', London, November 2005. www.statistics.gov.uk.

The trends in life expectancy correspond to the material quality of people's lives (see Graph 11:1). The average household 'disposable

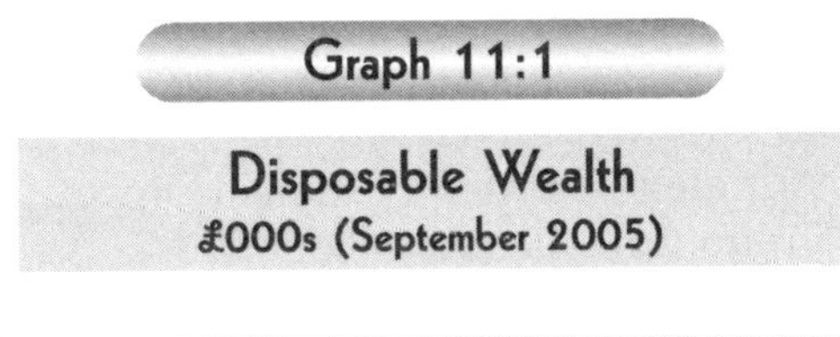

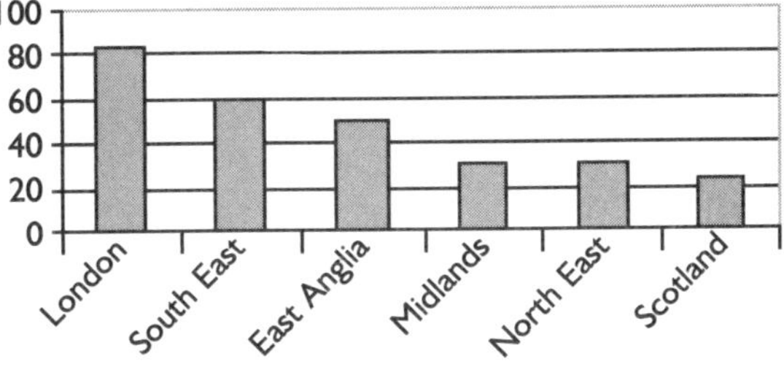

Source: KDB Quarterly Analysis of Disposable Wealth (May 2006).

wealth' – including savings, shares and housing equity – was four times greater for Londoners than for people in Scotland. The gap actually misrepresents the long-term trend; it is usually even larger. But the weakening in the London housing market in 2004 coincided with a catch-up phase in property prices in the North. In Teesside, in the North East, house prices in Saltburn-by-the-Sea increased by 41% in 2004. There were similar increases in Scotland, but starting from a very low level of prices. Even so, the gap between the rich and poor regions determined – literally – people's life-chances.

But the economic and biological contrasts cannot be interpreted in isolation from a history that demeaned the people of Scotland. That history is a harrowing one, an experience that has left its searing mark on the collective consciousness of the people. It is a story of betrayal that crushed the spirit and culture of millions of people who lived through the past two centuries. It has, at its heart, the struggle to control and dispose of the value that makes and breaks civilisation: the rents of land and of nature's resources.

11.2 Betrayal of the Lairds

THE LAND GRAB in Scotland was as callous as any in the colonial record. Psychically, the brutality was all the more grievous to the victims because it was the breach of ancient trust that left them traumatised.

To understand the social psychology of the people of Scotland today we need to appreciate the nature of the bonds that held the clans together in ancient times. On the face of it, the relationship was a feudal structure. But the reality was strikingly different.

Feudalism was a model of social organisation in which power flowed from the top down. The monarch reigned supreme and assigned rights to land to his tenants-in-chief in return for the services they would render to him. The tenants-in-chief then sub-let the land to others, who provided the labour services or goods in kind which fuelled the feudal economy.

In Scotland, however, the chief depended on the goodwill of the people of his clan. They exercised the power to remove the chief. The people rendered services to their lairds in return for leadership. The association was one of mutual support. The bonds had more to do with kinship than contract. The land was the domain of the clan, and the laird could rule as chief for so long as he kept the confidence of his clansmen.

Over the centuries, dynastic struggles led to the recognition of monarchs who were linked to the clans by means of charters. In about 1500 these charters were renewed, but as far as the clansmen were concerned this did not alter their territorial rights. But following the conflicts with England and the Union in 1707, the lifestyles of the English aristocracy began to attract the attention of the lairds. Conspicuous consumption – the lavish living in splendid country homes and in the court of Westminster – appealed to the lairds who would be lords.

But to finance the high life they had to increase the flow of rents into their pockets. To raise the rental potential of the highlands, new economic methods would be necessary. The choice of competing models of growth became a live issue. One option was to develop a diversity of agricultural activities and rural-based crafts. This would expand the employment opportunities, raise productivity and deliver a growing surplus (rent) that could be fed back into the funding of the highways and canals that were needed to foster further growth in the highlands.

Instead, the lairds chose to introduce the flocks of Cheviot sheep that would yield increases in rents. This strategy depended on depriving the clansmen of their traditional land rights. So the lairds began a process of asserting proprietary rights. By the middle of the 18th century, the lairds wanted to abandon their role as chiefs to adopt the status of aristocratic landowner. No longer was there recognition of a mutuality of interest. Now, the lairds relied on the charters from the Crown to assert their exclusive rights over the land. Those rights, they claimed, entitled them to demolish, by brute force if necessary, hundreds of settlements from the foothills of the highlands.

No one knows for sure how many people were ruthlessly cleared from the land, but at least 500,000 men, women and children were evicted from their dwellings and told to either migrate to Canada or squat on tiny plots of land, called crofts, on the rugged coast. This experience inflicted the trauma that was the human cost of the land grab. When the lairds issued their eviction notices, their vocal opponents were not the fearsome fighting men whose bagpipes and broad swords struck terror in the hearts of the enemy in foreign lands. When the sheriff or the laird's lawyer turned up with bits of paper to order the evictions, the men were struck dumb. In the main, it was the women who put up the physical opposition, taunting the soldiers who had been ordered to oversee the demolition of the hearths. It was the women who challenged: 'You have no right to do this.'

Box 11:1 Men, Morality and Manhood

THE GENERAL condition of young men has been tracked by the quality of those who enlist as soldiers. The highlanders who enlisted in their regiments over the past centuries came with a spirit that was second to none. When they were called upon to defend Britain against Napoleon, for example, a Major called David Stewart noted that the boys were 'healthy, vigorous and efficient, attached and obedient to their officers, temperate and regular ... possessing those principles of integrity and moral conduct which constitute a valuable soldier'.[1]

Between the times of Napoleon and the tyrants of the late 20th century who had to be opposed, something happened to the young men who reported for duty in the British army. And by the time it came to challenge Saddam Hussein in the second Iraq War, the verdict on the recruits was an indictment of the way that the young people of Britain were being raised.

According to the commander of the Army's 3rd Division, Maj. General Graeme Lamb, a 'morally corrupt and dysfunctional' society had incubated youngsters who were 'cocky and arrogant and brought up on a diet of football brats and binge drinking ... who are not educated in and able to recognise self-discipline'.[2]

Lamb was not referring specifically to recruits from the highlands, but his description fits with the sociological evidence to be gathered about the condition of the young men who volunteer to serve Queen and country.

1 Quoted in John Prebble, *The Highland Clearances*, London: Secker & Warburg, 1963, p.132.
2 Sean Rayment, 'Army risks losing its reputation, warns general', *Sunday Telegraph*, August 21, 2005.

Historians have noted that the fighting men, with a few exceptions, were as meek as the lambs that would be feeding off their land once they were despatched to a fate unknown in the New World. John Prebble, the author who revived our awareness of these terrible deeds with his book published in 1963, assessed the failure of the men to defend their land rights in terms of 'their childish faith in the laird'.[4] The men relied on their traditional understanding of their relationship with their chief. They could not believe that their rights were being usurped and the trust that held the clan together was being mercilessly cast aside in favour of sheep. So the men were driven from their ancient territories, cast adrift with no more than the clothes on their backs, elderly women literally dumped in ditches with nowhere to go, the screams of pregnant women wailing across the lochs.

The men were not cowards. In their Scottish regiments, they were the equal of the best fighting forces anywhere in the world. But nothing would persuade them to turn their broad swords against their chiefs. The humiliation to which they were subjected, a continuous process that ran from about 1770 through to 1850, caused the spirit of these brave men to ebb away (see Box 11:1).

It was not enough for the lairds to deceive by claiming to own superior rights to the land. To justify their cruelties they had to slander their clansmen. The story went out that these were lazy and retarded people who preferred lives of idleness to one of hard labour. The highlanders did enjoy their free time: their recreational pursuits were part of their culture which, at the time, they had no reason to trade for long hours of endurance in the factories of the Lowlands. Their dwellings were of a rude kind, sculptured into the hillsides, but they had no reason to want to trade them for the slum tenements of Glasgow. In fact, their pastoral economy was productive. We know that this was so because they were able to generate a surplus – a rent which was paid to their lairds. And when they were threatened with eviction, some sought to appease the chiefs by offering to pay higher rents.

The global economy of the 18th century was reaching into the highlands, and change was inevitable. But there was nothing about the highlander which said that he and she could not adapt the traditional lifestyle for everyone's benefit. These were not parasites: they were paying their way in this world, even supporting the lairds who were now adopting the airs and graces of the effete aristocrats from the South. But the lairds were not interested in economic development that would enrich everybody.

The notion that the highlanders were unproductive – and therefore had to be replaced by sheep – is exposed as a lie when we examine the hard life on the crofts. Crofters produced a surplus income which could have been ploughed back into the community. The case of the kelp industry is illuminating. Kelp was freely available for collection from the seashores. Crofters laboured on the beaches, packing and forwarding the raw material to the factories that turned it into agricultural fertiliser.

> The income from kelp was unequally distributed. Almost all went to the landlords. But because there was some benefit to tenants, rental levels were often increased, a fact which represented simply a surrogate means of benefiting landlords.[5]

If those rents had been invested in the community's infrastructure, the displaced highlanders *could* have enjoyed a contented existence after that shameful episode in the history of the clans, the clearance from their ancestral highlands. But the rents were not reinvested in their communities; they were appropriated by the lairds who squandered them in what economists today call 'conspicuous consumption'. Thus did the landlord class turn themselves into capitalists.

> Kelping was an important means of capital accumulation for the landlord class ... The collapse of kelping after 1830 had several effects on the crofting economy. For landlords, a vital source of cash income was removed. This was an important prompt to the sales of estates at this time.

The new owners turned vast regions of the highlands into sporting estates. They cleared the remaining farmers off the land to make way for deer stalking. All of this in the land of the Enlightenment. Enlightement? Why, then, did William Ogilvie, a professor of humanities at the University and King's College, Aberdeen, fear the consequences of publishing the remedy to his nation's problems? He wrote *An Essay on the Right of Property in Land,* which was published anonymously in 1782.[6] He convincingly explained that Scotland could enjoy economic improvement alongside the enrichment of the culture of all of her people. This would be achieved by reserving the rent as the fund out of which to defray the public services that everyone shared.

But the fabulous lifestyles of the Peers of the Realm were contingent on their appropriation of the rents. In stealing the land which had been the common property of the clans, the lairds also stole the humanity of their kinsmen. And in stealing their humanity, they became the arbiters of the spiritual and moral, as well as the material, condition of the nation. The theft of the land could deliver one outcome only – the impoverishment of the majority of the people in Scotland.

Who were the barbarians in Scotland?

11.3 Failure of the Social Immune System

THE PEOPLE of the clans evolved a culture that was resilient enough to see them through the vicissitudes of centuries. Suddenly, the immune system was destroyed by a virus from within that exposed them to a deadly infection. By the end of the clearances, the clansmen who found their way to the Lowlands were adrift in a world for which they were ill-fitted. A self-destruction was at work. The lethal effects were shrouded by the deaths in the trenches as the First World War removed one generation. The killing fields of the Second World War accomplished this for the following generation. Today, with no world war to destroy the new generation, we are able to ask whether the young of Scotland have been rescued by the socialist Welfare State.

The mortal evidence is forensically documented in the morgue in Edinburgh. Here, the man in charge is Professor Anthony Busuttil, regius professor of forensic medicine at the University of Edinburgh. His morbid routine is to examine 40 bodies a week, just over 2,000 people a year in a city with a population of 500,000. He summarised his findings in these terms:

> The deaths have become tinged with such despair. There are more suicides than there used to be. Suicide used to be the prerogative of the young, 18- to 25-year-olds. Now we're seeing more and more bodies that have been lying around for weeks. More than ever before, people are dying at home, on their own and nobody cares. No neighbours have knocked. No one has taken a blind bit of notice. We have, without doubt, become less and less of a caring society.[7]

The depth of the marginalisation was chronicled by Gordon Brown when he was Chairman of the Labour Party in Scotland. He edited books that outlined the socialist solution to the deprivation of the Celts. That there was a striking gap in the condition of his people compared with those who lived south of the border was beyond doubt. Writing in 1983, the future Chancellor of the Exchequer listed some of the inequalities.

- The top 1% of Scots owned 25% of personal wealth; the top 5% owned 50%, and the top 10% owned 80% of personal wealth.
- Five hundred people or companies owned half of Scotland's land.
- After tax, the top 10% of income earners took home more than the bottom 50%.[8]

An indignant Brown recorded that the main beneficiaries of public spending on education, housing, health and transport were the most advantaged social groups. The collateral effect of this distribution of income, in Glasgow, was cancer rates that were 80% higher in the poorer areas of the city than in the more prosperous neighbourhoods.

Another indicator of the pathological division of the population, according to Brown, was psychological. Now outraged, he described it as the 'fragmentation of people's consciousness'.[9] Equality was not possible because of 'inherited privilege or private power'. These were not based on merit or contributions to the community. They were the result of 'the vast inequalities in wealth that distort society'.

Capitalism was to blame, and the failure of governments to challenge and transform the malevolent forces that were at work. The solution lay with a therapeutic socialism. This would heal 'the split personality caused by people's unequal control over their social development'.[10] To reverse this condition, power had to be shifted to working people so that they could impose 'planned control of our economy and a transformation of democracy at all levels'. Taxation had failed to erode the power of private property. The need to redistribute income and wealth was central to the socialist agenda, and the tax system needed to be shaped by two basic principles.

- Those who cannot afford to pay tax should not have to pay it.
- Taxation should rise progressively with income.[11]

This tax philosophy was congenial to the feudal aristocracy. The chiefs had dispossessed their clansmen so that they could appropriate the rents to ape the knights and barons in England. The philosophy of progressive taxation was to become the confidence trick which bought off the firebrands and fooled the people. What it could not do was equalise wealth or empower the marginalised sections of society. It did not do so over the first 50 years of the Welfare State, and it did not do so under the chancellorship of Gordon Brown. In fact, incomes were as unequal at the end of Brown's second tenure at the Treasury as when he first entered the building in Whitehall in 1997.

The labouring masses that were denied the full benefits of their work sought refuge in a false consciousness and adopted strategies that subverted their ambitions. Labour and Capital turned on each other. Instead of forming an alliance against Land, they were deceived by their common enemy – the free riders – into embarking on a class conflict that would be fought to the death.

Historians offer a distorted assessment of the social malaise. This is how the unfolding trends of the 20th century are summarised by David Cannadine, who has taught at both Cambridge and Columbia universities:

> The conflict between the classes was the direct, *inevitable* consequence of the conflict between those who were differently related to the means of production, and it was this struggle which in the end determined the nature and the working of the political structure. Even if the dictatorship of the proletariat had not yet arrived, as Marx had predicted it should have done, his insights still seem to offer the best way of understanding the broad contours of the economic, social and political development of modern Britain – insights to which, it bears repeating, class formation, class identify, class consciousness and class conflict were central.[12]

The outcome was *not* inevitable. And the structure of power and conflict in the 20th century was *not* because people were differentiated by their relationship to the way they earned their incomes. That was Marx's version of history – a version driven by a doctrinal prejudice that was not consistent with reality.

Labour and Capital were united in the common objective of adding value to the wealth of the nation. They were opposed by the owners of Land, whose sole *raison d'etre* was to extract value out of the nation. Someone had to lose, and it was not going to be the owners of Land.

The intervention of the First World War helped to confuse people. Millions died in the trenches; even the aristocracy suffered. Still, the foundations of the social structure remained solid. So when the workers tried to negotiate higher wages through their collective actions on the factory floor, the police and army were ranged against them.

Sense might have prevailed if people had had access to the statistical evidence that revealed the reality. The distribution of the nation's income would have informed the owners of capital and their employees where the problem lay; but that information was not audited by Parliament in a form that revealed the true story of what was causing the stresses in the economy. Data on land and rents were secreted under headings such as 'capital', 'profits' and 'interest'. The disruptions caused by Land, and the financial sector that served its interests, were concealed from public gaze. So responsibility for low wages and bad housing was directed at the bosses of factories, and their shareholders.

The outcome for Scotland can be calculated on the basis of the British government's own yardstick of the damage caused by its tax policies. That damage stems from the 'excess burden' of taxes on people's work, savings and investments. The distortions to economic incentives result in 'deadweight losses': 30p for every pound raised from taxes such as Income Tax, VAT and Corporation Tax. For Scotland, the annual losses in wealth and welfare are about £8.5bn.[13] This was the value that the people of Scotland would have otherwise produced if they were not subjected to the kinds of taxes favoured by Gordon Brown. The losses exceeded the funds that are needed to provide all the services that are required by a civilised community.

11.4 On Social Solidarity

THIS WAS NOT the prospectus that Brown promoted for Britain under his stewardship. There would be 'symbiotic relationships between growth and investment in people and infrastructure [and] a new understanding of how labour markets really work'. His vision, he informed the people whom he wished to lead as Prime Minister, was of 'a Britain of ambition where there is no ceiling on talent, no limit to potential, no cap on ability'.[14] Brown's policies achieved the opposite of his declared objectives.

Box 11:2 Blaming Margaret Thatcher

NICK DAVIES, a *Guardian* journalist, documented the corrupted lives of young people on Britain's municipal housing estates. In moving detail he chronicles the hopelessness that leads to young girls embarking on prostitution, youths making money out of selling drugs, boys renting their bodies to earn the money they need to feed their heroine addiction. His book should be read for the convincing detail he provides about life beneath the economic margin. But missing is the explanation that might move impassioned reformers to take political action.

Davies blames Margaret Thatcher, who had claimed: 'The pursuit of equality is a mirage.'* After the 1979 election, Prime Minister Thatcher turned her doctrines into laws. For Nick Davies, the abandonment of equality resulted in a cutback in welfare programmes which injected hopelessness among young people.

And yet … for three weeks in November 2005 the young people who lived in France's 750 depressed suburbs rioted, torching people's cars, schools and community centres. Blame for the civil disturbances was directed at the French republic's official dedication to the concept of equality, which refused to adopt policies of 'reverse discrimination' to favour ethnic minorities. Many of the young outcasts were violent, trading and using drugs and resorting to crime. This was their alternative to the jobs that were not available to them in the labour market.

On November 14, 2005, President Jacques Chirac, in a televised address, insisted that the government would not budge from the principle that all its citizens were equal and that there would be no positive discrimination regardless of race or religion. *Égalité* would not be abandoned by the political elite of France – and yet, as in Britain, there was an underclass of disturbed and deprived young people whose lives were being corroded by forces beyond their control, and apparently beyond the control of politicians.

* Nick Davies, *Dark Heart: The Shocking Truth about Hidden Britain*, London: Vintage, 1998, p.286.

Commentators lacked a theory that could guide them to the root cause of the social problems, which is why a confusing variety of explanations were offered. But secret agent James Bond – 007 himself – knew exactly where to find the solution. His alter ego, Sean Connery, tried to persuade Brown to help the movie industry to locate studios halfway between Glasgow and Edinburgh. He offered £1m towards that job-creating project. 'Scotland could be made to work for film but you would need to improve the tax situation,' he said.[15] But the damaging nature of the Treasury's policies were not on people's radar screens, so scapegoats had to be found. An easy target was the hard-hearted Margaret Thatcher, who helped to undermine the consensus that supported the Welfare State. Closer scrutiny shows that Thatcher's critique of the concept of equality could not account for the profound corruption of culture at the heart of our urban civilisation (see Box 11:2).

But what of the land reforms introduced in Scotland as a result of the creation of a parliament in Edinburgh? The feudal traces of property rights were abolished and crofters were given the right to buy out their lairds under a 2003 law. But land reform was treated as an exclusively rural challenge. Crofting families could band together to buy land when the owner decided to sell and quit the highlands and islands. For those tenants who could beg and borrow money – and draw on the lottery funds gambled by other citizens – it became possible to purchase some estates. If all the proposed buy-outs that were mooted in 2005 were consummated, over 230,000 acres would be taken out of 'private hands' within a few years. The problem with this policy was that the shareholders in the communal land schemes would still be liable for the taxes imposed by Westminster.

This policy failed to equalise people's right of access to the community-created value of land in a way that would energise the people of Scotland. As a back-bench MP for Dunfermline East, Brown had lamented that 'the earning potential of the poorest tenth of workers is now no greater than it was 100 years ago'.[16] Under his stewardship of the economy, that marginalised 10% of the population continued to be excluded. The notion that power could be devolved from Westminster without a radical revision of the tax base was fraudulent.

The Parliament in Edinburgh could alter the property tax, which raised about 20% of what was spent by local governments. And income tax rates could be varied by 3p in the £. Exploiting these limited opportunities – untaxing buildings, and reducing the income tax – would reduce the burden that imposes a cap on capitalism. But even these modest shifts in taxes would require an imaginative leap that was not possible among politicians schooled in the conventional wisdoms. Should the outcasts of Scotland return to the migration trail in search of a better life in the Land of the Free? Gordon Brown would not go that far, but there was a surrogate. He disclosed it in a speech during the general election in May 2005.

Acutely aware of the threat from the East, Britain, he said, would have to be mobilised. The nation needed a new sense of social solidarity, which could be provided by the sense of Britishness. Brown invoked the iconic ideas of individual liberty and freedom of speech. Britain, after all, he reminded his audiences, was the birthplace of 'ideas that were exported to and became the foundation stone of the USA'.[17] For Brown, the American enterprise economy was a major point of reference during his years at the Treasury. But while eulogising American market-driven entrepreneurship he pursued Old Labour socialism.[18] Brown's problem was that he did not grasp the significance of Ricardo's Law.

Brown did enlist the name of Adam Smith in his attempt to define the terms of a new settlement, but he distorted the mechanism at the heart of the Smithian model of society. Smith, in his *Theory of Moral Sentiments*, provided a rich matrix of social values that ought to be synchronised with the economics of the free market, but the mechanism that secured a balanced relationship between the individual and society was not the version ascribed to him by Gordon Brown. Brown's revisionist history claims that Smith's 'invisible hand' of the free market was 'dependent upon the existence of a helping hand'.[19] That helping hand was the socialist's 'enabling state'.

Gordon Brown believed that education was the key. And yet, while he travelled to Mozambique in April 2006 to pledge $15bn (£8.5bn) of taxpayers' money to educate children in the developing world, back home in Glasgow a shocking 23% of children played truant from their classrooms. The young of Scotland were unhappy with their lot; as they were south of the border, according to the Archbishop of York, John Sentamu. He wondered: 'Why is it that young people in Britain, the fourth largest economy in the world, are the most depressed in Europe?'[20] That question demands an answer. Is it to be found in the Land of the Free, where happiness is a doctrine of the state?

REFERENCES

1 Gerard Seenan, 'Scotland has second highest murder rate in Europe', *The Guardian*, September 29, 2005.

2 Henry George, *Progress and Poverty* (1879); centenary edn., Robert Schalkenbach Foundation, New York, 1979, Bk X, Ch. 4.

3 Arthur Herman, *The Scottish Enlightenment*, London: Fourth Estate, 2003.

4 John Prebble, *The Highland Clearances*, London: Secker & Warburg, 1963, p.135.

5 Charles W.J. Withers, *Urban Highlanders*, East Linton: Tuckwell Press, 1998, p.48. One lie used to dispossess people of their crofts was that they had failed to pay rents, following the decay of the kelp industry. In fact, notes Prebble (*op. cit.*, p.273), 'Far from the rents being in arrears for years, they had in fact been paid with regularity'.

6 William Ogilvie, *Birthright in Land*, Edited by Peter Gibb, London: Othila Press, 1997.
7 Stephen Armstrong, 'Modern death: People are killing themselves and their children and no one seems to notice', *The Guardian*, January 14, 2006.
8 Gordon Brown, Introduction, *Scotland: The Real Divide* (eds: Gordon Brown and Robin Cooke), Edinburgh: Mainstream, 1983, p.12.
9 Gordon Brown, 'Introduction: The socialist challenge', in *The Red Paper on Scotland*, Edinburgh: EUSPB, 1975, p.7.
10 *Ibid.*, p.8.
11 *Scotland: The Real Divide*, p.22.
12 David Cannadine, *Class in Britain*, New Haven: Yale University Press, 1998, p.7. Emphasis added.
13 Peter Gibb and Fred Harrison, Evidence to the Local Government Finance Review Committee, Glasgow, November 14, 2005.
14 Gordon Brown, 'Britain's future lies in entrepreneurial talent', *Financial Times*, November 14, 2005.
15 Jasper Gerrard, 'I've a wee issue with the English', *The Sunday Times*, March 12, 2006.
16 *Scotland: The Real Divide*, p.13.
17 Michael White, 'Brown sets out vision for a new great Britain', *The Guardian*, April 28, 2005.
18 Gordon Brown lectured Europe's business leaders and finance ministers on September 9, 2005, on the need to adopt a new social model, citing the statistic that 'European living standards are one third lower than those of the US. The problem comes from a long-run failure to adapt to the new global economy' (Gordon Brown, 'Open trade is needed instead of blocking imports', *Financial Times*, September 9, 2005). Brown omitted to mention that Europe does not suffer the same level of deprivation as the US, where, for example, 40m people do not have health insurance.
19 Hugo Young Memorial Lecture, *op. cit.* p.6.
20 Maev Kennedy, 'Government accused of draconian treatment of asylum seekers', *The Guardian*, May 23, 2006.

12

America's Constitution of Unhappiness

12.1 Beyond the Land of the Free

THE DREAM lives on to this day as folklore. America is the land of the free. It was, once, for those who sought refuge from the aristocracies of Europe which had dispossessed them. The New World was a continental-wide bolthole to freedom. But once the land was liberated from its original occupants, staked out and the title deeds were assigned, something eerie happened. When the land ran out in the 1890s, the land of plenty turned into a hell of poverty.

Today, across the land, we find a depth of human tragedy not to be found in the worst of inner city slums in Europe. Even as the empire waves the flag of democracy under the noses of the populations of other cultures, the internal colonisation of the citizens of America proceeds unabated.

That is not how Americans interpret the crises that afflict their communities. Real estate is revered rather than held culpable as the root cause of their problems. But how, then, can they account for the fissures that split this metropolitan civilisation? Given the sacred character ascribed to the laws of their land, the fault had to be displaced onto the psychology of the individual. Racism was, and necessarily remains, a favourite explanation, and the statistics lend credence to this interpretation. A *New York Times* analysis highlighted the evidence that exposes the marginalisation of Afro-Americans.

- The proportion of black men (aged 22-30) without jobs had climbed relentlessly. In 2000, 65% of black male high school dropouts in their 20s were jobless – unable to find work, not seeking it or incarcerated.

By 2004, the share had grown to 72% compared with 34% of white and 19% of Hispanic dropouts.

- In 1995, 16% of black men in their 20s who did not attend college were in prison; by 2004, 21% were incarcerated. By their mid-30s, 6 in 10 black men who had dropped out of school had spent time in prison.[1]

Was America reviving racial segregation in schools? That was the view of one commentator.[2] Fears of racism are understandable in states located at the US margins – like Louisiana and Mississippi – but do those fears distract people from the causal roots that nourish discrimination? They do, in the view of a social activist who combined academic economics with concern for people addicted to narcotics – and who is also a landlord. Dr Polly Cleveland was a close observer of the real estate market from the inside, as co-owner of two rental apartment buildings in New York. In her view, the problem of deprivation is more complex than the psychology of whites *versus* blacks.

> Increasing racism? Or maybe a consequence of growing inequality of wealth and income *driven by a system of taxes, subsidies and regulation that directs resources to the top*? The system varies from state to state; it's no coincidence that the black poverty trap of New Orleans lies in Louisiana, which vies with Mississippi for most unequal state.
>
> *Growing inequality drives growing housing segregation by wealth and class, followed by growing psychological segregation.* It reduces empathy between classes. It makes it easier for officials to withdraw services from poorer neighbourhoods, and easier for employers to hire their own kind. It leaves the cities' young black men isolated and bitter. To fight racism, we must also challenge the rigged system that has now pushed wealth inequality back up to levels last seen in 1929.[3]

The poverty-stricken condition of some southern states is in part self-inflicted. Tax laws that impoverish, driving people into the zone below the economic margin, are wilfully adopted by local and state governments. That proposition was tested by economist Mason Gaffney and former newspaper proprietor Richard Noyes. Louisiana, for example, featured near the bottom of all US states in terms of *per capita* income. A people-friendly regime of state and local taxes would raise revenue from the property tax, preferably by exempting buildings and directing the charges at land. Louisiana was sixth from the bottom in the league that ranked states by the ratio of property tax to all taxes.[4] In other words, its revenue-raising policies were *designed* to impoverish its people. Low productivity employees are penalised for working while the owners of land are rewarded for accumulating assets whose value increases in line with tax-payers' investment in infrastructure.

This vicious funding-and-finance cycle drives the wedge ever deeper between those who rent their homes and those who own them. The impact as transmitted through the housing market was analysed by Wenli Li and Rui Yao, two economists at the Federal Reserve Bank of Philadelphia. They wanted to know how welfare would be affected as a result of a 10% increase in the price of houses. Families that rent their homes suffered a 4% drop in welfare, compared with a 5% increase for owners who had paid off their mortgages (see Graph 12:1).

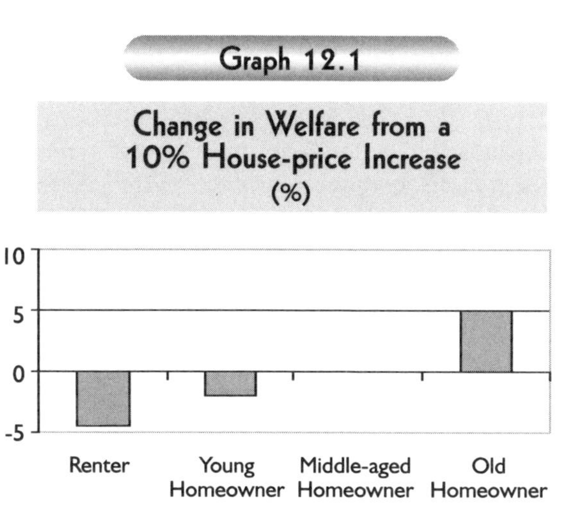

As employees' wages were taxed and invested in highways and other public amenities, the financial status of renters deteriorated while the asset-rich became increasingly prosperous. For the owners of real estate enjoyed two streams of income: the money they earned if they worked, and the money they could borrow from banks when they offered their houses as collateral. The re-financing of homes was a buoyant source of tax-free revenue. Over the life of the mortgage, about 45% of households refinanced their properties.[5]

Home owners increase their consumption by monetising their windfall gains. They can live beyond their means. How much more they consume depends on where they happen to be on the family life-cycle and the size of their mortgages. Graph 12:2 exposes the void between renters and property owners. The additional

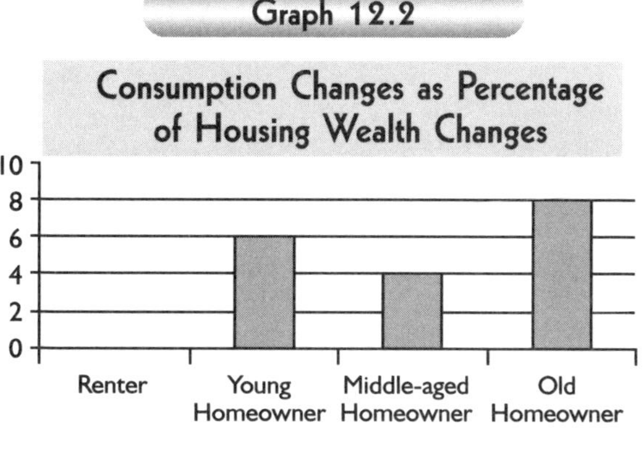

Source: Wenli Li and Rui Yao, *Your House Just Doubled in Value?* Federal Reserve Bank of Philadelphia *Business Review* Q1 (2006).

consumption by young owners is about 5 to 6 cents for every additional dollar in the price of their homes. This jumps to 8 cents for elderly owners. Similar effects have been identified for the UK, where the effect (11 cents) is largest for old homeowners, with zero effect for renters.[6]

As the value of residential assets increases over time, a contrary trend is observed among renting families. Campbell and Cocco, referring to the UK, found that 'Over the life-cycle, individuals who remain as renters typically have stagnating or declining incomes, while individuals with rising incomes tend to become homeowners'.[7] If public policy was not heavily to blame for the plight of renting families, we might accept a crude Darwinian interpretation of the differences of lifestyles. In fact, renters spend their lives locked in that unidentified battle with the state and its tax-take.

Thus is discrimination at its most elemental level built into the treatment of citizens. But unlike the racial segregation laws that disgraced the Deep South up to the time when they were outlawed in the 1960s, the discrimination sponsored by the Tax State's economics of real estate is not decoded for the public. An economic class structure divides the people, and yet they unite in celebrating the laws that segregate them. The facts are laid out in the official statistics, and yet no one interprets them in terms that can lead to calls for a renewal of the campaign for civil liberties.

Social scientists tend to avoid questioning the fundamental principles on which the US Constitution is based, but nature is brutal in its indifference to doctrinal sensibilities. Nothing was going to stop Hurricane Katrina from exposing the underbelly of American society.

12.2 Where's the Levy on the Levee?

NEW ORLEANS, one of the jewels in America's urban civilisation, was not a sustainable city. This thought troubled Mason Gaffney as his jetliner cruised over Louisiana one day in 1965. The city built below sea level was vulnerable, but not because of the thermal threats that lurked menacingly out in the Gulf of Mexico. Nor was the city's fate a matter of technology. Concrete walls shored up the sides of the levees that drained the land on which the city was built, but more sophisticated technologies were available for purchase elsewhere in the world. The litmus test for sustainability lay with the way New Orleans and the state and federal governments raised revenue to fund infrastructure.

Gaffney, at the time a professor of economics at the University of Wisconsin, was responding to an invitation from a civic group to advise them on urban economics. He would lay the truth on the line. To secure their lovely city's future, so that Mardi Gras and all that jazz would continue to lure the tourists, New Orleans would need to reshape the property tax. Gaffney mailed ahead of him the literature which he had published in the academic journals, and in the cordial precincts of a downtown hotel he explained how the city could fund the reinforcement of the levees. People who occupied the land should be charged rent for the benefits they enjoyed; with compensating reductions in the taxes levied on their earnings. By this means, the levees would be self-funding, and there would be no state-sponsored obstacles to the employment of the population, white or black.

By locking out the water, the land acquired immense value. The city stood at a confluence of world trade and, combined with the cultural diversity of its population, it was a highlight of the tourist circuit. The more valuable the land, the more money there would be to upgrade the levees in line with the technologies which, in Europe, had kept the North Sea from breaching London's defences, prevented the inundation of Holland and had bought a new lease of life to Venice.

The civic leaders listened to Gaffney with respect, entertained him royally at the home of one of their bankers – and despatched him on his way with no intention of taking his advice. Forty years later, Gaffney watched the result on his TV.

Katrina landed on the levees on August 29, 2005. By the time the hurricane had moved on, more than 1,300 people were dead. Bodies floated in the streets, homes levelled by the onrush of water from the Gulf as the concrete defences buckled and exposed to the rest of the world the real story behind the tax system: a shocking depth of poverty.

The President was in his bunker on his ranch in Texas. By satellite TV, George W. Bush had been warned that the levees might not stand up to the pressure. They didn't. As the residential areas were flooded, the people of the ghetto – the residents who could not afford to flee – paid the price. Poverty immobilised them in one of the transport hubs of the richest nation on earth.

It need not have happened. But someone would have had to pay if the levees were to be upgraded. True, the defences would have paid for themselves: barriers that excluded the Gulf raised the rents people were willing to pay to live in New Orleans. But America believed in privatising those rents and taxing people into poverty. So there was no impregnable wall between the people and Katrina.

But after the deluge, what then? Here was the chance of a fresh start. Surely, now, the political leaders – from the Mayor all the way up to the President – would champion the core principles of a sustainable community? Here was the opportunity for democratic governance and the social sciences to prove themselves. Would the correct tools be used to recreate a balanced city? The US Government had access to the wisdom of the best brains, and they do not come sharper than Thomas Schelling's. His concern for the welfare of America is indicated by the terms of his professorship at the University of Maryland: foreign affairs, national security, nuclear strategy and arms control. In 2005 he was awarded the Nobel Prize for Economics, 'having enhanced our understanding of conflict and co-operation through game-theory analysis'.

Schelling's understanding of the rules of the game has helped to shape public policy since 1945. So when reporter Peter Gosellin from the *Los Angeles Times* asked him how New Orleans could be rebuilt, his words would resonate in Washington, DC. He is quoted as stating:

> There is no market solution to New Orleans. It is essentially a problem of coordinating expectations ... But achieving this co-ordination in the circumstances of New Orleans seems impossible ... There are classes of problems that free markets simply do not deal with well. If ever there was an example, the rebuilding of New Orleans is it.[8]

Mason Gaffney, at home in the midst of a hilltop avocado orchard overlooking Riverside, read that diagnosis with horror. Now a professor at the University of California, he recalled his clash of words with Schelling in 1969. It happened at a seminar at the Brookings Institution in Washington. Gaffney was a research associate at Resources for the Future, a think-tank whose offices were in the same building as Brookings. He had been invited to present his analysis of the relationship between taxation, the land market and public policy. Schelling objected to his critique. Gaffney had stressed that the property market operated most effectively when the public's services were defrayed out of the rent of land. The switch to that policy, Schelling warned, would *break the social contract, destabilize people's expectations and shatter the confidence of investors*.[9]

Katrina – not Gaffney's tax agenda – had shattered New Orleans. Might it have been a different story if that city had adopted Gaffney's funding strategy 40 years earlier?

But Schelling was not just hostile to the tax plan that would reduce the silent civil conflict that was continuously rupturing the fabric of people's lives – a conflict resolving strategy absent from his influential *The Strategy of Conflict* (1960) and *Arms and Influence* (1966); he was also selling short the ability of the free market to work with the grain of people's needs in the rebuilding of New Orleans.

The burden of Gaffney's presentation to some of the leading social scientists in America was that the market *did* enable people to provide for their needs, *if* the tax obstacles were removed. The land market, for example, responds to all the influences that constitute an urban environment, including investment in a flood-control facility like the New Orleans levees.[10] Without this reform, warned Gaffney, the economy, urban communities and the environment are all seriously compromised.

Gaffney's diagnosis went to the heart of the US Constitution. He warned that the tax authorities might be flouting the constitution. The 16th Amendment authorised taxation of 'income from whatever source derived', but the tax rules provided owners with covert loopholes through which to exempt their rents. One of the most lucrative loopholes was the way land could be manipulated for depreciation purposes – as if it were a building that rotted with age. That trick was repeated time and again, for the same plot of land.

Gaffney was emphatic: 'Nothing less than a thoroughgoing shake-up of the tax treatment of land income will avail. And this is exactly the time when such a project, hitherto a pipe dream, may be seriously entertained'.[11] The consequences of not having this policy in place could be observed in everyone's neighbourhood. For when rent was privatised, people who obstructed the market were rewarded.

> [T]he income imputable to land is largely exempt from income taxes. This helps explain why landowners in high [tax] brackets hold out for higher prices than can be met by low-income workers whose wages are fully taxable. It helps explain the paradox of high and rising land prices in the face of a vast surplus of vacant and under-utilized land, and the twin paradox that islands of hyper-intensive, high-density land use, appropriate to high land values, arise in oceans of empty space with which they have little complementary linkage. It helps explain why the land market is not nearly as responsive to consumer demands as a market has to be to be functional in a complex modern economy.[12]

Schelling was not convinced. By his negative response to the plan he implicitly contributed to the perpetuation of the culture of inefficiency and injustice. Would this happen if scholars had to audit their doctrines, to inform the people of the wealth, welfare – and quality-of-life options – which they *could* enjoy if they adopted optimum policies such as the one advocated by Gaffney?

An estimate of the scale of the potential gains has now been calculated by Nicolaus Tideman. He began his teaching career at Harvard, served as a Senior Staff Economist at the President's Council of Economic Advisors in Washington, DC, and became Professor of Economics at Virginia Polytechnic Institute and State University. If the US government was sufficiently concerned about the well-being of its citizens to optimize the public's revenue raising policies, average earnings per worker after taxes would have been about $4,000 higher in 2005. Within 10 years, after-tax earnings per worker would be higher by an average of $7,000. And by consistently applying public charges to the rent of land, by 2025 – in an open economy, trading with China without fear – American workers would be earning an additional $10,000 per year after taxes, compared with their prospects under the current tax regime.[13]

We can infer what a difference this would make to the people of New Orleans. By swapping the constraint-on-trade doctrine for the freedom-to-produce philosophy, they could rely on their personal and community initiatives to rebuild their city, working in partnership with government and its agencies. If Katrina left the land worthless on the day she struck, that value would be restored on the day that people cleared the derelict buildings and began to reconstruct their homes.

After Katrina, all that the survivors needed was a plan that created the right combination of incentives to undertake the renewal work. The primary innovation was a land levy for the levee. The government's unique function is to provide the legal framework for ensuring that the value added to the land was recycled back into the public's services rather than allowed to leak through the colander of the current tax regime. People would hand over those land-rents if they knew that this was the best defence against Katrina's sister, who is waiting in the Gulf ready to strike. The Mayor of New Orleans could offer his citizens the off-the-peg plan for a sustainable city by drawing on the scholarly papers available on www.masongaffney.org.

But that is not what happened. The speculators moved into New Orleans as the water was driven back. Taxpayers would fund the renewal of the levees and raise the value of adjacent sites, a process described by Gaffney for the benefit of his Washington audience: 'The extraordinarily favourable tax treatment encourages speculators to buy and hold land, and retards their releasing it to developers and builders, whose income is fully taxable at ordinary rates'.[14] After Katrina, the biggest losers in New Orleans would be victimised a second time: excluded from their homes by the land speculators.

There are worse things than the wrath of nature. Katrina was unforgiving, but the state's abuse of power is unforgivable. Evidence of how it manipulates taxation to terrorise people was documented in the US Senate by William V. Roth, Jr., a Republican who represented Delaware and who, at the time, was chairman of the Senate Finance Committee (see Box 12:1). Here, in black and white, was an account of the perpetual civil war waged by the state against citizens. Witnesses testified to the abuse of power which challenged the official doctrines on which the Anglo-American model of society rested.

12.3 The Anglo-American Model Challenged

TERRORISTS LIKE Osama Bin Laden cast their critiques of the West in terms of strident cultural preferences and the blasphemous invocation of God to justify mass murder. The Anglo-American response was advocacy of the formal trappings of democracy. There was no meeting of minds in

Box 12:1 The State as Enemy of the People

WHEN ITS REVENUE is at risk, the state becomes an instrument of tyranny. That contention is consistent with the evidence that was documented in US Congressional Hearings chaired by William V. Roth, Jr.

The taxmen of the Internal Revenue Service (IRS) were rewarded with cash for their assault on the innocent and 'to feed the insatiable demands of Washington for revenue and more efficiency'.[1] People were driven to commit suicide to escape the abuse of state power. With an 83% compliance rate in the payment of taxes – the lowest in recent history – emergency measures were taken against dodgers. Fear was used as a tool by the IRS, for 'Fear leads to submission. Frightened Americans will more readily pay their taxes.'

The Roth hearings showed that the 'bribery, embezzlement, influence peddling, and rampant conflict of interest' which had been documented by Congress in the 1950s had continued unrestrained by the rule of law up to the end of the century. The lack of accountability within the IRS 'facilitated the abuse of power and denial of due process for taxpayers'.

> Many innocent taxpayers, denied due process and living lives on the edge of financial ruin, were forced and even bullied into paying more taxes than they owed, and the perpetrators of this abuse were being promoted, given cash awards, and allowed to carry on within a federal agency that is shrouded in more secrecy than the CIA.[2]

Errors were concealed through the use of intimidation that would have earned the admiration of Don Corleone. Senator Roth documented abuses such as "wrongful enforcement procedures, unaccountable managers with near-absolute power to ravage employees, an informal policy of omerta that results in threats and retaliation against those courageous enough to come forward".[3]

1 William V. Roth Jr. & William H. Nixon, *The Power to Destroy*, New York: Atlantic Monthly Press, 1999, p.120.
2 *Ibid.*, p.9.
3 *Ibid.*, p.120.

Box 12:2 People Property Rights?

ORIGINALLY, the enslavement of Africans and their sale to plantation owners in the New World was so inoffensive that this property right was exercised by the Church of England. The church did not perceive a tension between its pulpit theology and the revenue that flowed into its purse.

So confident was the church in the righteousness of its behaviour that the Society for the Propagation of the Gospel in Foreign Parts branded its slaves on the chest with the word SOCIETY to proclaim their property rights.

When slavery was abolished, and Parliament voted to pay compensation to former owners out of taxpayers' money, the church received £8,823 8s 9d for the loss of slave labour on its plantation in Barbados.

The abolition of slavery was the result of a major shift in the collective consciousness of British society. The nation's attitudes were upturned and property rights were negated. The attack on those private property rights did not inaugurate the end of the world.

this Clash of Cultures, so the mutual hostility of the fundamentalisms trapped the innocents in a process of violence.

The challenge to the Anglo-American model, however, is not confined to Muslim extremists. Within the West, the nations of the Enlightenment disagree over the direction that social evolution should take. This is an impasse that cannot be tolerated indefinitely, now, thanks to the intervention of China and India in the global market. For without a rescue plan, the cumulative weight of deprivation among the peoples on the peripheries of the West will drag everyone else down with them. Europe and North America have two choices. They either support the marginal regions with policies that would enable them to fund their way into the future out of the rents which they generate. Or they cut adrift the peripheral regions, which in Europe includes vast areas along the Mediterranean coastline, so that the core cities, those with the highest productivity, can operate as adjuncts to the new centre of industrial gravity in the East.

Few people would choose the second option. And yet, the first choice brings with it the anxieties associated with change. But the history of

Europe and America over the past 500 years has been a continuous medley of social experiments. The great reforms included radical changes to perceptions of moral standards and the way in which these required amendments to property rights. Americans would empathise with such an agenda, for they celebrate the association of their civil war with the notion of 'the land of the free' for African and well as European Americans (see Box 12:2).

In the labour market, the abolition of taxes that destroyed jobs would transform life at the margin and consolidate the values of the New World, based on the independence of the individual in the face of the adversities of nature. We can test this claim by comparing resource-poor countries – those that are traditionally assumed to be marginal locations – with resource-rich territories. Intuitively, we would expect resource-rich populations to enjoy higher standards of living. That deduction does not follow from the facts, and the reason is of profound significance.

Table 12:1

GDP Per Capita
(2004)

	GDP/per capita ($)	*Government Consumption of GDP (%)*
Norway	39,259	22
Japan	39,941	17.6
UK	26,391	21.3
USA	36,067	15.4

Source: Marc A. Miles, Kim R. Holmes and Mary Anastasia O'Grady, *2006 Index of Economic Freedom*, Washington DC: The Heritage Foundation, 2006.

In the 19th century, during the transition to urban commercial society, the peoples of Norway and Japan managed to retain their rural land rights. This exercised a major influence over the way their societies evolved during the industrialisation of the 20th century. The cultural differences between them were considerable, but they had one thing in common. Their home territories were very poor in the natural resources that were readily available in the UK and USA. But Norway and Japan preserved traditional values based on the ethics of social solidarity. So although they did not possess precious metals and fertile plains, the economic independence enjoyed by people on their family farms and small coastal and rural businesses enabled them to develop a quality of life that came to exceed those in Britain and America. The data on GDP *per capita* (an admittedly insufficient representation of a society's welfare) are shown in Table 12:1.

This comparison alerts us to the reality that the suffering caused by the dispossession of birthrights in land was not a precondition for the emergence of the capitalist economy. How the two resource-poor countries worked their way into the top of the income league by honouring people's rights to land will be the subject of a separate study.[15] The relevance of the comparison for our present problem is this: the restoration of social solidarity is imperative if the Anglo-American model is to adapt to the challenges of the 21st century. The aged and infirm, for example, are vulnerable, with the gains of the last 50 years under threat. Substantial changes in the pension arrangements are unavoidable. The Tax State's solution is to require low-income people to work until they drop dead. Similar challenges are arising in the health sector. Long-term spending in the UK is predicted to increase from 7.2% of national income to 12.7% by 2050. If people want access to the medical care made possible by scientists in their laboratories, they cannot rely on these being delivered by the Tax State.

In the United States, the private pension crisis faced by employers is resulting in the jettisoning of employees' pension plans. Private enterprise is covertly shifting responsibility onto taxpayers. What it distastefully calls Big Government is now being treated by Big Business as the escape route from the pension obligations which it assumed after the Second World War. So what looks like a low rate of tax-take in the US today will escalate to levels closer to other countries under the pressure of populist politics. This will erode the competitiveness of America, adding further stresses to an already overburdened economy which is suffering from record levels of national debt.

The Tax State is rapidly losing its financial viability. Because economic growth is now hostage to consumption funded by debt, in Britain, in 2005 families pushed their debts to £1,158bn. This was over £30bn more than the value of total economic output. The nation reached the point where it was no longer paying its way.

A similar escalation of indebtedness has surfaced in the US. But the national debt, for which the US is dependent on creditors like China, India and Japan, has to be seen in its historical context. We have to go back to the early 1960s to track the trends in wages and salaries.

For households in the bottom half of the income distribution, wages (in inflation-adjusted dollars) have been flat or declining. For those in the top half, and particularly the top 10%, income has escalated into the stratosphere. This is the financial context for investigating the sociological implications of indebtedness.

Stagnant wages have made it increasingly difficult to acquire homes. As the price of real estate escalated, those at the bottom of the income league have been locked deeper into mortgage debt. That debt increased by more than 190% for people in the lowest 20% of incomes, compared with 40% for families in the top 10% income band (between 1989 and 2001). Then there is the difference in the kinds of debt being incurred. Credit card debt is a fraction of the total held by homeowners compared with those who rent their homes. By 2005, total household spending exceeded after-tax income for the first time since the Great Depression. Americans were dis-saving, eating into the seed corn (to use one of their favourite agricultural analogies).

The financial pain, however, was cushioned for one class of indebted household: the owners of real estate. With property prices rising rapidly, owners were able to borrow to spend. But this has increased the fragility of family finances. For over the 25 years to 2005, despite rising prices, the percentage of the value of homes that families own has plummeted (from 67% in 1979 to 56% in 2004).[16] The extraction of equity bequeaths a multi-dimensional crisis. First, families are getting deeper into debt and exposed to the day of reckoning when China pulls the financial plug and interest rates rise. But, secondly, the upward drive in property prices is transferring much of the debt to the next generation of American working families.

Economic growth continued apace, but the rewards were not distributed in a way that left the nation happy. In the 1960s, something started to go seriously wrong. The nation's state of happiness did not improve alongside the aggregate increase in material prosperity. Why? Was this not offensive to the constitution of America?

12.4 Happiness: a Constitutional Right?

THE NATURAL right to possess property was affirmed by John Locke (1632-1704). His version of the social contract contained the memorable restatement of the right to *life, liberty and estate*. The word *estate* was the old English term for land. Locke argued that we all enjoyed the natural right to possess land, which was freely provided by nature. He explained in *Second Treatise on Civil Government* (1690) that government was obliged to secure the practical means by which this could be delivered.

Locke's treatise was an embarrassment to the feudal rent-appropriators. How could the noblemen of the kingdom justify the accumulation of vast estates by dispossessing others of their natural birthright? The patricians of the New World solved that conundrum. Even though they claimed to base their Declaration of Independence on the doctrines of the English philosopher, they dropped one of Locke's natural rights. They swapped the right to land for the right to pursue happiness. Everyone in the 'land of the free' enjoyed the right to 'life, liberty and the pursuit of happiness'. Little thought was given to how this right to happiness could be squared with the mal-distribution of land to a privileged minority.

Box 12:3 The Price of Sunny Smiles

SUNNY CALIFORNIA puts on a smile for the rest of the world, but much unhappiness lurks in the margins of that society. We can trace the workaday misery at the Mexican border, which day labourers cross at dawn to pick carrots and cabbages from the fields for $7.25 an hour (50¢ more than the minimum wage in 2006).

The work is long and hard, but better than employment prospects in Mexicali. But American farmers in Calexico are being tempted by richer pickings, thanks to the US government's tax code. Because of the privileged treatment of real estate, house prices 120 miles away in San Diego are unaffordable to many people. So farmland is being sold in Calexico for residential development, with houses sold to commuters for $400,000.

Farmland owners are pressured from above and below. From above, they face the overwhelming bargaining power of a market dominated by the purchasing power of five giant supermarket chains. From below, they are tempted by the ripples of riches from San Diego's real estate market. This complicates life for the Mexican day workers who now have to compete with the wage costs of farm hands picking vegetables in deepest China.

The implications of the interaction of these forces for the US food sector were expressed by the Western Growers Association: 'Our industry is going to rely on a foreign workforce. It's only a question of whether that workforce harvests crops in this country or in another country and builds up the economy of that country.'*

For San Diego's commuting employees, the long drive to and from the office exacts a price in family happiness.

* Dan Glaister, 'US crops left to rot as Mexicans leave the fields for better-paid jobs', *The Guardian*, February 4, 2006.

The spirit of Locke's thesis was written into the constitutions of some of the states, including California's. But a right is meaningless if it cannot be enforced. How can a marginalised person in the United States seek to enforce his or her right to the pursuit of happiness in a Supreme Court? It is not in the gift of the legal system to ensure a person's happiness, or to determine the means by which that happiness can be pursued in each case.

About 37m people are classified as poor in America, the blacks in the urban ghettos and the whites in the suburban trailer parks. It is reasonable to assume that many of them are involuntarily unhappy, but even if they could prove this, a court could not apply sanctions against others to ensure restitution.

Unhappiness on a socially significant scale is ingrained into the rich nations of the West. The scale of discontent is evident in our neighbourhoods. An obvious case is the stress associated with people's working lives. Family lifestyles are sacrificed as they work longer hours to make ends meet. This means less sleep than is needed, leading to physical and psychological deprivation.[17] Forced to commute long distances to work – by the need to move to locations where house prices are affordable – people skip meals (see Box 12:3). And so, even while medical science has learnt how to extend lives, the quality of life atrophies.

Does the proposal for tax reform address the problem of happiness? Discontent is heavily determined by the financial distance between the rich and the poor. In societies where the gap is relatively narrow, empirical research shows that the populations are relatively content. Happiness is not a function of the absolute level of prosperity. The United States, as the richest nation on earth, is also one of the unhappiest. The evidence was documented by Richard Layard.

Graph 12:3

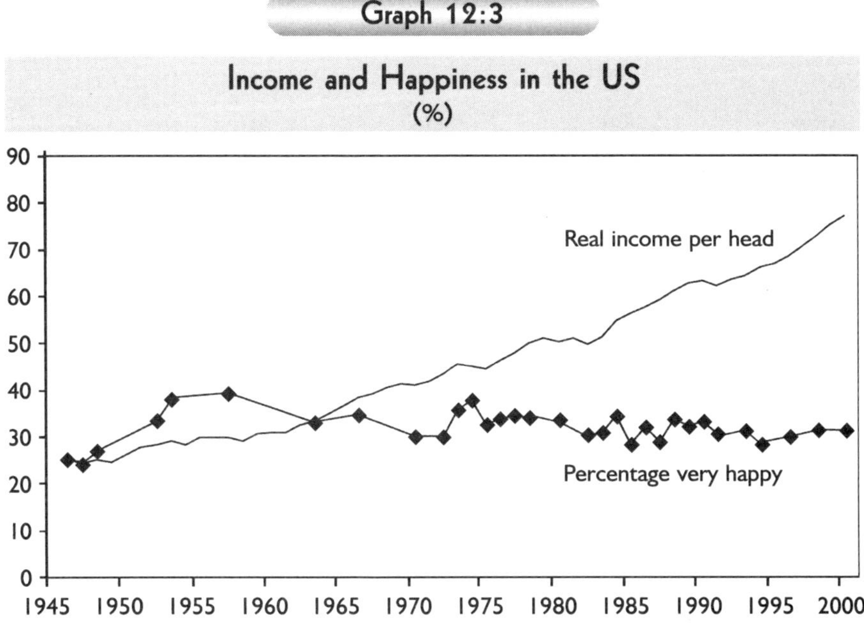

Source: Richard Layard, *Happiness*, London: Allen Lane, 2005, p.30.

Graph 12:3 tracks the growth of income in the US since 1945 and the index of happiness as reported in the General Social Survey. In general terms, there has been no increase in happiness since 1960. This confirms the common sense view affirmed by surveys which conclude that 'there appears to be little income-induced increase in life satisfaction once one's family income rises above the median income'.[18] But while happiness levelled off in the United States, it has risen in Europe where income *per capita* is significantly lower. How do we account for the disparity, and what can be done about it?

Layard is an influential academic whose work on unemployment and inequality helped to shape the Blair government's policies. His prominence as a policy advisor earned him a peerage. Startlingly, Layard concludes that we should impose *higher* taxes on people to persuade them to work less. And the data, if taken at face value, appears to support his shocking recommendation. In Table 12:2 we compare four countries where the hours spent at work vary by a considerable margin.

Table 12:2

Selected Quality-of-Life Indicators

	Hours worked in the Year (Full-time workers, 2002)[1]	*GDP per capita*[2]	*Top income tax rate (%)*	*Home ownership rates (%)*
USA	2,000	36,067	35	70
UK	1,990	26,391	40	71
France	1,660	22,723	48.1	55
Germany	1,650	23,002	44.3	40[3]/43

Sources: 1 Richard Layard, *Happiness*, London: Allen Lane, 2005, p.50.
2 Tax rates and GDP derived from Marc A. Miles, Kim R. Holmes and Mary Anastasia O'Grady, *2006 Index of Economic Freedom*, Washington, DC: The Heritage Foundation, 2006.
3 Owner-occupied housing for the Federal Republic in 1988.

Americans work 350 hours more, on average, than German workers. During the year, Germans enjoy 43 days of leisure more than Americans. British workers invest up to 42 days more in work than their continental partners. These extra days are reflected in the higher GDP *per capita*. And yet ... French and German workers enjoy their vacations and the quality of their lifestyles in general. They *expect* high quality public services. And from their vocal opposition and street protests against Anglo-American 'neo-liberal reforms', it is clear that they are reluctant to swap their social model for one that is underpinned by tediously long working hours.

We cannot be dogmatic in deciphering the meaning behind the statistics. Some generalisations are defensible, however. It does appear that continental Europeans do want more of their services delivered through the public sector, compared with Americans. And the Europeans are less discontent with taxation than their English-speaking cousins. But is it the higher tax rates in Europe that encourages workers to seek an escape from work through leisure? That is the logic of Layard's analysis.

> Taxes are clearly performing some useful function, beyond that of raising money to pay for public expenditure: they are holding us back from an even more fevered way of life.[19]

His recommendation – that we increase happiness by increasing taxes on incomes – is counter-intuitive. People would say that the reverse is consistent with common sense: if they were not taxed so heavily, they could afford to buy the things they need without having to work so hard. But in Layard's view, workers in Britain and America – who are subject to lower tax rates – suffer from 'addiction' to work. And since we deal with addictive expenditures – such as tobacco – by taxing them, the way to adjust the life/work balance is to reduce living standards by raising taxes on those who go to work!

To justify his prescriptions, Layard is obliged to challenge the traditional treatment of taxes as injurious. He does acknowledge that '£1 collected in tax actually hurts more than the simple loss of £1 – the difference being called the 'excess burden' of the tax. This makes taxes harder to justify'.[20] But he transforms the negative qualities of taxation. For by defining work as an addiction, a tax that deters people from going to work is transformed into something good, and the losses associated with taxation become acceptable.

Our competing thesis is consistent with reality. We have to factor in the impact of the real estate market. The reason why people are coerced into working harder is not just because of tax rates, but because of the distortions caused by the character of the taxes used by government. One impact is the unaffordability of houses, which forces (for example) mothers to work when they might prefer to devote their lives to nurturing their children. The result emerges in social surveys, such as the one which reported on the effects of the long hours worked by UK employees compared with their fellow citizens in the EU. With people in the UK having the longest working hours in Europe, more than one third of British men rely on alcohol to relieve the stress from overworking. Notably, men who found it most difficult to switch off from work had careers in property, with 52% saying it was hard to stop thinking about the job. Overall, more than 25% of men suffer from exhaustion through stress. According to Cary Cooper, Professor of Organisational Psychology and Health at Lancaster University: 'Employees are more autocratically managed and are intrinsically more insecure. These changing patterns of work seem to be having a negative effect on men's health'.[21]

But if raising the tax rate is at odds with reality, a solution to discontent is not to be found in merely lowering the rate of taxes. For lower taxes tend to be offset by a rise in land prices. Land prices are higher in the relatively low-tax Anglo-American countries compared with those in Germany, where people work the fewest hours and a larger percentage of the population lives in rented accommodation. German workers are not pressured by the burden of mortgages, which sit heavily on the shoulders of British and American employees. It is the two taken together – tax rates and land prices – that have to be weighed in the balance.

Culture plays a major role in the propensity of people to buy or rent their homes. In America, ownership has achieved the status of a cult-like quality, as one *Financial Times* correspondent saw it.[22] Security of possession (such as is provided by leases) rather than freehold tenure was sufficient for the majority of German families. This is reflected in their attitude towards home-owners, who are labelled as *spiessig*, or petit bourgeois.

From the conflicting sentiments over ownership rights spring financial costs that affect psychological health in America, where, in many residential areas, the premium for owning a house is a cost 40% higher than renting the home, according to research by the HSBC bank.[23] Is that extra burden worth it? What is not in doubt is that Americans have to devote more hours to earning money, and devote more time to commuting, to cover the extra costs of owning the freehold to their homes.

By combining the tax and tenure effects we arrive at a rounded assessment of the conditions that determine material prosperity and personal contentment. Superior results are achieved when we diminish the taxes that distort people's freedoms. As for the provision of public services, the best results are achieved when the payments are symmetrically tailored to the services that each of us wants to access from the locations where we want to live or work.

This agenda does not receive attention by governments. Instead, advisors like Lord Layard propose strategies that aggravate society's problems. Raising the tax rate, for example, does not help people to fund their mortgages out of post-tax incomes. Nor does it resolve the problems that flow from the propensity of high income earners to 'shelter' their wealth from taxation through investment in real estate, which consequently widens the gap between rich and poor. To the relatively poor, the robust equation is: Taxes = Unhappiness.

Is this reasoning beyond the comprehension of people like Lord Layard (who is an economist, not a psychologist)? Couldn't Layard have drawn on 'public economics', a sub-discipline of his specialty, to deepen his understanding of the way in which taxation damages people's efforts to achieve happiness? In fact, Layard had studied public economics, and he concluded that it needed to be radically reformed because it 'fails to explain the recent history of human welfare and it ignores some of the key findings of modern psychology'.[24] As evidence, he cited the book by Nobel Prize economist Joseph Stiglitz and his co-author Anthony Atkinson. This was a puzzling piece of evidence in favour of his tax-raising agenda. Can we unravel that puzzle?

In an article published in an academic journal in 1977, Stiglitz explained that it was possible to fund public goods out of land in place of those taxes that damaged economic incentives. And in the volume to which Layard referred, Stiglitz and Atkinson affirmed this tax theorem in which 'rents equal public goods expenditure. This has been dubbed the 'Henry George' theorem, since not only is the land tax non-distortionary, but also it is the 'single tax' required to finance the public good'.[25]

Stiglitz, who has served as Chairman of the President's Council of Economic Advisors and as Chief Economist at the World Bank, took the trouble to affirm the truth of an economic law that has a tradition which links Locke in the 17th century, Adam Smith in the 18th century, J.S. Mill in the 19th century and Alfred Marshall in the 20th century. Stiglitz provided the algebraic proof that confirmed the public policy virtues of rent and he exposed as injurious the taxes favoured by the economic fraternity. Those findings were at variance with Layard's eccentric psychology: '[W]e now know that people would work too hard if taxes were zero'.[26] Therefore, 'much of the addiction to general spending, like the addiction to smoking, is not foreseen. If we are willing to tax addictive substances, we should also be willing to tax other forms of addiction' – like work.[27]

In America, at least, what we will call the Layard theorem – 'raising the tax burden will make people happier' – will probably be put to the test. For if the US government wishes to balance its books by 2040, on present policies it must either *cut* total federal spending by 60% or *raise* federal taxes by 200%. These are projections by David M. Walker, head of the US Government Accountability Office (GAO). Walker is not in the business of exaggerating his forecasts. He warns: 'If America continues on its current course, it's only a matter of time before the ship of state hits the rocks'.[28]

We may assume that people would not want public services cut by 60%, but would they feel happier with a 200% increase in taxes? We know that UK taxpayers would not relish that prospect. One in five of them – nearly 10m adults – have reported that they are considering leaving the country because politicians had failed to deliver tax cuts.[29] Should we be surprised that this evidence contradicts the Layard theorem? If the Anglo-American model of society is to be redeemed, we need to apply economic analysis with greater rigour. Governments and their economic advisers may not like the results, but that is not a problem for the people.

REFERENCES

1 Erik Ekholm, 'Plight Deepens for Black Men, Studies Warn,' *New York Times*, March 20, 2006. The US had the highest percentage of its population in prison in the world.

2 Jonathan Kozol (author of *The Shame of the Nation: The Restoration of Apartheid Schooling in America*, New York: Crown, 2005) claims: 'It's not simply that segregation has returned with a vengeance to public education; it's worse than it's been at any time since 1968.' Interview in *Extra!* March/April 2006, (www.fair.org).

3 Personal communication to author, March 26, 2006. Emphasis added.

4 Mason Gaffney and Richard Noyes, 'The income-stimulating incentives of the property tax', in Fred Harrison, *The Losses of Nations*, London: Othila Press, 1998, p.211, Table 8:IV.

5 John Y. Campbell and João F. Cocco, 'Household risk management and optimal mortgage choice', Harvard University and London Business School Working Paper. April 2003, p.23.

6 Campbell and Cocco illustrate their analysis with a representative house in the UK in 2000 of £81,628. Given average consumption levels at the time, 'an increase in the value of the house by 1% or £816 would lead to an increase in annual consumption of £63, equivalent to 8% of the house price increase'. John Y. Campbell and João F. Cocco, How do house prices affect consumption? Evidence from Micro Data, Harvard Institute of Economic Research Discussion Paper No. 2045, October 2004, p.11.

7 *Ibid.*, p.21.

8 Peter Gosselin, 'On Their Own in Battered New Orleans', *Los Angeles Times*, December 4, 2005.

9 Gaffney recalls Schelling's 5-minute intervention: 'I am not quoting him verbatim, but giving the exact sense of what he said, and repeated several times in several ways. That includes 'bringing the world down in ruins' – or at least that part of the world that moved to land value taxation'. Email to author, March 6, 2006.

10 Mason Gaffney, 'Coordinating Tax Incentives and Public Policy: the Treatment of Land Income', Brookings Institution, May 1969, p.11; on www.masongaffney.org.

11 *Ibid.*, p.1

12 *Ibid.*, p.27

13 Email communication, Nicolaus Tideman to author, May 11, 2006.

14 *Ibid.*, p.12.

15 Fred Harrison, *The Pathology of Capitalism*, forthcoming.

16 Federal Reserve Board, 'Flow of funds accounts of the United States: Historical Data', December 5, 2005 (www.federalreserve.gov/releases/z1/Current/data.htm).

17 Andrew Jack, 'Workers losing sleep to job and family worries', *Financial Times*, February 18, 2006.

18 John F. Helliwell, 'Well-being, social capital and public policy: what's new?' *Economic Journal*, March 2006, p.C38.

19 Richard Layard, *Happiness*, London: Allen Lane, 2005, p.155.

20 *Ibid.*

21 John Carvel, 'Third of men drink to drown out job stress', *The Guardian*, June 8, 2006.

22 Christopher Swann, 'Soaring cost of homes turns spotlight on renting', *Financial Times*, March 3, 2006.

23 *Ibid.*

24 Richard Layard, 'Happiness and public policy: a challenge to the profession', *The Economic Journal*, March 2006, p.C24.

25 Anthony B. Atkinson and Joseph E. Stiglitz, *Lectures on Public Economics*, London: McGraw-Hill, 1980, p.525.

26 Layard, 'Happiness and Public Policy', p. C27.

27 Ibid., p. C29.

28 David M. Walker, Speech, World Future Society Conference, Toronto, July 28, 2006. Walker's data appears in 'Saving Our Future Requires Tough Choices Today', Speech, Atlanta Rotary Club, June 12, 2006. Both speeches are on www.gao.gov.

29 David Cracknell, '10m want to quit "over-taxed" UK', *Sunday Times*, August 27, 2006.

13

The Dis-abling State

13.1 The Aristocratic Coup

STATELESS SOCIETIES existed in the past, and they will probably exist again in the future. So why do we need the state? It is expensive to maintain, so it has to pay its way by serving a function that justifies its costs.

The state is defined by its activity. It evolved to provide people with security and to facilitate the benefits that they could gain from social complexity and an enlarged territory. It served an enabling role. It protected a defined geographical space from external aggressors. In return, the population granted it the monopoly of force to secure safety within its borders. In discharging its obligations, the state acquired its legitimacy.

That legitimacy could persist for so long as the state enabled people to enjoy their lives. But as it happens, the state itself, by the terms of its development over the past five centuries, de-legitimised itself. It did so by undermining the reasons for its existence. Instead of freeing people to optimise the pursuit of their private lives, the state actively obstructed the majority. It is not the champion of 'the common good'. How did this anomalous state of affairs arise?

By its actions, the state creates an economic value which is sufficient for it to pay its way. It is a self-funding institution. It can finance the military and its police and law-enforcing activities out of the value that people are willing to pay for the benefits which they receive from the state. If the state collected that value, it would not need to appropriate the value that people create by their personal activities. But that is not what happened. For even as the state was being established in 16th century Britain, a coup against it was in the making.

It was a coup in the literal sense. The revolutionaries wanted to grab revenue from the public purse, and to do this they had to fashion the state's levers of power to serve their private ends. Parliament was their vehicle for achieving this constitutional coup.

The aristocracy of the late feudal era determined to privatise what Marshall called the public value. In doing so, the feudal class subverted the state. Insofar as the state condoned this action, it undermined its legitimacy. For by allowing the rent of land to be sidelined into the pockets of the barons and knights, the state had to turn to brigandage against the people whom it was supposed to protect. It abused its power, by intruding into people's private lives. In doing so, it circumscribed people's freedoms. Consequently, the general welfare was diminished below its potential. The state lost its legitimacy, and therefore its right to exist.

This process in British history has been neatly summarised by Dominic Hobson in his review of the emergence of the post-feudal aristocracy.

> The Glorious Revolution of 1688 had made them more powerful than the monarchy. The King was subordinated to Parliament, the House of Commons was controlled by the House of Lords, and the executive and legislative arms of the state were exercised almost solely on behalf of the landed interest. Nobody who lacked property could vote, let alone hold public office: membership of the House of Commons was not open to people with landed incomes of less than £600 a year in the shires or £300 a year in the towns. The House of Lords could oppose all but financial legislation, and anyway dominated the House of Commons through a mixture of patronage, bullying and bribery. Some constituencies were uncontested, and the local aristocrat nominated the MP. Where elections were held, the outcome could be fixed by subsidising rents, paying campaign expenses, or bribing or bullying the voters (the ballot was not secret until 1872). As late as 1900 the Marquess of Hastings evicted a tenant who did not vote for his candidate.[1]

For the majority of people, the coup turned the state into a dis-abler. The evidence we have adduced so far appears to support this conjecture. But in the Age of Democracy, why did rational people allow the state to continue on these abusive terms? The answer is that, to complete the execution of their rent-grab, the aristocracy had to bend people's minds. That meant massaging the language of political philosophy to protect privileges that would otherwise outrage a clear-thinking, fair-minded citizenry.

This proposition is offensive to the intelligence of the people who pride themselves in leading the scientific revolution that was concurrent with the emergence of the modern state. But we have to try and visualise the barbaric methods that were used to intimidate the people into quiescence. Recall, for example,

> The ferocious 'Bloody Code' of the 18th century, which greatly increased the number of capital offences, [which] was at bottom no

> more than a determined defence of their property by the aristocracy. Crimes as petty as stealing a sheep carried the death penalty.[2]

By such coercive means – sanctioned by Parliament – the minds of free-born Englishmen were tortured into compliance. But surely people would not tolerate the state's transgressions once the vote had been extended to those who did not own land? And, in particular, surely the radical Left would not have been complicit in the self-serving agenda of the rent-appropriating class?

The tragedy for the working class was that the Left failed to puncture the propaganda. Concepts of social science and the application of common sense were perverted in a way that protected the landed class. The false paths to justice were strewn with signposts that misdirected the energies of reformers. The outcome, today, is that we order our minds in a way that subverts what we are trying to achieve. So incredible is this claim that we need an appreciation of the way the state evolved before we can contemplate the prospect of radically altering the structure of power. The story is one of how the aristocracy devised strategies to divide and rule the people of England.

13.2 Divide and Rule

IN THE 300 years of feudalism after 1066, public expenses were largely funded out of the rents of land.[3] Then something ruptured the integrity of that form of social organisation. We pick up the history at the point where Thomas More (1478-1535) penned *Utopia*, at the juncture in history which saw the beginning of the modern state.[4]

Thomas More was an envoy to Flanders when he wrote a novel about a mythical place he called Utopia. It was published in 1516. Book II was about the new society he visualised, one grounded in the communist principles of a monastery in which everyone lived a virtuous communal life. His critique of English society appears in Book I.

More was a close observer of England, over which he was to preside as Lord Chancellor. He caused one of his characters to condemn the enclosures of the common land on which people had grazed their cattle and raised crops. The commons were being enclosed so that the nobility could expand flocks of sheep. These had grown 'so greedy and fierce that they devour men themselves. They devastate and depopulate fields, houses and towns'.[5]

The displacement of villagers from the commons had a profound social and psychological effect. A proverb at the time held that 'when the fiend finds men idle, he puts in his heart foul thoughts of fleshly filth and other follies'.[6] For the pious, ascetic, hardworking Thomas More, this was a social tragedy that had to be explained. Daringly, he offered a fundamental critique of the state that exposed the ligaments of power. The landowners were fiercely criticised for the way in which they had induced people to turn to crime to relieve their poverty. He recalled how Cornishmen had been slaughtered in 1497 when they marched on London to protest against the rapacious taxation of Henry VII. But it was not just taxes that were tightening the screw on the working people of England.

> There are a great many noblemen who live idly like drones off the labour of others, their tenants whom they bleed white by constantly raising their rents. (This is the only instance of their tight-fistedness, because they are prodigal in everything else, ready to spend their way to the poorhouse.) What's more, these gentry drag around with them a great train of idle servants, who have never learned any trade by which they could make a living.[7]

But on top of this aristocratic edifice sat the monarch. Most kings, wrote More, preferred to pursue war rather than peace, to conquer new territories rather than govern well the lands already within their domain.[8] From this, we can infer two consequences.

- The monarchical state was derelict in its duty to its subjects. People were entitled to efficient stewardship of the public domain (the territory, and the social rights attaching to the land).
- Kings who indulged in foreign wars had to raise large sums of money. That put them in thrall to the aristocracy, who were able to negotiate further limits to the power of the monarch to their advantage.

Thus, the alienation of land, and therefore the rents, rendered the feudal state vulnerable from within. If the monarch could not rely on the natural source of revenue to fund the state's activities, he would be beholden to others; which necessarily imposed limits on sovereign power and therefore on the state. More's king was Henry VIII. Henry rendered himself financially vulnerable. This need not have happened, for the Crown had the right to the feudal obligations of the tenants-in-chief.

The aristocracy, for its part, was also facing a dilemma. The feudal role of the great magnates was being rendered obsolete by the emergence of modern institutions and systems – professional judges on circuit, professional civil servants at court, and an increasingly professional army. The only way for the feudal class to survive was to detach the land (which it held as tenants) from its social obligations. The aristocracy *had* to make a play for rent privatisation if it was to survive as a class. The privatisation of land became the political mission for the nobility and its hangers-on. But this could not be openly declared, for there would have been a reaction both from above (the king) and from below (the common folk of England). A subtle strategy was necessary. This necessitated the erosion of the powers of the state. This goal could be achieved by taking control of the public purse. This would enable them to determine two outcomes. First, they could reduce the Crown's claims on rent. Second, they could determine *how much* money the king could claim, and – more importantly – *how* that money would be raised.

Monarchs and the people, between them, could have secured the future of the nation. Unfortunately for the people, kings and queens failed to deploy the appropriate policies. The first major mistake was made by Henry VIII. He proved his determination as a personality in his wrestling match with Rome and the conscience of Thomas More, whom he beheaded in 1535. But – in terms of his regal obligations to serve his country – he lost his fight with the nobility.

Instead of developing the feudal financial arrangement so that it was fit for the emerging commercial economy, Henry took a short-cut: he grabbed a large slice of the land of England, which had been held by the monasteries. The land grab began in 1536 with the Act for the Suppression of the Lesser Monasteries. This transferred to the Crown all the lands and property of any religious house with an income less than £200 a year. In 1538 religious houses were closed at the rate of 20 a month and the last abbey to surrender, in March 1540, brought the Dissolution to its end. This made him 'the richest king in English history'.[9] The land held by more than 800 monasteries in England and Wales was transferred to the Crown estate, but by the end of Henry's reign two-thirds of it was 'dissipated'.[10] If that land had been husbanded within the public domain, *the rents would have provided in perpetuity all the revenue that the state could need*. The land could have been allocated to private users, in return for the best rents that the market could deliver.[11] And as one guide to the Dissolution commented, if Henry had retained possession of all those estates, the Crown 'would have acquired a very useful permanent endowment which might have released it from financial dependence upon Parliament – and thus altered the whole course of English constitutional history'.[12]

But the nation's territorial patrimony was not husbanded, either by Henry or his successors. We can judge him harshly, for he linked 'the welfare of the realm' with his performance as a monarch, on one occasion challenging the Commons to side with him in a dispute over the passage of an Act of Parliament.[13] The 'welfare of the realm': recall the definition of corruption which we used in the Indictments (pp.9-10). Did Henry act in the best interests of all his subjects to maximise welfare? By this test – *his test* – he was a failure. His abuse of the nation's finances reverberated down the ages. His mishandling of 'the monastic spoils' meant that every English monarch 'was perilously short of funds'.[14] By weakening the revenue base of the state, Henry weakened the monarchy, and thereby weakened that institution's capacity to defend the equal interests of all subjects. In doing so, he played into the hands of the aristocrats. They could drive their rent-seeking agenda deeper into the heart of the parliamentary process, enabling them to exercise ever increasing influence over taxation.

Parliamentarians, in short, connived with the monarch to shape land tenure to suit private ends. Stanford Lehmberg, a University of Minnesota professor of history who spent his life studying the history of Parliaments in the formative decades of the modern state, had no doubt that members of the House of Commons viewed Henry's grab of the land of the monasteries as a looming opportunity. They dutifully consented to his two Acts of Parliament in 1536 and 1539, 'no doubt gleefully enough since many members stood to benefit from this secularisation of land'.[15]

A key figure in the process, an architect of Henry's land grab legislation, was Thomas Cromwell (1485-1540). Regal vanity and bureaucratic venality intersected in his biography. Cromwell was first employed in the suppression of some of the minor monasteries in 1525; and then, with increased industry the suppression of the lesser monasteries in 1536. Cromwell was lord great chamberlain of England, raised to the peerage as the Earl of Essex and enriched with some of the abbey lands that he helped to confiscate. Alas, he did not live long to enjoy the spoils. With the land grab project completed in 1539, Henry ordered him to stand trial as a traitor, and he was beheaded in the Tower of London in 1540.

From Henry VIII to the present day, governments pillaged the landed wealth to fund activities by means that divided the nation. Historian R.H. Tawney summarised the formula developed by Henry and employed all the way through to the Blair government.

> What it did ... was to alienate most of the land almost immediately, and to *spend the capital as income*. For a decade there was a mania of land speculation. Much of the property was bought by needy courtiers at a ridiculously low figure. Much of it passed to sharp business men ...[16]

By the time of Henry's death in 1547, the fate of the modern state was sealed. Opportunities to reverse this fate did recur, but they were not taken. One opportunity came when Parliament challenged the Royalists in the Civil War of the 17th century, which led to the abolition of the monarchy. England became a republic. On what principles would the nation base its governance?

There was a ferment of ideas. The most coherent critique and programme were advanced by James Harrington. In 1656 he published *The Commonwealth of Oceana*, which he dedicated to Oliver Cromwell, the land owner from the fens whose shrewd tactics on the battlefield turned him into England's Strong Man.

Harrington was eminently practical, identifying the felt needs of the people of England. He sensed that the jockeying for power and privilege was not laying the foundations for a future built on something resembling a popular government. In *Oceana*, which he dedicated to the Lord Protector himself, he explained that a balanced society was possible only if the distribution of land rendered it impossible for anyone to abuse power. This entailed the break-up of the large English estates and a legal limit on how much land could be purchased. Harrington's authority was God. His treatise on government identified him as the most original political thinker of his time.

> This kind of law fixing the balance in lands is called agrarian, and was first introduced by God himself, who divided the land of Canaan unto his people by lots, and is of such virtue that, wherever it hath held, that government hath not altered, except by consent; as in that unparalleled example of the people of Israel.[17]

Harrington analysed the rules for sharing land by reference to previous civilisations. When the nobility held half the land, and the people were left with the other half, for example, 'there is no remedy but the one must eat out the other, as the people did the nobility in Athens, and the nobility the people in Rome'.[18] Harrington studied the divine laws on land tenure which included the Jubilee. This entailed (every 50 years) the restoration of land to people who had lost it through indebtedness (Leviticus, Ch 25).

Harrington could read the mood of his England. In a pamphlet published in 1659 he warned that Parliament was not to be trusted to reach a settlement that was good for the people, for it was likely to re-introduce monarchy. But it was not the love of kings that drove the gentry back to the monarchical model. They needed a political formula which protected their estates. Harrington's advice on the diffusion of land to those who had been excluded was at odds with their interests. They were not attracted to Harrington's prescriptions, which included compulsory education; election by ballot of the executive; and an executive drawn from all classes in rotation. Divinely ordained it may have been, but the Oceana model was not inviting to men whose power was contingent on their monopoly of the land. The aristocracy and gentry had established their pre-eminence, and they were not about to yield it to the masses of 'free-born Englishmen'!

The aristocracy – in defence of their class interest – needed to re-establish the legitimacy of the state in a way that enabled them to retain power over the public purse. This entailed the restoration of the monarchy, together with a set of fictions that would be sold as the English constitution. That constitution had to obviate the need for popular government because, as Harrington stressed, popular government entailed the diffusion of land rights. And so, a king in exile was invited to re-occupy the throne, on the understanding that, on money matters, the landed class would determine public policy.

Our account, because of its brevity, has smoothed the edges of a sequence of turbulent events. But our broad-brush canvas is faithful to the thrust of that history, in which the gentry divided and ruled the people of England to advance their cause: the privatisation of public value.

From then on, the aristocracy proved itself shrewd in the manipulation of the laws of the land. It had to respond to events like the agricultural revolution, and Parliament now that it held the whip hand over the raising of revenue had responsibilities that it could not duck. One result was the introduction of the Land Tax in 1692. In principle, this afforded the opportunity to eliminate the taxes that injured enterprise and the wealth of the nation. But the aristocracy had no intention of basing the revenue on the principles of justice. It continued to ensure that the fiscal burden was shifted onto others. In 1732, for example, Horace Walpole re-imposed the salt tax (which fell most heavily on the poor), to avoid having to raise the Land Tax. Walpole 'desired to placate the landed gentry'.[19]

With the onset of the Industrial Revolution, yet another opportunity to restore justice offered itself. In *The Wealth of Nations*, published in 1776, Smith elaborated the principles of a public finance that was fit for the emerging enterprise economy. A cornerstone of his proposals was public charges on rents, which he commended as the 'peculiarly suitable' source of the nation's revenue.[20] Instead, in 1799, Pitt the Younger – a self-declared fan of Smith's – invented the Income Tax.

But the Land Tax still existed, and a mechanism was needed to reduce the burden on rent. In 1798, owners were given the option to redeem the Land Tax by paying the state a price equal to 15 years rent. Within 17 years, one-third of the land was redeemed. The cultural consequences of this fateful fiscal arrangement were not discussed in Parliament. There was little doubt about the economic consequences, however. The rental income of landlords doubled between 1795 and 1815,[21] even as tens of thousands of souls went begging in the kingdom.

The shift in the revenue base pitted the state against the people in a silent war of attrition. A culture of coercion was complemented by the criminalisation of people who, to make ends meet, dodged their tax payments. The government fought back with official snitchers, who were rewarded with half of the revenue that was clawed from the tax dodgers.[22]

And so the uncoupling of land from its natural role as the source of revenue for the state continued apace. In the 19th century, while industrial entrepreneurs relied on the rational approach to book-keeping, the nation's natural wealth was shrouded in mystery: the state failed to maintain a database of land, its ownership and value. This well-served the aristocratic class: the state's bureaucracy seldom attempted to reassess values for tax purposes.

> Some land, particularly that which underwent enclosure, rose in value during the period covered by the assessments; yet there was no corresponding rise in the amount of tax paid on such land.[22]

By under-assessing the value of land, owners were relieved of their fiscal obligations and the burden was shifted further on to people who laboured. The under-assessment of property values continues to this day.

13.3 Of Leakages and Losses

THE SCALE of the state's dis-abling policies can be assessed in both quantitative and qualitative terms. We shall begin our analysis with some historical insights.

There is no mystery about the impact on people's lives, for discrimination was built into the fabric of the nation's financial architecture. To acquire a sense of the pervasive character of this pathological state of affairs, we may step back 200 years to see how the laws were framed to undermine the interests of working people even before Pitt's Income Tax of 1799. Our examples are taken from Thomas Paine's *Rights of Man* (1791).[24]

Paine scathingly attacked the aristocracy for its licentiousness and social insignificance. The only use that the landed interest made of its power '(and which it has always made,) is to ward off taxes from itself, and throw the burthen upon such articles of consumption by which itself would be least affected'. The goal was the shift of taxes onto people's consumption. The nation's finances for 1788 are summarised in Table 13:1.

Table 13:1

Taxes at Michaelmass 1788 (£)

Land Tax	1,950,000
Customs	3,789,274
Excise*	6,751,727
Stamps	1,278,214
Miscellaneous Taxes	1,803,755
Total	15,572,970

* Including old and new malt.

There was logic to the way the aristocracy rigged the taxes, as we can see in the case of beer.

> The tax on beer brewed for sale does not affect the aristocracy, who brew their own beer free of this duty. It falls only on those who have not conveniency or ability to brew, and who must purchase it in small quantities.

Paine was outraged. This tax was an affront to justice. The beer tax alone, from which the aristocracy were exempt, was nearly equal to the revenue from the Land Tax in 1788 – 'a fact not to be paralleled in the histories of revenues'.

The House of Lords, he pointed out, was nothing more than an institution to promote the class interest of landowners. Their mission was to diminish the state's share of the nation's rents, 'The consequence of which has been a constant encrease in the number and wretchedness of the poor, and in the amount of the poor-rates'.

To add insult to their humiliation, the poor were forced to fund those who were pauperised by the Tax State. The Poor Law was rigged to favour the aristocracy. The residences of the aristocracy, 'whether in town or country, are not mixed with the habitations of the poor. They lived apart from distress, and the expense of relieving it. It is in manufacturing towns and labouring villages that those burthens press the heaviest; in many of which it is one class of poor supporting another'.

Little has changed in more than two centuries. The losses in wealth and welfare over those 200 hundred years cannot be quantified. They are even beyond imagination. An abundance of wealth has now been lost in the sluices of time. But we can begin to quantify the amounts which are being lost to us today.

The first shocking statistic is that, over the course of the first nine years of Tony Blair's administrations, Britain lost about £1 trillion in spendable income. It was as if the nation stopped working for one year out of the decade. Somehow, 60m people were supposed to exist without earning for 12 full months. This loss was not voluntary. The population did not decide to take a sabbatical year of leisure. The loss was inflicted by the tax system over which a democratic government presided.

How is the figure computed? It is the British government's own assessment of what it calls 'the distortionary impacts of general taxation on the economy'.[25] The distortion, according to HM Treasury, is equal to 30p in every £1 raised through taxes. On that basis, Britain lost £120bn in wealth and welfare as a result of taxes levied in 2003/04 (£399bn), rising to £138bn in 2005/06.

But we are not surprised to learn that the Treasury's estimates are on the low side. Academic economists assess what they call the deadweight losses at an appreciably higher figure. One estimate goes as high as £2 for every £1 raised by 'bad' taxes.

This is such a grave gap in knowledge that one would have thought a responsible government and its ministry of finance would want to resolve the anomaly. I sought to unravel the puzzle by asking the Treasury for sight of its working papers on deadweight losses – the technical term being 'excess burden'. Astonishingly, I was informed:

> The Treasury does not hold any unpublished studies, working papers or any other documentation on the way excess burden estimates are calculated, as you have suggested. Particularly, it would not be the Treasury's role to calculate these.[26]

The one piece of information that would fascinate the taxpaying public does not exist!

But perhaps there is a good reason for not worrying about deadweight losses? If the Treasury was confident that its 30p/£1 loss was uncontested, there would be no need to refine the 101 different ways of milking the public. But, in fact, the Treasury admits that estimates of deadweight losses 'are not very reliable'. In that case, would it not be worthwhile assigning a project to some of its economists to calculate the damage it inflicts on the economy? After all, the Treasury is foremost in insisting that the other public agencies must deliver value for taxpayers' money. But, as it happens, the Treasury does not feel under such an obligation. It told me:

> Although raising revenue is the primary aim of taxation, the government also has a duty to consider that the taxation system is not wholly neutral, for example, in the context of addressing market failures. How and what is taxed sends clear signals about the economic activities which governments believe should be encouraged and discouraged, and the values they wish to entrench in society.[27]

This is puzzling. The government admits that it is in the business of re-engineering people's lives, and yet it abstains from undertaking the work that would enable it to employ the tax tools that would most efficiently deliver the changes it desires! Can this failure be the result of oversight? If so, the state convicts itself of being derelict in its duty to account for its actions. On the other hand, its reluctance to refine the impact of taxes may be intentional. In that case, the state is confessing a malevolent attitude towards those whom it taxes.

In the end, what is most revealing is what the modern state does *not* tax. Why does that matter? If we worked into our assessment the impact of a public charge on the rent of land and natural resources, we dramatise the injustice of those taxes which are imposed by the state. This is how a leading university teaching manual puts it:

> *[A] tax on rent will lead to no distortions or economic inefficiencies*. Why not? Because a tax on pure economic rent does not change anyone's economic behaviour ... Hence, the economy operates after the tax exactly as it did before the tax – with no distortions or inefficiencies arising as a result of the tax.[28]

A taxpayer, armed with this knowledge, might ask his MP: 'Why do you impose taxes on us which damage the economy when you could raise revenue in a way that does not distort people's behaviour?'

Once we ask such uncomfortable questions, the audit of losses caused by the state becomes exceedingly embarrassing. New anomalies come to the surface. For example, the current tax regime distorts the land market.

Property is underused within towns, and capital is wasted in the provision of infrastructure on the sprawling urban edges. If we computed the losses that stem from this misallocation of land and capital, the Treasury's estimate of deadweight losses is dwarfed. This new estimate of losses is based on a vision of what the economy *could* be, given existing knowledge and technologies. Our exercise is not utopian. As the Treasury readily admits, it is in the business of affecting people's behaviour to achieve its vision of what society ought to be like. Unfortunately, the people themselves are denied the opportunity to participate in that exercise because they are denied the vital information they need on which to base alternative strategies for achieving their personal goals.

To be fair, Tony Blair was one politician who did begin the attempt to visualise a new social framework. But his New Labour project could not struggle out of the linguistic bonds that shaped the Welfare State. His government was trapped in the mental landscape that was fashioned to serve the vital interests of a class that would not yield the public space which it had conquered. This proposition can be tested in terms of the purpose of 'progressive' taxation, which was supposed to narrow the gap between the rich and the poor. This did not happen. When Margaret Thatcher was elected as Prime Minister in 1979, almost 6% of the nation's income went to the top 1% of the population. Twelve years later the share rose to 9% and escalated to more than 13% during Blair's administration. *The socialists,* without intending to do so*, spent 60 years colluding with the rent-seekers to channel the income from the poor to enrich the asset values of the free riders.*

Now, in the 21st century, the question that exercises the Left is: what is the agenda beyond Blair? Blair intuitively understood that coming to terms with market economics was imperative, but he could not formulate the rules that would re-define the relationship between the individual and the state, the public and the private sectors. Labour traditionalists resented the intrusion of notions such as market prices into the delivery of public services. That doctrinal logjam inhibited fresh thinking.

The revisionist tendency on the Left coalesced around the idea that public policy had to 'give people greater control over their lives'. This anodyne declaration was one to which the conservative Right could subscribe. The devil, as ever, was in the detail. The Left hit on a new idea: *the enabling state*.[29] Equality continued to be a guiding principle, along with the demonisation of the free market; but the state would be cast in a new light, not as a centre of stern command but as a benign uncle, the *enabler*.

But theorists of the Left like Patrick Diamond (a former special advisor in the Prime Minister's Policy Unit in Downing Street) failed to identify an operating mechanism that could exercise the power to override the forces that thwarted the honourable aspirations of those who fathered

Box 13:1 Clean Slate Proclamations

THE PRIESTS and princes who provided the leadership for ancient civilisations learnt that survival depended on periodically doing two things. Debts that were accumulated as the result of taxes imposed by the city-states had to be cancelled. This was essential, to restore social stability. (Commercial debts were not cancelled.) And land had to be restored to families who were forced to yield their fields because they could not pay back money they borrowed. This outcome was achieved by what archaeologists call Clean Slate Proclamations.

Mesopotamian kings realised that society was disrupted when land fell into too few hands. Under these conditions, rents were increasingly used for the private benefit of a privileged minority, which gave rise to discontent. So when the failure of governance led to social crisis, a Clean Slate became necessary (and was usually proclaimed at the beginning of a new reign).*

In the Bible, this practice is known as the Jubilee. Debts were cancelled and land was restored to their former owners. Families could be rescued and the lifeblood once again course through their communities.

Clean Slate proclamations were appropriate for the earliest civilisations. Modern nations, however, are more complex in the way wealth is produced. Different techniques are needed to secure the continuous re-balancing of society. Even so, the philosophy of the Clean Slate remains as valid today as it was when people pooled the rent that made possible the creation of the first civilisations among the sand dunes of Mesopotamia.

A shift in the structure of taxation would constitute the modern version of the Clean Slate. The administrative infrastructure has been tried and tested in countries as diverse as New Zealand, South Africa and Denmark.

* Notable studies on ancient Clean Slates are works by Michael Hudson. See his 'Debt Forgiveness and Redemption: Where do the Churches now stand?', *Geophilos*, No. 2 (Autumn 2002); 'Reconstructing the Origins of Interest-Bearing Debt and the Logic of Clean Slates,' in Marc Van De Mieroop and Michael Hudson (eds), *Debt and Economic Renewal in the Ancient Near East*, Bethesda: CDL Press, 2002; 'The Economic Roots of the Jubilee,' *Bible Review* 15 (February 1999); 'Land Monopolization, Fiscal Crises and Clean Slate "Jubilee" Proclamations in Antiquity,' in Michael Hudson, G.J. Miller and Kris Feder, *A Philosophy for a Fair Society*, London: Shepheard-Walwyn, 1994.

the Welfare State. The failures are no longer contested. Socialists created the Welfare State to grind down the class system. And yet, as Diamond conceded, neither educational reform nor draconian income redistribution had modified class inequalities by the time of the arrival of Margaret Thatcher in 1979.[30] The democratic agenda had failed.

But is it feasible to contemplate a Clean Slate proclamation for the 21st century (see Box 13:1)? Such a radical departure would be resisted by those whose fears have been aroused by the myths that shroud the free market. But we must begin the analysis of the new public finance by asking the obvious first question.

13.4 Whose Money is it Anyway?

THE SOCIALIST PROJECT could not succeed because Labour governments were co-opted into accepting the tax system that served the interests of the class that dispossessed the people of the commons. The prospect of shifting to an egalitarian agenda appears to be no better after Blair if we are to believe the words of Gordon Brown. His incumbency of HM Treasury for a record nine years provided him with a unique opportunity to reset the course of fiscal history. But his stewardship of the nation's finances consolidated the injustices of income and wealth distribution. Would there be a turn for the better in a Britain under his leadership as Premier? Brown revealed his political routemap in a lecture in December 2005. The test of the success of a new constitutional settlement would be whether people were liberated to achieve their full potential, he declared. Fairness was a necessary ingredient but the private sector could not be relied on to deliver this on its own. People need 'a good enabling government' to make sure that every child was empowered.[31] But there was nothing in Brown's vision which suggested that the generation into which his first child had just been born had a better chance of a square deal under his Premiership.

His language slotted into the doctrines that had been framed by the Labour ideologists who clung to the belief that education provided the magic wand. Education would be even more important in the post-industrial society because 'In a knowledge-driven economy, access to education and skills is *the* central determinant of life-chances'.[32] What was the evidence to support this notion? Diamond acknowledged that 'Post-war socialists believe that educational reform would create a world of equal opportunities for all'. But the income gap was not narrowed and the class structure was not shaken by the diffusion of educational opportunities during the heyday of the Welfare State.

Brown wished to renegotiate the British constitution in favour of fairness and equality for all. His was a grand vision. He located his agenda in the traditions of British legal history from Magna Carta (1215) through the Bill of Rights (1689) to the Reform Acts of the 19th century. But Brown's version of the evolution of liberty was a caricature. The second millennium was the one in which the common property rights of the people were hijacked. Poverty was institutionalised – and there could be no back-door route to neutralising the power of the land monopolists, no matter how far the ownership rights were diffused in the population, how fragmented the title deeds in favour of a post-primogeniture settlement which protected the vital interests of the rent-privatisers. Brown failed to see through the landlords' agenda, so he was co-opted to serve their interests.

According to Brown, a new social contract entailed the idea of responsibility by everyone for his and her actions.

> The modern British way is of responsibility by all: of new opportunities matched by the obligation of *the unemployed* to work or to learn new skills.[33]

The conservative Right had long urged the unemployed to 'get on their bikes' and find work. This was its coded way of conveying the idea that jobless people were layabouts, the architects of their misfortunes. But why did Gordon Brown choose to illustrate his concept of responsibility with the same example? Unemployment, he had repeatedly insisted in defending his record at the Treasury, was not the most pressing problem in Britain.

If Brown wanted to stress personal responsibility, he should have developed a language fit for a democratised public finance. The key concept is the *obligation to pay for the benefits that one receives*. That is not a Red Revolutionary idea. In our private dealings with others we automatically acknowledge our responsibility to honour our half of the bargain, as when we enter a supermarket to obtain our groceries or when we engage someone to undertake a personal service on our behalf. There is an exchange between the contracting individuals which affirms that we do not expect to receive something for nothing. Why should this rule be suspended for land owners?

The logical way to fund society's infrastructure is not employed because politicians use perverted language and values that serve the interest of the rent-grabbers. This linguistic failure continues to compromise public policy to this day. We may see this by examining the terms on which Gordon Brown planned to raise revenue from developers who are granted planning permission. The words that are employed are designed to deceive.

When planning permission is granted for land to be developed, there is a change in the market price of sites. That increased price could be captured to fund the infrastructure that would give the land its value. The

Treasury decided to consult on the proposal for a charge on that value, calling it a 'planning-gain supplement'. In its consultation document, the Treasury indicated the scale of good fortune that could flow when a farmer secured permission to turn his hayfields into housing estates.

Table 13:2

Land Value per Hectare (£)

	Mixed Agricultural	*Residential*	*Industrial & Warehousing*	*Business (Class B1)*
England	9,287	2,460,000	632,000	749,000
Wales	8,628	2,180,000	280,000	264,000
Scotland	4,858	1,680,000	235,000	588,000

Source: Valuation Office Agency *Property Market Report*, January 2005, cited in HM Treasury, *Planning Gain Supplement: A Consultation*, December 2005, p.7.

The transformation when grazing fields are converted into housing plots is stupendous (see Table 13:2). In England, the uplift (in 2004) was from under £10,000 to nearly £2.5m per hectare! To whom did that value belong? The economic waters get muddied by the official language.

According to the Treasury and the Office of the Deputy Prime Minister (which was then responsible for land use) this added wealth is 'created by the planning system'.[34] If so, surely the value belonged to the community which, through its planning authority, granted the permission? But that characterisation is economically false; and so it should not be relied upon to justify the ownership of the public value.

The value of land is a measure of the productivity of the economy. The value attaching to a particular location is the price that people are willing to pay for all the benefits they assign to that location. That value is arrived at as a result of the demand by people who wish to use the site for residential, industrial or commercial purposes. If there was no demand for such use, the grant of planning permission to develop it would not make a single penny's difference to the value of that plot (see Box 13:2).

Unpicking the source of land's value matters. Ownership rights are at stake. Whoever creates wealth has the first and best claim to it. But this principle is an affront to the doctrines of the Treasury. It holds that Planning Gain Supplement 'should only capture a modest portion of the uplift'.[35] Why, if the community creates value, through investments by its public agencies, should the state settle for just a modest portion of the value? When you or I go to work, we do not expect to settle for just a

Box 13:2 The Siberian Plot

IF YOU were offered, as a free gift, 2,000 square metres of land in the south London borough of Southwark, or 20 square miles of land in the middle of Siberia, which would you choose? Your decision would be based on which plot of land was the most valuable. Assuming that there are no gold or diamond deposits under the land in Siberia, you would choose the site on the south bank of the Thames. Why? Because that is where people want to live and work.

What if the Siberian authorities tried to lure you with the added attraction of planning permission to develop their land? If you invest your capital, you can build as many 26-floor skyscrapers as you like on top of the permafrost. If you are rational, you would still resist that tempting offer: the mere grant of planning permission does nothing to change the value of the land. The grant of planning permission frees people to realise the latent market value. That value is inherent in the land irrespective of the planning system.

Few people want to live in Siberia. They did so in the Soviet Union because they were press-ganged by the state into doing so. Many of the Soviet settlements were 'closed'. Ostensibly, this was to keep Western spies out. In practice, it was to keep residents locked in.

In Southwark, 1 square foot of land beneath an office building of five storeys commanded a purchase price of £400 in 2006. But there was a growing demand from people who wanted to work within walking distance of the stations at Southwark and London Bridge. The demands for commercial space between Tower Bridge and Blackfriars Road rose to the point where investors priced a square foot at £1,200 beneath a skyscraper of 26 floors.

Planning permission does not create that value. It is the presence of people, and their preferences for work and leisure, which gives value to the locations in Southwark.

'modest portion' of our wages. When people invest their money in the shares of an enterprise, they do not settle for a 'modest portion' of the dividends which their investments generate. Why should the community, through its institutions, deny itself the full value of what is its by right?

But Brown and his colleagues decline to engage in debate on the fundamental questions concerning the justice of income distribution. Instead, they rely on rhetoric to persuade us that the issue is resolved in 'a principled approach to funding the infrastructure that makes growth possible and acceptable'.[36] Where is the principled approach to funding highways and schools out of taxpayers' money when the net gains are handed as windfall fortunes to a few people who do nothing, by their labour or entrepreneurship, to create it?

For the Tax State, fairness is sacrificed at the altar of expediency. The Planning Gain Supplement, we are assured, 'can be levied efficiently on this uplift'.[37] But the only way in which a tax on development land would not obstruct development is if the rate is so low that owners are indifferent to paying it. In other words, the government of the people was reconciled to setting its revenue policy to accommodate the attitudes of land owners!

But wasn't the Treasury under Gordon Brown's stewardship being realistic? Capturing a modest portion of the uplift was necessary, it declared, 'thereby preserving incentives to develop'.[38] This argument is also employed by the construction industry for reasons that are easy to understand. Developers make a large part of their profits out of hoarding and speculating in land. An example is provided by Persimmon, which became Britain's largest and most successful house builder by outperforming its rivals. In analysing that company's success, *Financial Times* reporter Lucy Smy wrote:

> Persimmon is good at buying land without planning permission at low prices and accurately predicting that it will be granted permission when local plans change.[39]

We should not be surprised at this astuteness. The founder of Persimmon, Duncan Davidson, the grandson of the 15th Duke of Norfolk, was a pageboy at the Queen's coronation at the age of nine. But primogeniture did not favour his blood-line, so he had to work his way into the position of a successful businessman who owned 20,000 acres in Northumberland.[40]

The Treasury believed that the development industry would go on strike if more than a modest part of the uplift in land values was captured. This expectation was prudent, for land speculators know how to defend their interests. One of them emphatically pronounced on the Planning Gain Supplement: 'We will object to it violently if the government goes ahead'.[41]

But if we accept the Treasury's economic logic, we are faced with the incredible claim that, if every penny of the value of land was used to fund infrastructure, no profits would be made from piling brick upon brick as houses and office blocks. If this were correct, it means that the building industry is a philanthropic institution in which investors lock up massive amounts of capital without making a profit. If so, this would be a unique sector of the capitalist economy!

In fact, the British government knows that development would take place even when construction firms made not a penny out of land. Britain, as a colonial power, administered such a system in Hong Kong for 150 years. There, to this day, construction takes place on publicly-owned land. When the land is released for use, developers bid at auctions to acquire the land use rights. They then erect buildings for commercial and residential use, and it is from this entrepreneurial activity that they derive acceptable profits.[42]

The policy failures of the British Treasury were all the more poignant because nurses, teachers and policemen were harangued into delivering full value in return for taxpayers' money. And yet, the Treasury's policies deliver waste wantonly on an epic scale.

The Tax State is a dis-abling state. A new financial architecture is needed, one that can improve everyone's life. Our proposals (as set out in Part IV) are not aimed at redistributing life chances from the top down. We need to elevate lives, from the bottom up. The problem is to identify a mechanism which preserves the freedom for people to move through the community spatially and vertically up the income scales, while protecting the equal rights of everyone else. What, in particular, does this entail in relation to the divisions that now originate in the classroom?

If people want to pay more to locate near high performing schools, the location values – *the public value* – should go into the public purse and contribute towards the improvement of under-performing schools. The institutional arrangements may vary according to people's preferences. One size does not fit all. So, for example, if the location premium was retained by the local school, as the result of working through municipal institutions, the school would need less funding from the central exchequer. This would free more taxpayers' money to be directed at schools whose academic achievements need to be raised.

But whatever the institutional variations, a society that wishes to honour the norms of justice cannot remain aloof from the way in which public values are deployed.

REFERENCES

1 Dominic Hobson, *The National Wealth: Who Gets What in Britain*, London: HarperCollins, 1999, p.71.
2 *Ibid.*, p.72.
3 The evolution of feudal laws and institutions was succinctly traced by Kenneth Jupp, a judge in the English high court, in *Stealing our Land* (London: Othila Press, 1997), a history that was ruptured by what he called 'A Plague of Beggars in Merrie England' (Ch. 9).
4 The political crisis in the 1530s was resolved with a clear rejection of papal authority and the creation of the English nation state. Alan G.R. Smith, *The Emergence of a Nation State: The Commonwealth of England 1529-1660*, London: Longman, 1984, p.17.
5 Thomas More, *Utopia* (1516); Cambridge: Cambridge University Press, 1989, pp.18-19.
6 Richard Marius, *Thomas More*, London: Phoenix, 1999, p.165.
7 More, *op. cit.*, pp.16-17.
8 *Ibid.*, p.155.
9 Joel Hurstfield, *The Illusion of Power*, London: Athlone Press, 1979, p.15.
10 *Ibid.*
11 One proposal was that some of the monastic land rents could have been used to establish an embryonic University of London, but 'that vision ... was too remote from the harsh realities of Henrician England'. Hurstfield, *Freedom, Corruption and Government*, *op. cit.*, p.179.
12 *Dissolution of the Monasteries*, Andover: Pitkin Pictorials, 1993, p.19.
13 Hurstfield, *The Historian as Moralist*, *op. cit.*, p.31.
14 Hurstfield, *The Illusion of Power, op. cit.*, p.25.
15 Stanford E. Lehmberg, *The Later Parliaments of Henry VIII 1536-1547*, Cambridge: Cambridge University Press, 1977, p.64. The main opposition was concentrated in the North, in what became known as the Pilgrimage of Grace. Most of the discontent was coded in the form of prophecies, with Bede as one of the cited authorities. Henry was ruthless in his response. Up to 200 people were executed for their part in the rebellion. Sharon L. Jansen, *Political Protest and Prophecy Under Henry VIII*, Woodbridge: The Boydell Press, 1991.
16 R.H. Tawney, *Religion and the Rise of Capitalism* (1926), London: Penguin, 1990, p.144. Emphasis added.
17 James Harrington, *The Commonwealth of Oceana* and *A System of Politics* (J.G.A. Pocock, ed), Cambridge: Cambridge University Press, 1992, p.13.
18 *Ibid.*, p.12.
19 C.R. Fay, *Great Britain from Adam Smith to the Present Day*, London: Longmans, Green, 5th edn., 1950, p.29.
20 The importance of land taxation to Adam Smith's theory of governance is explored in Ch. 5 of *Wheels of Fortune*, *op. cit.* (www.iea.org.uk).
21 Marshall, *Principles, op. cit.*, p.766, n.2.
22 The state's mobilisation of snitchers to protect the flow of revenue was refreshed in February 2006, this time with the aid of TV commercials inviting people to inform on their neighbours or the friends with whom they socialised in pubs. Britain's 'black economy' was estimated to be worth £75bn a year. The Chairman of Revenue and Customs (Sir David Varney) was quoted as condemning people 'who refuse to pay their way' (Rupert Jones, 'Shop your neighbour, tax-dodging ad urges', *The Guardian*, February 28, 2006). The sleuths who were searching for the missing millions in public revenue were not instructed to estimate the losses that were pocketed by the free riders.
23 H.G. Hunt, 'Land Tax assessments', *History*, Vol. LII (176), 1967, pp.285-6.
24 Thomas Paine, *Rights of Man, Common Sense, and Other Political Writings* (Edited with an introduction by Mark Philp), Oxford: Oxford University Press, 1995. The quotations and data are taken from Ch. V, Pt 2.

25 Department for Transport, 'Guidance on value for money', London: Department for Transport, 2004, para. 13.
26 Email to present author from John Adams, Correspondence Manager, HM Treasury, June 13, 2005.
27 *Ibid.*
28 Paul Samuelson and W.D. Nordhaus, *Economics*, 12th edn, New York: McGraw-Hill, 1985, p.605. Emphasis in original.
29 Patrick Diamond, *Equality Now: The Future of Revisionism*, London: Fabian Society, 2005, p.24.
30 *Ibid.*, p.23.
31 Gordon Brown, The Hugo Young Memorial Lecture 2005, London: December 13, 2005.
32 Diamond, *op. cit.*, p.28.
33 Hugo Young Memorial Lecture, *op. cit.*, p.9. Emphasis added.
34 Foreword to *Planning Gain Supplement: A Consultation*, London: HM Treasury/ODPM, p.3, December 2005, signed by John Healey MP, Financial Secretary to the Treasury, and Yvette Cooper MP, Minister for Housing and Planning.
35 *Ibid.*, p.8.
36 *Ibid.*, p.3.
37 *Ibid.*, p.7.
38 *Ibid.*, p.8.
39 Lucy Smy, 'Persimmon cheers while rivals weep', *Financial Times*, December 28, 2005.
40 Topaz Amoore, 'Persimmon's master builder', *Sunday Telegraph*, March 19, 2006. In 2006, Persimmon owned a land bank of 78,000 plots.
41 Jim Pickard, 'St Modwen blasts planning gains tax', *Financial Times*, February 14, 2006.
42 Harrison, *Wheels of Fortune*, pp.87-94. Developers who acquire leases on land owned by the Crown, or aristocratic estates such as the Duke of Westminster's in central London, pay the full ground rent to their landlord; and make their money out of sub-letting the buildings to tenants. There is no evidence to suggest that the dukes of the kingdom are willing to forego their ground-rents for the benefit of property companies.

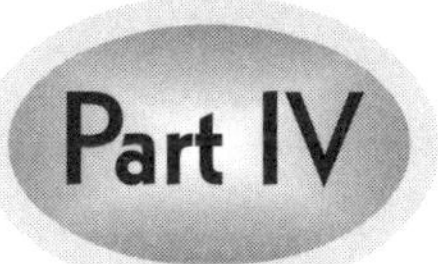

THE NEW FINANCIAL ARCHITECTURE

14

The Economics of Equality

14.1 The Measure of Justice

JUSTICE DOES NOT come in half measures. Either we want it, or we don't. The same stricture applies to efficiency. Ordinarily, a rational person does not plan to be less than efficient. To under-perform is to waste energy wantonly and to deprive oneself of the full satisfaction from accomplishing the task in hand. We see this in sport. When we play, we strive to give of our best. If we shirk, we know that we are cheating ourselves, our team mates and the spectators.

This rule applies to public policy. Rational people who engage in the quest for justice do not deliberately settle for second best. We may have to compromise in the face of insuperable problems; but we work towards the removal of these obstacles in our attempt to achieve the best possible results. But there is one area of life which is the exception to this general behaviour. When attention is turned to the use of land, we compromise as a matter of policy. Time and again we deprive ourselves of the rewards that ought to be ours, by resolutely denying the norms of justice and efficiency. This is a bizarre situation which rational people would not condone if they had an understanding of the behaviour and its implications. The pathological consequences, we believe, would be removed if people insisted on the consistent application of the norms of justice and efficiency in economics, which would encompass decision-making in the land market.

In Chapter 12 we began to explain why tax policy should be at the cutting edge of action that leads to the renewal of communities. The philosophy guiding this agenda is not revolutionary. It is based on the doctrine of the sanctity of the individual as a social being who cannot exist in isolation. We co-operate through the community to improve the fabric of our neighbourhoods because what is good for others is also good for ourselves. The economic rules for achieving this may be summarised by two principles. (1) We should not use the coercive power of the state to appropriate what belongs to the individual. (2) What belongs to us as members of a community should be pooled and divided equally between all of us. How this latter rule is applied may vary, according to the circumstances of time and place; but the principle should not be abused by treating some of us as more equal than others (and therefore entitled to more of the surplus than others). If we adopt these two principles, we redefine the interface between individual and society, and we rescue the state from its disabling proclivities.

Broadly speaking, these were the rules enforced through anthropological timescales. Civilisations broke down when they abused the principles, causing the ruptures that rendered communities unsustainable. Today, we suffer the consequences of the breach of the two rules because, thanks to the resilience of the values that were inculcated into society by the feudal aristocracy, Ricardo's Law was allowed to operate to the detriment of society. We need to re-learn how to synchronise justice with efficiency. This would remove intrusive government from people's private lives. *The primary practical policy for achieving this is the integration of public and private prices into a single mechanism.*

Because we have been co-opted into abusing the rules of best behaviour, the implications of applying the corrective policy come as a shock. John Calverley, the chief economist at the American Express Bank, correctly identified one of them. 'With a 100% land tax the modest cottage in Chelsea would be worth the same as its twin in Glasgow. Ouch!'[1] Are we sincere in our advocacy of justice? If so, we cannot shirk our responsibilities to the people of Glasgow, who are entitled to be treated as the equals of the residents of Chelsea. How this is achieved is the subject to which we now turn. We begin with an examination of exactly what we mean by the value of that 'modest cottage'.

The bricks and mortar invested in a cottage in Chelsea cost no more than a comparable structure in Glasgow. The labour content, the plastics and metals are equal in value, and the buildings depreciate at similar rates. The difference in the value is in the locations. Taken together, the amenities that can be accessed at any location in Chelsea are superior to those enjoyed by the residents of a comparable property in Glasgow. If they paid their way, the fees for the benefits that they received would be equal to the rent of the land they occupy. Newcomers to the Chelsea property market are *willing* to pay for all the services they are about to receive. It is the vendors who do not comply with the rule. For they pocket the value of those services as capital gains from their land. The amount of the value which they currently pocket is the measure of their failure to comply with the principle that we apply in all the other spheres of our lives:

the duty to pay for the benefits that we receive. And this delivers results that are neither efficient nor fair.

But notice that people are not seeking to avoid paying their way. In fact, as newcomers into the Chelsea property market, they *do* pay the full value of the amenities which they are about to receive. The problem, of course, is that they make that payment to the vendor of the property, not the providers of the services (such as the nearby Tube stations) which they want to use.

The outcome is unjust. Is there a good reason why the Glasgow taxpayer who rents his home should help to subsidise the private pleasures and social amenities of the Chelsea set? For that is what he is doing, through the public spending which, in part, gives Chelsea its unique value. Either we are consistent in championing the principles of fairness and efficiency, or we abandon them in favour of a public creed of parasitism. No one will (publicly) endorse the latter, so we need to adopt the policies that remove this virus from the body politic.

The cornerstones of the new fiscal philosophy are:

- *equality* of all citizens under the law of the land; and
- *market economics* as the institutional framework that makes it possible for people to optimise the accomplishment of personal and social goals.

This is a mixture that will bewilder people who have been weaned on the extreme philosophies of socialism or libertarianism. So we need to escape the doctrinal *cul-de-sacs* down which we have been led. Obstacles to comprehension are to be found in the prejudices that have been built into social psychology.

The first tenet with which we are concerned is not generally contested. People agree that we are entitled to own the products of our labour. We work, and we have a clear conscience about asserting our ownership of the fruits of our labours. We may dispose of that value in whatever way we see fit.

Vexatious problems arise when we turn to the property we share as a community. Communists believe that all the means of production – land and capital – should be owned by the state as the steward of the people. Libertarians believe that the state has no claim to property, and any control which it may exercise is grudgingly conceded as a necessary evil. How do we resolve this dispute?

Part of the value created in the community does not belong to any one individual. This becomes apparent, once we understand how this value is jointly created by the co-operative spirit in society. As individuals, we labour to create wealth for our own use. But by participating in the wealth-creating endeavour – that is, by accepting the competitive spirit of free people – we isolate part of our product as the rents that we are willing to

Box 14:1 The Consumer's Surplus

COMPETITION levels unit prices down to marginal costs, which are the costs of delivering the last additional article coming off the conveyor belt in a factory, or the one additional seat provided on a passenger train. Efficient enterprises make a profit out of revenue from these prices after defraying operating costs.

But people are often willing to pay more for a labour service or a manufactured product than its market price. How does this happen? What happens to the additional value, the amount that a prospective customer is willing to pay over the price that he is charged? Economists say that value is 'externalised'.

If a consumer was willing to pay £2 when the price of the product is £1, he enjoys a 'surplus' of £1. 'Good luck to the consumer!' would be our response. When that effect is multiplied by the million, the economic implications are dramatic. We may trace the impact all the way down the pricing chain to the point where the 'surplus' is transformed into the rent of land.

This outcome is the result of downward pressure on prices, which implies an increase in productivity, yielding gains that people can afford to pay as rent for the use of land.*

There are exceptions. One stems from the bargaining power of trades unions. Another relates to workers whose scarce skills command extraordinary remuneration (such as software programmers in the early years of the IT age). Sooner or later, however, these privileges are eroded, and landowners are ready to claim the net benefits generated by cost-cutting progress in the economy.

* Consumer surplus is treated at length in the standard economic textbooks. See, for example, Paul A. Samuelson and William D. Nordhaus, *Economics*, New York: McGraw Hill, 1985, pp.417-19.

pay for the use of nature's resources. No one individual makes a superior contribution – if he does, he is rewarded with higher labour remuneration. And no individual can be excluded from participating in this joint exercise in generating the rents of land. The mere presence of a person adds to the attractions of a community, for the larger the population, the greater the opportunities for profitable enterprise. As populations cluster in communities, so the productivity of the economy increases. People seek to share in those benefits by paying rents to gain access to the location. The technical terms that describe this rent-generating activity are given in Box 14:1.

Thus, through the marketplace, as free individuals we compete to offer our services to employers and consumers. We deliver goods and services, the prices for which are subject to the choices of consumers. On a like for like basis this tends to equalise the wages of labour across the economy. The same principle applies to the products and services available in the retail outlets. As a result of the equalising process, part of the value that we generate is hived off. This value belongs to no one person. Or, put more precisely, since we collectively produce it, that value belongs to us all.

But while that value attaches to land, we have seen that it does not do so as equal amounts on each plot across the country. The land market (meaning, people in free association) is a sophisticated mechanism for distinguishing the attractions of one site relative to another. This does not happen according to some magical formula. People determine the outcome by negotiating the relative values through the deals they strike with each other. They bid for the right to monopolise particular plots. Those with the highest preferences bid the most and earn the right of exclusive possession. The outcome is an elegant distribution of the rental surplus across the economy according to the attributes which give each location its unique qualities. Rents, in other words, are a symmetrical measure of all the benefits and disadvantages associated with each site. They are the price we are willing to pay to access the benefits, after subtracting the sum equal to the perceived disadvantages.

There are no losers in this competitive market – if, as citizens, we exercise our right to a share in the rents. We may be out-bid for the right to occupy a house in Chelsea, where we wanted to live, but the higher price paid by the winner for the right to use the land is pooled for the benefit of all of us. As citizens, we share the public goods that are funded out of the rents of land.

When we combine the three factor markets – for land, labour and capital – we end up with an efficient mechanism for producing wealth. But we achieve our goals, of optimum efficiency and of justice, only when we treat rent as a joint income. The particular institutional arrangements may vary from one community to another, but whatever the details, they should not deliver an unfair advantage to any one person or group. If we compromise on this principle, we dislocate the economy and community (see Box 14:2).

For conventional economists, this is a disturbing conclusion. According to the textbooks, most of the problems in society stem from 'market failure'. The market, apparently, is not up to the job. It obstructs people's aspirations in some fundamental ways. If this is correct, the market is too fragile a mechanism on which to rely for the attainment of justice and

Box 14:2 The Economics of Law and Order

TO REDEFINE people's rights and obligations, we need a comprehensive description of the way rents are formed – and who, or what, is responsible. There are three categories which have claims on this flow of income.

(1) **The state**. It adds to the sum total of surplus income through the provision of (i) law and order, and (ii) infrastructure.

(2) **Individuals-in-community**. The agglomeration of people in urban settlements is the beginning of the critical mass of economic activity that yields enormous gains in productivity.

(3) **Nature**. She does not demand a payment in cash, but someone has to intercede on her behalf if society is to operate efficiently and fairly.

Enforcing these claims is the reason why we need a social contract. Government must be authorised to collect the rents which, as individuals, we would not be able to do on behalf of others.

This leads us to an understanding of public prices. Take the case of the state. It is a primarily rent-creating institution. Its legitimate activities are those that deliver value in the form of rents. Law and order enforced at the borders and within the state's territorial domain are benefits that people desire. These military and civil functions enable people to increase their economic productivity. They are prepared to pay rent for the benefit of living and working within the secure confines of the state's territory. Even the state's non-rental charges are for services which are adjuncts, in the main, to its rent-generating activities. Fees for passports facilitate cross-border movements. Licences and charges regulate mobility within the territory.

If the state confined itself to its business, fewer bureaucratically-administered regulations would be needed, and damaging taxes could be abolished.

prosperity. Is this correct? Or could the doctrine of market failure be a camouflage for the failure of governance?

14.2 Blame It on the Market

SO INGRAINED is the doctrine of market failure that people take it for granted. We need to question the doctrine, which is pernicious in its effects on governance.

If ours is the age of abundance – we can manufacture as many cars as we want, from the cheapest run-around to the extravagantly luxurious – why do we persistently fail to equate demand with supply for those products and services that are attached to land? To blame 'market failure' is peculiar, since we can change the rules that determine the nature of markets. But we fail to do so. Instead, we subordinate ourselves to the corrosive effect of this doctrine. One consequence is echoed on the news bulletins almost daily. When confronted with personal problems, people now tend to seek solutions by asking: 'Why doesn't the government do something about it?' So deep is our state of dependency that we now automatically expect salvation from the paternalism of the state. The state, consequently, expands its functions to the point where it is not able to discharge the functions for which it is responsible, such as the enforcement of law within its territory and order on its borders. The state is now suffering from bureaucratic overload. Laws are multiplied faster than people can understand them, let alone its agents' capacity to enforce them.

This is the logical outcome of official economic practises which are preserved because the role of markets is methodically misrepresented. Scholars and politicians alike condone the vulgarisation of the concept of competition, allowing it to be detached from its twin, co-operation. Yet the market is no more than a rules-based procedure for mediating the competing claims of two or more individuals. But instead of investigating deeper into the causes of discontent (by questioning the rules), we resort to a straw man. We invoke shorthand terms like *laissez faire* to vilify something that is not of us, as individuals, and then ascribing the defects in the caricature to *the market*. We have allowed ourselves to be persuaded that this dysfunctional entity subverts the welfare of the individual, operating on logic of its own, disengaged from the common good. Adam Smith is subtly vilified, his writings trawled for terms like 'the invisible hand' which are taken out of context and ridiculed. The outcome is resignation to the notion of 'market failure'. This is how the authors of a bestselling textbook on economics put it:

> We know that the market sometimes lets us down, that there are 'market failures.' Two of the most important market failures,

> running as themes through this book, are the *absence of perfect competition* and the presence of *externalities*.[2]

But while we can understand why the enemies of the market should adopt this device, we have to accept that the market is also sold short by its friends. This is a puzzle. We are obliged to ask: who gains from the tactic of smearing the market? If we dig deep, might we find that this exercise preserves the monopolistic arrangements associated with land ownership? To test this conjecture, we shall examine the views of a philosopher who is one of the gurus of the free market fraternity.

Friedrich von Hayek (1899-1992) made a dramatic appearance in political philosophy with *The Road to Serfdom* (1944). He was to earn a Nobel Prize for his economics in 1974. Today, he is cited for the stress that he placed on the market pricing mechanism as an information gathering system. In a world of imperfect knowledge, pricing signals enable people to transmit their preferences as efficiently as humanly possible. One of Hayek's starting propositions was that, in an ideal world, each of us would be rewarded for all the benefits that we create; and we would accept personal responsibility for the costs of the damage we inflict on others.

The problem with Hayek's idealisation, however, is that it is *impossible* for the private pricing system to deliver the full value direct to those who create it. Competition, by equalising prices between people and places, denies individuals of some of the value which they create. This value is *externalised* out of the labour and capital markets, *and deposited in the land market*. The same problem applies to some of the costs created by an individual or enterprise: the pricing mechanism in competitive markets cannot *internalise* all of these, to impose the consequences on those who create them. Fortunately, however, the land market provides the institutional mechanism for solving this pricing problem. That it is not allowed to do so, in practise, is not the fault of the market, *per se*, but the social rules that determine the outcomes. To understand the significance of this, we need to take a closer look at the land market.

The land market does not serve the same function as the other markets. In the labour and capital markets, participating individuals are engaged in the value-creating process. But individuals as owners in the land market are anomalies. The rents they claim are a pure transfer of income. There is no *quid pro quo*, no exchange of like for like value. Thus, Hayek's ideal is undermined by the laws of competition which he prescribed as necessary for the market economy (see Box 14:3).

We are led by this analysis to formulate two moral imperatives. (1) People who own the property rights to labour and capital have a shared stake in the rents which, by their co-operation, they help to create. (2) People who own the title deeds to land do not have an equivalent claim

Box 14:3 Whose Failure is it Anyway?

A CURIOUS feature of the doctrinal war of the 20th century – between capitalism and socialism – was the consensus that the market was intrinsically disposed to 'failures'. This was an assumption in the work of F.A. Hayek, a champion of the libertarian Right.

Hayek would make no concession to socialist planning. For him, the private market provided the optimum approach to allocating resources. But, conceded Hayek, there were cases in which the legal arrangements could not ensure efficient outcomes. Ideal outcomes were achieved only when 'the owner benefits from all the useful services rendered by his property and suffers from all the damages caused to others by its use.'*

When it was not possible to make the enjoyment of certain services dependent on the payment of a price, competition and the pricing system are ineffective. Hayek cites the case of damage caused to others by certain uses of property that cannot be effectively charged to the owner of that property.

Resolving such problems was 'a wide and unquestioned field for state activity. In no system that could be rationally defended would the state just do nothing. An effective competitive system needs an intelligently designed and continuously adjusted legal framework as much as any other.'

Hayek acknowledged that there was still much to be done to create 'a suitable framework for the beneficial working of competition'. Oddly, however, one issue was off-limits: a challenge to the legitimacy of private property in land. Abuses associated with the landed privileges of the nobility belonged to a bygone age, and 'to call private property as such, which all can acquire under the same rules, a privilege, because only some succeed in acquiring it, is depriving the word privilege of its meaning'.

The one area where reform was necessary to enhance the pricing system and to enforce his rule on personal responsibility was off-limits as far as Hayek was concerned.

* F.A. Hayek, *The Road to Serfdom* (1944), London: Routledge & Kegan Paul, 1962, pp.28-9, 60.

Box 14:4 Supermarkets Bank on Land

THE FORMAL right to buy land does not compensate for the privileges that flow from its private ownership under the current tax regime. This is illustrated by the UK's retail sector. In May 2006 the Office of Fair Trading (OFT) called in the Competition Commission to conduct an inquiry into the dominance of the four big supermarket chains. Evidence had surfaced that the land banks held by Tesco, Sainsbury, Asda and William Morrison could be a constraint on competition. The OFT's Chief Executive, John Fingleton, said that his "primary concern" related to the land banks as barriers to entry into the retail sector.

Supermarkets steadily increased their share of the market at the expense of 39,000 independent retailers. The corner shops on the nation's high streets were constantly shrinking in number as customers switched to out-of-town superstores with their accommodatingly large car parks.

- The OFT had discovered that 75 sites acquired by one of the big four had been re-sold with a covenant which prevented the buyer using the land for retailing food.
- The big four had purchased, or had options to buy, 468 strategically located sites across the country "which can be used to restrict entry by potential competitors".*

Some sites had been held vacant for up to eight years. This added to urban sprawl and the cost of funding infrastructure which was underused – thereby depriving investment within towns where it was needed.

In the five years up to 2005, 5% of small shopkeepers had gone out of business. It was little comfort for them to know that, legally, they could compete with the Tesco giant to purchase land. They lacked the financial power to compete in the land market, and once covenants had been written into the title deeds, those sites were beyond their reach forever.

* Julia Finch, 'Small shops get chance to fight back', *The Guardian*, March, 10, 2006.

to the rent that is created by others. Insofar as the owner retains any part of rent, he is undermining Hayek's ideal that 'the owner benefits from all the useful services rendered by his property'. The landowner's gain is the labourer's unjust loss.

The land market is the *social collection agency* that assesses the value of land. It facilitates the distribution of rent to those who create it. As it happens, the land market was compromised by the corrupted aristocracy of the late feudal era, whose rent-privatising project was enthusiastically supported by the gentry.[3] But although privatised, rents remain a socially constituted value in the way that wages and the returns to capital are not. Privatisation was not, and cannot be, a process for de-socialisation of value that is collectively generated. Unfortunately, through the failures of social science and the success of propaganda, people like Hayek failed to perceive the social function of the land market. Hayek resorted to a simplistic argument, in which the formal right of everyone to acquire land meant that there was no privilege associated with its ownership. This was an astonishingly naïve treatment of the power that is exercised by those who accumulate land. The right to receive lottery-like windfalls on a regular basis – by virtue of one's name on title deeds – looks like a privilege to most rational people. Likewise, the ability to sidestep the full costs of services delivered to the occupant of a location is also an awesome privilege. These opportunities are not shared by the propertyless. They *are* required to pay the full market price of the locational benefits which they rent.

The privilege of ownership runs deep. An owner can quarantine his assets and deprive people of a finite resource that cannot be replaced by importing land from (say) Outer Mongolia, where it is in surplus supply, to make up the deficit in Central London or downtown New York. If people decline to work, they are replaced by migrants. If the owner of capital destroys his assets on a bonfire, new capital is manufactured or transported from places where it is underused. But the owner whose land is located in places where people need to live and work exercises enormous destructive influence by withdrawing his sites from use, and the loss in that location cannot be replaced. That is privilege with power to the nth degree. An illustration is provided by Britain's Big Four supermarkets which have cornered the retail grocery trade and driven thousands of retailers out of their high street stores (see Box 14:4).

The 'market failure' doctrine is damaging to public welfare, for it shifts attention from root causes to symptoms. It legitimises the panoply of government interventions – regulations, subsidies and taxes – imposed on people and enterprises as surrogates for the remedy that would work.

14.3 Conflating Land with Capital

IF THE information-gathering technique of the market – the role played by prices – is imperfect, as Hayek affirms, why should we expect a more informed performance from government? This conundrum has led political discourse into the endless dialogue of the deaf between the Left and the Right.

The view from the Right is expressed by Philip Booth, the Professor of Insurance and Risk Management at London's City University.

> Government cannot correct market failure because it is itself imperfect. Governments fail. Governments have imperfect information. Governments impose social costs ... as a result of this, it is rare to find intelligent graduates who believe in free markets who do not then go on to say, 'But we need the government to intervene to correct market failures.'[4]

If we cannot rely on the free market to apportion all the risks and the rewards of our labours correctly, and if we cannot secure full compensation by government intervention – because it, too, suffers from imperfect information – politics and economics are left in a shambles. And that, indeed, is the state of economics and public policy today. Politicians will not admit this, of course, but they have perfected the art of self-deception. That is the lesson of history, as Joel Hurstfield noted:

> Politicians are the last people to learn from history, if indeed anyone can. But they understand the processes at work in contemporary politics and they erect elaborate machinery of public relations, supplying the new, vast media of communication and dedicated to burying reality under new illusions of power and virtue.[5]

The irony is that it is the champions of the market economy who have contributed most grievously to the perception that the market keeps failing. Again Hayek illustrates our point, as illustrated by his failure to differentiate between land and capital.[6] By treating land as capital, the unique characteristics of rent as public value are obliterated, and that opens the way to theorising that favours the 'market failure' thesis.

One important difference concerns the long-run trends in the distribution of income. Because land is finite in supply, over time – as populations grow and communities expand on a fixed territorial base – it receives a rising share of the nation's income. Marshall confirmed what the classical economists had written a century earlier. Capital goods can be multiplied without limit, so their share of national income declines over time. In the land market, however, economic growth 'tends on the whole to raise the value of land'.[7]

Another distinguishing characteristic is that the earnings of land 'is a surplus in a sense in which the earnings from other agents are not a surplus ... there is this difference between land and other agents of production, that from a social point of view land yields a permanent surplus, while perishable things made by man do not'.[8] By erasing these differences, Hayek could treat land as if its impact on the economy and society was similar to a reproducible commodity like a car or computer. One result is that Hayekian advocates of the free market fail to champion private enterprise in ways that are convincing to people who are excluded from the riches that do, undoubtedly, flow from the capitalist order. And that, in turn, enables government to sidestep its responsibilities and continue with policies that damage the nation's wealth and welfare.

14.4 The Failures of Governance

ECONOMISTS AND politicians assume that private and public prices must necessarily work as separate categories, wholly distinct like oil and water, rather than combining as a single operating mechanism.

Conceptually, the separation divides society in a literal sense, with profound personal consequences. The psychological effect is to divide us as personalities. Somehow, we are supposed to be both a private individual and, as a separate entity, a socially-engaged person. This separation disintegrates the human personality. In the process, we end up with a system for producing and distributing wealth that works against the grain of human welfare.

The flaws are not with prices in private markets. Cartels have rigged prices in the past, and they would do so again if people dropped their guard. But price-rigging is not the legitimised outcome of an institutional process; rather, it results from the abuse of people's freedom to compete in the offer of goods and services without being constrained by monopolists.

The problem with public prices – the taxes that governments charge – is of a wholly different character. Taxes are crude tools which have nothing to do with matching supply and demand (which includes considerations of social welfare). There is no symmetry between the services provided by public agencies and the payments for the benefits that are distributed, the principal beneficiaries of which are the rich. This failure of governance is the cause of stresses that surface in the economy, but we shall turn, first, to the sociological implications.

The glue that holds a community together is the composite of inherited customs and the formal rules that are enacted from time to time. Conventions and laws support the individual and ensure the integration of everyone in a functional system that facilitates people's needs and aspirations.

We see this at work in traditional societies, where outcasts were people who seriously transgressed their community's conventions. They lost the right to protection and the other benefits associated with membership of, and residence in, the clan's territory. They were literally cast out of the land. This status of the outcast is a key indicator of the difference between our contemporary and pre-modern societies. Today, a person does not have to offend the rules for him or her to be cast out from the mainstream of society. Innocent people are routinely excluded by a process that is sanctioned by law. But in this age of democracy, governments will not acknowledge that our outcasts are the by-product of their laws, let alone the victims of a dysfunctional pricing mechanism. Consequently, exclusion has to be treated as a personal failing that requires corrective action with the aid of paternalistic intervention by the state.

The result is resource-sapping experiments in compensatory action. But the outcasts cannot be rescued, because they are the victims of the state's primary laws. Sticking plaster 'remedies' are necessarily weaker than the fundamental causes of the exclusion. Effective remedies would constitute a direct challenge to the power of the state itself. This cannot be countenanced, and the state is aided by the myths created by social scientists. Among these is Marx. He attributed what is now called 'social exclusion' to the private ownership of capital. Again, ironically, we find the Left in league with the Right in fostering this diagnostic confusion. Hayek, for example, added to the disarray with his analysis of what, in the late 19th century, became known as the Single Tax.

In *Progress and Poverty*, Henry George traced the poverty amidst nature's plenty to the private appropriation of rent. Working with both common sense observation and theory, he concluded that rent was society's natural source of income. But, he stressed, this did not mean the land *per se* should be nationalised. Government need not control the use of land. Wise fiscal policy could be made to work *with* people, harnessing the power of the marketplace for everyone's benefit. As people revealed their preferences – through the rents they were willing to pay for the exclusive use of particular plots – so the public revenue base of the community was voluntarily declared; all that remained was for the community to collect those rents to defray public expenses.

Hayek reviewed this sophisticated model of governance in *The Constitution of Liberty*. He conceded that, if the factual assumptions on which the policy was based were correct, 'the argument for its adoption would be very strong'. But he perceived fatal practical difficulties, so 'we will find in it no solution to any of the problems with which we are concerned'.[9] His pessimism stemmed from a false representation of George's model of property rights and public finance.

Hayek claimed that Henry George's pricing model entailed the transfer of ownership of land to the state. In fact, Henry George stressed that this was not necessary: possessory rights under existing title deeds need not be disturbed. This is how he stated his position:

> I do not propose either to purchase or to confiscate private property in land. The first would be unjust; the second, needless. Let the individuals who now hold it still retain, if they want to, possession of what they are pleased to call *their* land.[10]

Hayek also claimed that it was difficult to break commercial rents down into its components parts, separating that element that was due to the enterprise of the individual owner from the value that arose from communal influences. No such practical problem exists. Most people would recognise how this separation occurs in relation to their own homes. They pay insurance on the value of the bricks and mortar. The premium is for a value that excludes land (which will never be stolen by a thief or burnt down by an arsonist). And in countries like Denmark, Australia and New Zealand, which employ direct charges on land, fiscal authorities have no difficulty in agreeing with owners about the value that is liable to taxation.

The objections raised by Hayek were nebulous. They were calculated to deter the advocates of the free market from examining George's fiscal solution to systemic failures. This helps to explain why libertarians turn their hostility on government without understanding the primary cause of the friction in the economic junction boxes that are the interface between the individual and society.

Once correctly analysed, we are led to a formulation of the pricing system which would unite the Left and the Right in a common understanding of the obstacles that prevent people from realising their dreams. I assert that the state's prices can be integrated with the prices that people use to facilitate their private transactions. This public finance is not hostile to private property. In tracing what this means, in practical terms, we will discover that there need be no conflict between the spirit of competition and people's natural desire to co-operate with others to fulfil their aspirations. If public and private prices were synchronised, the psychological obstacles to political consensus for constructive change evaporate. How this would happen, through the shift in people's behaviour, needs to be carefully articulated. It leads to a new view of the relationship between the individual and the state.

REFERENCES

1 John Calverley, 'Boom Bust: House Prices, Banking and the Depression of 2010', *Economic Affairs*, Vol. 25(4), December 2005, p.90.

2 Paul A. Samuelson and William D. Nordhaus, *Economics*, 12th edn. New York: McGraw Hill, 1985, p.46.

3 Alan G.R. Smith, *The Emergence of a Nation State: The Commonwealth of England 1529-1660*, London: Longman, 1984; see, especially, pp.30, 54, 77, 80, 91, 225 and 260.

4 Philip Booth, '364 economists and economics without prices', in Philip Booth (ed), *Were 364 Economists All Wrong?* London: Institute of Economic Affairs, 2006, p.101.

5 Joel Hurstfield, *The Illusion of Power in Tudor Politics*, London: Athlone Press, 1979, pp.29-30.

6 Marshall (in the 1898 edition of *Principles of Economics*, p.609, n.1) discusses this problem in relation to the Austrian school of economics, of which Hayek was a member.

7 *Ibid.*, p.767. See, also, note 2 on p.766.

8 *Ibid.*, pp.626-7.

9 F.A. Hayek, *The Constitution of Liberty*, London: Routledge & Kegan Paul, 1960, p.353.

10 Henry George, *Progress and Poverty* (1879); New York: Robert Schalkenbach Foundation, 1979, p.405. See also p.367.

15

First Law of Social Dynamics

15.1 The Philosophy of Prices

HUMAN COMMUNITIES emerged 100,000 years ago, as part of a process of colonising the planet. To ensure a successful voyage through time and space, people developed laws that secured their well-being. The deep social fractures in post-industrial society suggest that we have forgotten how to abide by rules that bind societies in ways that deliver protection and prosperity.

To identify the desirable reforms, we shall not rely on people's better natures; nor shall we pre-empt people's preferences by constructing a complicated programme for an ideal society. Rather, we propose a single, simple change in the way that people pay for the goods and services which they want. This, we shall explain, would *automatically* realign behaviour in ways that begins to solve problems that have so far defeated apparently all-powerful governments.

The pricing mechanism that we have inherited from the past is the legacy of a 500-year history of land grabbing. That history is implicit in the way that the current pricing mechanisms operate. These need to be adjusted to comply with the philosophy of an integrated pricing system. Such a mechanism, we claim, would simultaneously deliver behaviour in the best interests of both the individual and the community. The pricing policy that is prescribed by the integration of public and private prices into a single working system constitutes the core of what I call the First Law of Social Dynamics.

The integration of private and public prices into a single mechanism is a fundamental challenge to the cherished beliefs of both the Left and the Right. I advance two propositions that warrant this reform. First, there need be no conflict between private aspirations and all the values and

Box 15:1 The Time for Renewal

WHEN IS an 'old' country entitled to renew itself? Never, according to one argument against tax reform. This claims that the rent-as-public-revenue policy cannot be introduced in an 'advanced' or 'settled' country because it would disturb arrangements to which people had adjusted themselves. This was the contention, for example, of Garrett Hardin, who authored the notion of the 'tragedy of the commons'. Two hundred years ago, he wrote, the rent-revenue policy would have been appropriate as the 'ground rules for the development of the New World'.[1]

But if this is true, we have a dilemma. For if an 'old' country wants to function properly, and with justice, it cannot do so without the policy. That point was well made by Alfred Marshall.

> [F]rom the economic and from the ethical point of view, land must everywhere and always be classed as a thing by itself. And in an old country this distinction is vital for a broad survey of the causes that govern normal value. For the net income derived from the inherent properties of land is a true surplus, it does not directly enter even in the long run into the normal expenses of production.[2]

One of the great truths of economics followed from this, as Marshall reiterated. By collecting rent as 'public value', private enterprise would not be distorted. Even established societies could do without the burden of the deadweight losses that they currently impose on themselves.

1 Quoted in R.V. Andelson (ed), *Commons Without Tragedy*, London: Shepheard-Walwyn, 1991, p.viii.
2 Marshall, *Principles*, *op. cit.*, pp.717, 718.

processes which we associate with the idea of the common good. Second, the major forms of deviant behaviour result *not* from the irrationality of the individual, but from the perversity of public pricing policies.

This suggests the need to start again with a new approach to the pricing mechanism that helps us to produce and distribute wealth. The one important change is the adoption of rents as the prices that people ought to pay for the use of public services. This proposition had been addressed in the past and accepted as correct, in theoretical terms, but brushed aside with the excuse that it is only appropriate for newly established countries. We reject that argument on two grounds. First, even old countries are entitled to renew themselves (see Box 15:1). Second, the abolition of injustices in the past – such as slavery – would have been disallowed on the grounds that, once property rights had been established, they should not be disturbed.

At present we rely on two distinct pricing systems.

Prices in the private sector help to determine what will be produced and consumed. For producers, prices must be sufficient to cover costs. For consumers, prices must satisfy a person's needs or desires. If the bargain cannot be struck in the market place, the product is not brought into existence.

A wholly different philosophy exists in the public sector. Governments separate expenditure (on services to be rendered) from revenue (which is needed to defray costs). Governments determine their spending priorities, and then set about raising revenue. Unlike the private sector, there is no symmetry between the service to be rendered to the individual and the tax imposts which pass for the public sector's prices. So whereas in the private sector the individual accepts personal responsibility for what is to be enjoyed, and pays a price to cover costs, in the public sector there is no such personal equivalence. Political doctrines are invoked to justify this deviation from the principles that are applied in the private sector.

Governments make decisions by ostensibly taking into account considerations that are alleged to be beyond the logic of the pricing mechanism. We reject this contention, and we maintain that the mark of personal freedom and of a mature society is the ability to unite the two sectors. Crucially, an integrated pricing mechanism would relate benefits to payments in the public sector for those goods or services which we share in common. That doctrine recognises the individual's social obligations, an aspect that is denied to the present pricing mechanism in the markets.

The justification for the present arrangement is presented as if the division of the two sectors is rational, and that we therefore need two distinct pricing philosophies. Thus, it is argued that private markets cannot produce all the goods that a community needs, so we should not be constrained exclusively by the logic of prices as they apply in private markets. But once we decline to accept the assumptions and probe the reasoning, we discover that the arguments are derived from special pleading. They camouflage the interests of the free riders.

On the Left, market prices are rejected for public goods on the grounds that health and education are so important that they should be available 'free at the point of need'. This doctrine emerged as a second-best solution to the problem of income distribution. Its retention damages people's best interests.

The need for the free access philosophy emerged because people were denied the freedom to retain their share of the total wealth of the nation. The consequence of this was that they were, indeed, prevented from defraying the costs of the health and education which they needed. Property rights and public finance were structured to exclude people, both from employment opportunities and their share of public value. Because Parliament refused to remedy this perverse structure of rights, the socialist doctrine of state power found favour with the people. They used the muscle of the state as a counter-weight to the power of the free riders, to create the Welfare State.

But preserving the Welfare State plays straight into the hands of the free riders. For the Welfare State declines to enforce a symmetry between the services delivered and the prices paid by the individual. *The absence of the cast iron moral connection between what we want and what we are willing to give in return is the defining feature of the land owner's creed.* He literally lives a free life. But the reciprocal of this was the exclusion of people from their share of the fruits of the land, which consequently spawned the tax regime that is now used as the government's pricing mechanism.

This leads us to a distasteful conclusion, but one that we have to confront. The Welfare State accommodates the custom and practice of the free rider. It does so not for dishonourable reasons, for it seeks to ameliorate the plight of the people who are excluded from society. But we now know that it has failed to achieve its goal, while nonetheless perpetuating the perverted pricing arrangement in the public sector. But the damage is not confined to the distortions that consequently arise in the public sector. There is a feedback effect into the private sector. Taxes are added to prices. These prices, consequently, do not reflect the costs of production or the needs of consumers. This distorts private enterprise and the fulfilment of people's needs and desires. The losses arising from this are a measure of what it costs to carry the free riders on our backs.

We need to stress the important single point of the argument so far. Because the aristocracy and gentry de-socialised rent, they had to inculcate into our collective consciousness the philosophy of free access to the services they wanted, with others paying for what they received. The problems that flowed from this hijacking of public value could not be remedied by extending the philosophy to include the victims who were dispossessed from their share of the land.

We now turn to the argument that private markets cannot produce certain goods, which justifies intervention of government. The two examples most often cited are the military defence of the nation's territory, and the enforcement of law and order within the territory. Economists rationalise the current philosophy on the grounds that the private sector could not provide these services for the simple reason that those who did not pay their share of the costs could not be excluded from the benefits. Thus, we need taxes to compel people to bear their share of the cost of an army, the police force and the administration of the judicial system. Again, we reject this conventional wisdom on the grounds that it is special pleading to protect the free riders.

Under the present pricing regime, the logic of this argument is correct. There is a disconnection between the citizen and the state, and compulsory taxes are necessary to bridge the gap. But how did the disconnection between public prices and public services come about? The clues are to be found in Adam Smith. His maxims on taxation are cited by economists to this day, as if they accept the wisdom in *The Wealth of Nations*. Smith argued that people should pay in proportion to the benefits which they received. And he applied this principle to the relationship of the individual and the state. This was a direct relationship, one that was registered by the value which the state made possible for people to create. This established a financial obligation. This is how Smith put it in *The Wealth of Nations*:

> Nothing can be more reasonable than that a fund which owes its existence to the good government of the state, should be taxed peculiarly, or should contribute something more than the greater part of other funds, towards the support of that government.[1]

The mutual benefit was clearly laid out by Smith in the paragraph preceding the one we have just quoted. The rent of land, he wrote, was

> a species of revenue which the owner, in many cases, enjoys without any care or attention of his own. Though a part of this revenue should be taken from him in order to defray the expenses of the state, no discouragement will thereby be given to any sort of industry. The annual produce of the land and labour of the society, the real wealth and revenue of the great body of the people, might be the same after such a tax as before. Ground-rents, and the ordinary rent of land, are, therefore, perhaps, the species of revenue which can best bear to have a peculiar tax imposed upon them.[2]

No such claim can be advanced for other forms of raising revenue.

Smith was explaining that when the state secured the protection of its territory, the benefits were measured by the amount that people were willing to pay in rents for the use of land. If they defrayed the costs of the army or the police force out of land rents, the direct connection between benefits received and prices paid is established and preserved. The amount we paid would vary according to the scale of the benefits. Thus, if I possess 1,000 acres, and you make your living on 10 acres, I would pay more than you because I rely more heavily on the benefits that I accrue from the state. Why should you pay the same amount as me when we benefit disproportionately?

This principle of paying for benefits received from the public sector is exactly the same as the one that we apply in the private sector. The provider is not a commercial organisation. The state is not seeking a profit. So what? The population has freely decided that it wants a certain service, driven by personal and collective welfare (I want my neighbour to be protected, like me, because how else would I make a living out of economic intercourse?). We agree to a pricing regime proportionate to the benefits that each person receives to defray the full costs.

The case for not changing the present fiscal regime is allegedly reinforced by the free rider argument. We are told that the provision of public goods is associated with the problem that some people cannot be excluded from the benefits of law and order. *Ergo,* it is necessary to capture some of their earnings by means of 'broad-based' taxes. Are there such free riders in a community where rents are the prices charged for public goods? Don't we all live on land, and pay *someone* for the benefit of doing so? The rent pricing mechanism is inclusive: there are no free riders. We all pay rents for the space we need on which to live, to work and to recreate.

Thus, the reasons offered as justification for preserving the present system are spurious. They are designed to legitimise perverse arrangements that abuse people's natural rights. Whether this is intentional or not, those reasons serve as camouflage for the free riding landowners.

When we substitute rents for taxes as public sector prices, we end up with a single pricing system. This is an inclusive arrangement in which people accept personal responsibilities and share in the benefits of living in community.

So far, our case has been presented in terms of general principles. We now need to put it to the test to see how it would work in a particular case.

15.2 Testing the Hypothesis

THE THEORY of the single pricing mechanism needs to be assessed in terms of knowledge gleaned from the laboratory of everyday experience. We want to know if this is a comprehensive solution to the allocation of resources in the complex society. For example, it must work with the grain of the environment. Nature has served mankind in a most generous way, but it is not our servant. Nature exists independently of humans. In the past, humans acknowledged this through folklore and rules that guided collective behaviour. Errors were made, sometimes with disastrous cultural consequences.[3] But armed with scientific knowledge, there is now no excuse for compromising the welfare of future generations by damaging nature's ability to flourish.

The impact which we claim for an integrated pricing system will be analysed by placing centre-stage that most worrisome of individuals, the self-serving, congestion causing, gas-guzzling motorist. He is the bane of governments that are searching for international agreement on how to deal with 'global warming'. He is the archetype of the selfish individual, the hate figure of the Left who is invoked to prove that 'the market' has to be tamed by government intervention. He is the consumer who enjoys the open highway without compensating the losers for the damage inflicted on the fabric of urban civilisation. I contend that, if we adopt the integrated pricing system, that individual could be left free to act in his best interests, without government intervention, and in the process he would behave *as if* he were equally concerned with the welfare of others and of nature.

The anti-social behaviour of the carbon-spewing motorist is the product of a pricing system that emits confusing signals. The costs that are currently incurred are not designed to deliver the best results primarily because the individual is subsidised and a major part of the costs he creates are transfers to others. The result is the worst of all worlds.

When the motorist buys his vehicle and purchases his fuel, he incurs fixed tax liabilities. Thereafter, providing he has insurance protection against third party injuries in an accident, he can drive without considering the welfare of others. If he drives at peak times, he may sit in lanes of stalled vehicles, engines running and polluting the environment, everyone frustrated because they cannot arrive at their destinations on time. Journeys are made regardless of the gains that would be achieved by making fewer trips, or by driving at off-peak times, or by switching to public transport. All motorists suffer. So do residents whose homes border the highways, who are subjected to noise and the waste that is poured into the air around them. The motorist imposes costs and does not suffer the consequences. Everyone loses. This is neither fair nor efficient.

We have, here, what looks like a case of market failure. People are competing for a scarce resource – nature's finite time and place on the highway – without consideration for others. The overuse of that resource – and its under-use at other times – suggests an inefficient market mechanism. But is the fault intrinsic to the market, or can the blame be laid elsewhere? We consider this question by reviewing the alternative pricing regime.

Let us assume that the motorist is invited to pay for all the benefits that he receives. He does so, already, in the private market: he pays the full cost when he purchases the vehicle and the fuel that goes into the tank. Problems start with the prices ordained by government. Missing is the price for using the road, and for depositing the carbon waste into the air. This failure is the responsibility of Parliament, which passes the laws, but is *this* failure of governance the cause of highway congestion?

What would happen if government integrated its prices with those that are negotiated between individuals in the private sector? First, the motorist would be charged a rent for using the highway. The charge would vary according to demand. Peak time driving would incur higher charges than off peak periods. Then there would be a charge for the carbon emitted into the atmosphere. The carrying capacity of the heavens is finite. That charge would also take into account the damage to the fabric of the communities through which the highways traversed. What would be the outcome of this bipartisan pricing arrangement?

The motorist, being rational – albeit selfish, according to our caricature – would adjust his motoring habits according to the new pricing regime. For some people, it would no longer be worthwhile driving at peak times. The effect of this is to spread trips on the highways so that cheaper, under-used time slots are occupied and congestion is relieved at peak times. Some journeys would be deemed unnecessary, so the volume of pollution would be reduced. Everyone gains – other motorists, and nearby residents – even though our motorist is behaving in a purely selfish way. Because he has adjusted his behaviour to accommodate the integrated pricing system, he makes decisions *as if* he cared about the interests of other motorists, for the environment and for the communities through which he drives.

Suddenly, market behaviour is responsive to the needs of everyone equally, and it is accommodating non-market imperatives such as nature's. But the change is not brought about by the market *per se*. The change is in the way government raises its revenue. It has tailored its prices to fit the needs *and the obligations* of the individual. The payments are symmetrically related to the benefits that people receive from using a public resource. The technologies for this pricing regime could have been developed a century ago if government had applied the principles of charging people for the benefits they received at the time of the automobile revolution.

The Blair government announced that it wants Britain to introduce road pricing after a 10-year public debate. Whatever the motives for postponing the policy, there is no doubt that the technical requirements for road pricing can be resolved in that time. A glimpse of how road pricing would work went on display on the roads of London in 2004, and Stockholm in 2006 (see Box 15.2).

We now relax our caricature of the individual. In truth, people do care about the feelings and interests of others, and about the quality of the urban and the natural environments. People do not wilfully set out to damage the interests of others, because they respect the community in which they live. The perverse outcomes that are undoubtedly displayed are, ultimately, the result of perverse pricing policies employed by government.

Box 15:2 Stockholm's Road Rents

LONDON'S Congestion Charge is a crude road price, with a uniform charge (£8 in 2006) irrespective of the time of travel. The term Congestion Charge is a misnomer. While the charge certainly spread the traffic more evenly through the day and thereby relieved congestion at peak travel times, the charge was actually a general price for the right to traverse the inner city roads between the appointed hours. A flat rate was charged whether the motorist was inside the charging area during peak or off-peak times. The ideal rental charge would vary according to demand. Peak times ought to incur a higher rental charge than off-peak driving. Even so, this was a valuable beginning, with refinements to the charges as the wisdom of the policymakers was deepened.

A rental charge that would vary in relation to the time of travel was the arrangement introduced in Stockholm in 2006. The Swedish city's road prices cut twice as much traffic as London's scheme, despite the fact that drivers paid an average of only £2 a day. The tolls started at 75p between the off-peak time of 6.30 am and 7.00 am and rose to a maximum of £1.50 between 7.30 am and 8.30 am, the peak travel time.

The response of drivers illustrated how people adjust their behaviour on the basis of private interests while simultaneously delivering social benefits. Easing congestion in Stockholm adds to the attractions of living and playing in that city, and consequently enhances the rents that people are willing to pay for residential and commercial locations within the area where motorists were obliged to defray more of the costs of their use of automobiles.

The further benefit of the integrated pricing system is that government can begin to scrap taxes that damage economic incentives. If the road price was refined to include the costs of pollution, for example, the tax on petrol could be abolished.

Whether government will adopt the enlightened road to reform depends, however, on whether it continues to listen to the conventional wisdoms of the experts who advise them. Some of them are flagging up revisions that would further deepen the social divide. A study commissioned from researchers at Imperial College, London, suggested that some of the revenue from road prices could be used to cut the local property tax (the Council Tax). For political reasons, this attracted the Treasury and Department for Transport.[4] But such a use of revenue would undermine the principle of requiring people to pay for the benefits they received. It would raise property prices, further destabilise the housing market and deepen all the collateral damage that we reviewed in Part II. A more sensible proposal was aired by *The Financial Times*, which suggested that the revenue from road pricing 'could replace three or four pence of the basic rate of income tax'.[5] By reducing the payroll tax, new employment opportunities would be created, which would automatically reduce the welfare costs on government – yielding a further reduction in government tax-take.

We have just described the virtuous circle delivered by the integrating pricing mechanism. The principles of good governance yield benefits that surface in the private sector. And meeting personal obligations yields benefits that surface in the public sector. This interaction, self-propelled and driven by a mutuality of interest, is the fastest and smoothest route to rebalancing complex societies. But the philosophy will not be turned into practical politics if the language of public finance continues to be a victim of political prejudice. What, for example, is a tax? That this is a serious question was illustrated by arguments over the charge for using London's roads. The US Ambassador decided that the Congestion Charge was a tax from which he – as a diplomat – was exempt. This upset the Mayor Ken Livingstone, but the ambassador from the Dominican Republic agreed with his fellow diplomat. Indignantly, he wrote to *The Times*:

> To equate the Congestion Charge with a payment for a service rendered, for example parking or use of a toll road, is to forget the essential character of taxation: compulsion.[6]

Transport *for* London's Director of Congestion Charging replied that the then Foreign Secretary, Jack Straw, had told the House of Commons: 'The congestion charge does not constitute a form of direct taxation under the Vienna Convention, but is a charge analogous to a motorway toll and … they [diplomats] are expected to pay'.[7]

A charge for the use of space on the highway is a rent, not a tax. Users defray the costs on the basis of the benefits which they receive. It is a voluntary payment: no one is forced to traverse the London inner city highway. This conforms to principles that we use to pay for what we receive, when we receive it, and for how much we receive.

Policies will not be reformed until these linguistic confusions are resolved. That confusion does abound is suggested by the answers to questions that appear in Table 15:1. It seems that most people (57%) would resist an increase in the cost of motoring to encourage less driving. At the same time, a large majority (74%) agree that much higher taxes should be imposed on cars that use a lot of petrol. But what if people were invited to pay for the full costs of their motoring to meet their personal responsibilities to others and to nature? I believe that the majority would agree, if the charges were proportional to the benefits they received.

Table 15:1

Paying For the Roads

In percentage terms		*All Voters*	*Labour Voters*	*Conservative Voters*	*Lib Dem Voters*	*18-24*	*45-54*
Increase cost of motoring to encourage less driving	Agree	41	47	33	55	40	49
	Disagree	57	53	65	41	60	48
Much higher taxes on cars that use a lot of petrol	Agree	74	71	70	88	68	78
	Disagree	24	28	29	12	32	21

Source: Populus for *The Times*, April 11, 2006.

People need to come to terms with the fact that the users of highways are heavily subsidised. Under the present pricing regime, they do not pay their way. Others cover the costs for a range of services which they enjoy. An example is the policing of highways. The costs ought to fall directly on road users by means of a direct charge. This principle is employed in New Zealand. The police are contracted for a particular level of enforcement service and that cost is defrayed out of the National Land Transport Fund, which receives income from petrol taxes and road user charges.[8]

A public debate in which all the information was made available would enable people to distinguish between a tax and a rental charge; and to agree on the redistribution of costs so that they fell on users rather than people who are currently forced to defray other people's costs out of taxes.

The integrated pricing system resolves anomalies in individual behaviour. It would remove much of the personal discontent that nurtures public displays of aggression. Debate on public policy would consequently lead to the kinds of mutual understanding on which enlightened public policies must be based (see Box 15:3). But could the new pricing system also resolve the crises associated with irrational mass behaviour?

Box 15:3 Knocking the NIMBYs

WHEN RUTH KELLY was appointed as the British government's Secretary for Communities and Local Government, her first BBC radio interview was reported by the *Daily Telegraph* (May 10, 2006) under the headline: 'Kelly declares war on middle-class Nimbies over more homes'.

In discussing the need to provide affordable housing, Kelly launched a mission statement that was perceived as threatening to home owners. She talked of 'changing the social culture in this country where too often the case has been that people have been protective of their own space and not wanted to see more affordable housing being built. That is something we really have to root out.'

Some people do resist the construction of housing in their localities. They enjoy, and wish to preserve, the congenial *milieu* of low density/green/intimate surroundings, which give their locations high value.

Under the present pricing regime, residents in those low density/green/intimate communities are subsidised by people in high density/brownfield/impersonal urban environments. The integrated pricing system would enable an automatic mediation between the two without the need for intrusive governmental action.

NIMBY communities tend to be located on high-value land – the measure of the benefits that the residents enjoy. If they paid into the exchequer a land rent proportionate to those benefits, they would be compensating the people whom they wish to exclude from their localities. Those who were excluded would have their community infrastructure enhanced out of public funds up to the level where a balanced lifestyle matched the distribution of population in a way that was acceptable to everyone as both fair and efficient.

Ideological war, and screeching media headlines calculated to whip up tension in the population, would be consigned to the dustbin of class history.

15.3 The Counter-cyclical Policy

THE SELF-INTEREST of the individual can be 'enlightened' by good public policy. But what about mass behaviour of the type that drives (say) the 'manias' associated with booms and busts? Periodically, and collectively, people lose sense of reason as they bid up property prices to unaffordable heights. This is the prelude to the painful crash. The property cycle has disrupted the capitalist economy for three centuries. Could this repetitive property syndrome, the cause of mass unemployment, also be due to the failure of governance?[9] Does the integrated pricing system have the power to smooth out the property cycle?

That this question is relevant to current public policy is indicated by a study published by the bankers' bank, the Basle-based Bank for International Settlements (BIS). It used the coded language of the financial institutions to call for policies that would diminish the violent swings in prices, thereby reducing the risks of the 'boom-bust cycle'. Its censure of governments was cautiously framed, noting that 'it is odd that domestic financial imbalances are not ranked higher on policymakers' list of priorities, since international imbalances have been a source of concern for centuries'.

But what kinds of policies would neutralise the boom/busts? The BIS economist was not trying to communicate with the untutored layman when he wrote about 'the desirability of a more symmetric policy response to the expansionary and contractionary phases of the financial cycle. Implicit in this would be a greater focus on long-term outcomes of policy decisions than currently seems fashionable'.[10] What would count as 'a macro-prudential regulatory framework'? On which parts of the financial architecture should we focus our attention? The author, William White, offered clues when he summarised the booms and busts of the 20th century. The persistent theme was the way in which asset prices – especially 'house' prices – explode and implode. Now, however, the disturbances have gone global.

> [I]t is not an exaggeration to say that this house price phenomenon now has almost global reach, with a number of emerging market economies (especially China) also showing large increases. Among the major economies, only Japan and Germany have avoided such increases, presumably because they are still recovering from the bust phase of the last credit, asset and investment cycle.[11]

The 'property bubble' is acknowledged, but no attention is given to the economics of the land market. So we will ask: does the integrated pricing mechanism deliver a 'symmetric' solution to instability that originates in the land market? Is the principle of paying for benefits received tantamount to a counter-cyclical strategy? Would the payment of land rents into the public purse dampen down the price fluctuations?

The violent amplitudes are illustrated by the most recent British cycles. The prices of new houses increased 700% in the years from 1979 to 2005, for example, whereas the price of land rose by 1,700%.

During the upward ride of the property helter-skelter, the owners of land amassed fabulous windfall fortunes. The media reported the get-rich-quick stories of fortunes from buying and selling properties. I have described this history in detail elsewhere, and of how the inevitable outcome is protracted recessions.[12] For people who own land, the losses of the recession years are more than offset in the following boom. From Graph 15:1, we see that the price explosions were led by property owners in the Greater London area, where price instability far exceeded the trends in the South East and in the rest of the country.

After the recession of 1992, the economy recovered in time for the arrival of Tony Blair in 1997. That was when the next land boom was triggered. As New Labour's 'prudent' economic policies were applied by Gordon Brown, the poorest sections of the community were made to

Graph 15:1

Residential Land with Planning Permission
(£m per hectare)

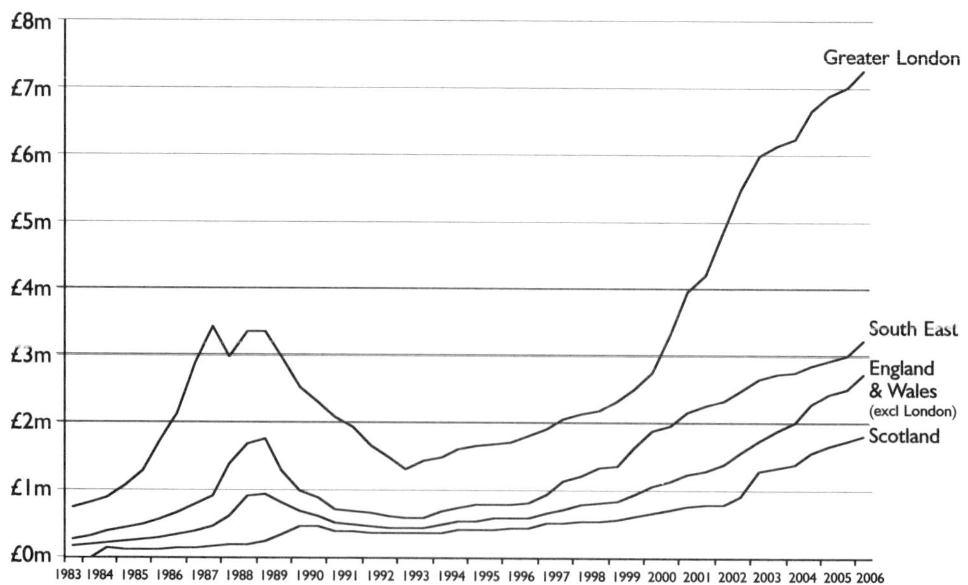

Box 15:4 Life in the Concrete Jungle

WHEN THE Conservative Party elected David Cameron as its leader, he sought to prove that Tories could move beyond the image of the country squire and NIMBY home owner. He brought Michael Heseltine – who had retired to his country mansion with a peerage – out of retirement.

In the 1980s, Heseltine led the Thatcher government's attempt to deal with the aftermath of a riot in the Toxteth suburb of Liverpool. Heseltine decided that the inner cities needed to be rehabilitated. Within a mile of Liverpool's city centre and Toxteth were 1,000 acres of abandoned industrial wasteland. In London, 6,000 acres of 'forgotten wasteland' were located around the docks in the East End.

Heseltine was appalled. In his autobiography he refers to the 'alienated population' and his anger at observing 'the immense tracts of dereliction ... The rotting docks ... the crumbling infrastructure ... and vast expanses of polluted land.'* His twofold solution:

- **Invest taxpayers' money in infrastructure to attract private enterprise**. This delivered windfall gains to owners of adjoining land and raised the cost of rented accommodation to low income families.
- **Exempt real estate from the property tax**. This attracted warehouse-type investment with low labour content to areas of high unemployment – of little help to the marginalised dwellers of the decaying hearts of Liverpool and London.

Heseltine did not understand that private landowners were as responsible for the dereliction which he observed as was 'the large-scale hoarding of land in the hands of the public sector'. When he was escorted back to Liverpool in March 2006 by David Cameron, it appeared that a future Tory government would repeat the mistakes of the Thatcher years. Heseltine commended investment in capital-intensive infrastructure. There was no hint that the Conservative Party would require the owners of land to pay for the extra services that would make their assets valuable.

* Michael Heseltine, *Life in the Jungle*, London: Hodder & Stoughton, 2000, pp.211-12.

suffer even more as land values took off into the stratosphere. By 2005, about 43,000 homes in Britain were worth more than £1m. Nine out of 10 of them were in London and the South East.

Now reflect on that history in terms of the integrated pricing mechanism. If people paid for their public services out of the rent of land, the incentive to speculate in land would be removed. Rents that were paid to the exchequer, or otherwise used to fund infrastructure, could not be capitalised into selling prices. This means that there would be no windfall gains to animate financial fever. The property cycle would be smoothed, with prices responding to supply and demand rather than 'irrational exuberance', as Alan Greenspan, the former Chairman of the US Federal Reserve Bank, put it. The disruptive forces would be neutralised. Rent would be transformed into a power for good rather than evil. Paralleling the switch to this method of funding public services, people's wages and consumption would be untaxed. The rise in real disposable incomes would more than compensate for the public charges paid for the land occupied.

Compare this outcome with the arrangement in which taxes abuse families that rent their homes and reward landowners with windfall gains. When a recession hits, renters have no private safety net to help them through the bad times. The prospects are quite different for property owners, especially those who have paid off their mortgages. Although house prices decline, owners can still borrow against the value locked into their assets. This wealth effect has been quantified for the US market crash between 1999 and 2001. The dot.com bubble burst, but home owners increased their consumption by approximately $100bn.[13] This cushioned the trauma for home owners, but it was small comfort when set against the wider social costs.

The reshaping of mass behaviour is reflected in other changes in the land market. The under-use of land, for example, which indicates urban sprawl, would be corrected. High-value sites would be brought into use before low-value greenfield sites on the urban edge. Why? Because land owners would be required to pay for the services delivered to their sites – which gave their land its value – even if they decided not to make the land available to people who need to use it. The failure to understand this chain of cause-and-effect is one of the major blind spots of governance (see Box 15:4).

The scale of the financial gains from an effective counter-cyclical policy are illustrated by the impact of land speculation in Australia. In the 30 years to 2006, the four economic downturns driven by real estate booms and busts caused a loss of GDP of about A$768bn. This is the additional income that would have been distributed among the population if the economy had not gone into recession in 1976-8; 1983; 1991-2 and 1999-2003, according to estimates by Bryan Kavanagh of the Melbourne-based Land Values Research Group.

Box 15:5 The Upside Down Distribution of Income

BRYAN KAVANAGH, a founding director of Westlink Consulting, a Melbourne-based real estate valuation company, is director of the privately-funded think tank, The Land Values Research Group. Aided by estimates of Australia's land and natural resource rents by former Treasury civil servant Dr Terry Dwyer, Kavanagh was able to profile the continent's income in the following terms:

- Less than $30bn (12%) of Australia's publicly-created $245bn in resource rents was collected for the public purse in 2004.
- As rentiers and homeowners were able to privatise $215bn in resource rents, it was necessary to tax incomes, goods and services to that extent.
- One consequence: household debt has risen from $289bn in 1996 to $818bn in 2004 ($41,000 for every man, woman and child).
- As a proportion of GDP since 1972, net incomes have declined by 40%, taxes have grown by 28% and annual resource rents have grown by 150%.*

Using real estate data, Kavanagh has developed an Economic Barometer which has proved accurate in forecasting the direction of the Australian economy.

* Bryan Kavanagh, 'The Economic Consequences of Bubbles', International Union for Land Value Taxation conference, London, July 4, 2006.

But this understates the GDP that could have been available for distribution. For compound interest ensures that, had investment continued during the recession years, GDP in 2004 (A$810bn) would have been appreciably higher. The multiplier effects of economic activity – from continued consumption, higher savings, the accumulation of capital equipment – would have delivered an appreciably higher level of *per capita* incomes by the beginning of the 21st century. But even that adjustment would fail to convey the true scale of the long-term benefits of the integrated pricing mechanism. If we want to know what the Australian economy *could* have looked like, we have to revise the figures to take into account the benefits of untaxing wages and savings, and from the efficient use of land. These would deliver a rate of growth of productivity much higher than the historical average (2.5% for Australia). If we adjust GDP since 1972 to take account of that higher level of productivity, Australia's national income today would be A$2,200bn from just capturing half of its rent as prices for the use of land.[14] Thanks to Australia's use of land taxation, we can piece together a reasonably accurate picture of the consequences of using taxes that damage the economy (see Box 15:5).

15.4 Unpicking the Tax State

THE INTEGRATED pricing system is the essential step towards identifying and quantifying the true surplus of the economy. We cannot rely on government to produce an honest estimate of this chargeable revenue. It resorts increasingly to taxation-by-stealth so that it can conceal the full impact of its policies on the nation's welfare.

But even now, we can offer a numerical sense of what is implied by switching to a rational and just system of public prices. By integrating these into the workings of people's private lives, productivity would be significantly increased. The synergy that would flow from emancipating people and liberating the land market would raise the annual rate of growth.

Britain's Treasury pessimistically projects a *decline* in both productivity and GDP over the years to 2035. It assumes annual percentage growth declining from 2% to 1.75%.[15] Our reform would deliver an increase of at least an additional 1% per annum. Is this realistic? The rate for the world throughout the 20th century was 3%, and countries like China and India are achieving rates of between 7% and 10% per annum. Given the scale of inefficiency and underused resources, there is no reason why Britain's historic trend of 2% should not be increased to 3%. What does this mean, in terms of hard cash? The estimates are shown in Table 15:2.

The 3% growth rate was calculated by Rana Roy, who has specialised in the economics of infrastructure. He calculated the degree to which Britain has seriously under-

Table 15:2

UK Real GDP Growth

Alternative long-term projections and results
Real GDP in £billions (2006 prices)

Real Growth @	*2005-6*	*2035-6*	*2105-6*
3% per annum	1,224	2,971	23,524
2% per annum	1,224	2,217	8,867
The difference		**754**	**14,557**

Source: Rana Roy, *Investing in the New Century: Toward an Undistorted Appraisal Process*, London: The Railway Forum, May 2006, p.7.

performed in its investment policies even compared with its European and North American competitors, let alone in relation to what it *could* achieve under optimal pricing policies.

If the 2% average was sustained over the 30 years to 2035, Britain's GDP would double to £2.2 trillion. But by shifting to the integrated pricing policy, GDP in 2035 could be greater by at least £754bn. If Britain remained reconciled to the 2% average for the next 100 years, the economy would increase from £1.2 trillion to £8.8 trillion, an 8-fold increase. But by removing the Tax State's obstacles to achieve a sustained 3% growth, GDP in 2105 would be £23.5 trillion – a difference in that year of more than £14 trillion. That is a 20-fold increase. £14 trillion per annum by the end of this century is the price that future generations in Britain would pay for failing to act in their best interests.

Realistically, it is not possible to move from a 2% (or worse) yearly growth rate, to a sustained 3% rate overnight. We would propose a 10-year phase-in period. The transition is necessary to enable people to adjust their financial arrangements, and to allow for the psychological changes to the new ways of living and working. If we began the tax shift in Year 1, by Year 10 the process would be completed. The benefits would come thick and fast, for people would move swiftly to take advantage of the new opportunities. In the first three years, the annual gains would not reach the long-run average. During the middle years of the decade of transition, there would be above-average gains due to the 'catch-up' effects, before the economy settled to the path of balanced growth.

I calculate that, over a 10-year transition period, Britain would be better off by an accumulated £240bn. That revenue, split between the private and public sectors, would be sufficient to remove personal deprivation and public degradation that mar our communities. By Year 10, Britain would be cruising on the sustainable 3% per annum growth path. This is what I describe as the Free State.

Figure 15:1

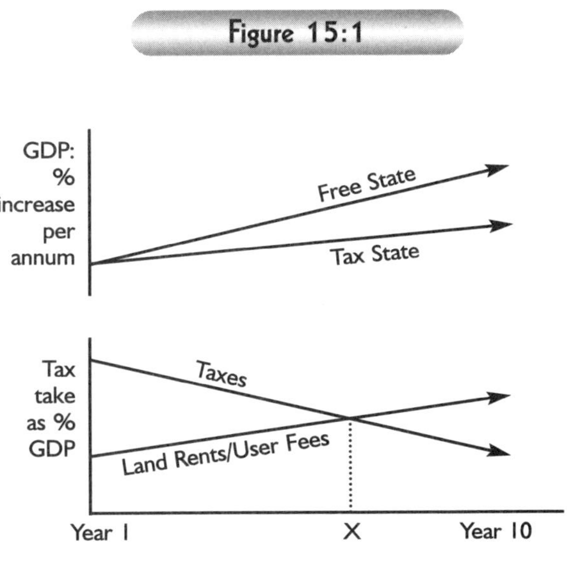

The interaction of the processes of change is illustrated in Figure 15:1. The two bottom lines show a declining tax-take, as people shifted to direct payments for the services they accessed at the locations where they live and work. The top two lines illustrate the adjustment in the annual rate of growth. Under the present tax regime (represented by the lower line, for the Tax State), the UK would remain locked into its historical 2% annual growth rate. But as the integrated pricing mechanism was brought into play from an agreed date (Year 1), there would be a progressive increase in the trend growth towards the Free State.

The state would continue to take its share of the nation's income to fund the services that only it can provide. If people want their land to be protected by an army or police force, they should pay directly out of the value which those services create. There are few other services that are uniquely associated with the state. Many of them – such as health and education – were brought into the public sector precisely because of the past failures of governance. The Tax State intervened in the 20th century to provide such personal services for one reason only: the tax system, as it was evolved by the aristocracy and gentry, marginalised people to the point where for many of them their incomes were not sufficient to pay for their health insurance and education fees. Under the new funding arrangements, people would reclaim control over how they spent their money. That would include a determination of which services should continue to be provided by the state.

The proposal that we should pay fees, or insure ourselves, to cover schooling and hospital services will initially trouble people who have been raised in the expectation that an omniscient state was the default mechanism in our lives – the safety net that provided our essential needs. And so, a variety of spurious arguments was used to legitimise that arrangement (see Box 15:6). But the state is not the reliable, all-powerful guardian for all of us, as we have seen with the failures of the Welfare State. To denigrate the public sector, however, for not being perfect is as pointless as denigrating the private sector for also being imperfect. In any event, we are not proposing an overnight transformation. People need time to adjust, and they are entitled to deliberate on how public services might be restructured to meet their future needs.

This debate will not progress if it becomes the opportunity for scoring cheap points against ideological enemies. Linguistic clarity, and respect for other people, is of paramount importance. I believe that a mature debate will lead to a profound reassessment of the world around us. On the future of the Welfare State, for example, what people actually mean when they defend the *status quo* is that 'Nobody should be deprived of health and education by others'. But the Welfare State offends this principle, because of the funding tools that were bequeathed to it from the past. They also mean: 'Nobody should be involuntarily deprived of health and education'. But humanitarian provision for people who are disadvantaged could be funded out of a source of revenue that is *theirs by right*, which preserves

Box 15:6 Of Pizzas and Public Goods

ONE LEGACY of the doctrine of the Welfare State is that 'public goods' are sacred, that they are different – in some peculiar way – from private goods. This thesis is routinely advanced by the Left to resist proposals from the Right that the bureaucratically administered public sector would benefit from being reformed into manageable pieces with the help of private enterprise.

The coloured language that bedevils this debate was illustrated by Jonathan Freedland in an important article in which he noted that the state itself now needed to be refashioned. He wrote: 'Nor will aping the private sector, pretending government can be run like Domino's Pizza or DHL, work – because health, education and public safety are not like garlic bread or packages. They are much more complex to deliver.'*

No one claims that government is equivalent to running a pizza parlour. There is a difference between pizzas and education. However, many people tend to devote greater care and attention to the price and quality of their pizzas than they do to the tax-funded school to which they send their children. The reason: they pay for one with cash over the counter, while they leave it to others to deal with the school.

The aristocracy long ago demonstrated that *they* can pay for the health and education of their families without recourse to the state. Is there something peculiarly different with the rest of us – those who are not free-riders – that we cannot take control over personal needs? Why can we be trusted to spend large sums on buying cars and houses but not on running or selecting schools and hospitals?

Public and private goods can be distinguished, but the essential difference relates to *how* goods are funded, not *what* goods are funded.

* Jonathan Freedland, 'Blair's failure is to think public goods can be delivered by private means', *The Guardian*, May 10, 2006.

their dignity in the way that the progressive taxation of other people's earnings does not.

The prize for the change that we propose is actually beyond financial calculation. In the labour market, for example, the abolition of taxes that destroy jobs would result in a personal independence and dignity which has not existed since the enclosures and the clearances. The new partnership between Labour and Capital would turn the workplace into a pleasure rather than the civil war zone that it has been for the past two centuries.

I am not arguing for the abolition of all taxes tomorrow. A few may be retained, but they need to be renegotiated. The rules regulating their use need to be carefully framed to rebalance the distribution of power between the individual, civil society and the state. Most importantly, harmful taxes should *not* be acceptable if their sole purpose is raising revenue for general expenditure. A bad tax, if it is to be retained, must be justified *because* of the damage that it does, to convert it into a weapon for the common good. An example is the tax on tobacco. People who smoke wilfully place themselves at risk of cancer. Why should others fund their medical treatment? A tax on tobacco has the negative effect of dissuading some people from inhaling nicotine. But others are not deterred, and some of them will contract cancer. So a tax on tobacco may be retained as a hypothecated charge, the revenue to be invested in a fund dedicated to the treatment of cancer patients and to fund research into this terrible disease. Some smokers do not contract cancer, of course, but that is not a reason for not taxing their habit. After all, some motorists do not crash their cars, yet we regard it as socially responsible to oblige them to take out insurance against the risks of causing injury to others.

This tax rule harnesses the destructive power of taxation for a responsible purpose. But it also serves to place limits on the power of the state. Governments should not be free to extract revenue from anybody, from whatever source it wishes, for whatever purpose it deems necessary, whenever it wishes to do so. *The state's right to collect revenue should be directly tied to the value it adds to the wealth of the nation.* No Value = No Revenue. This imposes an invigorating discipline on government. It shifts power back to the people, and it drives those who are entrusted with thc levers of power to serve the community in ways that add to wealth and welfare.

Thus, some 'bad' taxes may be retained for good purposes. In the case of the tobacco tax, individuals who recklessly place their health at risk derive a direct benefit from their tax payments. And society is entitled to impose that responsibility on them: for some would fail to take out private health insurance, but then expect others to pay for their stay in the cancer ward. Similar issues arise with alcohol, in which costs are inflicted on others by those who drink to excess. We need an obligatory insurance system to compensate the victims, as well as treating alcoholism. The tax on alcohol is the insurance premium that is reserved to cover the costs of the negative consequences of alcoholism.

As a result of this reform, what would happen to free riding landowners? Will they be materially better off? Figure 15:1 depicts the dynamic interaction that results in the enhancement of the quality of people's lives. By phasing in the changes, there would come a point at which the rent revenue would exceed the taxes (point x on the graph). As this process proceeded, the rate of increase in the growth of GDP would accelerate as people rearranged their working and saving habits. Landowners would have the time to rearrange their affairs, so that, like the rest of us, they worked for their living. Notice that their non-land assets – buildings on the land, investments in enterprises, their personal labour remuneration – would be untaxed even as they were being required to accept responsibility for the services delivered to them on their land. The energy that they now expend in avoiding taxes would be rewarded when invested in creative activity that added to their wealth and to the welfare of the nation.

From the point of view of society at large, lifestyle choices would improve immensely. People could opt for more leisure rather than a higher material standard of living. That choice would be theirs, for individual freedoms are expanded as the powers of both the Tax State and the free riders are reduced. That is the nature of the Free State.

By engaging democratically in the demand for reform, everyone acquires the right to renegotiate the social contract. But while this process needs to be conducted in a cool manner, in my view the project cannot safely be postponed. For adjustments in the relationship between the state and citizen are already under way, but not for the right reasons. If we fail to set the terms for the new social contract, the end result will be the further erosion of our liberties.

REFERENCES

1 Smith, *The Wealth of Nations*, Bk B, Ch. II, Pt II, Art. 1 (p.371of the Canaan edn).

2 We have cited Alfred Marshall as having endorsed the efficacy of the economics of rent as the appropriate source of public revenue. Economists throughout the 20th century continue to affirm the correctness of Smith's insights. These include a raft of Nobel Prize winners for economics, including William Vickrey, Robert Solow, Franco Modigliani and James Tobin. See Richard Noyes (ed), *Now the Synthesis: Capitalism, Socialism and the New Social Contract*, New York: Holmes & Meier, 1991, pp.225-9. That even the gurus of libertarian free market economics acknowledged the rent-as-public-revenue thesis may be seen from

the statement by Milton Friedman: 'In my opinion the least bad tax is the property tax on the unimproved value of land'. Quoted in Fred Harrison, *The Power in the Land*, London: Shepheard-Walwyn, 1983, p.299.

3 Jared Diamond, *Collapse: How Societies Choose to Fail or Survive*, London: Allen Lane, 2005.

4 Ben Webster, 'Road toll money may be used to cut council tax', *The Times*, April 24, 2006.

5 'Time to give road pricing the green light', *Financial Times*, May 22, 2006.

6 Anìbal de Castro, 'Congestion Costs', *The Times*, April 5, 2006.

7 Malcolm Murray-Clark, 'Congestion Charging', *The Times*, April 6, 2006.

8 I owe this information to Roger Toleman.

9 The history of the property cycle is reviewed in Harrison, *Boom Bust*, *op. cit.*

10 William R. White, *Procyclicality in the Financial System: Do We Need a New Macrofinancial Stabilisation Framework?* Basle: Bank for International Settlements, BIS Working Papers No. 193, January 2006, p.17.

11 *Ibid.*, p.3.

12 *Boom Bust*, *op. cit.*

13 Wenli Li, 'Moving up: trends in homeownership and mortgage indebtedness', Federal Reserve Bank of Philadelphia, *Business Review*, 2005, pp.26-34 (www.philadelphiafed.org).

14 Bryan Kavanagh, 'The economic consequences of bubbles', International Union for Land Value Taxation conference, London, July 4, 2006.

15 HM Treasury, *Budget 2006: A Strong and Strengthening Economy: Investing in Britain's Future*, London: Stationery Office, 2006.

16

The New Mercantilism

16.1 Fool's Gold

WEALTH came without pain, from beyond the blue horizon. Gold and silver flowed from beneath the earth of a mysterious land on the other side of the ocean. *Money galore!* The monarchs of the nation states that were emerging in the 16th century had to control this wealth. As the source of the new commerce, the supply lines would need to be jealously guarded against the covetousness of others. Since Adam Smith, that model of state power and monopoly economics has been known as mercantilism.

Mercantilism concentrated power in the monarch and privilege in the merchant. The letters patent legalised a monopolistic distribution of wealth that narrowed people's liberties. Adam Smith wrote *The Wealth of Nations* to debunk that system of economics. He exposed the fallacies that imbued England, Spain, Portugal and France from around 1500 – fallacies that provoked wars as monarchs truncated the rights of others to prevent them from producing and exchanging their products with whomsoever they wished. In Book IV, Chapter 1, Smith went straight to the confusions that equated wealth with money. 'To grow rich is to get money; and wealth and money, in short, are, in common language, considered as in every respect synonymous.'

Today, we are in danger of embarking on a new mercantilism. Like the monarchs who presided over the transformation from feudalism to capitalism, *we the people* have found a new and painless source of wealth. It, too, flows in from the blue beyond, the money for a new prosperity. Like the bullion which did not require work for its riches to be enjoyed, the new 'wealth', the currency that fuels the state and economy in the post-industrial age, is also a gain without pain.

That 'wealth' is coming to the aid of the Western state, which is cornered, fearful of the economic power of the Eastern countries which are asserting their right to sell their manufactured goods on the world's markets. But with the competitive advantage in the manufacturing sector gravitating to the East, how will Europe and America continue to raise tax revenue from its eroding economic base? Refuge is being sought in the new source of wealth. The propaganda is subtle, designed to lull us into believing that prosperity is assured – if we agree to be guided by the agents of the state.

From whence is this new wealth arriving? Western consumers are now in the grip of a new cargo cult, the ritual that originated in the South Seas during World War II.

The islanders of the Pacific had a foretaste of manna from heaven by courtesy of the allied forces. Cases full of exotic goods parachuted from the skies, dropping onto their beaches, no questions asked – and with no price tags attached. To this day, some islanders continue to pray for the return of those wondrous miracles. They ritualise their hopes through cargo cults. Westerners in the 21st century are indulging in a sophisticated version of the cargo cult. The wealth still cascades from the heavens; curiously, however, most of us know as little about its origins as the loin-clothed Pacific islanders of yesteryear.

That wealth is in the land beneath our homes.

For no apparent reason, and without any effort on our part, it grows in value year after year. When we need cash to buy the latest gadgetry from China's factories, banks will lend us money when we tell them that we are the owners of residential property. As the price of property climbs higher and higher, so we convince ourselves that the key to eternal prosperity is within our grasp. All we have to do is *sit tight*. Fears about a shortfall in pension funds, the end of a job-for-life culture, the inability of the state to fund our health and our children's education – all will be well, the deficits in the state budget plugged by our personal wealth.

The original mercantilists deluded their victims as they re-engineered society to suit their private interests, and they are doing it today to make sure that *they* will not suffer as the curtain comes down on the Welfare State. The outcome will be a savage disappointment to millions of families.

The 'wealth' in our homes is actually debt. It is a debt which, because we do not accept responsibility for it, we impose on our children and grandchildren. The delusions of the 'property owning democracies' will lead to enormous political chasms as the realities strike home over the next two generations. By 2050, the world will be a different place. We can shape that future for everyone's benefit, but not if we yield our fate to the new mercantilism of the sclerotic state.

The delusional basis of wealth in residential property was analysed by William White, the Head of the Monetary and Economic Department at the Bank for International Settlements. Real wealth, he reminds us, 'is generated by increased saving, investment and/or increases in total factor productivity'. These changes can drive up the price of equities in enterprises where, 'unlike the case of house prices, there are winners but no offsetting losers'.[1] The losers are locked into the wrong end of land-based property deals. Governments would prefer to keep us ignorant about the economics of debt. This is understandable. As White explained:

> [A] large part of what statisticians (and common sense) define as wealth at the level of the individual is not obviously the same thing at the aggregate level. It could be argued that the higher house prices are simply a change in relative prices and do not increase wealth in aggregate. In effect, the higher price of a house (or benefit to the owner) is offset by the discounted costs of higher rents in the future (either explicit, or implicit, for owner-occupied dwellings). Any associated increase in net spending generated by such 'wealth' is a borrowing from the future that will have to be repaid. If house prices fall, the homeowner, who borrowed against higher equity, will have to retrench. If house prices do not fall, then those purchasing more expensive housing services will have to economise on something else.[2]

The significance of a fall in house prices is that this would serve as a reality check, an antidote to the delusions created by the short-term machinations of governments. For the new mercantilism is leading Western countries into a trap. By encouraging the expansion of credit on the back of land held as collateral by banks, it is eroding further the competitiveness of Western economies. In the 19th century, the outcome of global competition was heavily determined by the cost of labour. That cost was mainly the result of the price of food. Today, the key factor is rent. We can see the reversal of the importance of these costs in the USA. The Bureau of Labor Statistics estimated that, in 1900, food, alcohol and tobacco accounted for 43% of average New York City spending. Housing costs absorbed 15% of the average New York family's income. Today, the numbers have been reversed. The rent-take has increased to 38% and the cost of food, alcohol and tobacco accounts for just 13%.[3]

This has exposed Western economies to a fragile situation, one of heavy dependence on the stability of their financial sectors. And the banking sector, in turn, is dependent on stability of the real estate market. If property prices were to crash, they would render financial institutions vulnerable to bankruptcy. And that, in turn, puts the whole economy at risk. This heightened risk is stressed by the shift in the fortunes of the various employment sectors in the UK over the past 20 years. From Table 16:1 we see that the food and manufacturing sectors suffered a serious net loss of jobs, whereas there was a significant rise in the real estate and retail sectors. The latter two are interdependent: if real estate prices crash, the cut-back in consumption will savage the retail sector. There is little comfort to be drawn

Table 16:1

Proportions of UK Employment by Selected Sectors (1983 and 2001)

Sector	*Percentage of Total Employment 1983*	*2001*	*Percentage Change*
Retail	8.7	11.2	29
Other Business	6.1	11.1	82
Computer	0.5	2.0	280
Real Estate	0.7	1.4	103
Fabricated Metals	2.5	1.4	-42
Machinery	2.4	1.3	-45
Chemicals	1.6	0.9	-43
Food	2.6	1.8	-30

Source: *Annual Business Inquiry* (2001), *Annual Employment Survey* (1983); cited in GLA Economics, *Why Distance Doesn't Die: Agglomeration and its Benefits*, London: GLA, 2006, p.13, Table 4.1.

from the substantial increase in employment in the computer sector. For computers raise the productivity of the economy, contributing much of their net gains to an increase in land values.

The West relies on history not repeating itself to avoid a generalised depression. I do not believe that the developed countries can buck the trends of history: the remedial policies have not been put in place. The employment growth sectors are the ones most vulnerable to the financial crises which are a continuing threat to the European and North American economies.[4]

Politicians are resigned to superficial calculations of the public interest. With the wealth-creating capacity ebbing away to the East, the fiscal base is being eroded even as the demands on the state for welfare support are increasing. How can these economies maintain social stability? People need to feel that they have money in their pockets – money that can be spent in the shops, generating consumption that secures employment. But, while global output has expanded by 34% in the 10 years to 2006, Britain's share of world manufacturing fell from 3.8% to 3%. Japan, the second biggest manufacturer after the US, increased its manufacturing output by 12.6%, but its share of the total global output also dropped. China was the winner. Its output rose by 156%, with its share of world manufacturing output doubling over the decade from 4.2% to 8%, according to the Vienna-based UN Industrial Development Organisation.[5] If these trends are not addressed by raising the productivity of Western economies, the consequences will extend well beyond the next property-led recession.

The West has yet to discover the formula for perpetual wealth – for basing a new prosperity on secure foundations. The easy solution is to propagate the illusion that rising house prices – which stimulate debt-driven consumption – are the solution.

This is the financial basis of the new mercantilism: a commercialism that arrogates extraordinary power to the state and privileges to the financial corporations that are favoured with the patent right to execute policy.

It is an agenda built on the illusion of wealth and debt that will exact a heavy price on the majority of people.

Like its original version, the tenets of the new mercantilism are not made explicit by the nation's leaders. Indeed, they rely on smokescreens to conceal the significance of their decisions. One of these is that the core economies – such as, in Britain, London and the South East – have to be protected; their welfare secured even at the expense of their hinterlands.

An early account of the new mercantilism was offered by Mason Gaffney in his analysis of the US. He likened the relationship between the core and periphery to that of old-style colonialism.

> It is a relationship between the capital and the provinces in what is known as the mercantilist mindset. In this view, trade is not mutually beneficial but entails one party taking advantage of, or at least dominating, another. Mercantilist thinking exalts the capital and subdues the provinces to their purpose.[6]

The new mercantilism is at its embryonic stage, so we can still influence the international relations and institutions that will determine geopolitics for the rest of the 21st century. But this will entail the expression of as much concern for the fate of the people of China as for our own citizens. The internal tensions in China stem from the same sources as those in the West. After 30 years of economic growth 'with a Chinese face', the gap between rich and poor has reached a crisis level. The poorest fifth of city dwellers receive 2.75% of urban incomes, less than a twentieth of the richest fifth. The 'great leap forward' of the post-communist era created nation-wide social stress that alarmed the National People's Congress. In March, 2006, the Prime Minister, Wen Jiabao, analysed the traumatic social conditions in the countryside, where poverty was at its extreme (see Box 16:1).

China has eclipsed Britain as the fourth largest economy in the world, and by 2050 she will be joined by India and others as among the leading economic powerhouses. Western statesmen are not analysing this prospect in terms that will secure prosperity for everyone. Instead, they are seeking refuge in the new mercantilism to protect the core regions.[7] If current trends continue, the central economies will covertly abandon their regional hinterlands to their fate. This will deepen the imbalance, with the backwaters held as reserves to replenish the labour and capital markets of the privileged centres of power and wealth. This scenario is not articulated by politicians who rely on the votes of the under-class. But we can read the trends in the logic of the public's finances. Governments realise that they cannot maintain public services at Welfare State levels. Something – or someone – has to be sacrificed. And of one thing we can be sure: the merchants of finance will not be among the losers.

Box 16:1 Care about China's Coolies

EAST NOW meets West at the global economic margin, the farmland around China's villages. More than half of the 1.3bn population (750m people) live in the countryside, tens of millions subsisting on less than $1 a day.

The low economic margin benefits the West's financial institutions, which, with the aid of the internet, are transferring back-office operations to call centres in the East. As western consumers saddle themselves with increasing personal debts, their credit card transactions are sorted by lower-wage workers in countries like India. The connectedness of this global relationship is monitored in the world's land markets, for productivity gains – wherever these are achieved – are ultimately reflected in the higher rents that people are willing to pay for the use of land.

One way to deliver global economic security is to raise living standards at the margin. We all have a vested interest in the welfare of China's rural workers. But China has yet to resolve its land policy. In 2005, there were 87,000 protests, riots and other 'mass incidents' related to the forcible appropriation of farmland by local governments. This was a rise of more than 6% over peasant protests in 2004.

Through the ripple effects, social tensions at a volatile economic margin are transmitted to China's coastal cities, and onwards through trade to the heartlands of Europe and North America. We have as much of an interest in encouraging the correct tax-and-tenure policy for China as for our own countries. Otherwise, the escalation of destabilising debt will multiply its effects through interactions around the globe. The failures of geopolitical diplomacy would most likely lead to the temptation to solve problems in the traditional way, through a renewed struggle for domination over other people's territories, to extract their rents.

16.2 The Finance Merchants

WESTERN GOVERNMENTS began to develop protectionist policies within two years of China's accession to the World Trade Organisation. The pressures were enormous, from Greece to Seattle on the West coast of the United States. Rising poverty levels fuelled popular discontent (in Greece, 21% of the population lived below the poverty line in 2006). Free trade politicians were suddenly attracted to the virtues of preferential treatment for domestic entrepreneurs – even at the risk of jeopardising the European Union.[8] In America, alarmed Wall Street moguls warned the Senate banking committee of the risks of protectionism to US interests.

Former colonial powers like France and Spain, which once thrived on the free flow of capital across borders, began to raise barriers against the takeover of their corporations by foreign entrepreneurs. The retreat from the open economy was sold as patriotism, throwing the veil of ignorance over what politicians called the 'knowledge' economy that was supposed to be the West's salvation. And with the increase in migration from Eastern Europe, jingoism (and worse) surfaced in the countries along the Atlantic seaboard.

The cards are being stacked in favour of finance capital against labour. The finance merchants will survive, for two reasons. One is the preferential tax treatment they enjoy – much of their revenue is rent disguised as interest on mortgages. The other reason is that electronic money transfers make it very easy to launder 'dirty' money. Money laundering is now estimated at $2,500bn each year from the financial centres (the US washes about half of this money, while Britain probably accounts for over $300bn, according to one professor of accounting[9]).

As the money merchants amass their fluid fortunes, the legitimacy of the state – dependent on its ability to raise revenue – is called into question. The solution would be to transform tax policy in favour of the one asset that cannot be stashed in tax havens: land. But that reform would not commend itself to the administration of George W. Bush, who tried to buy time by channelling taxpayers' money to faith groups ($2.15bn in 2005). This was his attempt to shift some of the state's social obligations onto charities.

Free trade, not protectionism, is the global framework within which nations ought to address the crisis of power and legitimacy. David Ricardo provided the theory on which this trading arrangement is based: the theory of comparative advantage. This explains how each community, region and nation can secure its prosperity by specialising in the activities at which it is particularly good. The theory is sound, but it does not work out that way in practice. The explanation is to be found in the way the world economy was seriously distorted by the tax-and-tenure model that was spread throughout the world by colonialism.

The full exposition of the free trade case will be the task for another book. But we must stress, here, that current tax policies are biased in favour of the core economies, with the peripheries being increasingly left to fend for themselves. The injustice of this is evident in Britain. Fiscal philosophy is biased in favour of London and the South East, layering privilege on top of the comparative advantage of the FIRE sector – finance, insurance and real estate. China and India need the services of the City of London. They do not need the high-labour-cost products from the North East. But the City of London's bankers owe a debt to the peoples of the regions, for it is their money – pensions, insurance premiums and savings – that in large measure are channelled to London for investment. If the finance merchants fail to support the democratic interests of all citizens, they will deepen the trap in which we will all be caught.

16.3 Democracy's Trap

WHEN ALL ADULTS finally secured the right to vote, the hope was for a society in which everyone could be included in the cultural mainstream. To achieve this, however, the vote was not enough. The public's finances also had to be democratised. Strenuous efforts were made in the first three decades of the 20th century to achieve this, with little result in the US and none in the UK.[10]

Without a change in the structure of taxes, the system was rigged against the individual. The outcome was logical. Working people had to develop collective forms of coercive behaviour, notably through trades unions, to try and improve their living standards. Their defeat in the General Strike of 1926 left them in no doubt that the power was with those who controlled the instruments of the state. So that would have to be their objective.

The Labour Party finally secured its political mandate in 1945. But the socialist experiment was foredoomed, and its end came with the demise of the Soviet Union in 1990. It was at this point that the trap laid by the trappings of democracy was sprung on Britain. Without a democratised form of public finance, people would have to adopt the institutions and values of the landed elites which had created Parliament in their class image. Thus it was logical that a socialist Chancellor, Gordon Brown, should resolve to deepen the 'property owning democracy' agenda.

The doctrine was that people who had their names on title deeds would share in the prosperity of the nation. But in Britain, 50% of people who were living in poverty were the owners of their homes.[11] They were trapped by the tax-and-tenure laws into paying for homes that they could not afford; paying taxes that reduce them to the breadline; and pocketing capital gains on their properties that they dare not spend in the supermarket, for fear of a lapse into negative equity with the onset of the next property crash. In this way, citizens are turned into supplicants, claiming subventions from the state: taxes are raised further to subsidise people whose difficulties originated with the tax system.

The Blairite Third Way agenda crashed against the brick wall of fiscal reality when it tried to merge market values and methods with state-run public services such as health, education and transport. It was a valiant attempt to move society beyond the Welfare State. It could not succeed because the contact points between the public and private sectors could not be synchronised. It was like a Soviet satellite trying to link up with an American space platform, when both structures used different specifications for their docking platforms.

Puzzled politicians did not realise that they were missing a vital component. They were not working with a pricing mechanism that integrated the private prices of the markets with the public prices of the state. The principles on which each of these were based were completely different. There was no logical coherence between them. The result was comfort for both the extreme Left and extreme Right. Drawing attention to the policy tensions in the centre, they promoted either the return to the nationalisation of the 20th century or the privatisation of the 19th century.

The sophisticated strategy required a vision beyond the Welfare State. It is for the people to redefine the communal and individual ethos in new institutional forms. But the politicians feared the risks of venturing into the philosophical unknown, so a mature discussion could not take place. Their conversation with the electorate was impoverished because they lacked the language for a progressive agenda.

This is an impasse that cannot be tolerated indefinitely. For without fiscal reform, the cumulative weight of deprivation among the peoples of the peripheries will drag everyone else down with them.

The tax change we propose would complete the reform agenda that began with the Enlightenment, in which campaigners dedicated themselves to abolishing injustices that were the currency of a corrupted feudal aristocracy.

Tax reform of the kind we envisage, however, is not confined to a financial transaction. It is the first step in the direction of the new community. People who recalibrate their relationship with the state's political centre would automatically create new moral and cultural centres. These are the powerhouses for a new renaissance.

16.4 Not *How Much*, but *How*

THE ANGLO-AMERICAN fiscal philosophy is now the major obstacle to the evolution of a socio-economic system that can be sustained in the face of the challenge from the East. In the first instance, the solution is not to be found in a reduction in the amount that government takes from the economy. This is a red herring: Norway and Japan are not out of line with the UK and the USA over the size of government consumption (as a percentage of GDP), and yet (as we noted in Chapter 12, p.189 above) they produce higher *per capita* incomes. What matters is not (so much) *how much* government taxes out of the economy, but *how* it raises its revenue. The evidence from Japan is illuminating.

After a 20-year period in which the Meiji government funded infrastructure out of taxes on the value of land, the Emperor agreed to a democratic Diet (Parliament). The landowning samurai grasped this opportunity to shift the tax structure away from land rents. This rendered the country vulnerable to land speculation and the property cycle which I claim drives the business cycle. Japan's 20th century booms and busts were reviewed in *The Power in the Land*,[12] so we shall pick up the story with the fall-out from the mania of the 1980s.

The lessons are twofold. By abandoning the rent-as-public-revenue policy, Japan abandoned the counter-cyclical tool that would have afforded it protection from the disruption of land speculation. The corrosive effects of land speculation consequently undermined the cohesiveness of Japan's culture. As we have dealt with the counter-cyclical features of the rent policy in Chapter 15 (p.251), we will examine here the hypothesis that the fabric of society is at stake when governments fail to employ the enlightened revenue policy.

When Japan went into recession in the early 1990s, her governments resorted to an early form of the new mercantilism. They placed a premium on protecting the banks against the bad loans tied to land. But someone had to pay for the bad debts: the people. The depression set in, which lasted for more than 10 years. The outcome was a damaging shift in the psychology and sociology of the population. *The Financial Times* correspondent identified one of the results.

> During Japan's heady bubble, when land prices could only go up and sprinkled gold was a culinary imperative, a full three-quarters of the population considered themselves middle-class. Now, a Nikkei survey says, only 54% feel that way – and a once unthinkable 37% classify themselves as lower class.[13]

Homelessness, rootlessness, hopelessness – these all intruded into the once solid social culture, surfacing in public in ways familiar to Europeans and North Americans: rising suicide rates, people sleeping in the streets, despair as workers shifted from one job to the next instead of enjoying the benefits traditionally associated with the job-for-life corporation. Inequality rates began to reflect the characteristics of American society.

The West needs to be concerned about the welfare of the Japanese population as much as with China's coolies. We know from the past that social dislocation can lead to imperial adventures. Japan fought China over the energy resources in neighbouring territories, and that dispute (over oil under the sea) lingers on to this day.

For the mercantilist agenda, if consolidated in a new protectionism, has the capacity to bring about a new kind of world war without end. The only way to head off this prospect is to renegotiate the powers of the state, and to reach a global settlement on the rents of nature's resources.

We have argued that this can be achieved in a non-violent way, with the transformation of the public's finances; non-violent, but revolutionary in its consequences for the fabric of communities and relationships as people adapt to a heightened sense of personal and civic responsibilities.

This fiscal strategy for change will be resisted by politicians, for it entails an open discussion on issues that are readily manipulated by the rent-seekers. It is safer to comply with the norms of the *status quo*. In Britain, this was made clear in the general election of 2005, when both the Labour Government and the Conservative Party published plans for reviving the fortunes of regional cities. Their refusal to acknowledge the link between rents and the quality of people's lives made a mockery of the idea of urban regeneration. The proposals, which favoured the construction industry, were calculated to serve the interests of rent-seekers.

If politicians wish to assist people to consolidate the civilised society, they will need to relearn their trade. No one expects them to be superhuman; all that we can ask is that they display the honesty that is expected of the rest of us. For a start, they ought routinely to *tell the truth*. For opportunistic reasons, that is perceived as difficult for politicians who depend on votes. One erstwhile political leader, however, has confessed, to his credit. Charles Kennedy led the Liberal Democrats in Britain for seven years, through two general elections. He admits that he and other politicians 'play down the big, divisive issues' that were relevant to people's lives, 'because the debate wouldn't have helped win votes'.[14]

When politicians fail to treat people as mature citizens, we can expect the evil men lurking in the wings to attempt a coup against the weakened state. This happened too often in the 20th century, and the vulnerability of democratic institutions to another takeover is now increased by the way in which the state is not able to fund the demands being imposed on it. When vulnerable, low-income people observe the rich escape their obligations, should we be surprised if they turn to false prophets? In the United States, for example, the rich conceal their taxable income in tax havens, costing the US government between $40bn and $70bn a year in revenue.[15] So effective are the tax dodgers that they are beyond the reach of the law enforcement agencies, according to Carl Levin (Democrat). His staff ran the Senate investigation that revealed the scale of the problem. So, while the US was chasing terrorists in the mountains of Afghanistan, some of its own citizens were undermining the nation's laws from within; and the US government was unable to defend its homeland fiscal base. According to Levin: 'Tax cheating has become so large that no one, not even the United States government, could go after all of it.'[16]

Thus, to excuse their failures, governments sponsor vacuous analyses of the impact of the public's morality on governance. This relieves politicians of their responsibilities.[17] What those in power will not do is assess their direct impact on people's lives through the tools over which they exercise exclusive responsibility: taxation. An example is the pontificating of Gordon Brown. In June 2006 he called for the creation of millions more skilled jobs, while offering no plan for ameliorating the way in which his tax policies were undermining the labour market.[18] According to one tax consultant's estimates, Brown's welfare benefits and irksome taxes have reduced the potential number of jobs by at least 1.6m, in a country with 8m people aged under 65 who were not working.[19]

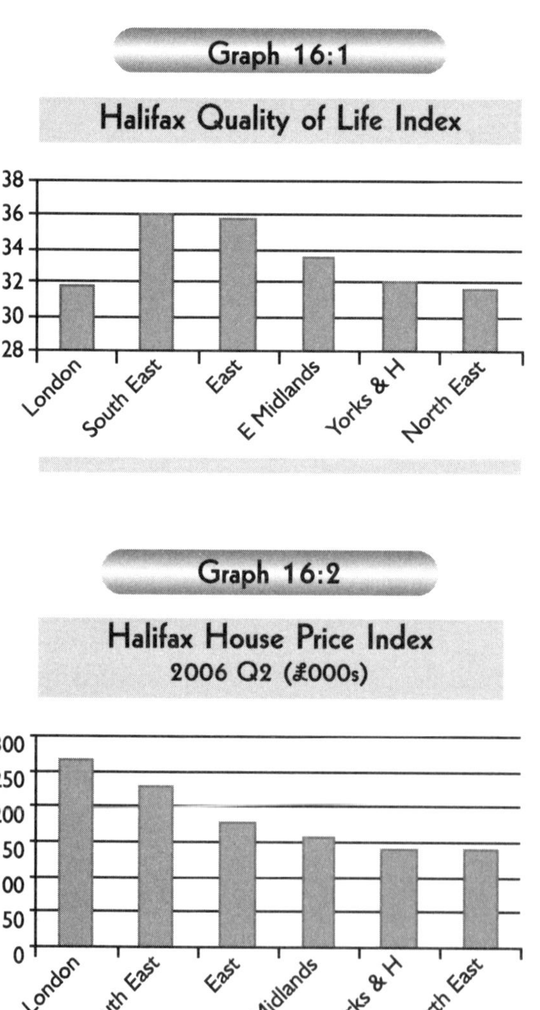

If democratic governments really want to improve people's prospects, they should start by understanding the way in which Ricardo's Law is compromised by taxation. The theory of land rent provides the single most illuminating way to track the dynamics of the enterprise economy. But to make sense of the reality on the ground, we need to 'read' the nation's tax code with open eyes.

By applying Ricardo's theory, we have exposed a grievous injustice in that tax code. The discriminatory impact explains statistics such as the quality-of-life index compiled by Halifax Home Insurance.[20] This ranks every district in Britain according to factors that include housing, employment, earnings, environment, education, health and the weather. They *all* affect the amount of money people are willing to pay for specific locations. But the distribution of location values ought not to be correlated with the quality-of-life index. There is no universal law that predetermines a pattern – similar to the profile of land values – in the quality of people's lives across the nation. And yet, the two sets of data are correlated, as we can see by comparing the trend in Graph 16:1 with the average price of houses tracked in Graph 16:2. The one deviation from the expected trend is with London. Here, the quality-of-life average is reduced by the concentration of deprived neighbourhoods in the capital (as we noted in Chapter 5). The residents of Richmond upon Thames, however, whose area tops the index for London, would not swap the quality of their lives for that experienced by people in the North East.

To equalise people's life-chances in an upward direction, with the biggest gains in the peripheral regions, we need to democratise the public's finances in the way that we explained in the last two chapters. This would deliver new relationships not just between individuals, but between regions and nations.

- Tax-and-tenure reform equalises opportunities between core towns and their hinterlands, by sharing the benefits that naturally accrue to locations, such as proximity to sea-ports or landscapes of natural beauty and close relation to centres of trade. Every region is placed on an equal footing. Each community would flourish on the basis of the creative energy of its inhabitants, rather than by monopolising the advantages provided by nature and the investments of previous generations.
- Areas with fewer natural advantages would not be disadvantaged by underfunded infrastructure. The extra gains in the central locations – which were in part financed by the flow of money from the periphery – would be shared with others, to level up the productivity of the economy as a whole.

The transformative consequences of this spatial convergence of economic opportunities need to be understood and accepted if people are to renew the democratic mandate.

REFERENCES

1 William R. White, 'Pro-cyclicality in the financial system: do we need a new macro-financial stabilisation framework?' BIS Working Paper No 193, Basle, 2006, p.10, n.31.
2 *Ibid.*
3 I owe this point to Michael Hudson.
4 Harrison, *Boom Bust, op. cit.*
5 Peter Marsh, 'Share of world production falls as China surges', *Financial Times*, May 23, 2006.
6 Mason Gaffney, 'Counter-colonial land

policy for Montana', *Western Wildlands*, Winter 1977, pp.16-25; available on www.masongaffney.org.

7 This was the burden of the argument by London's mayor, Ken Livingstone, in 'Being most global is London's trump card', *The Sunday Times*, June 18, 2004.

8 In April 2006, the European Commission was forced to launch 28 cases against 17 member states which, in one way or another, were retreating from the idea of a single European market.

9 Prem Sikka, 'The corporate scams that aid terrorist money launderers', *The Guardian*, February 23, 2006.

10 Some modest gains were achieved in some US cities, as elected mayors – influenced by Henry George and *Progress and Poverty* (1879) – stimulated municipal reform. But the forces of reaction managed to contain attempts to reform the property tax. Some British colonies, notably Australia, New Zealand and South Africa, did forge ahead with land taxation; but the glowing start fizzled over the course of the century. South Africa finally buried the direct public charge on land values in 2004.

11 R. Burrows, *Poverty and Home Ownership in Contemporary Britain*, Bristol: Policy Press, 2003.

12 See Harrison, *The Power in the Land*, Chapters 11 and 12.

13 David Piling, 'Land of the rising inequality co-efficient', *Financial Times*, March 14, 2006.

14 Charles Kennedy, 'How we lost people's trust', *The Guardian*, August 4, 2006.

15 *Tax Haven Abuses: The Enablers, The Tools and Secrecy*, Washington, DC: US Senate Permanent Sub-committee on Investigations (chairman: Norm Coleman), 2006, p.1 (http://levin.senate.gov/newsroom/supporting/2006/PSI.taxhavenabuses.080106.pdf).

16 David Cay Johnston, 'US blows the whistle on tax cheats', *International Herald Tribune*, August 2, 2006.

17 An example of political philosophy that fails to address the fatal shortcomings of governance in the sphere of public finance is offered by Geoff Mulgan in *Good and Bad Power: The Ideals and Betrayals of Government* (London: Allen Lane, 2006). Mulgan has served as chief adviser to Gordon Brown, director of Tony Blair's Strategy Unit and head of policy in Downing Street. After this influential service at the heart of government, he published a report which claimed that 'there will always be poverty' (Geoff Mulgan and Alessandra Buenfino, 'Pressing needs', *The Guardian*, July 12, 2006). Having resigned himself to the bleak prospect of a continuation of poverty, Mulgan refreshed his think-tank enthusiasm by going in search of deprivation in 'unexpected new guises'. Might the advisers to government do well to resolve the old kinds of poverty before adding new manifestations of deprivation to their hit lists?

18 The skills shortage was reported by the Learning and Skills Council to be greatest in Yorkshire and Humberside, and in the North-East. Larry Elliott, 'Skill shortages reduced but north still fares worst', *The Guardian*, June 22, 2006.

19 Mark Wadsworth, *Tax, Benefits, Pensions: Keep it Simple Part 2: Ten Steps to Simplicity*, London: Bow Group, 2006, p.3. Wadsworth proposed the scrapping of Inheritance Tax, Council Tax, Stamp Duty, Capital Gains Tax on the sale of land, and the TV licence, in favour of a revenue neutral land value tax. If that modest reform would deliver 1.6m new jobs, one is left to wonder how quickly full employment would be achieved by swapping other damaging taxes for higher charges on land values.

20 Halifax Home Insurance Quality of Life Survey, News Release, August 10, 2006.

The Judgement

WHEN VITALITY ebbs away from culture's immune system, signs of the emerging catastrophe are visible in the decomposition of the laws and institutions that are society's buttresses.

Western nations have been in a state of transition since the Second World War. Following the mass slaughter on the killing fields of Europe, the survivors and their children made it clear that they would no longer defer to those who had previously ruled them. But those who were paid to think and act on their behalf have generally failed to enrich the hollowed-out communities on which the predators had feasted. Ideas capable of animating the renewal of communities were missing.

When the 21st century dawned, people were intuitively aware that a dangerous void existed. Russia had just been lost to the oligarchs, but the significance of the way in which the de-socialisation of the Soviet Union had been mishandled was not understood. Is the West at risk of going the same way as Russia, a society defined by corruption and the casino? I fear that the risk is a serious prospect, but it need not be so. The philosophical void can be filled by invoking the twin principles of justice (between people) and efficiency (in the use of nature's treasures). But substantive change will not occur until people are convinced that those who represent them have failed, and are not competent to redeem themselves.

To assess the evidence as it relates (to a greater or lesser degree) to all of the Western nations, I articulated four indictments levelled specifically at the UK. If the facts I have accumulated are sufficient to convict the state and its agents in the court of public opinion, the time has come for the citizen to reclaim his and her destiny. The reader who has remained with me on this journey through the files of evidence will have reached a conclusion as to whether I have made a convincing case. I will offer my judgement.

Indictment I

The state is derelict in its duty to citizens

HISTORY, WHEN we step back to observe its contours, may be seen primarily as the struggle to adjust to new forms of land tenure. The anthropological record reveals finely tuned adjustments of communities to their ecological habitats to ensure long-term survival. The historical record is more complex. The adjustments ranged from the territorial conquests of early civilisations and empires through to the land grabs of colonialism. In all cases, it was the struggle for land or its extractable resources that underpinned the episodic highlights of history.

The forces that shaped the modern state, and therefore the character of the power that it exercises, were disputes over land and its rent. The struggle over public value may be tracked at several levels. One is cross-border conflict over territory. The level that we have chosen for analysis is domestic politics and the machinations to control the public purse. The outcome was the privatisation of rent. Marshall elegantly described the economics that preceded this privatisation, and the need to invest large amounts of capital in the 'public goods' that create the 'public value in land'. He wrote:

> Large expenditure is needed to secure air and light and playroom. And the most appropriate source from which that expense can be defrayed seems to be those extreme rights of private property in land, which have grown up almost imperceptibly from the time when the king, representing the State, was the sole *landowner*. Private persons were but *landholders* subject to the obligation to work for the public well-being.[1]

The state cannot discharge its obligations if the natural source of its revenue is withheld from it. Thus, the state was undermined almost at the outset by the aristocrats' coup. Land lords disengaged themselves from the social obligations associated with the rents they received. This established the class system that continues to dis-unite Britain. Tony Blair's Equalities Review concluded that the single largest contributor to inequality in most cases was without doubt the class into which people were born.[2]

Gordon Brown did nothing to unravel the financial vortex which spins the inequalities that disgrace Britain. He continued with Henry VIII's policy of alienating state assets so that the proceeds could be spent as income. In his budget on March 22, 2006, for example, he announced the sale of £30bn of 'fixed assets' by 2010 to raise cash for 'front line priorities'. Rental revenue, if it were retained in the public domain – but using market mechanisms like auctions to determine values – could fund public goods in perpetuity. Instead, Brown embarked deeper into the sale of land owned by the public's hospitals. The outcome is an artificial cap on the productivity of the economy.

To prove our case that the state is derelict in its duty to citizens, we had to prove that it is responsible – as Hurstfield put it – for subverting the welfare of its members; and that 'we may define corruption as the subversion of that object for other ends'.[3] We have quantified the under-production of wealth and welfare as a result of state policies. We can, therefore, safely conclude that *the Tax State has been derelict in its duty to treat all citizens as equals. The result is the severe deprivation of people's welfare; and the unjust distribution of income.*

The state needs to be disciplined by the people. As James Harrington presciently noted in the 17th century, democracy is contingent on a democratised form of land tenure. We are attracted, in particular, to his concept of 'balance', which denotes a sustainable arrangement. Balance was secured when land was diffused in a way that deprived law-makers of the ability to abuse their power against the interests of the 'free and equal commonwealth'.[4] Harrington called this 'the only practical settlement' for a government of the people.[5] His particular formula may have been appropriate for the economy of the 17th century, but it would not meet the needs of the post-industrial society. Nonetheless, we can easily translate the philosophy of land-sharing in terms of the democratisation of the public's finances. In practice, this means viewing rent – rather than the land itself – as the shared resource. To achieve this, we need rules that limit the power of the state to tax people's earned incomes. We need to distinguish between two kinds of expenditure. The first is revenue that is needed to support the state itself. The second is the expenditure that is for and by citizens who, in a mature democracy, do not need the support of state paternalism. *To secure this outcome, we need a new constitutional settlement; one that guarantees everyone's right of access to the rents from the land of their birth.*

We can never recover the wealth and welfare that was lost over the past two centuries as a result of abusive taxation. But a new prosperity for future generations would go some way to redeeming Europe and the USA for the policy errors that deprived its peoples of the economy of abundance.

The lessons from which we must learn may be summarised in the following terms.

The state compromised itself from the outset by the way in which it relinquished control over the land to a minority class. From that point onwards, it was bound to lose its ability to represent the common good. The arrangements are no better today, despite the 20th century experiment in democracy. The Welfare State (given the political circumstances prevailing in 1945) was an understandable attempt to rescue an ailing economic model. It tried to reclaim the public value. It failed. European models – variations on a common theme – are equally unviable in the 21st century. The Tax State imposes not only material losses; it also impoverishes culture and community. It is in everyone's interests to discuss the terms of a new social contract that would re-regulate relationships. This could lead to a richer, more satisfying quality of life for everyone.

Change is now unavoidable. The arrangements that suited Henry VIII and his successors are now obstacles to progress. As a unit of power controlling a defined territory, the state in its present form is obsolete. We need an institution that is more flexible and sophisticated. Power needs to be both devolved downwards to territorial sub-units, and evolved upwards to trans-national units. This triadic model is a formula for curbing political conflict, if people agree on the one essential principle of good governance: the allocation of public value among the participating political units on the basis of the principles of justice. People will understand the need for this kind of revenue allocation, once it is explained that *they* generate the rental revenue as neighbours in a local community, as citizens of a territorial state and as humans on the global stage. Earth, through the resources of nature, is capable of playing its part in this moral agenda. Are we humans?

Indictment II

Parliament has failed to use its democratic mandate to remedy the injustices of the Tax State

THE FORMAL democracy of the 20th century failed to reverse the fiscal fortunes of the nation. This was not for the want of trying. At the end of the 19th century the people of Britain mobilised themselves through the ballot box. With a landslide vote they mandated the Liberal Party to reform taxation through the Finance Act (1909). Parliament was served notice: the people wanted governance for the common good. The people understood that this was conditional on democratising the nation's finances.

If Parliament had performed its duty, it would have redeemed itself for its role in the Scottish clearances, the English enclosures and the Irish appropriations. Those land-grabbing episodes were rationalised as 'improvements' that would add wealth to the nation. In fact, *because of the pricing system favoured by the aristocrats*, fields were left vacant where people wanted to live and work. David Lloyd George published his audit of the great land larceny when he presented the People's Budget in 1909. He offered a scathing assessment of the stewardship of the lords of the land. There were, he said,

> Millions of acres … more stripped and sterile than they were, and providing a living for fewer people than they did, even a thousand years ago – acres which abroad would either be clad in profitable trees or be brought … to a higher state of cultivation.[6]

Lloyd George intended to offer grants to improve the farming sector. But his plan, of putting the nation's territory to its best economic use, did not commend itself to their lordships. For Lloyd George also proposed to tax the rents. He needed that revenue to introduce pensions for the aged who lived in poverty, and to establish employment exchanges to help the jobless to find work. The peers of the realm drew their proverbial swords and went in search of blood. Few Chancellors have been the target of such venom as was directed against Lloyd George.

The fiery Welshman retaliated. In a speech at the Edinburgh Castle, a pub in Limehouse, East London, he dissected the economics of the land market. Nearby marsh land that was worth £2 or £3 an acre for farming could be sold for up to £8,000 an acre as residential and commercial land.

> Who made that golden swamp? Was it the landlord? Was it his energy? Was it his brains? – a very bad look-out for the place if it were … it was purely the combined effort of all the people engaged in the trade … of the Port of London … everybody except the landlord … in future those landlords will have to contribute to the taxation of the country on the basis of the real value – only one halfpenny in the pound! Only a halfpenny! And that is what all the howling is about.

The aristocrats were outraged, and the king came to their defence when he spoke to the Prime Minister, Herbert Asquith. What was Lloyd George's offence? His speech, according to the king, was 'a menace to property and a Socialistic spirit'.[7] The landed elite fought a running battle through the courts, and key clauses in the Finance Act – on the valuation of land – were not implemented. Without valuations, there could be no taxation.

The next opportunity for working people to reassert their birthrights came in 1945. Exhausted by two world wars, they gave the Labour Party a mandate. The survivors of those who were in the front line of the bombing of London have now delivered their verdict: the Welfare State has failed its part of the bargain (see Chapter 5.4). The state did redistribute some of the nation's wealth to those in need. Measured in *material* terms, many people are better off today than they would have been without the intervention of the Welfare State. But because the tools were those of socialism, society was not re-based on sustainable foundations.

It need not have been so. Before the Second World War, the labour movement favoured the fiscal and free market approach to land values. Although it used the language of Marx, the political wing of the labour movement (the Labour Party), in its manifesto of 1906, advocated the taxation of market-based land values. It retained this approach through to the manifesto of 1923, but in 1929 it adopted the socialist concept of nationalisation. In 1945, armed with an overwhelming majority for the first time in the House of Commons, Clement Atlee's Labour government went into full throttle in favour of the Marxist model of land ownership.[8] Labour's successive revenue-raising novelties, however, which disrupted the construction industry, were repeatedly deleted from the statute book as impractical.

By its use of force, the Tax State on both sides of the Iron Curtain was able to remain viable during the years of the Cold War. With the coming down of the Berlin Wall, everything changed. In Russia, not only did the oligarchs appropriate the natural resources of Russia; some of them also turned their attention to the tax revenue of Western nations. In doing so, they challenged the viability of the state itself. Britain found itself humiliated by crooks operating a VAT scam. This nets them an annual sum equal to a dozen fully equipped hospitals or 300 secondary schools. The loss in 2005 was about £5bn, the sum that the crooks tricked HM Customs & Excise into 'reimbursing' them for goods allegedly exported out of the country. The links with the Russian mafia were identifiable.[9] If a state cannot hold on to its own revenue it is no longer viable. When it hands over its revenue to criminals, it is self-certifying its own institutional bankruptcy.

The viable alternative, one that would defeat the mobsters (and protect citizens who would rather remain within the law) is a fiscal base that cannot be moved across borders. But to this day *Parliament continues to avoid its responsibility to promulgate a democratised public finance.*

Indictment III

Tony Blair's New Labour administrations were constructed on a grand deception

TONY BLAIR launched his first administration with the promise of nothing less than the revitalisation of the nation. 'New' Labour would energise the people, modernise archaic institutions like the House of Lords and emancipate people by extending the freedom to choose.[10] If that happened, it would be the start of the climb out of the corner into which Britain had been boxed by a class history that emerged to de-socialise the rent of land.

The political trends had arrived at their logical conclusion in the 1980s when Margaret Thatcher abolished the property tax. Owners would be relieved of the last direct payment for the services that gave their land its value. Instead, local government would levy a Poll Tax on the head of every citizen, including those who did not own property and therefore did not share in the capital gains that are funded by taxes.

The first Poll Tax, in 1381, ended in abject failure. Peasants led by Wat Tyler fought back. Tyler confronted Richard II at Mile End, at the head of a march of men from Kent and Essex. The king backed down, but the peasants were unleashed. They roamed London, and in a further meeting with the king, Tyler was struck dead by the Lord Mayor. The tax, however, was scrapped. When Thatcher decided to revisit the Poll Tax, it was the turn of the urban proletariat to riot (in 1990). The tax, again, was abandoned. The struggle of the state with the people over the public purse had ground to a stalemate. A new course needed to be charted, and Tony Blair offered himself as the champion of the people.

In Part II we offered a portrait of Blair's Britain. Perhaps the most poignant judgement on that record was offered by the Prime Minister himself when, after eight years in power, he addressed his party in Scotland.

> We must be honest. For some, those who from generation to generation, are brought up in workless households in poor estates, often poorly educated and frankly sometimes poorly parented, the rising tide has not helped lift them. We intervene too late. We spend without asking how effective is the spending. These are the children who are the clients of many agencies of government but the charges of no one, prey to drugs, into crime and anti-social behaviour, lacking in self-belief ... it isn't good enough.[11]

Some of the costs of that inequality were quantified by Blair's Equalities Review panel. This concluded that, if inequality was reduced by just 30%, the nation's welfare would gain by no less than £43bn – equal to £1,700 per household. 'This is the benefit of reducing inequality, and could be interpreted as the 'cost' of inequality in the UK.'[12] A more ambitious reduction of inequality would deliver gains of up to £82bn. This would enrich each household by £3,342.[13]

Who – or what – should be held accountable for this pathetic record? The answer is contained in the terms of reference of the Equalities Review.

> Despite 40 years of legislation to protect people from discrimination, evidence suggests that there are still social, economic, cultural or other factors that individually or in combination may limit or deny individuals the opportunity to make the best of their abilities and to contribute to society fully.

Unless we resort to supernatural explanations for the constraints on people's freedoms, we must place the responsibility for failure on the lawmakers. They have failed to define the framework for a society of equals. Blair admitted as much when he launched his party's Let's Talk conversation with the public, in which he admitted:

> If we are frank about it, there is a group of people who have been shut out against society's mainstream and we have not yet found a way of bringing them in properly ... If we are to change that we need a different way for government to operate and we need different systems of delivery.[14]

Was this not a confession of systemic failure? Despite determined efforts on the party of government, the record was one of failure so far as the most vulnerable individuals in society were concerned. But mortified though he was by the lack of change at the bottom of society, Blair would not place the blame on the way his government had administered the nation's finances. On the contrary, he commended his Chancellor, Gordon Brown, for the tax credits which he claimed had helped the poor.

Then how did Blair explain the failures? Britain, he insisted, 'is not a caring country while we allow such hopelessness to go unchecked'. Britain? The people themselves? But their hands are not on the levers of power! They do not control the junction boxes through which flow the information that shapes political attitudes and frames public policies. But elected representatives like Blair *do* exercise immense power over people's destinies, and they do not conceal their desire to re-engineer people's lives. Take the case of the fetish over the private ownership of homes. Blair argued for the need to raise ownership rates from 71% up to 80%.[15] But he failed to take into account the way that taxation, combined with the privatisation of public value, discriminated against families that rent their homes. Diminishing the number of those families by one third would still leave two-thirds – 10,000,000 people – at the mercy of the Treasury and the land market. That discrimination is directly responsible for curbing people's 'capabilities'. It is, therefore, a state-sponsored offence against the principle of equality.

Politicians are not entitled to assign blame elsewhere. They bear personal responsibility for the expectations they create when they seek power. The failure to protect citizens is central to the case against Tony Blair. As we noted on pp.9-12, the legitimacy of monopoly power is contingent on the state securing people's safety. In opposition, Blair promised that he would be not only tough on crime, but also tough on the *causes* of crime. More money was, indeed, spent on policing, but the attack was on symptoms, not causes. So some citizens felt obliged to arrogate unto themselves the power to protect their interests. In doing so, they further de-legitimised the state.

- The rich paid for private security systems to secure their families and property. They purchased their way into gated communities, the high-value locations where uniformed guards patrol neighbourhoods to expel prowling intruders.
- The poor could not afford to fund their own protection. The streets were

Box 1 The State of Disarray

IF THE STATE has reached systemic crisis, the evidence of stress should surface in the primary institutions of government. These should reveal a diminished capacity to fulfil the functions that define the state, most especially over the control of its borders and over the enforcement of law and order. In Britain, many of these functions are the responsibility of the Home Office. It is responsible for the movement of people across the borders, and the incarceration of over 77,000 people in prison in April 2006 (more people than in any other European country and more *per capita* than in Libya or Burma).

In 2006, over 1,000 foreign criminals who had served sentences for murder, rape, drug peddling and paedophilia were freed into the general population without supervision. They disappeared, and at least 200 of them re-offended. And yet, the courts had ordered that these men should be considered for deportation when they had served their sentences.

The verdict on the Home Office was pronounced by Home Secretary John Reid: it was 'not fit for the purpose: averse to a culture of personal responsibility, technologically ill-equipped for an era of mass migration and led by officials that are incapable of producing facts or figures that remain accurate for even a short period of time.'[1]

The Financial Times, in an editorial (April 27, 2006), characterised the Home Office as 'a sick institution'. The malaise went to the heart of the state itself. The state was failing in its duty to protect its citizens and was not able to enforce its own laws. On the financial front, it was not even able to hold on to its revenue. Detected fraud from public authorities reached a record £111m by 2005, and many of the biggest increases involved claims from people who were dead. Also on the increase were claims from failed asylum seekers, housing benefit fraud, and double claims for salaries from two different public bodies.[2]

1 Patrick Wintour, 'Reid vents fury at Home Office over prisoners fiasco', *The Guardian*, May 24, 2006.
2 David Hencke, 'Big increase in bogus benefit claims for dead people detected', *The Guardian*, May 23, 2006.

> not safe for them from the stray bullets of drug peddlers engaged in turf wars. So Glasgow teenagers formed street gangs for their personal protection.[16]

That the state had lost control of order within its territory was evidenced by the bureaucratic *débacle* involving the Home Office (see Box 1). But Blair confessed to his part in this failure in a letter to his new Home Secretary, in which he instructed John Reid to ensure 'that the criminal justice system is shaped around targeting the offender and not just the offence, in order to enhance public protection and ensure that the law-abiding majority can live without fear'. Why, after nine years in power, was Blair now issuing such an instruction? Because, he confessed, 'Despite our attempts to toughen the law and reform the criminal justice system ... the criminal justice system is still the public service most distant from what reasonable people want'.[17]

Britain is a caring nation whose people show compassion in many ways towards those in need. The problem is not with an uncaring people, but with an uncaring public finance. Over the course of his three administrations, Blair did not challenge the logic on which taxes were based. His opportunity to understand the injustices of the past occurred when he reviewed The People's Budget of 1909. But he failed to perceive the significance of the fiscal philosophy of the Liberal government whose welfare provisions he admired.[18]

As a result, the time would come when spending by the Welfare State would have to be cut back. The Institute for Fiscal Studies warned that retrenchment was imminent, and that the reversal of inequality 'still seems an unlikely prospect any time soon'.[19] Meanwhile, however, despite pressure from backbench MPs who wanted to know when he would resign, there was time for another policy initiative before the end of his premiership. Blair, refreshed by his 2006 summer vacation, announced that the state would clamp down on anti-social children by identifying the culprits before they were born. The government could predict children who would be 'a menace to society' and pre-emptive action taken 'pre-birth'.[20]

Who is to blame for the illusions of the Third Way? On May 5, 2006, the Prime Minister sacked Home Secretary Charles Clarke because of the Home Office's failure to enforce law and order. He also relieved John Prescott of his departmental responsibilities – not because of failures in the realms of land use or community development, for which he was responsible, but because the Deputy Prime Minister's diary secretary revealed that they had conducted a torrid sex affair on the other side of the open door of his office. The flaws in the structure of the state cannot be remedied by sacking cabinet ministers. *But if any person is responsible, it is Tony Blair. For the Prime Minister appoints the Chancellor of the Exchequer, the Home Secretary and the other members of his Cabinet.*

Indictment IV

Experts who advise government muzzle our collective consciousness

EARLY HUMANS, from the day they invented abstract concepts, began to live in two parallel universes. The first was the material world in which symbols were employed to redefine their biological existence. The other universe tantalised them with a landscape of the mind, which could be transformed into reality if they strove hard enough. Today, that universe of the mind – some would say of the soul – is a blur. I hold responsible the philosophers and social scientists who have abetted those who impoverish our lives. Between them, they have deprived people of the hope that a better world is waiting to receive us – on earth.

We are the victims of a process that dumbs down our minds and our moral senses. Responsibility for this cannot be placed on the shoulders of any one person. Individually, the gatekeepers to our minds would be horrified at the accusation that they were debilitating the way we viewed the world – and the way in which we might create a better future. But taken together, they have orchestrated an intellectual and emotional impoverishment for which we all pay a terrible price. Those whom we can least excuse are the scholars who, adopting the methods of science, are supposed to be 'objective' in their treatment of facts. We have seen, in this study, the recurrent cases of people who have failed to match their theories with reality.

Knowledge is cumulative. With it, we solve problems. In medicine, we no longer use leeches to bleed people's bodies back to health. Instead, we transplant hearts to give them new leases on life. In physics, we no longer believe that the rest of the universe orbits around earth. We can now put astronauts on the moon. In economics, for 200 years, we have tried to solve mundane problems like poverty and homelessness. And yet, these persist, and we still – apparently – do not have a firm grip on the *causes*. The reason is shocking: knowledge in the social sciences is not cumulative. The 'experts' bud off into 'schools of thought', competing for attention not on the strength of their ability to solve the problems that blight our communities but to secure the fame and research contracts that bring rewards of celebrity. We are victims of knowledge atrophied.

It would not be fair to suggest that the academics and consultants who were hired to advise Tony Blair's government were uniquely inadequate. The failure of the social sciences is a systemic problem, the origins of which may be tracked back over two centuries.[21] Nonetheless, we do have to assess the performance of a consultancy industry that now draws rewards from the public purse measured in the hundreds of millions of pounds every year.[22] Some of the wisdom sold to government is laughable. Politicians hire consultants for fabulous fees whose reports are likely to accumulate dust on shelves. But the Blair government's 10-year Transport Plan – championed by John Prescott – also failed because the politicians lacked the political willpower to deliver an integrated system. With the foregoing comments in mind, we are obliged to spotlight the case of Kate Barker.

We have just asserted that the experts fail to draw on the accumulated knowledge that yields lessons on which improved policies can be built. Our claim is that knowledge counts for little in the social sciences when the evidence threatens the material interests of those who have their hands on the levers of power. Specifically, we have equated that power with the ownership of the income from land. The relevant test for our argument, then, entails a review of the treatment of the land market and the implications for public policy.

Gordon Brown acknowledged – during his budget speech in March 2004, while standing at the despatch box in the House of Commons – that the 'unearned increment in land' was relevant to the supply and price of housing. He appointed Kate Barker to conduct an enquiry, and she had no difficulty in pinpointing the blockage in the system. She identified 'land supply as the major constraint on housing growth'.[23] From this, it followed that the overriding need was for a more fluid supply of land at prices people could afford. Did Barker examine the historical evidence with dispassion and *build* on that knowledge base to recommend a solution that *might* work? The public was entitled to expect such an outcome for the money that it made available for Barker's nationwide search for answers.

Barker came with the best credentials. She was on the Bank of England's panel of specialist economic advisers, the Monetary Policy Committee (MPC). This made her one of the most influential of unelected public servants. Members of the MPC, through their manipulation of interest rates, affect the lives of people in a thousand ways – not least, through the cost of borrowing money to buy homes or to keep businesses going. As a member of that committee, Barker was obliged to display 'independence, judgment and technical economic expertise' – the standards acknowledged by four former members of the MPC.[24] To suggest that Barker trimmed her conclusions to suit the preconceived wishes of the Treasury (which *was* acutely sensitive to the politics of taxing land), would be to cast unwarranted aspersions on this distinguished economist.

The evidence that Barker assembled, and her recommendations, appeared in *Delivering Stability: Securing our Future Housing Needs*. This stressed the need for 'evidence based' solutions, and evidence was what Barker stacked up in her report. A vital piece of that evidence was the way

Box 2 Tyranny of the Experts

BANK OF ENGLAND economist Kate Barker's Final Report on Britain's housing crisis summarised the history of failed land development taxes.[1]

1947 Development charge A tax of 100% of value of land after planning permission granted. It resulted in the reduction of land made available for development and produced less revenue than expected.

1967 Betterment levy A tax on land values which reached 110% of the value prior to development. Designed to encourage land sales and protect some development profits. Introduced at 40 per cent but proved too complex and less revenue was raised than expected.

1973 Development gains tax Taxed as income the gains from disposals of land possessing development potential – 82% for individuals, 52% for companies. Undone by changing market conditions and change in government.

1976 Development land tax Levied on land sales and assumed disposals where development projects had begun prior to sale. It was deemed too complex, was unfairly weighted against small landowners, and led to a proliferation of avoidance schemes.

Despite this evidence, Barker recommended a tax on development at the point where planning permission was granted. She offered the caution that the 'tax rate should not be set so high as to discourage development'. How low? Why should land owners wait to find out? Barker's Report triggered the expected disruption in the market. There was no excuse for the diagnostic failure on her part. The historical evidence had been amply analysed.[2]

1 *Delivering Stability: Securing our Future Housing Needs*, London: HMSO, March 2004, p.78, Box 4.2.

2 V.H. Blundell, 'Flawed Land Acts 1947-1976', in Nicolaus Tideman (ed), *Land and Taxation*, London: Shepheard-Walwyn, 1994.

in which taxes levied at the point of property development had failed when they were tried and tested in the past. In fact, they had failed on *four* occasions since 1947. So what did Barker recommend? She proposed a Planning Gain Supplement, *aka* a development land tax! The tax, Barker noted, would be paid by the owners when they sought permission to develop their land. But why, if it had failed on four occasions in the 20th century (see Box 2), would it work in the 21st century?

As it happens, her recommendation – that developers could be taxed at the point when they secured permission to develop land – *did* resonate with the Treasury's preference. But was this not a curious turn of events? A tax that had failed four times was now to be the tool for a Labour government's further attempt to fund highways that serviced new homes. Surely, as with previous development land taxes, it would have the reverse effect? Barker tried to skirt round the awkward historical evidence by proposing that her tax, if 'applied at a sensible rate', would enable landowners to 'enjoy significant potential development gain and thus land sales can still profitably proceed'.[25]

The repetitive failures of the past suggest that this was not likely to happen. Land owners are rational people. They maximise their capital gains by taking into account the tax regime. They are not deluded by soothing assurances that a tax rate will remain low, once it has come into force. Consider, for example, the potential cost to an owner in Oxford, where land commanded £8m a hectare in 2006.[26] If the Planning Gain Supplement was 20%, the tax on the owner would be £1.6m.[27] Why would an owner part with his property and meet such a liability, when he could lock up his land and raise money by other means? Two options were available. First, he could borrow money from a bank, offering his land as collateral: so his decision not to sell would not deprive him of spendable cash, even if this did deprive others of the homes they needed in Oxford. Second, by going on strike with other owners, he would dislocate the property market. This would create the discontent that would cause a future government to delete the tax. Then he could sell.

Is this a plausible prospect for Kate Barker's Planning Gain Supplement? Even as the Treasury was consulting 'stakeholders' in 2005 the owners of land silently registered their intentions. In 2006, they began to withdraw their sites from sale. One property consultant explained: 'They will simply sit on it and wait for a change of government. Some have been sitting on the land for 17 generations so they can wait a few more years'.[28]

Thus, the expert hired to advise the Treasury declined to build on the lessons of history. And the politician who was responsible for enshrining the advice in law declined to learn the lessons of past failure. In his budget speech on March 22, 2006, Gordon Brown confirmed that Barker's proposal was government policy.

Barker could not claim that she was ignorant of the scientific evidence in favour of a correctly structured charge on the rent of land. She summarised the theory in these terms:

> The combination of a potentially wide tax base and the fact that land is physically 'fixed', which makes avoidance and concealment of the asset and its tax liability very difficult, point to land value taxation as a good method for raising revenue without distorting behaviour; indeed, it could encourage better behaviour.[29]

To achieve that outcome, however, the public charge has to be correctly formulated: an *ad valorem* charge on market values, to accurately reflect the rents that people willingly pay for the stream of services they access at the locations where they live and work. Barker's development land tax flouted the principles of this policy, ignored the historical evidence and failed to honour the tenets of justice (she was concerned that the tax might be 'unfair' to some owners).[30]

But it would be wrong to leave the reader with the impression that this farcical exercise in formulating economic policy was peculiar to one economist. Kate Barker kept good company. Her boss at the Bank of England, the governor, Mervyn King, had also short-changed the science of political economy – at least, when he turned his attention to land and its stream of rents. In a book he co-authored – when he was a professor of economics at the London School of Economics – King did offer an objective assessment of economic rent. The 'underlying intellectual argument for seeking to tax economic rent retains its force', he wrote.[31] And to demonstrate the integrity of the theory, the authors of this Open University textbook presented their students with a Ricardian diagram (on p.179) similar to those that we employ in Part I of this book.

Surely, here was the basis for an informed assessment of fiscal policy? Ah, but there was one problem:

> It is apparent that the total of economic rents, of all kinds, is not now a sufficiently large proportion of national income for this to be a practicable means of obtaining the resources needed to finance a modern State.[32]

This claim dissembles, at best, and is false, at worst. If its equivalent appeared in a textbook on geology, biology, physics or medicine, the authors would be censured by their peers. In economics, however, authors are free to take liberties with the facts.

King and his co-author John Kay could not support their assertion with the published statistics, because these are compiled in what can be described as either an appallingly slipshod way; or, expertly filleted to serve a doctrinal prejudice. Whatever the explanation, the nation's statistics, which purport to assemble information on the incomes of the factors of production, conceal more than they reveal. Specifically, they conflate land into 'capital', so economic rent is disguised under the headings of other sources of income.

That ought not to have deterred Professor King from reaching a reliable conclusion as to whether rent was a worthwhile source of public revenue, however. For, in the absence of empirical evidence, he could have tested his conjecture with theory. One probing question that ought to have been asked is this: to what extent do conventional taxes actually fall, indirectly, on the rent of land? If taxes on labour, capital and consumption reduce disposable incomes, they diminish the surplus that can be offered as rent. This leads to a vital insight: if we abolish conventional taxes, not only would we free people from the disincentives that shackle production; economic rent would automatically increase. This hypothesis was tested as far back as John Locke and Adam Smith. Locke, for example, in *Some Considerations of the Lowering of Interest* (1691), demonstrated that taxes on wages or the profits of merchants would be passed on as reductions in the rent paid for the use of land. As a generalisation, this retains its scientific force; and it dispels the glib dismissal of economic rent as a viable source of revenue for the state.

But while other taxes are subjected to investigation by state treasuries, the revenue raiser that is treated in a cavalier way is the one that would directly tap the rents of land. The Blair government's decision to review local government finance is a case in point. In 2004, the UK Treasury appointed Sir Michael Lyons to enquire into locally administered taxation. This was the government's ploy to avoid the reassessment of property values, which would have required the owners of houses that had risen in value to pay a higher Council Tax. Gordon Brown then postponed publication of the Lyons report. When it does appear, we should not expect it to venture beyond the bounds of the politically correct tax philosophy that continues to dis-unite the kingdom.

REFERENCES

1 Marshall, *op. cit.*, p.803. Emphasis in original.
2 Equalities Review, *op. cit.* p.28.
3 Joel Hurstfield, 'Political corruption in modern England: the historian's problem', *History*, Vol. LII (174), 1967, p.19; Joel Hurstfield, *Freedom, Corruption and Government in Elizabethan England*, London: Jonathan Cape, 1973, p.141.
4 Harrington, *Oceana*, *op. cit.*, pp.12, 113.
5 Harrington, *Works*, *op. cit.*, p.750.
6 Quoted in John Grigg, *Lloyd George: The People's Champion, 1902-1911*, London: Penguin, 2002, p.191.
7 *Ibid.*, p.208.
8 The land policies of the 1945 Labour government were a jumble. They included the provision for 'fair compensation' to land owners, which meant paying

them the rent instead of using this revenue to fund public expenditure. The one principle to which the government consistently adhered was the rejection of the free market as the framework for achieving fiscal justice.

9 Ashley Seager and Ian Cobain, 'Bogus deals keep Customs in a spin', *The Guardian*, May 9, 2006. By 2006, statistics compiled by the Office of National Statistics suggested that there had been nearly £10bn of criminal activity aimed at fraudulently reclaiming VAT from HM Revenue and Customs, and 'the actual VAT losses could run to £20bn – the equivalent of 6p on the basic rate of income tax' (Ashley Seager, 'VAT criminals may force tax rises as scams near £30bn', *The Guardian*, August 10, 2006). But the fiscal base of the transnational supra-state was no more secure than that of the nation-state. The European Union reported that cross-border VAT fraud was costing its members about ?50bn (£34bn). As ever, under the present tax regime, the losers are the low income families whose payroll taxes would have to make up the shortfall in state revenue.

10 In the year before his election victory, Tony Blair published a collection of speeches which he called *New Britain: My Vision of a Young Country*, London: Fourth Estate, 1996.

11 Tony Blair, Speech, Scottish Labour Party, Aviemore, February 24, 2006.

12 The Equalities Review (chairman: Trevor Phillips), *The Equalities Review: Interim Report for Consultation*, 2006, p.69 (www.theequalitiesreview.org.uk).

13 *Ibid.*, Table 3, p.110.

14 Patrick Wintour, 'Blair admits failing most needy children', *The Guardian*, May 16, 2006.

15 Roger Blitz, 'Blair's 10-year homeownership goal', *Financial Times*, January 25, 2005.

16 Peter Seaman, Katrina Turner, Malcolm Hill, Anne Stafford and Moira Walker, *Parenting and Children's Resilience in Disadvantaged Communities*, London: National Children's Bureau, 2006, funded by the Joseph Rowntree Foundation, pp.19-20.

17 Will Woodward, 'Blair's new bid to 'rescue' public services', *The Guardian*, May 15, 2006.

18 Blair, *New Britain*, *op. cit.*, p.15. Blair admired the Liberals who formed the government of 1909, but the philosophy of their tax plans eluded him. Their ideas, he wrote, 'drove the 1910 government, which legislated for reform of the House of Lords, improved working conditions, an embryonic welfare system and progressive taxation'. The progressive taxation promoted by the Liberals was aimed at shifting public finance onto the rent of land within the market economy, which was different from what socialists mean by 'progressive' taxation.

19 Institute for Fiscal Studies, *Poverty and Inequality in Britain: 2006*, London, March 2006.

20 Lee Glendinning, 'We can clamp down on antisocial children before birth, says Blair', *The Guardian*, 1 September, 2006.

21 This theme will be explored in the present author's forthcoming *The Pathology of Capitalism*, with special reference to the fateful influence of Herbert Spencer on the origins and evolution of sociology. In the mid-19th century, Spencer's seminal contribution to that discipline was marred by his dishonest retreat from his own insights – under pressure from his social 'betters', whose approbation he sought. This crippled the science of society which, in turn, inflicted immense damage on the knowledge base that people needed to shape policy in the 20th century.

22 Management consultants were paid £52.5m in the six years to 2006 in the health service alone. But that sum represented only the 'tip of the iceberg' according to former health secretary Frank Dobson. Taking into account fees paid by hospital trusts and other health service bodies, payments probably exceeded £200m. Brendan Carlin and Celia Hall, 'NHS advisors "cost £200m" as key jobs go', *Daily Telegraph*, March 30, 2006. Over the lifetime of Tony Blair's three administrations, the bill for management consultancy within government was predicted to reach £20bn. The

estimate was by a former consultant, David Craig, who concluded that the total expenditure on outside expertise was worth £70bn from 1997 to 2009 (the figure included spending on implementing IT projects in the NHS). Ben Hall and Matthew Campbell, 'Public sector consultants to cost £20bn', *Financial Times*, August 7, 2006. An investigation by *The Guardian* (David Hencke, 'Labour's £2bn army of consultants', September 2, 2006) found that the annual cost of consultants advising the Blair government had reached £2.2bn. Some of the bizarre cases included consultants (daily fee: £750) working alongside civil servants who performed the same work for £120. There was difficulty in estimating the total paid to consultants, however, because of the reluctance to disclose some of the payments. The worst offenders for withholding information were identified as John Prescott and the Home Office.

23 Kate Barker, *Delivering Stability: Securing our Future Housing Needs*, London: HMSO, March 2004, p.71, para. 4.7.

24 Willem Buiter *et al.*, 'New MPC member must be professional economist', *Financial Times*, February 25, 2006.

25 Barker, *op. cit.*, p.85, para. 4.71. That charge, she went on to advocate, should be 'set at a relatively low level'. Kate Barker, 'UK housing economics in the 21st century', *Planning in London*, 57, April-June 2006, p.35.

26 Anna Hutchings, 'Ready to drop', *Property Week*, March 3, 2006 (www.propertyweek.co.uk). Hutchings, a district valuer for south-east England, cited data from the Valuation Office Agency.

27 In a survey, planning authorities reported a preference for a 30% levy. The builders of houses in the social sector favoured a 20% rate. Ben Walker, 'Development Tax: the View from the Ground', *Regeneration & Renewal*, March 17, 2006, p.22.

28 Roger Blitz and Jim Pickard, 'Development tax alarms landowners', *Financial Times*, February 23, 2006. Landowners expected that an incoming Conservative government would abolish the tax. Their expectations were not unrealistic. The shadow Chancellor of the Exchequer, George Osborne, was quoted as saying that the Planning Gain Supplement 'will not work'.

29 *Op. cit.*, p.73, para. 4.22.

30 *Ibid.*, p.71, para. 4.11.

31 J.A. Kay and M.A. King, *The British Tax System*, 5th edn., Oxford: Oxford University Press, 1990, p.179.

32 *Ibid.*

Epilogue

A Personal Word

And now, Dear Reader, over to you ...

IN EUROPE, we have reached the point where tens of millions of people – including a significant proportion of home owners – have to rely on state support to compensate for the handicaps they suffer. Those handicaps, in the main, are the product of state taxation. This is a maniacal situation that cannot continue.

The crises that continually defy political remedy stem from the failures of governance. As such, the remedies must be sharply focussed on tax reforms that could deliver both freedom for the individual and the renewal of culture and community. Who should assume responsibility for this change? It would be easy to place responsibility on elected representatives, but this would be unfair. In Britain, politicians have a prejudicial interest in preserving the *status quo*. Through Parliament, they have granted themselves the means for personal enrichment funded by taxpayers. How this works further illustrates the financial problem that compromises our collective interests.

To conduct their business, MPs claim the cost of lodging if their constituencies are located outside London. The Additional Costs Allowance includes the costs of the mortgage on a second home, plus repairs and utility bills. This means that, at the end of their political careers, MPs not only walk away with one of the best pension plans imaginable, but also with the windfall gains on the properties.

- Tony Blair purchased his Sedgefield home in 1983 for about £30,000. He re-mortgaged the property in 2003 for at least £200,000, thanks to the 'unearned increment' on the property that was funded with the aid of money from taxpayers.[1]
- Ruth Kelly, who was appointed by Blair to assume John Prescott's departmental responsibilities, was reported to have paid £109,000 for

> her Lancashire home. On the basis of the allowances she claimed, she would have paid off the mortgage in about five years in a period that spanned the property bubble of 2000-5.[2]

As one price of democracy, it is appropriate that MPs should receive a cost of living allowance when they go about their constituents' business. But are taxpayers not entitled, by right of ownership, to the increase in the value of a property which they funded? The capital gains are enormous, sometimes running into hundreds of thousands of pounds. MPs of all parties, with multi-million pound property portfolios, claim tens of thousands of pounds in expenses. Nine of the wealthiest parliamentarians each claimed at least £50,000 over four years to finance their second homes. According to an investigation by *The Sunday Times*: 'Many own three or more properties, including landed estates and mansions abroad'.[3]

In my view MPs should disqualify themselves from sitting in judgement on the reforms that the nation needs to adopt. Property rights need to be re-examined. The people of the commons must be free to determine, in a democratic way – and it would be the first time since the defeat of the English at the battle of Hastings in 1066 – what is in *their* best interests.

The reform which I propose will court controversy. Some defenders of the present regime will argue for the sanctity of existing rights. But these were *not* established for eternity. The case of slave owners has been cited (above, p.188). Slave owners discovered that they could be deprived of their property in the name of human rights. More recently, in a judgment in September 1985, the European Court of Human Rights ruled that the 'compulsory transfer of property from one individual to another might constitute a legitimate means for promoting the public interest. The enhancement of social justice within the community could properly be described as being in the public interest'.[4]

Tax reform is necessary because the state converts much of its revenue into an asset that is handed over to those who have financial claims to land (these include banks and mortgage institutions). If we are to abolish this inequity, people themselves must initiate the action that leads to the democratisation of their public finances. They need to specify what, precisely, they regard as 'the common good', and how this can be delivered.

To aid a new constitutional settlement, insights can be drawn from three models of knowledge. The *theological* model was employed by James Harrington to develop his proposals for a commonwealth of citizens. For those who would prefer a secular approach, the *anthropological* model is compelling; sufficient comparative evidence has been collated to enable us to define the key elements of a balanced society. The *scientific* model would resonate with many people. Unfortunately, as I have begun to show, the social sciences have been bankrupted by the way that they have been practised. Introspection is necessary before social scientists can release themselves from their 'schools of thought' to reach a consensus on the verities that favour the common good.[5]

But whatever the method for reasoning out solutions to the fundamental problems that confront all nations in the West, there is no avoiding the clash between the individual and the state. The proposition that you, the reader, should challenge it might appear daunting. But in the past, history was made when people mustered the strength to draw on their reserves of reason and morality.

As residential property owners, many of us will be tempted to resist the policy of public charges on our prize asset. But that resistance is not in the interests of anyone, including home owners. That is why we need clarity in the way we discuss these issues. For a start, we must respect other people's intelligence. Our minds are coloured by the words that are used by vested interests. An example of how not to conduct the debate is provided by the Council of Mortgage Lenders (CML). It represents Britain's banks and the financial institutions which provide mortgages.

The CML presented itself as the champion of the home-owner when it calculated how much was paid as Stamp Duty and Inheritance Tax. Up to the year 2000, owners were subsidised through tax relief on the interest they paid for mortgages. In the previous 10 years, owners pocketed £2.6bn per annum at the expense of taxpayers. Then the rules were changed so that, in 2005, home-buyers and people who died paid £7.5bn as a net contribution to the Treasury. The CML was outraged on behalf of people who were buying or dying. It condemned the 'iniquities' of Inheritance Tax, and agonised on behalf of owners who were 'suffering'. These victims had 'worked hard to accumulate assets to pass on to their dependants'.[6]

The CML failed to acknowledge that the home owners' net contribution to the public coffers of £7.5bn in 2004/2005 was dwarfed by a capital gain of £352bn in 2004 alone. Compare that £352bn with the total net contribution to the Treasury of about £35bn over the previous few years! In the decade to 2005, as home owners we enjoyed a capital gain of £2.2 *trillion*. How can that be presented by the CML as home owners being 'out of pocket'? Furthermore, this good fortune was *not* the result of hard work. *Most of the increase in value was in land, the appreciation of which had nothing to do with owners in their role as the proprietors of land*.

Most home owners are also taxpayers. This does not alter the point I am making. If we cloud the debate with misleading language, we limit our freedom to choose policies that are in our best individual and social interests.[7] The build up of debt among home owners, for example, has created a precarious situation. If it is not addressed in a controlled way, it will destroy many lives and dreams. Between 1990 and 2005, household incomes doubled while mortgage debt trebled to £967bn. The house purchase debt as a percent of GDP was 23% in 1980. By 2003 it had reached a staggering 72%.[8] But according to the financiers, this was not threatening a 'debt meltdown' because interest had levelled off at low rates and mortgages could be financed. It was not such a rosy outlook for people living in rented accommodation who did not enjoy the safety net of windfall capital gains. Their unsecured borrowing as a percentage of household income was equivalent to 41% of their income, double the national average.

The enhanced dignity that would flow from our proposed reform is of incalculable value to everyone. The lowest-income people already pay more than they receive in state benefits, so they are not dependent on others. They pay for the services which they use when they pay commercial rents to their landlords. Asset-rich free riders do not enjoy a dignified life, but under the integrated pricing system they would also pay their way. Their contributions to the public purse would be greater than the payments from the poor, because they enjoy greater benefits from the locations they occupy. They would no longer receive the windfall gains from land, but nor would their earned incomes be taxed.

In this debate, pensioners are vulnerable. They will be panicked with scare stories by opportunists. Many of them rely on the value of their homes for some financial security during their retirement years. They will be told that the rent-as-public-revenue policy will confiscate their asset and leave them at risk. In truth, pensioners are already being deprived of income during their retirement years: a million more British pensioners were ensnared by Gordon Brown's tax dragnet since 1997.[9] The state has failed to provide a secure financial framework for people reaching pensionable age. For those who live through the years of transition to the Free State, a safety plan is needed that substitutes for the loss of land value.

The soft option – of leaving governments to muddle along – is not one that we can contemplate. Even without applying the full audit of the impact of tax policies (Chapter 1), the public's finances in the dis-united kingdom are a disgrace that brings shame on all of us. For if we limit analysis to the way the tax burden and social benefits are distributed, during Gordon Brown's tenure in the Treasury the poor paid more and received a lower share of the benefits than the rich.[10] Brown had promised (in his second budget, in 1998) that the Blair government would be 'modernising ... the entire tax and benefits system of our country' to 'advance the ambitions not just of the few but of the many'. Brown failed lamentably. *And this is without taking into account that tax revenue extracted from the lowest incomes were capitalised into the land values of the rich.*

An informed debate is now needed if we are to reclaim our lives from those who have a vested interest in keeping us imprisoned in mental straightjackets. I have provided tools which, if the reader works with them, lead to the liberation of the mind. That is the first step towards the liberation of our selves in a society built on freedom and prosperity for everyone.

If we fail to act, we are not entitled to blame anyone else for the damage that each of us will suffer as the global crises of the 21st century unfold.

REFERENCES

1 Gareth Walsh and Jon Ungoed-Thomas, 'Revealed: the "black hole" in Blair's expenses', *The Sunday Times*, April 9, 2006.

2 David Cracknell, ' "Black hole" in Ruth Kelly's expenses', *The Sunday Times*, March 19, 2006.

3 Steven Swinford, 'MPs with mansions get second home perk', *Sunday Times*, May 7, 2006.

4 The case was brought by the Duke of Westminster, who objected to being forced into selling leasehold properties to his tenants. Cited in Hobson, *op. cit.*, p.81.

5 My contention that the social sciences are not built on cumulative knowledge (see above, p.287) is illustrated by a letter in the *Financial Times*. The writer, who identified himself as Senior Economist at a firm of stockbrokers in Dublin, denied that Ireland had experienced a tax-led housing 'bubble', and he added: 'Yet, is it not the case that, in a global economy, the mostly "fixed" resource on which a tax base can be built is labour?' Eunan King, 'The 'fixed' resource on which tax base can be built', *Financial Times*, April 20, 2006. If readers are unable to challenge that claim with authority, the author of *Ricardo's Law* has failed in his mission to remove the blinkers from people's eyes.

6 'Inheritance Tax and home-ownership', *CML News & Views*, January 24, 2006, pp.1-4.

7 An example of the way in which the CML's number-crunching was translated into emotive manipulation of our collective thinking was provided by the *Daily Telegraph*. Above the by-line of Rosie Murray-West, its headline shrieked: 'Home-owners 'are £550 a year poorer under Labour' (January 25, 2005). In fact, home-owners were vastly richer under Labour than under the previous Conservative administration. Property value could be translated into spendable income by transforming equity into cash.

8 Wilcox, *op. cit.,* Tables 17d and 45.

9 Gary Duncan, 'A million more pensioners caught in the tax net than before 1997', *The Times*, May 8, 2006.

10 Charlie Elphicke, *Robin Hood or Sheriff of Nottingham? Winners and losers from tax and benefit reform over the last 10 years*, London: Centre for Policy Studies, September 2006 (www.cps.org.uk).

Select Bibliography

Aldridge, Stephen (2001), 'Social Mobility', Discussion Paper, London: Cabinet Office (www.cabinet-office.gov.uk).

Amin, Ash, Doreen Massey and Nigel Thrift (2003), *De-centering the Nation: A Radical Approach to Regional Inequality*, London: Catalyst.

Andelson, R.V. (2000), *Land Value Taxation Around the World*, 3rd edn, Oxford: Blackwell.

Apps, Patricia (1981), *A Theory of Inequality and Taxation*, Cambridge: Cambridge University Press.

Arnold, A.J., and S. McCartney (2004), *George Hudson: The Rise and Fall of the Railway King*, London: Hambledon and London.

Atkinson, Anthony B., and Joseph E. Stiglitz (1980), *Lectures on Public Economics*, London: McGraw-Hill, 1980.

Attwood, John (1988), *Dick Whittington: Fact and Fable*, London: Regency Press.

Barker, Kate (2006), *Delivering Stability: Securing our Future Housing Needs*, London: HMSO.

– (March 2004), 'UK housing economics in the 21st century', *Planning in London*, 57, April-June.

Beckett, J.V. (1977), 'English landownership in the later 17th and early 18th centuries', *Econ. Historical Review*, Second ser., XXX.

Bede (1969), *The Ecclesiastical History of the English People* (edited with introduction by Judith McClure and Roger Collins), Oxford: University Press.

Bédoyère, Guy de la (1992), *Roman Towns in Britain*, London: B.T. Batsford.

Blair, Tony (1996), *New Britain: My Vision of a Young Country*, London: Fourth Estate.

Blanden, Jo, Paul Gregg and Stephen Machin (2005), 'Inter-generational mobility in Europe and North America', London: Centre for Economic Performance, LSE.

Booth, Philip (2006) (ed), *Were 364 Economists All Wrong?* London: Institute of Economic Affairs.

Brown, Gordon (1975), *The Red Paper on Scotland*, Edinburgh: EUSPB.

– (1983), Introduction, in *Scotland: The Real Divide* (edited by Gordon Brown and Robin Cooke), Edinburgh: Mainstream.

Burrows, R. (2003), *Poverty and Home Ownership in Contemporary Britain*, Bristol: Policy Press.

Cabinet Office (1999), *Sharing the Nation's Prosperity. Variation in Economic and Social Conditions Across the UK*, London.

Calverley, John (2005), 'Boom bust: house prices, banking and the depression of 2010', *Economic Affairs*, Vol. 25 (4).

Campbell, John Y., and João F. Cocco (2003), 'Household risk management and optimal mortgage choice', Harvard University and London Business School Working Paper.

— (2004), 'How do house prices affect consumption? Evidence from Micro Data', Harvard Institute of Economic Research Discussion Paper No. 2045.

Cannadine, David (1998), *Class in Britain*, New Haven: Yale University Press.

Churchill, Winston S. (1970), *The People's Rights*, London: Jonathan Cape.

Cobbett, William John (1926), 'The development of the Duchy of Normandy and the Norman conquest of England', *The Cambridge Medieval History: Contest of Empire and Papacy* (Vol. V), Cambridge: The University Press.

Cole, Ian, Paul Hickman and Kesia Reeve (2004), *Interpreting Housing Market Change: The Case of Leeds*, Sheffield Hallam University (www.shu.ac.uk/cresr).

Coward, Barry (2003), *The Stuart Age: England, 1603-1714*, London: Pearson, 3rd edn.

Dench, Geoff, Kate Gavron and Michael Young (2006), *The New East End: Kinship, Race and Conflict*, London: Profile Books.

Department for Transport (2004), 'Guidance on value for money', London.

Department of Health (1999), White Paper, *Saving Lives: Our Healthier Nation*, London: Stationery Office.

— (2005), *Tackling Health Inequalities: Status Report on the Programme for Action*, London.

Diamond, Jared (2005), *Collapse: How Societies Choose to Fail or Survive*, London: Allen Lane.

Diamond, Patrick (2005), *Equality Now: The Future of Revisionism*, London: Fabian Society.

Equalities Review (2006) (chairman: Trevor Phillips), *The Equalities Review: Interim Report for Consultation* (www.theequalitiesreview.org.uk).

Fay, C.R. (1950), *Great Britain from Adam Smith to the Present Day*, London: Longmans, Green.

Federal Reserve Board (2005), 'Flow of funds accounts of the United States: Historical Data', www.federalreserve.gov.

Fiscal Studies, Institute for (2006), *Poverty and Inequality in Britain: 2006*, London.

Fujita, Masahisa, and Jacques-François Thisse (2002), *Economics of Agglomeration*, Cambridge: Cambridge University Press.

Fujita, Masahisa, Paul Krugman and Anthony J. Venables (2001), *The Spatial Economy*, Cambridge, Mass: The MIT Press.

Fukuyama, Francis (2005), *State Building: Governance and World Order in the 21st century*, London: Profile Books.

Gaffney, Mason (1969), 'Coordinating tax incentives and public policy: the treatment of land income', Brookings Institution, www.masongaffney.org.

— (1977), 'Counter-colonial land policy for Montana', *Western Wildlands*, www.masongaffney.org.

— (1978), 'The Synergistic City', *Real Estate Issues*, www.masongaffney.org.

Gaffney, Mason, and Fred Harrison (1994), *The Corruption of Economics*, London: Shepheard-Walwyn.

George, Henry (1879), *Progress and Poverty*, New York: Robert Schalkenbach Foundation, centenary edn, 1979.

Gibb, Peter (2000), 'Civil Society, Governance and Land Reform', *Geophilos*, Autumn (01).

Gibbons, Stephen, and Stephen Machin (2006), 'Paying for primary schools: admission constraints, school popularity or congestion?, *The Economic Journal*, March.

GLA Economics (2005), *Growing Together: London and the UK Economy*, London: Greater London Authority.

— (2005), *Our London, Our Future: Planning for London's Growth II*, Main Report.

— (2006), *A Fairer London: The Living Wage in London*, London: Greater London Authority.

— (2006), *Why Distance Doesn't Die: Agglomeration and its Benefits*, London: Greater London Authority.

Goodwin, Barbara, and Keith Taylor (1982), *The Politics of Utopia*, London: Hutchinson.

Graham, Daniel J. (2005), 'Wider economic benefits of transport improvements: link between agglomeration and productivity', Stage 1 report, Imperial College, London.

Grigg, John (2002), *Lloyd George: The People's Champion, 1902-1911*, London: Penguin.

HM Treasury (2005), *Planning Gain Supplement: A Consultation*, London: HM Treasury/ODPM.

— (2006), *Budget 2006: A Strong and Strengthening Economy: Investing in Britain's Future*, London: Stationery Office.

— (2001), *Productivity in the UK: 3 – The Regional Dimension*, London.

— (2001), *Productivity in the UK: Progress Towards a Productive Economy,* London.

Harrington, James (1992), *The Commonwealth of Oceana* and *A System of Politics* (edited by J.G.A. Pocock), Cambridge: Cambridge University Press.

Harrison, Fred (1983), *The Power in the Land*, London: Shepheard-Walwyn.

— (1998) (ed), *The Losses of Nations*, London: Othila Press.

— (2005), *Boom Bust: House Prices, Banking and the Depression of 2010*, London: Shepheard-Walwyn.

— (2006), *Wheels of Fortune: Self-funding Infrastructure and the Free Market Case for a Land Tax*, London: Institute of Economic Affairs.

Hayek, F.A. (1944), *The Road to Serfdom*, London: Routledge & Kegan Paul, 1962.

— (1960), *The Constitution of Liberty*, London: Routledge & Kegan Paul.

Health Statistics Quarterly (2000), 'Geographic inequalities in mortality in the United Kingdom during the 1990s', Autumn.

Helliwell, John F. (2006), 'Well-being, social capital and public policy: what's new?' *Economic Journal*, March.

Herman, Arthur (2003), *The Scottish Enlightenment*, London: Fourth Estate.

Hill, Christopher (1980), *The Century of Revolution 1603-1714*, London: Routledge.

Hobson, Dominic (1999), *The National Wealth: Who Gets What in Britain*, London: HarperCollins.

Hoffman, John (1995), *Beyond the State*, Cambridge: Polity Press.

House of Commons Select Committee on Transport, Local Government and the Regions (2002), Sixth Report.

Hunt, H.G. (1967), 'Land Tax assessments', *History*, Vol. LII (176).

Hurstfield, Joel (1967), 'Political corruption in modern England: the historian's problem', *History*, Vol. LII (174).

— (1973), *Freedom, Corruption and Government in Elizabethan England*, London: Jonathan Cape.

— (1975), *The Historian as Moralist: Reflections on the Study of Tudor England*, London: Athlone Press.
— (1979), *The Illusion of Power in Tudor Politics*, London: Athlone Press.
Jansen, Sharon L. (1991), *Political Protest and Prophecy Under Henry VIII*, Woodbridge: The Boydell Press.
Jupp, Kenneth (1997), *Stealing our Land*, London: Othila Press.
Kay, J.A., and M.A. King (1990), *The British Tax System*, 5th edn, Oxford: Oxford University Press.
Kynge, James (2006), *China Shakes the World: The Rise of a Hungry Nation*, London: Weidenfeld & Nicolson.
Lakin, Caroline (2004), 'The effects of taxes and benefits on household income, 2002-03', *Economic Trends*, London: Office for National Statistics.
Layard, Richard (2005), *Happiness*, London: Allen Lane.
— (2006), 'Happiness and public policy: a challenge to the profession', *The Economic Journal*, March.
Lehmberg, Stanford E. (1977), *The Later Parliaments of Henry VIII 1536-1547*, Cambridge: Cambridge University Press.
Li, Wenli (2005), *Moving Up: Trends in Homeownership and Mortgage Indebtedness*, Federal Reserve Bank of Philadelphia *Business Review* (www.philadelphia fed.org).
Lumley, Robert, and Jonathan Morris (1997) (eds), *The New History of the Italian South*, Exeter: University of Exeter Press.
Marius, Richard (1999), *Thomas More*, London: Phoenix.
Marshall, Alfred (1898), *Principles of Economics*, London: Macmillan, Vol. 1.
— (1909), 'Rates and taxes on land values', *The Times*, London, November 16.
— (1930), *Principles of Economics*, London: Macmillan, 8th edn.
McCarron, Peter (2003), 'North, South: changing directions in cardiovascular epidemiology', *Stroke*, November.
Miller, George J. (2000), *On Fairness and Efficiency: The Privatisation of the Public Income over the Past Millennium*, Bristol: Policy Press.
— (2003), *Dying for Justice*, London: Centre for Land Policy Studies.
Moorsom, N. (1975), *The Stockton and Darlington Railway: The Foundation of Middlesbrough*, Middlesbrough: J.G. Peckston.
More, Thomas (1989), *Utopia*, Cambridge: Cambridge University Press.
Morris, R.W., P.H. Whincup, J.R. Emberson, F.C. Lampe, M. Walker and A.G. Shaper (2003), 'North-South gradients in Britain for stroke and CHD', *Stroke*, November.
Mulgan, Geoff (2006), *Good and Bad Power: The Ideals and Betrayals of Government*, London: Allen Lane.
Noyes, Richard (ed) (1991), *Now the Synthesis: Capitalism, Socialism and the New Social Contract*, New York: Holmes & Meier.
ODPM (2003), 'Market renewal programme: learning lessons,' Manchester. Website.
Office for National Statistics (2003), *Cancer Statistics: Registrations*, Series MB1 No. 31, London.
Ogilvie, William (1997), *Birthright in Land* (edited by Peter Gibb), London: Othila Press.
Oxford Economic Forecasting (2005), *Time is Money*, London, GLA.
Paine, Thomas (1995), *Rights of Man, Common Sense, and Other Political Writings* (edited with an introduction by Mark Philp), Oxford: Oxford University Press.

Pickard, Duncan (2004), *Lie of the Land*, London: Land Research Trust/ Shepheard-Walwyn.

Pitkin Pictorials (1993), *Dissolution of the Monasteries*, Andover.

Prebble, John (1963), *The Highland Clearances*, London: Secker & Warburg.

Reid, A., and S. Harding (2000), 'Trends in regional deprivation and mortality using the Longitudinal Study', *Health Statistics Quarterly* (5).

Rice, Patricia, and Anthony J. Venables (2003), 'Equilibrium regional disparities: theory and British evidence', http://econ.lse.ac.uk/staff/ajv.

Riley, Don (2001), *Taken for a Ride*, London: Centre for Land Policy Studies.

Roy, Rana (2006), *Investing in the New Century: Towards an Undistorted Appraisal Process*, London: Railway Forum.

Samuelson, Paul A., and William D. Nordhaus (1985), *Economics*, 12th edn, New York: McGraw Hill.

Seaman, Peter, Katrina Turner, Malcolm Hill, Anne Stafford and Moira Walker (2006), *Parenting and Children's Resilience in Disadvantaged Communities*, London: National Children's Bureau.

Sephton, Robert S. (2003), '"Small Profits on a Large Trade": James Morrison MP [Part 1]', *J. of the Railway and Canal Historical Society*, Vol. 34, Pt. 6(186), November.

Sidney, Edwin (1845), *The Life of Lord Hill*, London: John Murray.

Smith, Adam (1976), *The Wealth of Nations,* Chicago: University of Chicago Press.

Smith, Alan G.R. (1984), *The Emergence of a Nation State: The Commonwealth of England 1529-1660*, London: Longman.

Stenton, F.M. (1971), *Anglo-Saxon England*, Oxford: Clarendon Press.

Stephen, Leslie, and Sidney Lee (eds) (1891), *Dictionary of National Biography*, Vol. xxvi, London: Smith, Elder.

Tawney, R.H. (1990), *Religion and the Rise of Capitalism*, London: Penguin.

Venables, Anthony J. (2003), 'Evaluating urban transport improvements: cost-benefit analysis in the presence of agglomeration', London: Department for Transport (http://econ.lse.ac.uk/staff/ajv/).

Wadsworth, Mark (2006), *Tax, Benefits, Pensions: Keep it Simple Part 2: Ten Steps to Simplicity*, London: Bow Group.

Wannamethee, S. Goya, A. Gerald Shaper, Peter H. Whincup and Mary Walker (2002), 'Migration within Great Britain and cardiovascular disease: early life and adult environmental factors', *International J. of Epidemiology* (31).

Weber, Max (1964), *The Theory of Social Organisation*, London: Macmillan.

— (1970), *Max Weber: The Interpretation of Social Reality* (edited by J.E.T. Eldridge), London: Michael Joseph.

White, William R. (2006), *Procyclicality in the Financial System: Do We Need a New Macrofinancial Stabilisation Framework?* Basle: Bank for International Settlements, BIS Working Papers No. 193.

Wilkinson, Adam (2006), *Pathfinder*, London: SAVE Britain's Heritage.

Wilkinson, Richard G. (2005), *The Impact of Inequality: How to Make Sick Societies Healthier*, London, Routledge.

Withers, Charles W.J. (1998), *Urban Highlanders: Highland-Lowland Migration and Urban Gaelic Culture, 1700-1900*, East Linton: Tuckwell Press.

Index

Acknowledgements

TWO OF my co-workers passed away before they could see the results of the support they provided which has resulted in *Ricardo's Law*. Sir Kenneth Jupp MC and Prof. George J. Miller were relentless in their search for justice. I treasured my association with them; our loss is profound.

Inevitably, with a work of this magnitude, the author accumulates debts. I have pleasure in acknowledging the assistance I received from Mason Gaffney and Michael Hudson, and the kind support of Ed Dodson, Don Bruce and my publisher Anthony Werner. Once again, my wife Rita rendered editorial assistance, an acknowledgement that does not fairly represent the support she provided during the years that went into the preparation of this volume. A grant from the Robert Schalkenbach Foundation of New York enabled me to follow Hurricane Katrina's trail into the ghettoes of poverty in America.

The usual disclaimer applies: the author is solely responsible for errors and omissions.

About the Author

FRED HARRISON is a graduate of the Universities of Oxford and London. His journalistic career in Fleet Street was followed by a 10-year sojourn in Russia, where he sought to help the people to adopt the market economy without the flaws identified in *Ricardo's Law*. *Inter alia*, he was an adviser to the federal Parliament, and to the Economics Department of the Russian Academy of Sciences. He is now Research Director of the London-based Land Research Trust.